An Introducti
Business L

2nd Edition

Vaeni Mac Donnell

Chartered Accountants Ireland

Published in 2015 by
Chartered Accountants Ireland
Chartered Accountants House
47–49 Pearse Street
Dublin 2

www.charteredaccountants.ie

ISBN: 978-1-910374-33-7

Typeset by Datapage

Table of Contents

Chapter 1

THE IRISH LEGAL SYSTEM

A Definition of Law

Law has been defined in *Murdoch's Dictionary of Irish Law* (2008) as:

> "the written and unwritten body of rules, derived from custom, formal enactment and judicial decisions, which are recognised as binding on persons who constitute a community or state, so that they will be imposed upon and enforced among those persons by appropriate sanctions".

The law can be classified as municipal (domestic) or international, public or private, criminal or civil.

Classification of Laws

An important distinction must be drawn between the areas of criminal and civil law.

A crime is conduct prohibited by law, for example larceny under the Larceny Act 1916. Criminal prosecutions are generally brought by the State but in rare cases an individual can maintain a private prosecution. The Garda Síochána or the Director of Public Prosecutions (the DPP) will take the initial decision to prosecute. The State prosecutes because it is notionally the community as a whole, which suffers when the criminal law is infringed.

Civil proceedings have as their object the resolution of disputes between individuals and the compensation of those who have been wronged under the civil law. The main areas of civil litigation comprise the law of contract, torts, employment and family law.

The table overleaf illustrates the comparison between civil law and criminal law in Ireland.

Table 1.1 Comparison of Criminal and Civil Law

	Criminal Law	**Civil Law**
Classification of Law	Public law	Private law
Parties	Prosecution (State), and defence.	Plaintiff and defendant.
Objective	Punishment – as well as: incapacitation, retribution, deterrence and rehabilitation.	Compensation, ceasing the unwanted action and specific performance.
Tests applied to determine liability	'Beyond all reasonable doubt.'	'Balance of probabilities.'
Finding	Guilty or not guilty	Liable or not liable.
Commencement of proceedings	State/People/DPP by summons or indictment.	By way of pleadings.
Penalties/Remedies	Fines, imprisonment, probation orders, community service orders, etc.	Damages, injunctions, court orders, account for profits, etc.
Courts	Criminal Court	Civil Court
Types of Court	District Court, Circuit Court, Central Criminal Court, Special Criminal Court, Court of Appeal and Supreme Court.	District Court, Circuit Court, High Court, Commercial Court, Court of Appeal and Supreme Court.

SOURCES OF LAW

All Irish law derives its validity from the Constitution of Ireland. The Irish legal system is broadly similar to the legal systems that exist in the United Kingdom, the United States and many of the present and former member states of the British Commonwealth. This is because Ireland is a common law jurisdiction. In a civil law jurisdiction, an attempt is made to codify or put in legislative form all law applicable in that country.

The law is contained not merely in the statutes passed by parliament, but in the corpus of judicial decisions, some of them concerned with the interpretation of statutes and others with the evolution of legal principles to be applied to situations for which the legislature has not provided. That corpus of law in turn consists of two great sections: the common law and the law of equity. The Irish legal system comprises the following elements:

- the common law;
- law of equity;
- the Constitution of Ireland;
- statute law;
- judicial precedent;
- custom;
- the courts system; and
- European law.

The Common Law

Following the Norman invasion of England in 1066 (Ireland: 1169) a system of centralised administration of justice was established whereby judges went on a 'circuit' throughout the realm, dispensing justice in accordance with the wishes of the King. This system attempted to avoid local law-making and, in turn, was aimed at strengthening the power of the King. In this way the "common law" developed.

However, the term 'common law' has more than one meaning. It is also used to distinguish 'judge-made law' from statute law. The former originates in the courts, while the latter is a product of the legislature's law-making power.

The common law is based on the system of **precedent**. The judge in a given legal case will examine previous cases (precedent) and if a similar dispute has been resolved previously the judge is bound to follow the decision. In cases were there is no authoritative statement of law, the judge has the authority to make law and create a precedent that future cases will be bound to follow. A general rule of precedent is that the lower courts are bound by decisions of the higher courts (e.g. the Circuit Court is bound by decisions of the High Court and the Supreme Court).

The Law of Equity

Following the Norman invasion, as discussed above, litigants throughout Great Britain and Ireland suffered the same disadvantages when attempting to bring a suit or action at common law:

- they had to bring their actions within one of the pre-existing suits (the writ system) – if one did not exist, the litigant would be without a remedy;

- many powerful defendants could use their resources to pervert the course of justice;
- in some areas, the common law was not effective and the judge's decisions were simply ignored; and
- the range of remedies available at common law was limited. By far the most usual remedy was damages; however, this was an ineffective remedy in many situations, for example where the plaintiff sought to have the defendant restrained from doing an unlawful act.

Therefore it is not surprising that there was great dissatisfaction with the common law courts. The Lord Chancellor ("the holder of the King's conscience" and his chief law officer) began to accept petitions from individual litigants circa 1150. After a time, the procedure for hearing petitions developed and was formalised to some degree (leading to the creation of courts of equity or Chancery) and in this way litigants were able to avoid the confines of the writ system.

Courts exercising equitable jurisdiction introduced the rights of parties to be witnesses in their own case and the right of a party to subpoena a witness (i.e. require the attendance of that witness before the court). Furthermore, the courts of equity introduced a whole new range of remedies for plaintiffs such as:

- specific performance;
- rescission;
- rectification; and
- the injunction.

Specific Performance

An order of specific performance is an order of a court directing parties to perform their contractual duties under a contract. Specific performance is an equitable remedy and so is discretionary in nature. The courts may order specific performance where a remedy of damages is inadequate in the circumstances. Orders for specific performance are frequently granted in disputes over the sale of land and can operate to oblige a party to complete the sale of a piece of land. An order of specific performance would **not** be granted to enforce contracts for personal service as it would be considered inequitable.

Rescission

The remedy of rescission aims to restore the parties to the position they were in prior to the contract being formed. There are limited grounds on which a court will agree to order rescission, such as where the contract has been entered into as a result of fraud or undue influence exercised by one of the parties.

Rectification

An order of rectification is made to amend a written instrument so that it accords with the true agreement reached by the parties.

Injunction

An injunction is an order of a court which requires a party to do or refrain from doing a particular act. The aim of an injunction is to preserve the *status quo* between the time of granting the injunction and the determination at a full trial.

The 'Campus Oil test' set out in *Campus Oil Ltd v. the Minister for Industry and Energy* (1983) details the three elements to be considered in deciding whether to grant an injunction:

1. there must be a serious/fair issue to be tried (and not a frivolous matter);
2. damages are not an adequate remedy (i.e. will the payment of damages be adequate compensation for the wrongful action?); and
3. the balance of convenience lies in favour of granting or refusing the application.

This third element, regarding balance of convenience, is usually only involved where damages are not an adequate remedy. The court then considers which party the balance of convenience favours while taking into account the parties' positions prior to the application of injunctive relief.

A plaintiff seeking an injunction will also be obliged to provide an undertaking as to damages to compensate the defendant for any losses which may accrue from the granting of an injunction should the plaintiff later lose the case.

Some examples of injunctions are as follows.

- **Mandatory injunction** – requires the defendant to take some positive action.
- **Prohibitory injunction** – requires the defendant to refrain from a course of action, e.g. an injunction against playing loud music at certain times.
- **Interim injunction** – an injunction prior to the main hearing of the action which is made in cases of extreme urgency where the plaintiff could suffer irreparable damage should an injunction not be granted.

- **Bayer injunction** – this is an extremely rare injunction as it effectively restricts a person's liberty and requires the person to offer up their passport.
- **Mareva injunction** – this is granted in circumstances where there is a fear that defendants will dissipate their assets before the main hearing of a case. Mareva injunctions can freeze a defendant's bank account or restrain them from disposing of other assets.
- ***Quia timet* injunction** – this is granted where there is a fear of a legal right being infringed: the plaintiff must have a well-grounded apprehension of injury. This type of injunction requires an anticipated or threatened injury to a plaintiff's rights.

Injunctions can be perpetual (of indefinite duration) or granted on an interlocutory basis, granted to maintain the *status quo* pending the full determination of an issue at trial. An interlocutory order is an order made at an interim stage during a trial.

The Maxims of Equity

The maxims of equity are principles developed by courts with equitable jurisdiction. They form a general set of principles which may be deviated from rather than a rigid set of rules that must be absolutely followed.

Equity regards as done that which ought to be done Where a specifically enforceable obligation exists, equity regards the parties as being in the position in which they would have been, had the obligation been performed.

Equity will not suffer a wrong to be without a remedy By adopting this maxim, the courts of equity have intervened to protect a right even where that right is not enforceable at common law. An example of this maxim in action is the injunction. At common law, the plaintiff only has a remedy when an actionable wrong has been committed against him or her. However, the *quia timet* injunction may be granted to restrain a wrong which is about to be committed against the applicant.

Equity acts in personam This maxim derived from the fact that courts of equity exercised jurisdiction over the parties personally, rather than against particular property owned by them.

He who seeks equity must do equity This maxim requires a party seeking equitable relief to act fairly towards the other. It has been said that there are many applications and almost no exceptions to this maxim.

He who comes to equity must come with clean hands This maxim is fundamentally distinct. It concerns the previous conduct of the party seeking relief. If the applicant has been guilty of misconduct in the events leading up to the application, then relief will be refused.

Delay defeats equity It is said that the law does not aid those who sleep on their rights. The maxim has been robbed of most of its practical importance by the Statute of Limitations 1957 which imposes strict time limits for bringing an action but continues to apply to those equitable claims which are outside the act.

Equity is equality Where two or more persons are entitled to an interest in the same property, then the principle of equity is equal division, provided there is no good reason for any other basis for division.

The Constitution of Ireland

The Constitution of Ireland 1937 (Bunreacht na hÉireann), is the basis of Ireland's constitutional law and the most important source of domestic law. The Constitution is superior to all other forms of Irish law (subject only to EU law). Article 29.10 of the Constitution provides:

> "No provision of this Constitution invalidates laws enacted, acts done or measures adopted by the State which are necessitated by the obligations of membership of the European Union."

The Constitution deals with such matters as the national territory, the President, the legislature (or Oireachtas, which is the National Parliament, consisting of the President, Dáil Éireann and Seanad Éireann), the Executive (i.e. the Government comprising the Taoiseach and ministers), the judiciary, and fundamental rights, which relate to (1) personal rights (2) the family (3) education (4) religion (5) private property and which are contained in Articles 40–44. There are also certain 'unenumerated' rights not written in the body of the text, but which are nonetheless protected by the Constitution. The courts have recognised many 'unenumerated' personal rights, such as the right to privacy, the right to earn a livelihood and the right to bodily integrity.

In the case of *Ryan v. Attorney General* (1965) the plaintiff claimed that a local authority scheme involving the fluoridation of the water supply violated her family's rights by subjecting them to a form of medication that they had not sought. Mr Justice Kenny **held** that the "personal rights" of the citizen as guaranteed by Article 40 of the Constitution were not confined to those specified.

Certain unspecified rights flow from what the judge called in his decision, "the Christian and democratic nature of the State". He concluded that the plaintiff *did* enjoy an unenumerated constitutional right to "bodily integrity". Having considered scientific evidence, he was satisfied that this right had not been violated by the fluoridation scheme. This was upheld by the Supreme Court, which also endorsed the finding that constitutional rights are not confined to those specified in the text of the document.

In *McGee v. Attorney General* (1974) the plaintiff was a married woman and she and her husband decided that for medical reasons they did not want to extend their family any further. She issued proceedings claiming that the prohibition on contraception violated her right to marital privacy. She lost her case in the High Court but, upon appeal to the Supreme Court, a majority found in her favour in accordance with the approach adopted in the *Ryan* case. Of the majority of four, three treated the right to marital privacy as forming part of the personal rights not specified in the Constitution.

Statute Law

"Statute" denotes that body of law enacted by the parliamentary process. Statutes or Acts are, as a source of law, subject only to the Constitution and EU law and always prevail in the event of a conflict with the common law.

Legislature: the Oireachtas

The Constitution provides that the Oireachtas has "sole and exclusive" law-making power and that no statute repugnant to the Constitution shall be enacted; any repugnant statute is invalid. The principal role of the Oireachtas is to legislate.

The Oireachtas consists of the following.

- The Dáil – initiates legislation.
- The Seanad – consults and provides advice on Bills initiated in the Dáil.
- The President – guardian of the Constitution.

The Dáil

- The number of Teachtaí Dála (TDs) cannot be more than one for every 20,000 of the population and cannot be less than one for every 30,000 (the current number is 166).
- The country is divided into 42 constituencies and every constituency must elect at least three members to the Dáil. As far as possible, the ratio of population to TD must be equal in each constituency.

The constituencies must be revised at least once every 12 years, although in practice they are revised after the census is published every five years.
- The maximum life of the Dáil is five years, although at any time the Taoiseach may advise the President to dissolve the Dáil.
- A Bill may be commenced in either the Dáil or the Seanad but it must be passed, by both Houses to become law. Usually, Bills are commenced in Dáil Eireann.

The Seanad

The Seanad has 60 members, 49 of whom are elected in the Seanad elections and the remaining 11 are appointed by the Taoiseach.
- To be eligible to become a senator, you must be over 21 and an Irish citizen.
- A Bill may start life in either the Dáil or the Seanad. In practice, the vast majority of Bills originate from the Government and are passed by the Dáil first. They are then sent to the Seanad for debate and consideration. Within 90 days, the Seanad may propose amendments, reject or pass a Bill. The Dáil has the power to override the Seanad's rejection of a Bill.
- The Seanad's powers in relation to Bills for Government spending (money Bills) are very restricted. These Bills cannot start life in the Seanad, they must come from the Dáil. The Seanad has only 21 days to consider a money Bill and cannot make amendments to it.
- The Seanad has other functions, which it shares with the Dáil, such as the removal from office of the President or a judge, declaring a state of emergency and annulling statutory instruments.

The President

The President's duties under the constitution are twofold:
- ceremonial duties as Head of State; and
- the guardianship of the Constitution.

Guardian of the Constitution The most important power that the President holds is under Article 26 of the Constitution. The President may, after consultation with the Council of State, refer any bill to the Supreme Court for a decision on its constitutionality.

Election of the President The President is directly elected by the people for a period of seven years and may be re-elected only once. Presidential candidates must be Irish citizens, be at least 35 years old and be nominated by at least 20 members of the Oireachtas or by four county councils.

Removal of the President The President is not answerable to the Oireachtas or to any court for the exercise of his or her functions. There are two constitutional mechanisms for the removal of the President:

- permanent incapacity: Article 12.3.1 of the Constitution provides that a President may be removed for permanent incapacitation if five Supreme Court judges are satisfied of this.
- impeachment for stated misbehavior (Article 12.10.1).

Delegated Legislation

Primary legislation is created by the legislature. Secondary or *delegated legislation* is law made by an executive authority under powers delegated by primary legislation in order to implement and administer the requirements of that primary legislation. Examples of those who have power to create delegated legislation include Government ministers, local authorities and professional or specialist bodies.

Examples of Delegated Legislation

Ministerial Orders Orders are generally made in respect of a single exercise of a delegated power and are administrative in nature. An example is the Misuse of Drugs Act 1977, which prohibits the possession of approximately 250 drugs. The Government is empowered by the Act to make an order adding additional prohibited substances to this list.

Statutory Instruments, Regulations and Rules These are enacted by ministers empowered to do so under various statutes or Acts and usually flesh out the matters contained in the parent statute. For example, under the Road Traffic Act 1961, the minister can present statutory instruments covering a wide variety of legislation. **Rules** are also legislative in nature but are usually of a procedural type. For example, the Rules of the Superior Courts 1986, as amended, regulate the practice and procedure of the High Court and Supreme Court.

Schemes These are orders involving figures and the calculation of fees or charges.

Bye-laws This is an ordinance affecting the public, or a portion of the public, imposed by an authority with statutory powers, ordering something to be done or not to be done, and accompanied by some sanction or penalty for its non-observance. For example, local authorities are empowered by various statutes with limited power to enact bye-laws.

Advantages and Disadvantages of Delegated Legislation

The advantages of delegated legislation are as follows.

- **Time-saving** – delegated legislation can be introduced quickly and necessary changes can be made without having to go through the entire debating process in the Oireachtas.
- **Access to particular skill and expertise** – given the highly specialised and extremely technical nature of many of the regulations that are introduced through delegated legislation, the majority of members of the Oireachtas simply do not have sufficient expertise to consider such provisions effectively.
- **Flexibility** – delegated legislation responds on an *ad hoc* basis to particular problems as they arise. It limits the need for the formal legislative process for dealing with administrative details.

The disadvantages of delegated legislation are:

- **Accountability** – the Oireachtas is presumed to be the source of statute law but, with respect to delegated legislation, Government ministers, and the civil servants who work under them to produce the detailed provisions, are the real source of the legislation.
- **Bulk** – given the sheer mass of such legislation, members of Parliament and the general public face difficulty in keeping abreast of delegated legislation.

Constitutional Limits Regarding Delegated Legislation

Although the Constitution facilitates the delegation of legislation (Article 15.2.1), this delegation is limited to the power to make regulations that give effect to the principles and policies contained in a principal Act/piece of legislation. In addition, the delegated legislation must not attempt to "change, amend or repeal" the law.

Controls Regarding Delegated Legislation

Parliamentary control over delegated legislation Power to make delegated legislation is ultimately dependent upon the authority of the Oireachtas. Secondary legislation is controlled by the powers that the Oireachtas delegated in the primary legislation.

Judicial control over delegated legislation The ultimate safeguard in ensuring that secondary legislation does not go beyond the power delegated by primary legislation is judicial control. The general principle is that a power may only be exercised by the authority in which it is vested. Additionally, this power must be exercised in a manner that is reasonable, and not arbitrary, unjust or unfair. In *Cassidy v. Minister for Industry and Commerce* (1978) the court declared that a minimum prices order, which controlled the price of intoxicating liquor sold in the urban district of Dundalk, was invalid based on unreasonableness of the exercise of the delegated power in that it only affected one area of the country.

Delegated legislation can also be challenged through a process of judicial review, on the basis that the person or body to whom the Oireachtas has delegated its authority has acted in a way that exceeds the limited powers delegated, or has failed to follow the appropriate procedure set down in the enabling legislation. Any provision made in this way is said to be *ultra vires* and is void.

Miscellaneous controls Other safeguards regarding delegated legislation include the Statutory Instruments Act 1947, which requires the **publication** of all delegated legislation. A copy of every statutory instrument to which the Act applies must be sent to certain listed libraries within 10 days of being made, as well as a notice of making it and a list of the places where it can be obtained. It must be published in *Iris Oifigiúil*, and the Government Stationery Office must publish the instrument itself. Similarly, section 42 of the Local Government Act 1994 requires the local authority to publish a notice of making a bye-law in *Iris Oifigiúil*, and also to publish it in one or more newspapers circulating in the area to which the bye-law relates.

Delegated Legislation and Presumptions

There are also **presumptions** made with regard to delegated legislation. In outline, it is presumed that the Oireachtas will *not*:

- delegate the power to raise taxes to a Government minister;
- delegate power to undermine the jurisdiction of the court;
- delegate power that encroaches upon the liberty or constitutional rights of a citizen; and
- propose any order that would give retrospective power to delegated legislation.

The Interpretation of Statutes

If the words of a statute are absolutely clear, there will be no need for statutory interpretation. However, interpretation will be necessary where there is either:

- ambiguity (the words used are capable of two meanings); or
- uncertainty (where it is unclear what the words are referring to).

Unless the statute contains express words to the contrary, the following presumptions apply:

(a) a statute does not alter the existing law nor repeal other statutes; and
(b) a statute does not have retrospective effect, i.e. it only governs the law in a particular area from the day it is signed into law.

Generally, a statute deals expressly with these matters to avoid doubt. Common law judges have developed a system to guide them when interpreting statutes in addition to the presumptions outlined above. The three fundamental rules are known as the '**three canons of construction**'.

The Literal Rule

The literal rule means that the courts give the words of a statute their ordinary, everyday meaning. In using this rule of interpretation, a judge will be concerned with what the statute actually says.

Rahill v. Brady (1971) concerned an objection by two publicans to the granting of a licence to sell intoxicating liquor to the proprietor of a cattle mart. The licence (an "occasional licence") was granted on the basis that cattle marts, held twice weekly throughout the year, were "special events" for the purposes of section 11(1) of the Intoxicating Liquor Act 1962. "Special" was not defined by the Act. On the ordinary literal interpretation of the word "special", it would have appeared that the mart, which occurred twice weekly throughout the year, could not reasonably be regarded as "special". It was argued that the history of intoxicating liquor acts showed an intention to exempt marts from the ordinary licensing laws. The court **held** that the evidence failed to establish clearly that a literal meaning would conflict with the intention of the legislature.

The Golden Rule

The golden rule is considered an extension of the literal rule and is used in circumstances where the application of the literal rule would lead to absurdity. In the case of *Re Sigsworth* (1935) a son had murdered his mother, who had not made her will. Under the Administration of Justice Act 1925, her estate would be inherited by her next of kin (i.e. her son). There was no ambiguity in the words of the Act but the court **held** that the golden rule should apply in order to prevent the repugnant situation of the son, in these circumstances, receiving his inheritance.

The Mischief Rule

The courts may look at the purpose of the legislation to see what 'mischief' it was trying to remedy. In looking at a law prior to the enactment of the statute to ascertain the defect that the legislation was intended to remedy, the court is guided in interpreting the terms of the statute.

In *Nestor v. Murphy* (1979), the statutory provision in question was section 3(1) of the Family Home Protection Act 1976, which states:

> "[W]here a spouse, without the prior consent in writing of the other spouse, purports to convey any interest in the family home to any person except the other spouse, then ... the purported conveyance shall be void."

The case concerned a married couple whose family home was *held jointly* and who were refusing to complete a contract on the ground that the wife had not consented in writing to the sale before the contract was signed. The purpose of this section was to afford the non-owning spouse of a family home some protection in law. Mr Justice Henchy delivered the judgment for the Supreme Court and commented:

> "The basic purpose of the sub-section is to protect the family home by giving a right of avoidance to the spouse who was not a party to the transaction ... The sub-section cannot have been intended by Parliament to apply when both spouses join in the 'conveyance'. In such event no protection is needed for one spouse against an unfair and unnotified alienation by the other of an interest in the family home . . . When both spouses join in the 'conveyance', the evil at which the sub-section is directed does not exist."

Other Rules of Statutory Interpretation

The ejusdem generis rule ("of the same kind") Statutes often list two or more specific words and then follow these with general words. The wide meaning of general words must be restricted to the same class as the preceding specific words.

For example, the case of *DPP v. Farrell* (1978) concerned the construction of section 30 of the Offences Against the State Act 1939. The legality of detaining the applicant centred on whether a garda car could be regarded as a "convenient place" in accordance with the legislation. Mr Justice O'Higgins considered that it could not, since the *ejusdem generis* rule required that the term be construed in the light of the other places of detention listed: "Garda Síochána station, a prison, or some other convenient place". The rule required that, as a minimum, "convenient place" be a building of some kind.

Expressio unius est exclusio alterius To express one thing is by implication to exclude everything else, e.g. a statutory rule concerning dogs does not include cats.

The rule of context A word should be construed in its context – in other words it is permissible to look at the statute as a whole in order to discover the meaning of any word in it.

The Advantages and Disadvantages of Statute Law

The advantages of statute law are:

- statute law is in written form and is easily available;
- statute law can be used to clarify or supplement the common law; and
- in Ireland, the Oireachtas can make law on any subject it thinks fit, subject to the Constitution. The Oireachtas can take public opinion and social policy into account in making new laws.

The disadvantages of statute law are:

- statute law can become so bulky and complex that it may be difficult to ascertain its intended meaning;
- bad drafting may create ambiguities;
- if the meaning of a statute is uncertain judicial interpretation may be necessary, which is costly for the litigants involved;
- it is difficult to change a major piece of legislation, as any change requires a new Bill; and
- legislation may be rushed through without adequate care or attention due to scarcity of parliamentary time.

Judicial Precedent

'*Stare decisis*' is a Latin term meaning 'let the decision stand'. It is a policy whereby the courts adhere to principles established in earlier cases in order to provide legal certainty. A principle or precedent may be binding or persuasive on the court, depending on the particular circumstances.

Both the common law and equity have evolved from decisions of the courts, and judicial precedent is another important source of law. A **precedent** is a judgment or decision of a court of law that is cited as an authority to justify a decision in a case involving a similar set of facts.

There are different types of precedent:

- **authoritative** – precedent is binding and must be followed;
- **persuasive** – precedent is worthy of consideration, but need not be followed (e.g. based on an *obiter dictum* – see below);
- **declaratory** – precedent is where the precedent merely applies an existing rule of law; and
- **original** – precedent is where it creates and applies a new rule of law.

A precedent is said to be **applied** when it is followed. It is said to be **distinguished** where a judge holds that there are important differences between the case on which the precedent was based and the case now being considered.

The operation of the doctrine of precedent depends on the hierarchy of the courts. The hierarchy of the courts regulates which decisions are binding on which courts and helps to ensure that the law is applied uniformly. The Irish Supreme Court binds all courts, although it is not bound by its own decisions (see *State (Quinn) v. Ryan* (1965). In this case, the Supreme Court declined to follow a previous decision of its own in which it had declared a statutory provision to be constitutional).

The High Court binds the Circuit and District Courts, i.e. a Circuit or District Court judge in applying the law in a given case must follow the decisions of the High Court. The Court of Criminal Appeal binds the Central Criminal Court, the Special Criminal Court, and Circuit and District Courts on criminal matters.

The growth of formal law reporting in Ireland has made the system of precedent more workable. *The Irish Reports* and the *Irish Law Reports Monthly* report on and publish all the important decisions, and so make it easier to refer to previous decisions and determine precedent.

Although the Irish courts are not bound by decisions in other jurisdictions, these can provide persuasive authority that may influence the Irish courts in applying the law in this country. The courts frequently look at decisions in other common law jurisdictions such as England, Australia and Canada to assist them in making a decision.

The Advantages and Disadvantages of Binding Precedent

The advantages of binding judicial precedent are as follows.

- **Consistency** – in order for the law to be decided fairly, consistency and uniformity of decision-making must be maintained. Ideally, it should be possible to predict the ruling of a court in a particular set of circumstances based on previous decisions of the court involving a similar set of issues.
- **Flexibility** – the law is capable of change and development – new decisions are always being added as new factual situations come before the courts.

The disadvantages of binding judicial precedent are as follows.

- **Expense** – the law can often only be known after an expensive court action.
- **Limitations** – the binding force of precedent can have the effect of limiting judicial discretion.

- **Complexity** – in order to avoid having to follow precedent legal counsel may often persuade judges that there are distinctions in the facts of cases which have no real substance and have the effect of complicating the law.

Otherwise binding precedent can be avoided:

- by 'distinguishing the facts' – the court may do this if the facts are not identical and the differences appear significant;
- when a previously decided case is said to be in conflict with a fundamental principle. (For example, the court may find that to follow an earlier decision of a parallel court would interfere with a fundamental principle of law and may refuse to do so);
- by declaring an earlier precedent to be too wide;
- because the earlier decision has been subsequently overruled by another court or by statute; and
- by declaring the previous decision made *per incuriam* – that it was made without taking account of some binding point of law.

Ratio Decidendi *and* Obiter Dicta

The system of judicial precedent is not as rigid as might first appear. Not everything that a judge (or court) says in the course of his or her judgment becomes a binding precedent. The binding part of the decision is known as the *ratio decidendi*. The *ratio decidendi* is the reason for a judicial decision. It is the ratio that forms the precedent for other similar cases.

If a judge's statements of legal principles do not form the basis of the decision then such statements are known as *obiter dicta*, or statements said 'by the way'. Examples of this would be where the statements are not based on the facts of a case but on hypothetical facts, or if his or her judgment is dissenting (dissenting judgments arise where one or more judges in a case have reached a different conclusion to the majority of their colleagues). These statements do not bind a later court, but they are of persuasive authority, especially if made by eminent judges.

Custom

Custom denotes rules of conduct which, by virtue of long usage, have the force of law. A valid custom must have been exercised since "time immemorial" (1189). In practice, if this is not possible, the court will accept evidence that it existed in living memory. If, however, it can be shown that it could not have existed in 1189, the custom will fail.

Simpson v. Wells (1872) involved a claim that custom of statute sessions (a type of fair) entitled the plaintiff to set up a stall on a public pathway. It was shown that the first statute session took place in the Fourteenth Century, and so could not have existed in 1189.

Custom must be certain, reasonable and not contrary to statute.

THE COURTS SYSTEM

Though a courts system has existed under Irish jurisdiction since 1924, the hierarchy of courts that exists today was formally established by the Courts (Establishment and Constitution) Act 1961. There must, by virtue of the Irish Constitution, be a Supreme Court and a High Court which are known as the Superior Courts. Other courts of a limited and local nature have been established by statute and are known as inferior courts. These are the Circuit Court and the District Court. *Jurisdiction* means the power of a court to hear and determine a case.

The District Court

Article 34 of the Constitution permits the establishment of courts of "local and limited jurisdiction". The District Court was established by section 5 of the Courts Act 1961. The country is divided into 24 districts, with one or more judges permanently assigned to each district and the Dublin Metropolitan District.

Composition of the District Court

The District Court is presided over by the President of the District Court and, in addition, 63 judges. The monetary jurisdiction of the District Court was increased from €6,348.69 to €15,000.00 by the Courts and Civil Law (Miscellaneous Provisions) Act 2013. It deals with actions based in tort and contract law. The decision of a District Court judge who sits alone when hearing the case can be appealed to the Circuit Court. Either party to a case may appeal a decision to the Circuit Court and the appeal takes the form of a *full rehearing.*

Jurisdiction of the District Court

The jurisdiction of the Circuit Court when hearing an appeal from the District Court is the same as for an original District Court action. It is a final appeal on a question of fact. If a question of law arises (e.g. the interpretation of a statute), either party may request that the District Court judge, or he or she may decide to, state a case to the High Court (i.e. skip a court level) on a question of law. The question is decided in the High Court, which sends its answer back to the District Court judge, who applies it to the case before him or her.

The District Court can deal, *inter alia*, with the following matters.

- **Liquor licensing** – the District Court can renew spirit and liquor licences.
- **Family law** – the District Court can deal with applications for maintenance and access to children and can grant barring orders.
- **Landlord and tenant** – the District Court can grant orders to landlords for the ejectment of tenants.

Criminal Jurisdiction of the District Court

The majority of criminal cases heard in the District Court are summary offences (offences for which there is no right of trial by judge and jury). They are exclusively statutory in origin and punishment does not usually exceed 12 months' imprisonment and/or a fine of up to €1,905.

Indictable offences (more serious offences to which there is a right to a trial with a judge and jury) can be tried summarily in the District Court with the consent of the accused and the DPP and where the judge is of the opinion that the offence constitutes a minor offence.

The Circuit Court

Composition of the Circuit Court

The Circuit Court is a court of local and limited jurisdiction. It was established by section 4 of the Courts Act 1961. The State is divided into eight circuits with one or more judges assigned to each circuit. The Circuit Court consists of the President of the Circuit Court and 37 ordinary judges. The judges travel to different towns in the circuit at prescribed times of the year to hear local cases. There are also approximately eight judges permanently assigned to the Dublin Circuit.

Jurisdiction of the Circuit Court

The civil jurisdiction of the Circuit Court is a limited one, unless all parties to an action consent, in which event the jurisdiction is unlimited. The monetary jurisdiction of the Circuit Court was increased from €38,092.14 to €75,000 by the Courts and Civil Law (Miscellaneous Provisions) Act 2013, with the exception of personal injury actions, which are limited to €60,000. Examples of the types of cases heard by the Circuit Court include actions in tort, contract and family law.

The Circuit Court judge may, during the proceedings, consult the Court of Appeal for clarification on a question of law. A decision of the Circuit Court may be appealed to the High Court and once again this is by way of a **full rehearing**. The appeal to the High Court is the final appeal on all questions of fact.

The Circuit Court can deal, *inter alia*, with the following civil matters.

- **Liquor licensing** – the Circuit Court can grant new spirit and liquor licences.
- **Family law** – the Circuit Court can grant orders of judicial separation, decrees of divorce and orders of nullity.
- **Landlord and tenant** – the Circuit Court can grant orders determining the ownership of parcels of land, etc.
- **Contract law** – the Circuit Court can grant orders relating to breach of contracts.
- **Tort** – the Circuit Court can grant orders relating to tortious actions (e.g. personal injuries).

The Circuit Court hears trial by jury of criminal, indictable offences other than those which must be tried in the Central Criminal Court, which deals with serious crimes, such as murder, rape, aggravated sexual assault and piracy.

The High Court

Composition of the High Court

The High Court consists of a President, who is an ex-officio judge of the Supreme Court and a member of the Council of State, and not more than 37 ordinary judges. The President of the Circuit Court and the Chief Justice are, by virtue of their office, additional judges of the High Court.

Civil Jurisdiction of the High Court

The High Court has full original jurisdiction over all matters whether of law or fact, civil or criminal. The High Court has unlimited jurisdiction. Since the passing of the Courts Act 1988, juries are rare in civil cases.

The High Court deals with:

- cases where the damages claimed exceed €75,000 or €60,000 in personal injury actions;
- cases questioning the validity of any law or legislation in relation to the Constitution (except references under Article 26);
- cases under the Companies Acts;
- cases under the Bankruptcy Act 1988;
- judicial review of the decisions of lower courts or tribunals;

- appeals from the Circuit Court; and
- rulings on questions of law submitted by the District Court.

The Commercial Court

The Commercial Court was set up in 2004 as a subdivision of the High Court with the specific purpose of facilitating speedy resolution of commercial disputes. It is "effectively a fast track division of the High Court … [and] has garnered a … reputation for dealing with commercial litigation in a practical and cost-effective manner". (Source: www.dilloneustace.ie)

Entry into the Commercial Court List A special application must be made to enter the Commercial Court list and only certain cases will be admitted. Generally the court deals with high-value disputes that involve a claim of €1 million or more.

The Commercial Court Rules (Order 63A of the Rules of the Superior Courts (S.I. No. 2 of 2004)) set out a series of categories that are classified as 'commercial proceedings' in respect of any claim or counterclaim relating to:

- a business document, business contract or business dispute;
- the purchase or sale of commodities;
- the export or import of goods;
- the carriage of goods by land, sea, air or pipeline;
- the exploitation of oil or gas reserves or any other natural resource;
- insurance or re-insurance;
- the provision of services (not including medical, quasi-medical or dental services or any service provided under a contract of employment);
- the operation of markets or exchanges in stocks, shares or other financial or investment instruments or in commodities;
- the construction of any vehicle, vessel or aircraft; and
- business agency.

In addition to this, the court has jurisdiction to hear cases involving intellectual property and judicial review, both with no minimum value threshold.

There is no automatic right of entry into the Commercial Court and the judge retains discretion to refuse entry. A common ground for refusal is where the moving party has caused delay in bringing about the action. Although there is a minimum value limit on cases, the judge may decide to grant an exception to the rule based on the complexities of the issues in the case.

Composition of the Commercial Court The Commercial Court has one judge assisted by other judges presiding over the list. Judges of the Commercial Court have commercial expertise and can deal with complex issues.

Operation of the Commercial Court Recent statistics demonstrate that a quarter of the cases entered into the commercial list of the High Court "conclude in less than 4 weeks and over 90% conclude within a year".

> "[The] Court has its own specific set of rules which dictates the manner in which the Court issues directions to the parties and the way it conducts proceedings once at trial. The Rules are designed to encourage litigating parties to agree as many issues as possible between them before the matter goes to trial so that the hearing can focus only on relevant issues that remain in dispute." (Dillon Eustace)

Cases may also be adjourned to allow for mediation on application by the parties or at the judge's own discretion.

Examples of Commercial Court Actions

One of the striking features of the Commercial Court is the nature of proceedings the court is willing to hear.

In *MCD Productions v. Nelson* (2008), MCD had sued the singer Prince (real name Prince Rogers Nelson) and his agents William Morris Endeavor Entertainment for €1.7 million over the cancellation of a concert at Croke Park in 2008. The case was entered into the Commercial Court list as it fell within the definition of a 'commercial dispute' and involved a claim of €1.6 million. Ultimately, the case was settled.

In *Irish Bank Resolution Corporation Ltd v. Quinn* (2012), a €2 billion judgment was obtained against John Ignatius Quinn, also known as Seán Quinn, in the Commercial Court in 2011. The Irish Bank Resolution Corporation (IBRC), formerly Anglo Irish Bank, successfully applied to transfer its case for summary judgment to the Commercial Court claim to fast-track the procedure. The judgment arose out of personal guarantees provided by Mr Quinn over unpaid business loans, and it is the highest monetary judgment made by the Court to date.

Criminal Jurisdiction of the High Court

The High Court in its criminal guise is known as the Central Criminal Court. Certain offences must be heard by the Central Criminal Court sitting with a judge and jury. These include murder (including attempted murder and conspiracy), treason, rape, aggravated sexual assault and attempted aggravated sexual assault under the Criminal Law (Rape) (Amendment) Act 1990.

Special Criminal Court

Special Criminal Courts are established where the ordinary courts are inadequate to secure the effective administration of justice and the preservation of public peace and order. There is no jury in the Special Criminal Court and it comprises three judges, usually one High Court judge, one Circuit Court judge and a District Court judge. Criminal cases are transferred from the ordinary criminal courts to the Special Criminal Court for two reasons:

- they may be a **scheduled** offence, i.e. any offence under the Offences Against the State Act 1939.
- the offences may not be scheduled but the DPP has issued a certificate stating that, in his or her opinion, the ordinary courts are inadequate to secure the administration of justice and the preservation of public peace and order.

An appeal against a conviction or sentence may be taken to the Court of Appeal.

The Court of Appeal

As a result of an amendment to the Constitution in October 2014, significant changes were made to the Supreme Court's appellate jurisdiction. The Court of Appeal has appellate jurisdiction in both civil and criminal matters and sat for the first time in November 2014. The introduction of the Court of Appeal came about to streamline the work of the Supreme Court as the waiting time for an appeal to the Supreme Court had reached over four years. It also replaced the Court of Criminal Appeal. It is the default appeal court from decisions of the High Court and its decisions are final (save in very limited circumstances). Additionally, questions of law which could previously be referred by the Circuit Court to the Supreme Court for determination are now determinable by the Court of Appeal.

Composition of the Court of Appeal

The court is presided over by a President and nine ordinary judges. It sits in divisions of three judges.

The Supreme Court

The Supreme Court was established pursuant to Article 34 of the Constitution, which provides for a 'court of final appeal'.

The Supreme Court comprises nine ordinary judges and the Chief Justice. The President of the High Court is *ex officio* a member of the Supreme Court. The court usually sits with three or five judges and, in exceptional circumstances, seven judges. In all constitutional cases, the court consists of five judges. The decision of the court is that of the majority, although each judge may deliver a separate judgment, except in a decision on the validity of a law having regard to the Constitution, when one decision only may be delivered.

Original Jurisdiction of the Supreme Court

The Supreme Court has original jurisdiction under Articles 26 and 12 of the Constitution:

- the President of Ireland may consult the Supreme Court to test the constitutionality of any Bill before the Oireachtas under Article 26 of the Constitution.
- under Article 12 of the Constitution, the Supreme Court can remove the President for "permanent incapacity".

Appellate Jurisdiction of the Supreme Court

The appellate jurisdiction of the Supreme Court was modified in 2014 by the insertion of Article 34.5.4 of the Constitution which brought about the introduction of the Court of Appeal. The Supreme Court now operates appellate jurisdiction in two circumstances, as outlined by the Courts Service:

> "(a) from a decision of the Court of Appeal if the Supreme Court is satisfied that the decision involves a matter of general public importance, or in the interests of justice it is necessary that there be an appeal to the Supreme Court (Article 34.5.3 of the Constitution) and
>
> (b) from a decision of the High Court if the Supreme Court is satisfied that there are exceptional circumstances warranting a direct appeal to it – a precondition for the Supreme Court being so satisfied is the presence of either or both of the following factors – the decision involves a matter of general public importance; the interests of justice (Article 34.5.4 of the Constitution)."

(Source: www.courts.ie)

ARBITRATION

Arbitration is an alternative means of dispute resolution to litigation in the courts. Parties agree to refer their dispute to an independent third party known as an 'arbitrator'. Arbitration is governed by the rules set out in the Arbitration Act 2010. An arbitration hearing is similar to a court case in that it normally involves pleadings and a full hearing is based on the law of

Table 1.2 Structure of the Courts

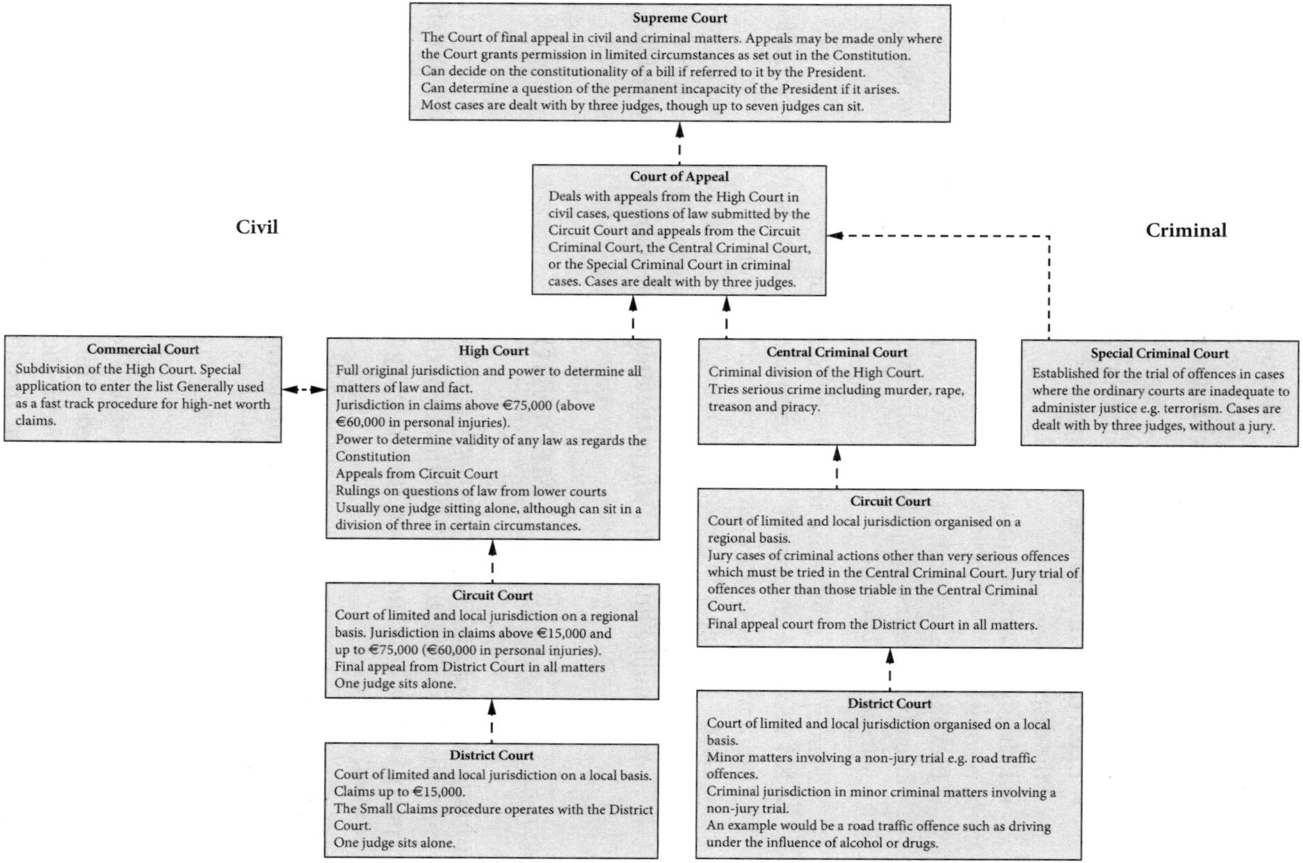

evidence applicable to court proceedings. An arbitrator has the same powers as a judge to award costs against the unsuccessful party.

Arbitration is commonly used as a dispute resolution process in the construction industry, and arbitration dispute clauses are included in terms and conditions of contracts in the travel industry. The decisions of an arbitrator are fully binding on the parties.

Advantages to arbitration include the following.

- **Expertise** – the arbitrator is normally an expert in the subject matter of the dispute.
- **Privacy** – arbitration is a private and confidential means of dispute resolution.
- **Flexibility** – arbitration provides greater flexibility: an arbitrator can usually be found quickly, thereby avoiding the long delays associated with court actions.

Disadvantages of arbitration include the following.

- **No recourse to appeal** – an arbitrator's award is normally final and binding without recourse to appeal in the courts.
- **Cost** – though arbitration may reduce costs in certain areas of dispute, the parties have the financial burden of paying for the arbitrator and venue, unlike litigation, where the judge and court are provided for.

MEDIATION

Mediation is a method of alternative dispute resolution where the parties of a dispute come together with the assistance of an independent third party known as a 'mediator' for the purpose of resolving a dispute themselves.

Mediation can be used as an alternative to going to court, or the parties may adjourn proceedings in an effort to reach a resolution through mediation. It is particularly successful in areas of family law, employment law, partnership disputes and other areas where parties may have ongoing relationships.

Mediation works on the premise that it is 'without prejudice', i.e. what is said at mediation cannot later be referred to in a court of law. Parties often enter into 'mediation agreements' that govern the confidentiality of what is said at mediation, therefore giving them the freedom to discuss matters openly and honestly. Mediation is non-binding until the point at which an agreement is executed, and parties are free to try mediation and commence proceedings or return to court should it not succeed.

TRIBUNALS

There are two types of tribunals used in Ireland, quasi-judicial and investigative tribunals.

Quasi-judicial Tribunals

Quasi-judicial tribunals are permitted by Article 34 of the Irish Constitution for matters other than criminal. Permanent in nature with specialised functions, these tribunals are made up of individuals who have specialist skills and knowledge in the particular area at issue. They can make binding decisions and enforce sanctions against the persons called before them and may be judicially reviewed by the High Court to ensure that they comply with fair procedures.

Examples of such tribunals are the Employment Appeals Tribunal, Solicitors Disciplinary Tribunal and An Bord Pleanála.

Advantages of quasi-judicial tribunals include the following.

- **Specialist skills** – the tribunal consists of specialists in a particular area, e.g. planning or employment.
- **Speed** – tribunals are usually heard on a specific date and are not subject to the vagaries of the court system.
- **Informality** – tribunals are supposed to be informal in order to make them less intimidating than full-blown court cases. The stricter rules relating to evidence, pleading and procedure, which apply in the courts, are not binding in tribunal proceedings.
- **Flexibility** – tribunals are not bound by the strict rules of precedent, although some pay more regard to previous decisions than others.

Disadvantages of a quasi-judicial tribunal include the following.

- **Appeals procedures** – appeals are allowed to the High Court but only for the purposes of ensuring compliance with fair procedures, and on the basis of a review of the decision, not the facts of the case. The function of the High Court is to judicially review the decision to ensure it was reached in a procedurally fair manner.
- **Costs** – although these tribunals are less formal than the courts system, an individual, given the seriousness of the sanctions imposed, often appoints a solicitor as well as a junior and senior counsel to represent them at tribunals; for instance, at the Solicitors Disciplinary Tribunal, which deals with complaints of misconduct.

Investigative Tribunals of Inquiry

Tribunals of inquiry are set up to investigate matters of public importance and report back with their findings to the Oireachtas. Established under the

Tribunals of Inquiry (Evidence) Act 1921, they serve a fact-finding purpose, are set up with powers to investigate specific matters and are temporary in nature. Once its investigation is complete, the tribunal presents a report of its findings to the Oireachtas. A tribunal of inquiry may also have the power to make recommendations with a view to preventing the same problem arising in the future.

This type of tribunal does not have the power to make judgments on individuals, as it does not have a judicial function. It simply reports on the results of its investigations and the findings of fact it has made. Examples of such investigative tribunals include: the Laffoy Commission, which investigated claims of child abuse in the State's industrial schools; the Moriarty Tribunal, set up to investigate payments to politicians; and the Morris Tribunal, which was established to investigate complaints concerning some gardaí of the Donegal division.

Advantages of investigative tribunals of inquiry include the following.

- **Public importance** – they fulfil an important function of public importance in investigating and providing information to the Oireachtas as to how certain matters occurred.
- **Recommendations** – for example, recommendations in relation to law reform to prevent a reoccurrence of the issue before them.
- **Flexibility** – tribunals are not bound by the strict rules of precedent, although some pay more regard to previous decisions than others.

Disadvantages of investigative tribunals of inquiry include the following.

- **Appeals procedures** – the terms of reference (what needs to be investigated) are decided by the Oireachtas, and the chairperson of the tribunal may have to go back to the Oireachtas to have them amended, which could delay the whole process.
- **Time/delay** – some tribunals have been prolonged for many years.
- **Cost** – some tribunals have cost the Irish taxpayer millions of euro.
- **Limited function** – a tribunal of inquiry cannot make binding decisions or penalise individuals; only the results of its investigations and the findings of fact are reported.

EUROPEAN UNION LAW

Although the Constitution of Ireland 1937 represents the fundamental law in the State, it is not supreme in all respects since Ireland joined the EEC in 1972. Membership requires that Community law should become part of the internal law of each Member State and be applied in the national courts. The primary law of the Community, which is contained in the principal Treaties, applies automatically to Ireland and takes precedence over domestic law (even provisions of Member State's constitutions), provided it is necessitated by Ireland's membership of the European Union.

In *Internationale Handelsgesellschaft mbH v. Einfuhr- und Vorratsstelle für Getreide und Futtermittel* (1970) the applicant company obtained an export licence for a quantity of maize, which expired on 31 December 1967. Under Council Regulation 120/67 the licence could be obtained by lodging a deposit which would be lost if goods were not exported within a specific period. The applicant lost a portion of his deposit as he had not exported the full amount of maize when it expired. He challenged the validity of this and the national court found that the deposit system was contrary to its constitutional law. It was decided by the European court that recourse to national legal rules or concepts in order to judge a community measure would have an adverse effect on community law. Validity of such measures can only be judged by reference to community law. A community measure cannot be impugned on the basis that it is contrary to the national law of a Member State.

Ireland formally joined what was then known as the 'European Economic Community' on 1 January 1973. Membership necessitated an amendment to Article 29 of the Constitution of Ireland and the ratification of the Treaty of Accession 1973. The original treaty, the Treaty of Rome 1957, had six signatories: France, Germany, Italy, Belgium, the Netherlands and Luxembourg. A number of fundamental principles underlined the original Treaty, in particular the founding of a common market and the development of ever-closer union between the peoples of Europe. As of July 2015, there are over 500 million EU citizens in 28 Member States.

What was the European Economic Community is now, since the ratification of the Single European Act, properly referred to as the European Union. The European Union is unique in that it is an international organisation having its own legal system and enforcement procedures.

The primary sources of **European Union law** are:

- the three basic Treaties: the European Coal and Steel Community Treaty, the Euratom Treaty and the European Economic Community Treaty;
- the Merger Treaty (1965);
- the Treaty on Budgetary Matters;
- the Accession Treaties;
- the Treaty on European Union of 1992 ("Maastricht Treaty");
- the Treaty of Amsterdam 1997;
- the Treaty of Nice 2002; and
- the Treaty of Lisbon 2007.

These Treaties are self-executing and apply automatically in Member States.

Sources of Secondary European Union Law

The secondary sources of European Union law are governed by Article 288 of the Treaty on the Functioning of the European Union (TFEU) and are created by either the Council of Ministers or the European Commission. They consist of:

Regulations

A Regulation is a legal measure that has general application, is binding in its entirety and is directly applicable in all Member States without the need for national legislative implementation. The main objective is to achieve uniformity in the laws of the Member States. It confers rights and imposes obligations to which it is addressed.

An example of a Regulation that is applicable to all Member States is Regulation 178/02 regarding food safety. This Regulation applies to all companies which are handling, processing, storing or moving food in the European Union. It is directly applicable and national governments did not have to undertake any local measure prior to it having effect.

Directives

Directives are addressed to Member States and not individuals, and are binding as to the result to be achieved, though Member States may adopt their own method of implementation. They are used to bring the laws of the Member States into line on relevant topics, such as company law. An example of a European Directive giving rise to a national implementation measure is the Directive on Liability for Defective Products 1985, which led to the implementation of the Liability for Defective Products Act 1991 in this jurisdiction.

Decisions

Decisions are acts that are directed at individual addressees which may be Member States or individuals, and are specifically named. Decisions are binding in their entirety and they are used to regulate specific situations. An example is *Commission of the European Communities v. Tetra Pak* (1996) where the Commission decided that the company had breached Community competition law and was liable to pay fines as a result.

Recommendations and **Opinions** may also be issued but these are merely persuasive and not binding.

The Effect of European Union Law in Ireland

As a consequence of the supremacy of EU law, any provision of national law that conflicts with EU law is invalid.

THE INSTITUTIONS OF THE EUROPEAN UNION

As outlined by Europa.eu, the official website of the European Union, the three main institutions are:

- the **European Parliament**, which represents the EU's citizens and is directly elected by them;
- the **Council of the European Union**, which represents the government of the individual member countries; and
- the **European Commission**, which represents the interests of the Union as a whole.

(Source: www.europa.eu)

EU laws and policies are produced by these institutions through the 'ordinary legislative procedure', which allows the European Parliament and the Council of the European Union to decide jointly on proposals given by the European Commission in a wide variety of areas, such as economic governance or the environment. In essence, new laws are proposed by the European Commission and the European Parliament and the Council adopts them. Member States implement the new laws and the Commission ensures that they are implemented and complied with.

The two other important institutions are:

- the **Court of Justice of the European Union**, whose role is to uphold the rule of EU law; and
- the **Court of Auditors**, which is responsible for checking the financial management of the EU's activities and implementation of budgets.

Council of the European Union

The Council of the EU is made up of a government representative of each Member State and is the means through which ministers meet to adopt laws and coordinate policies. There are no fixed members; at each Council meeting, each state sends the minister dealing with the particular area, e.g. the Minister for Agriculture attends meetings on the Common Agricultural Policy.

Functions of the Council of the EU include:

- passing EU laws;
- coordinating the broad economic policies of EU Member States;
- signing agreements between the EU and other countries;
- approving the annual EU budget;
- developing the EU's foreign and defence policies; and
- coordinating the cooperation between courts and police forces of Member States.

(Source: www.europa.eu)

The European Parliament

Every five years, the European Parliament is directly elected by EU voters. Along with the Council of the European Union, it is one of the EU's main law-making institutions.

"The European Parliament has three main roles:

- debating and passing European laws, with the Council
- scrutinising other EU institutions, particularly the Commission, to make sure they are working democratically;
- debating and adopting the EU's budget, with the Council."

(Source: www.europa.eu)

The European Union Commission

The EU Commission comprises 28 Commissioners one from each EU Member State and each is assigned a specific policy area of responsibility by the EU President.

> "The Commission upholds the interests of the EU as a whole. It drafts proposals for new European laws as well as managing the day-to-day business of implementing EU policies and spending EU funds."

The principal functions of the Commission are:

- proposing new laws to the European Parliament and Council;
- managing the EU's budget and allocating funding;
- enforcing EU law, working with the CJEU (the Commission can take actions against Member States that they believe are infringing EU law); and
- representing the EU internationally, e.g. at the World Trade Organisation.

Court of Justice of the European Union

The function of the Court of Justice of the European Union (CJEU) is to interpret EU law and to ensure that it is applied uniformly and consistently in all EU Member States. Any disputes that arise between EU institutions and Member State governments are also settled by the CJEU. Additionally, individuals and companies within the EU can bring cases to the court.

The CJEU is comprised of one judge from each EU Member State. There are also nine 'advocates-general' who assist the court by impartially presenting opinions on the cases brought before it. Judges and advocate-generals are appointed for a renewable six-year term.

Following the Lisbon Treaty in 2007, a General Court was introduced due to the high volume of cases brought to the Court of Justice. The function of the General Court is to offer better legal protections to citizens by dealing with cases brought by private individuals, companies, etc., and competition-related cases.

The five most common types of case brought before the CJEU are as follows:

"1. requests for a preliminary ruling – when national courts ask the Court of Justice to interpret a point of EU law
2. actions for failure to fulfil an obligation – brought against EU governments for not applying EU law
3. actions for annulment – against EU laws thought to violate the EU treaties or fundamental rights
4. actions for failure to act – against EU institutions for failing to make decisions required of them
5. direct actions – brought by individuals, companies or organisations against EU decisions or actions."

(Source: www.europa.eu)

The European Court of Auditors

The European Court of Auditors is responsible for auditing the EU's finances, reporting on the use of public funds and improving financial management. One of the court's key roles is compiling and presenting an annual financial report to the European Parliament and the Council. "Auditors frequently carry out inspections in EU institutions, member countries and countries receiving EU aid."

The European Court of Auditors is independent from the other EU institutions and comprises a member from each EU Member State. The Council appoints each member for a renewable term of six years, and the president of the court is appointed by the members. The president is elected for a renewable term of three years.

EUROPEAN CONVENTION ON HUMAN RIGHTS

The European Convention on Human Rights was created following the atrocities of the Second World War with the aim of ensuring respect and dignity for human life. It is separate to EU law, although many Member States of the EU have ratified it and incorporated it into their national law.

Ireland ratified the Treaty in 1953, but did not incorporate it into its national law until 2003. The Convention has had a prominent effect on human rights' issues in this country in areas such as rights for single fathers and decriminalisation of homosexual behaviour following applications to the European Court of Human Rights.

The European Convention on Human Rights Act 2003 (ECHR Act 2003) became enforceable on 31 December 2003 and is described as "an Act to enable further effect to be given, subject to the Constitution," to the rules of the European Convention on Human Rights. Section 2(1) of the Act provides that, in interpreting and applying any statutory provision or rule of law, an Irish court must, insofar as is possible and subject to the rules of law relating to such interpretation and application, do so in a manner compatible with the State's obligations under provisions of the European Convention.

In addition, section 4 provides that judicial notice must be taken of the provisions of the Convention and of:

1. any declaration, decision, advisory opinion or judgment of the European Court of Human Rights established under the Convention on any question in respect of which that court has jurisdiction;
2. any decision or opinion of the European Commission of Human Rights so established on any question in respect of which it had jurisdiction; and
3. any decision of the Committee of Ministers established under the Council of Europe on any question in respect of which it has jurisdiction.

The same provision further states that, when interpreting and applying the Convention provisions, a court must take due account of the principles laid down by those declarations, decisions, advisory opinions, opinions and judgments.

Section 5(1) of the ECHR Act 2003 provides that the High Court and the Supreme Court may make a declaration that a statutory provision or rule of law is incompatible with the State's obligations under the provisions of the Convention.

Section 6(1) provides, however, that the Attorney General and the Human Rights Commission must be given notice of the proceedings. Under section 5 a declaration of incompatibility will not affect the validity, continuing operation or enforcement of the statutory provision or rule of law in respect of which it is made. The making of such a declaration, however, does not prevent a party to the proceedings making representations in respect of the matter in any proceedings before the European Court of Human Rights. Furthermore, section 5(4) makes provision for the Government to make an *ex gratia* payment of compensation to a party to proceedings in which a declaration of incompatibility is made.

The effect of the ECHR Act 2003 on the manner in which the Irish courts interpret legislation is that national courts must now take cognisance of the principles of the Convention and their methods of legislative interpretation. However, national courts do not have the authority to declare legislation invalid if it violates the Convention. Thus, the Constitution remains superior to the European Convention on Human Rights. Unlike the English Human Rights Act 1988, the Irish legislation does not provide for the provision of remedial legislation through a fast-track procedure.

Application of the ECHR in the Irish Courts

In *M. O'Donnell (a minor) v. South Dublin County Council* (2007), the court found that South Dublin County Council had failed in its obligation under Article 8 of the ECHR (right to respect for one's "private and family life, his home and his correspondence", subject to certain restrictions that are "in accordance with law and [are] necessary in a democratic society".) The council had failed in its obligation by failing to provide or help obtain a properly-adapted mobile home to provide proper care for disabled family members.

In *Oguekwe v. Minister for Justice, Equality and Law Reform* (2008), the Supreme Court upheld a decision of the High Court to quash the deportation order of an Irish child's foreign national parent for failing to give adequate consideration to the child's rights under the Constitution and also Articles 3 and 8 of the ECHR.

REVIEW QUESTIONS

(See Solutions to Review Questions at the end of this text.)

Question 1.1

Briefly outline the differences between civil and criminal law.

Question 1.2

BCG is expanding its business and has decided to purchase land in Waterford from Mr Elis. BCG has agreed a purchase price of €100,000 with Mr Elis and it is the intention of BCG to build the company premises on the land. Contracts have been signed between Mr Elis and BCG and a completion date has been finalised for the transfer of the land and monies to be exchanged. However, Mr Elis has recently been told that he could have received twice the price for the land and has just phoned his solicitor to say that he no longer wishes to sell the land and is refusing to complete the transfer document.

BCG is extremely annoyed at Mr Elis withdrawing from the contract. You explain to BCG that it could sue Mr Elis in the High Court for breach of contract.

Requirement Explain to BCG Ltd the civil jurisdiction of the High Court in Ireland.

(Based on Chartered Accountants Ireland, CAP 1 Law for Accountants, Autumn 2014, Question 2(c))

Question 1.3

When Bella contacted her solicitor about her problems with Premier he informed her that, if this case proceeded to litigation, precedent would be used to determine the meaning of merchantable quality and fitness for purpose. Bella does not understand the meaning of the word 'precedent' and seeks your advice.

Requirement Define the meaning of the term 'precedent' **and** discuss the precise rules of precedent, with reference to the hierarchy of the courts.

(Based on Chartered Accountants Ireland, CAP 1 Law for Accountants, Summer 2014, Question 1(c))

Question 1.4

Last year Dylan Accounting College ('Dylan') experienced a 20% drop in student numbers. Dylan has just discovered that another college has been established in the same locality and it is calling itself Dillon Accounting School ('Dillon'). Dylan is now considering taking a legal action against them for 'passing-off'. Dylan is unsure as to whether this action should be set down for hearing in the High Court or in the Commercial Court.

Requirement:
(a) Discuss the jurisdiction of the Commercial Court.

(b) State whether the Commercial Court has the right to hear Dylan's 'passing-off' action.

(Based on Chartered Accountants Ireland, CAP 1 Law for Accountants, Autumn 2014, Question 1(c))

Question 1.5

The European Union is currently considering passing a Directive regulating the disposal of chemical waste.

Requirement Explain the nature of EU Directives and advise ABC as to whether it is bound to comply with EU Directives when enacted.

(Based on Chartered Accountants Ireland, CAP 1 Law for Accountants, Summer 2013, Question 1(c))

Question 1.6

Your firm has acquired a new client, BlueSky Ltd. You are part of the team on the first audit of BlueSky Ltd. One of your tasks in the audit is to audit the travel expenses incurred by the company's management team in the past year. In doing so, you discover that Gary, the company's accountant, made numerous claims for trips abroad that he claimed were work-related. Further investigation has revealed that these trips were personal holidays and completely unrelated to his work. The firm's solicitor has advised that there could be both civil and criminal proceeding against Gary based on his fraudulent claims.

Requirement Explain to BlueSky Ltd the distinction between criminal law and civil law, under any **four** headings.

(Based on Chartered Accountants Ireland, CAP 1 Law for Accountants, Autumn 2012, Question 2(a))

Question 1.7

Explain any **four** differences between civil and criminal law, and explain the jurisdiction of the Special Criminal Court.

(Based on Chartered Accountants Ireland, CAP 1 Law for Accountants, Autumn 2011, Question 3(c))

Question 1.8

XYZ is aware that it is required to enforce a statutory instrument prohibiting smoking in the workplace. It knows that statutory instruments are a form of delegated legislation, but is unaware of what this is. Define delegated legislation, giving **three** examples of the forms that delegated legislation can take, and outline any **three** advantages of delegated legislation.

(Based on Chartered Accountants Ireland, CAP 1 Law for Accountants, Autumn 2010, Question 4(d))

Question 1.9

Shoreland recently discovered that one of its employees was stealing large quantities of stock from the company. This employee has since been dismissed and the company is considering reporting the incident to the police and having criminal charges brought against the worker. In this regard, outline to the company the distinction between a summary offence and an indictable offence, and the various classifications of the criminal courts.

(Based on Chartered Accountants Ireland, CAP 1 Law for Accountants, Summer 2010, Question 1(c))

Question 1.10

Daffodil and Dandelions Ltd is involved in commercial litigation with a competitor for breach of some of its intellectual property rights. The case is listed for hearing in the Circuit Court.

Requirement:
(a) Explain the composition of the Circuit Court.
(b) List any **three** classifications of cases heard in the Circuit Court.

(Based on Chartered Accountants Ireland, CAP 1 Law for Accountants, Summer 2011, Question 4(d))

Question 1.11

Explain briefly the nature of a quasi-judicial tribunal, outlining any **three** advantages and any **one** disadvantage of these tribunals.

(Based on Chartered Accountants Ireland, CAP 1 Law for Accountants, Summer 2012, Question 3(a))

Chapter 2

THE LAW OF TORT

Definition of a Tort

A tort has been defined as a **civil wrong** arising from a breach of duty created, not by agreement, but by operation of law. The law imposes both rights and obligations in certain situations; if these obligations are breached, the person who suffers injury may bring an action in tort seeking redress from the person who has committed the wrong. Of course, not every wrong resulting in injury is a tortious act. A person must be shown to be under a duty to take care to have avoided this wrong and this duty must have been breached. Whether this is so is decided on the facts of each case.

Torts and Contract

Tort law is also defined or described by contrasting it with the law of contract. A contract exists where there has been an agreement between parties, where the parties intended to create legal relations and have supported their agreement with consideration (something of value in the eyes of the law). The contractual relationship is denoted by the concept of privity, which means that only a party to a contract can sue on it. The law of torts exists outside the confines of the doctrine of privity of contract. The case that best illustrates this is *Donoghue v. Stevenson* (1932) (see below). A breach of contract may also amount to a tortious act. For example, the selling of a car with faulty brakes.

Examples of common torts include:
Defamation The definition of defamation is the publication of a false statement that lowers the reputation of the subject in the eyes of reasonable people. Defamation may occur either by words, writing, broadcasting, Internet, caricatures, etc.

Nuisance Nuisance causes offence, annoyance, trouble or injury. There are two types of nuisance, public and private.

- Private nuisance is a violation of one's use of quiet enjoyment of land. It often takes the form of emitting noise, smell, pollution, etc.
- Public nuisance is a nuisance that affects the community at large.

Trespass Trespass is direct interference with the person, goods or land of another.

Occupiers' liability The Occupiers' Liability Act 1995 regulates the area of occupiers' liability. The statute governs the occupier's duty to people who come onto the property with or without permission.

Product liability Product liability deals with the law relating to the responsibility of the manufacturers, wholesellers, or retailers for the damages or injuries caused by the use of defective products to the ultimate consumers.

These and other types of tort are discussed later in this chapter.

NEGLIGENCE

Negligence is a specific tort and may be described as the failure to exercise the care that a reasonable man would exercise in all the circumstances of the case. Therefore, negligence may consist of omitting to do something which ought to be done, or doing something which ought to be done either in a different manner or not at all. In *Blyth v. Birmingham Waterworks* (1856) Baron Alderson said:

> "Negligence is the omission to do something which a reasonable man, guided upon those considerations which ordinarily regulate the conduct of human affairs, would do, or doing something which a prudent and reasonable man would not do."

However, liability in negligence will not exist unless a duty of care exists between the parties. The duty of care, if it does exist, is owed only to those persons who are in the area of foreseeable danger.

The tort of negligence consists of **three essential elements**:
1. the duty of care;
2. breach of that duty (by the defendant); and
3. damage resulting from the breach.

Duty of Care

Modern negligence law was born out of the decision in England by the House of Lords in the case of *Donoghue v. Stevenson* (1932). This case abolished the privity of contract rule. Prior to this, the plaintiff, Mrs Donoghue, would not have been able to seek redress in this situation as she did not have a contract with the manufacturer.

Lord Atkin set out in *Donoghue v Stevenson* what is known as the 'neighbour principle'. It is a question of law whether, in any particular circumstances, a duty of care exists and, before *Donoghue v. Stevenson*, there was no general principle.

In this case, Mrs Donoghue alleged that she suffered gastroenteritis as a result of drinking the contaminated contents of a bottle of ginger beer. This bottle was manufactured by the defendant, Stevenson. Mrs Donoghue had no contract, as her friend had bought her the drink. The House of Lords by a bare majority **held** that, if Mrs Donoghue could prove that which she claimed, she would have a good cause of action.

Lord Atkins outlined "a general conception of relations giving rise to a duty of care, of which the particular cases found in the books are but instances". He stated:

> "The rule that you are to love your neighbour becomes in law, you must not injure your neighbour; and the lawyer's question Who is my neighbour? receives a restricted reply. You must take reasonable care to avoid acts or omissions which you can reasonably foresee would be likely to injure your neighbour. Who, then, in law, is my neighbour? The answer seems to be – persons who are so closely and directly affected by my act that I ought reasonably to have them in contemplation as being so affected when I am directing my mind to the acts or omissions which are called in question."

The landscape of the tort of negligence was changed utterly by this principle. The neighbour principle set out a guide in deciding the categories of person to whom a duty of care is owed.

English Development of the Duty of Care

The House of Lords reviewed the development of the tort of negligence in England in the case of *Anns v. Merton London Borough Council* (1978), where Lord Wilberforce introduced his two-stage test in deciding if a duty of care arises. This focuses on:

1. proximity of relationship and, if this is found, the court considers; and
2. whether any considerations ought to negate the scope of the duty of care.

Lord Wilberforce set out this two-tier approach as:

> "[Is there a] sufficient relationship of proximity or neighbourhood [between the alleged wrongdoer and the person who suffered damage] such that in the reasonable contemplation of the former, carelessness on his part might be likely to cause damage to the latter, in which case a *prima facie* [at first sight] duty of care arises".
>
> "If the first question is answered affirmatively, it is necessary to consider whether there are any considerations which ought to negative, or to reduce or limit the scope of the duty or the class of persons to whom it is owed."

Much debate has ensued over the interpretation of this two-tier approach. McMahon and Binchy in *The Irish Law of Torts* (3rd edition, Butterworths, Dublin, 2003) point out that it can be interpreted as expressing Atkins' neighbour principle "in more expansive language, without implications of its embracing a wider scope of duty. On another view, Lord Wilberforce's formula hints at precisely the extension of this duty".

Lord Wilberforce's two-tier approach fell out of favour in England as it was criticised for adopting an overly-broad approach in mixing elements of proximity and foreseeability. In *Governors of the Peabody Donation Fund v. Sir Lindsay Parkinson & Co Ltd* (1984) Lord Keith noted that there was a tendency creeping into the law to treat this formula as definitive and that:

> "This temptation is to be resisted . . . [In determining duty of care] ... it is material to take into consideration whether it is just and reasonable that it should be so."

This is indicative of the change in the attitude towards the *Anns* decision. The approach taken in *Anns* case was overruled by *Caparo Industries plc v. Dickman* (1990) in which the House of Lords advocated a new **three-tier test** to replace *Anns* for establishing a duty of care. The key concepts in establishing a duty of care are:

- relational proximity;
- reasonable forseeability; and
- whether in **all the circumstances** it is fair, just and reasonable to impose a duty of care.

A plaintiff may succeed in establishing:

1. relational proximity;
2. foreseeability; and
3. must then go on to show that it is just and reasonable to impose a duty of care.

This approach differs to Lord Wilberforce in *Anns* where, once proximity and foreseeability is established, a duty of care is presumed.

Irish Development of the Duty of Care

Irish courts have long endorsed the neighbour principle propounded by Lord Atkins in *Donoghue v. Stevenson*, and there has been a strong emphasis on proximity in relation to the duty of care.

In *Ward v. McMaster* (1985) it was **held** that the duty of care arose from the proximity of the parties and the foreseeability of the damage. In this case the plaintiff bought a house with the assistance of the local authority housing grant. He later found out that the house was structurally unsound. He brought an action against the builder, local authority and the valuer.

The law required the local authority only to provide the grant on a valuation of the house. This valuation was conducted by a person who had never put himself forward as a person competent to value a house. It was **held** that the local authority was negligent as it had failed to employ a competent person to carry out the valuation. The local authority maintained that it had only failed in a duty to the public whose rates and taxes went into funding the local authority, and not the plaintiff. The Supreme Court ruled that the duty owed would be to avoid foreseeable harm and also to avoid any financial harm that might arise from having to repair defects in the house. Mr Justice McCarthy stated that the duty arose "from the proximity of the parties, the foreseeability of the damage and the absence of any compelling reason based upon public policy".

However, a retreat from this approach and an adoption of the English approach was seen in the case of *Glencar Exploration plc v. Mayo County Council* (2001). The plaintiff was a mining company granted renewable mining licences in County Mayo by the Minister for Energy since 1968. The defendant introduced a mining ban in 1992 as part of its strategic development plan. The plaintiff initiated proceedings declaring the ban *ultra vires* (outside of the council's authority), and claimed damages for negligence and breach of duty.

The action in *Glencar* failed due to a lack of relational proximity. The council exercised its powers for the benefit of the entire community and not for the benefit of a defined category of person (mining company) to which the plaintiff belonged. In the course of his judgment, the judge considered both *Caparo* and *Anns* and, although he did not reject *Anns*, he made a number of *obiter* (non-binding) comments.

> "It seems to me that no injustice will be done if they are required to take the further step of considering whether, in all the circumstances, it is just and reasonable that the law should impose a duty."

In *Breslin v. Corcoran* (2003) the court approved the passage of Chief Justice Keane in *Glencar*. Mr Justice Fennelly had regard to policy considerations and said:

> "In addition to the elements of foreseeability and proximity, it is natural to have regard to considerations of fairness, justice and reasonableness."

Breach of the Duty of Care

The defendant will be deemed to have breached the duty of care owed to the plaintiff if his conduct does not meet the standard that would be reached by the reasonable person. Defendants will not be excused if, throughout their impugned course of conduct, they did their best, if that merely amounted to doing their incompetent best. However, the issue of negligence can properly be determined only in the particular context in which the defendant has acted.

There is a fourfold approach taken by McMahon and Binchy in *The Irish Law of Torts* in answering the question: "What would the reasonable man have done?" Regard is had to:

- the probability of the accident;
- the gravity of the threatened injury;
- the social utility of the defendant's conduct; and
- the cost of eliminating the risk.

The Probability of the Accident

The greater the probability of an accident, the higher the standard of care imposed. In *O'Gorman v. Ritz Cinema (Clonmel) Ltd* (1947), the plaintiff was watching a film in the defendant's cinema when her leg became caught in a hinge as the person sitting in front of her stood up. The defendant was able to show that one million patrons had used those seats in the previous seven years and that no similar complaint had ever been made. The plaintiff was not successful. It was **held** by the court that:

> "to prevent such injuries would require precautions of a well-nigh fantastic nature, which could not reasonably be expected."

The Gravity of the Threatened Injury

The more grave the threatened injury, the higher the standard of care imposed. In *Paris v. Stepney Borough Council* (1951) a workman with only one sighted eye was not provided with safety goggles by his employers. A splinter to his good eye rendered him blind. The court found that the defendants should have shown greater care towards the plaintiff since they were aware of his disability. In effect:

> "The more serious the damage which will happen if an accident occurs, the more thorough the precautions which an employer must take."

The Social Utility of the Activity

Where there is a social benefit to the negligent behaviour, the court may decide that the standard of care was not breached. In *Whooley v. Lord Mayor, Alderman and Burgesses of Dublin* (1961), the plaintiff's foot was caught in a fire hydrant which had been opened by vandals. The defendant avoided liability by showing that the hydrant was designed to allow easy access to the fire brigade. The court

held that "no other type of fire hydrant that could be devised, consistent with the necessary purpose, would be safe from malicious interference".

The Burden of Eliminating the Risk

Where the cost of eliminating the risk is low and the probability or gravity of injury is high, then failure to eliminate the risk may be a breach of the standard of care. In *Muldoon v. Ireland* (1988) the court refused to find the defendant liable for injuries inflicted by one prisoner on another and **held** that the prison authorities (at Arbour Hill) were not expected to search each prisoner for weapons every time they moved from one part of the prison to another, as the cost of eliminating the risk would be too high.

Damage

Causation

Damage is essential to liability in negligence, and the law has been shaped by many considerations. In the first place, it has to be shown that the damage complained of was caused by the defendant's carelessness. Causation is the tool that the courts use to determine whether the defendant is responsible for the damage complained of. The test that is applied when determining the issue of factual causation is the 'but for' test. The court asks: "Would the harm to the plaintiff not have occurred but for the defendant's negligent act or omission?"

In *Barnett v. Chelsea & Kensington Hospital Management Committee* (1969) the plaintiff's husband went to the hospital feeling unwell and was sent home without seeing a doctor. He died of poisoning. The plaintiff's case failed on a causation basis as expert evidence established that, even if her husband had been treated at the relevant time, the poisoning could not have been contained.

Factual and Legal Causation It is important to distinguish factual and legal causation. The former arises where the defendant is linked in a factual or scientific way to the plaintiff's injuries. Factual causation is a prerequisite for legal causation. The 'but for' test is the test of factual causation. However, it can cause substantial problems where multiple causes operate to bring about the same event or damage.

Having established factual causation, the plaintiff is then obliged to establish legal causation. *Prosser and Keaton on Torts* (5th edition, 1984) defines it in the following terms:

> "The defendant's conduct is [the legal] cause of the event if it was a material element and substantial factor in bringing it about."

The material element and substantial factor test is the test applied by the courts to determine legal causation once factual causation has been established.

Novus Actus Interveniens

A defendant's negligence will sometimes form part of a sequence of events leading to injury or harm to the plaintiff. If part of this sequence is a *novus actus interveniens,* the court will deem it to have broken the chain of causation between the defendant's negligence and the damage suffered by the plaintiff. As a result, the defendant will not be held liable in negligence. The intervening act may be that of a third party, or of the plaintiff himself, or it may be an intervening act of nature.

Novus actus interveniens simply means that an act or event has intervened to break the chain of causation that was set in motion by the defendant's negligence which is independent of both the plaintiff and the defendant. In *Lamb v. Camden* (1981), the defendant's negligence resulted in flooding of the plaintiff's premises. The plaintiff, who lived abroad, arranged for the premises to be vacated and furniture removed. Squatters moved in causing further damage. It was **held** by the court that the squatters' actions were not reasonably foreseeable and so the defendant was not liable for the further damaged caused by the squatter who had moved in.

Remoteness of Damage

If damage is deemed too remote by the courts, the plaintiff's claim will fail. The test that the courts use relies on the proposition that a wrongdoer is liable only for the damage that was intended by him or her or which, though not intended, was the reasonably foreseeable consequences of his or her unlawful act.

The test of reasonable foreseeability was accepted in *Overseas Tankship (UK) Ltd v. Morts Dock & Engineering Co. ("The Wagon Mound (No. 1)")* (1961), which is discussed below. However, the traditional approach, which was considered to be too harsh, was first adopted in *Re Polemis & Furness Withy & Company Ltd* (1921). This is known as the *direct consequence test.*

The Traditional Approach – The Direct Consequence Test In *Re Polemis* (1921) it was **held** that, if the damage caused was a direct consequence of the defendant's negligent act, then the defendant would be liable for that damage. It was irrelevant that the defendant could not have anticipated the extent of the damage.

This approach differentiates the test to determine whether liability exists (foreseeability) from the test for limiting the extent of liability (directness of consequence).

In *Re Polemis*, two workmen negligently dropped a plank into the hold of a ship. The impact caused a spark, which ignited petrol vapours and caused an explosion that destroyed the ship. The owners sued the ship's charterers (who employed the two workmen) and it was **held** by the court that the charterers were liable for all the direct or natural consequences of their negligent act.

The Modern Test – The Reasonable Foreseeability Test The Privy Council in *The Wagon Mound (No. 1)* (1961) stated that it was illogical and unjust to adopt two different standards: one for determining liability; the other for setting a limit on the damage recoverable. Instead, there should be one uniform test of liability and remoteness: the reasonable foreseeability test.

In the *The Wagon Mound (No. 1)*, a steamship, *Wagon Mound*, was taking in bunkering oil some 600 feet away from a wharf in Sydney Harbour. As a result of the carelessness of those on board, a large quantity of oil spilt into the bay. Some 60 hours later the oil ignited; a fire spread rapidly and did considerable damage to the wharf, and also to ships adjoining the wharf. The outbreak of fire was due to the fact that wind and tide had together carried under the wharf some inflammable debris that caught fire. These flames, in turn, set floating oil on fire. The Judicial Committee (the judicial branch of the Privy Council) **held** that the test of remoteness of damage was reasonable foreseeability and on the facts of the case the damage in question was not reasonably foreseeable at all.

The *Egg-shell Skull Rule* This rule, also known as the thin skull rule, states that the defendant takes the plaintiff as he/she finds him/her, i.e. the tortfeasor takes the victim as he/she finds him/her. This rule is the exception to the rule that the damage suffered must be reasonably foreseeable. Usually in these cases, the type of injury is foreseeable but the extent of it is not.

A classic example is the case of *Smith v. Leech Brain & Co* (1962). In this case, the widow of the victim brought a claim for the death of her husband. He was employed by the defendant and, as a result of their negligence, he incurred a burn to his lip by molten metal which was a promoting agent of a cancer. The lip contained pre-cancerous cells which were triggered by the injury sustained. But for the burn, the cancer may never have developed. The husband died three years later.

Held: the burn was a foreseeable consequence of the defendant's negligence and therefore the defendant was liable for his death. It was not necessary to show that death by cancer was foreseeable, nor that an ordinary person would not have died from the injury. The egg-shell skull rule applies and the defendant must take his victim as he finds him.

Negligent Misstatement

In our study of negligence, we have examined how someone can be held to be liable for their acts or omissions. We turn now to examine the law on liability for negligently-made statements that result in economic loss. The harmful effects of a statement can carry further than the effects of an act, and it is probably easier to make a careless statement than commit a negligent act. This type of negligence is restricted by the courts for policy reasons and there are special requirements, which we will examine here, that a plaintiff will need to prove in order to establish a duty of care.

In 1964, the House of Lords heard an appeal in the case of *Hedley Byrne & Co Ltd v. Heller and Partners Ltd* (1964). The plaintiffs, Hedley Byrne & Co, were advertising agents who intended to engage in an advertising programme for Easipower Ltd which would cost about £100,000. They asked their own bankers, National Provincial Bank Ltd, to obtain a reference about Easipower, and National Provincial wrote to the defendants, Heller and Partners, who were Easipower's bankers. They replied in a letter, which said that it was:

> "For your private use and without responsibility on the part of the bank or its officials", and went on to say that Easipower was a "respectably constituted company, considered good for its ordinary business engagements. Your figures are larger than we are accustomed to see".

Easipower went into liquidation and the plaintiffs lost £17,000. The House of Lords **held** that on the facts there was no liability (valid disclaimer absolved them of liability in the circumstances). Importantly, however, the House of Lords accepted the principle that a duty could arise not to make a careless statement that leads to economic loss. This requires a special relationship of trust and advice, usually given in a professional capacity, and which is relied upon.

Special Relationship

The courts have established that special rules of proximity apply in the area of negligent misstatements so that a special relationship must be established between the parties and, to a large extent, this depends on the defendant knowing that the plaintiff is justifiably relying upon him/her for his/her special skill, expertise or knowledge. The *Hedley Byrne* decision makes it clear that the duty extends to all relationships where the inquirer trusted the other to exercise a reasonable degree of care, and where the other knew or ought to have known that the inquirer was relying on him.

The 'special relationship' requirement can be divided into three elements:

1. that the plaintiff relied on the defendant's skill and judgement or ability to make a careful inquiry;

2. that the defendant knew or ought reasonably to have known that the plaintiff was relying on the advice given;
3. that it was reasonable in all the circumstances for the plaintiff to rely on the defendant.

Hedley Byrne has been accepted in Ireland on a number of occasions. One such example is the case of *Wall v. Hegarty* (1989) where the defendant, a solicitor, failed to ensure that a will was witnessed in accordance with the law. As a result, the plaintiff lost out on a gift made to him in a will and incurred legal expenses in his role as executor in attempting to have the will admitted to probate. The court imposed liability on the basis of the neighbour principle, but also stated that the legal expenses would have been recoverable under the precedent set out in *Hedley Byrne*. The solicitor sent the will to the plaintiff knowing that it did not meet the legal requirements for a valid will, which amounted to a negligent misstatement (written). The court **held** that, in drafting the will, the solicitor owed it to the people receiving a gift under it to ensure that the intentions of the person who drafted the will were not frustrated by his own professional carelessness.

Where there is no Special Relationship

In the English decision of *Caparo Industries plc v. Dickman* (1990) a shareholder in Fidelity plc bought shares in a company after receiving the audited accounts and later made a takeover bid. Following the takeover, the plaintiff sued the auditors alleging that the audited accounts were misleading in that they showed a profit where in fact there had been a loss. It was **held** by the court that auditors of a public company owe no duty of care to the public at large who rely on accounts when purchasing shares in a company; nor was any duty owed to individual shareholders who purchase additional shares. Liability for economic loss due to negligent misstatement is confined to cases where the statement or advice had been given to a known recipient for a specific purpose of which the maker was aware and upon which the recipient had relied and acted to his detriment.

The precedent of *Caparo* has been endorsed in Ireland in *Glencar Exploration plc v. Mayo County Council* (2002) but has not been adopted.

A recent successful claim for negligent misstatement in the Irish courts occurred in *Walsh v. Jones Lang LaSalle* (2007). The defendant auctioneers issued a brochure for a Dublin property for which they were the selling agents. The sales brochure included particulars of the total floor area, representing it to be 23,057 square feet. At the bottom of the brochure in small print the following was included:

> "Whilst every care has been taken in the preparation of these particulars, and they are believed to be correct, they are not warranted and intending purchasers/lessees should satisfy themselves as to the correctness of the information given."

The purchaser calculated the total potential rental income based on this information and he estimated that the overall value of the property to be in the region of €2.5 million. Accordingly, the purchaser offered to purchase the property based upon the floor area as stated in the sales brochure. The purchaser had the property surveyed as to its condition, but in accordance with the standard practice did not arrange to have the floor area verified. Following completion of the sale he discovered that the floor area was 20% less than what was represented in the sales brochure. **Held**: it was to be expected that the potential purchasers would rely upon the information in the brochure when deciding whether or not to offer to purchase. The defendant is a large firm, which has been in existence for a considerable period of time and holds itself out as a company with particular skills and expertise in the commercial property market. The waiver was not sufficient to relieve the defendant of liability. The High Court described the waiver as:

> "a quite inadequate means of notifying prospective purchasers that the seemingly precise measurements of the floor areas so prominently published within the sales brochure were wholly unreliable".

Damages were accordingly awarded as a result of the overstatement of the floor area.

Professional Negligence

There is no distinct tort of 'professional negligence'. Instead, this area consists of a group of cases concerning the conduct of professionals, which have been decided on the basis of general negligence principles.

The first question to be addressed is 'who is a professional'? In *Kelly v. St Laurence's Hospital* (1989), it was decided that nurses are not 'professionals' in the eyes of the law. However, Mr Justice Blayney in the High Court in *Hughes v. JJ Power Ltd* (1988), **held** that mechanics were persons "exercising and professing to have a special skill".

Thus, if a member of a profession can show that he or she adhered to the customary practice of his or her profession, this should normally be sufficient to relieve him or her of the accusation of negligence. However, the courts reserve to themselves the power to have the last word on the question, though it is a power they will exercise sparingly, in only the clearest of cases.

Legal Professional Negligence: Barristers

For many years, it had been assumed that barristers could not be sued in respect of negligence in the course of their work. This approach was based on policy considerations, including the need to maintain the existence of a free and independent Bar, and the fact that a barrister owes a primary duty to ensure the proper administration of justice.

In *Rondel v. Worsley* (1969) the House of Lords **held** that barristers acting as advocates were immune from liability in negligence. Then, in *Arthur J.S. Hall and Co v. Simons and Others* (2000), the court **held** that it was no longer in the public interest that immunity for barristers remain in place.

For non-advocacy work, a barrister has the same liability as any other professional. This point was illustrated in the English case of *Saif Ali v. Sydney Mitchell & Company* (1980) where the defendant was found guilty of negligence in failing to institute proceedings within the limitation period against certain defendants.

(**Note:** the situation in Ireland is unclear as there is no decisive precedent on the subject.)

Legal Professional Negligence: Solicitors

While solicitors are in a contractual relationship with their clients, it is settled law that they may also be liable in tort as well as in contract if they fail to exercise the due skill and care required. Solicitors' duties may extend to third parties where public policy justifies it.

In *Doran v. Delaney & Others* (1998) the Supreme Court found that conveyancing solicitors acting for the vendor of a property owed a duty of care to the purchaser as well as to their own client in the circumstances of the case. In *Doran v. Delaney*, the plaintiffs purchased a plot of land on which they intended to build a house. After completion of the sale, they discovered that this plot was effectively land-locked; that the land providing access was not owned by the vendor and had not been included in the purchase. They were not informed that the adjoining owner claimed to be the owner of part of the land; nor that there was an ongoing dispute. In requisitions prior to the purchase, the vendor's solicitor was asked whether there were any disputes and replied: "Vendor says none". They replied to this only after taking instructions from the vendor. A partner in the firm acting for the vendor was aware of a dispute, but believed it to be settled. The solicitors did not ascertain from the vendor the terms on which the dispute had allegedly been settled.

In the High Court, damages were awarded to the plaintiffs against their own solicitors and the vendor of the property and, on appeal to the Supreme Court, the vendor's solicitors were also found to be liable. The fact that there was no contract between the plaintiff and the solicitor did not of itself negate the existence of a duty.

There are number of factors relevant in deciding whether a solicitor, while acting for a client, owes a duty to a third party:

1. the solicitor must assume responsibility for information;
2. the solicitor must hold out that he or she has the necessary skills and expertise; and
3. the solicitor must be aware that a third party would rely upon information.

Professional Negligence: Auditors and Accountants

The principal authority with regard to the professional negligence of accountants and auditors is *Hedley Byrne & Co. Ltd v. Heller and Partners Ltd* (1964) (see the facts of this case cited above under Negligent Misstatement). The *Hedley Byrne* decision makes it clear that the duty extends to all relationships where the inquirer (person seeking advice) trusted the other to exercise a reasonable degree of care and where the other knew or ought to have known that the inquirer was relying on him.

Auditors may be liable in negligence where they fail to exercise due skill and care. In *Re Thomas Gerrard & Sons Ltd* (1967) a managing director falsified accounts by including non-existent stock. As a result of the overstated profits, additional taxes were paid by the company and dividends were declared, which otherwise would not have been. The auditors became suspicious when they discovered that invoices relating to the stock had been altered. They did not investigate the matter further, having accepted the managing director's explanation. **Held**: both the managing director and the auditors were liable to the company for the amounts paid by way of dividends and excess taxes. In deciding whether an auditor has failed in his duties, the court will have regard to the standard statement of accountancy practice and auditing guidelines for the profession.

In *Kelly v. Haughey Boland & Co* (1989), Cavan Crystal expressed an interest in taking over Royal Tara Ltd, and asked to have a look at their accounts for the years 1972–1976. The years 1972–1974 had already been prepared by the auditors and handed over to Cavan Crystal. They subsequently prepared the years 1975–1976 with knowledge of the plaintiff's interest. The defendant had not attended physically at stocktakes over a 20-year period. **Held**: physically attending stocktakes, although not compulsory, was considered by the court to be 'good practice' in the industry. While not attending all of the stock-takes would not amount to a breach of duty, failure to attend any over a 20-year period amounted to negligence. The defendants should have foreseen at the time the second set of accounts was audited that the third party would rely upon them.

In *Caparo Industries plc v. Dickman* (1990) (see also above), the English Court of Appeal adopted a narrow approach to the duty owed by auditors to third parties in tort. An audit is conducted to comply with the Companies Acts, not to provide information to the general public or to potential investors. The auditor did not owe a duty of care to potential investors as he did not know that the information was going to be relied upon for that purpose. The precedent of *Caparo* has not yet been adopted in Ireland. In effect, this means that Irish auditors and accountants are potentially exposed to a broader obligation than their English counterparts.

EXAMPLES OF OTHER COMMON TORTS

As discussed previously, other torts are governed by more specific rules than negligence. The following is a brief discussion of:

- occupiers' liability;
- vicarious liability; and
- strict liability.

Occupiers' Liability

Occupiers' liability is the area of the law of tort that applies to the situation in which a person suffers injury while on another's premises.

Occupiers' liability was governed by common law rules until the introduction of the Occupiers' Liability Act 1995, which came about as a result of lobbying by landowners. The occupier's duty of care now depends upon which category under the Act the entrant who suffers the injury belongs to. There are three categories of entrants:

1. visitors (section 3(1));
2. recreational users (Section 4); and
3. trespassers (Section 4).

(**Note:** since the introduction of the Occupiers' Liability Act 1995, both recreational users and trespassers are owed the same duty.)

Visitors

A 'visitor' under the Act is someone who is present on the property with the consent or permission of the occupier. The person may be present on the property by contract, invitation or permission of the occupier or their family. Section 3(1) states that the occupier owes a duty of care to all visitors onto their property.

In *Power v. Governor of Cork Prison & Ors* (2005) liability was imposed where a prisoner slipped on the wet floor of a toilet. The defendant was aware of the persistent problem of water spillages on the floor and took no effective steps to remedy the problem or the foreseeable risk of injury.

Recreational Users

Section 1(1) of the 1995 Act defines a 'recreational user' as:

> "An entrant who, with or without the occupier's permission or at the occupier's implied invitation, is present on the premises without a charge being imposed for the purpose of engaging in a recreational activity."

Section 4(1) of the Act outlines the duty that is owed by occupiers to recreational users as a duty:
(a) not to injure the person or damage the property of the person intentionally; and
(b) not to act with reckless disregard for the person or the property of that person.

'Reckless disregard' amounts to something more than mere negligence. In *Weir-Rodgers v. SF Trust* (2005), a recreational visitor was sitting near the edge of a cliff. She stood up, lost her footing and rolled down the cliff ending up in the sea and suffering injuries. She sued the landowner under the Occupiers' Liability Act 1995 claiming that there should have been a fence and a warning sign. The court **held** that the landowner had no case to answer and emphasised the difference between ordinary negligence and reckless disregard. The judge went on to say that:

> "a person sitting down near a cliff must be prepared for oddities in the cliff's structure or in the structure of the ground adjacent to the cliff and he or she assumes the inherent risks associated therewith".

This is not to say, however, that a landowner does not need to erect a warning sign in all circumstances.

Trespassers

A person who is neither a visitor nor a recreational user is a 'trespasser'. The duty that is owed to a trespasser is the same as to a recreational user.

In the case of *Raleigh v. Iarnród Éireann* (2003) the court overturned an award of €110,000 in favour of an injured trespasser who had been struck by a train in circumstances in which he had been drinking and fell asleep for six hours beside the railway track. The court **held** that the trespasser was the "author of his own misfortune". The company could not be expected to foresee the "folly" of adults who came onto its property. The court also rejected the suggestion that the company ought to have erected a fence at the point where the plaintiff entered onto the embankment beside the tracks.

Disclaimers

The 1995 Act allows for modification of the duties owed by the occupier in certain circumstances.

- Section 5(1) provides that occupiers may by express agreement or notice extend the duty they owe towards the entrants.
- Section 5(2) provides that an occupier may by express agreement or notice, restrict, modify or exclude his liability towards visitors only. The disclaimer is only valid if it is:
  (a) reasonable in all the circumstances; and
  (b) reasonable steps are taken to bring the disclaimer notice to the attention of the visitor.

Although the duty can be reduced by disclaimers, the landowner will still owe a duty not to act in reckless disregard of the visitor's safety.

Note: liability may be imposed in certain circumstances without proof of wrongful conduct.

Vicarious Liability

Vicarious liability is the imposition of liability for the negligence of another. Liability is imposed even though the other party is not personally at fault. The most common context in which vicarious liability is imposed is the employer–employee relationship. Employers may be held vicariously liable for the negligent acts or omissions of their employees which occur in the course of carrying out their jobs.

The guiding principles used by the court in cases of vicarious liability in the employer–employee context are as follows.

1. Does the relationship of employer–employee exist?
2. Was the employee acting in the course of employment when the tort was committed?

The employer is only vicariously liable for acts committed in the course of employment. If employees engage in an independent act outside of the scope of their employment (sometimes referred to as 'a frolic of their own') then liability is not imposed on the employer.

Where an employer expressly authorises a wrongful act, the employer will be liable. The employer may also be liable for employees who carry out their duties in a wrongful manner. This is illustrated by the case of *Rose v. Plenty* (1976) where employees were expressly prohibited from employing children on their milk round to assist them with their deliveries. The plaintiff,

Rose, who was aged 13, suffered injuries due to Plenty's negligent driving after being invited by Plenty to assist on the milk round. **Held**: the employer was liable, as the purpose of being invited on the round was to assist in the employer's business, even though the employee was acting outside the scope of his employment.

In *Limpus v. London General Omnibus Co* (1862) an employee was under strict instructions not to race with other vehicles; however, the driver ignored these instructions and caused a collision. **Held**: in the circumstances, the employers were liable for the damage caused as the driver was acting during the course of his employment.

An employer is not liable for wrongful acts of his employee simply because they are committed at the time when he is performing the job he was employed to do. In *O'Keeffe v. Hickey* (2009) the plaintiff sought to attach liability to the State and the Minister for Education for the sexual assaults suffered by her on the grounds that both the State and the Minister for Education were vicariously liable for the acts which were carried out by her teacher, Mr. Hickey. Her action was dismissed as there was no employment relationship between the school principal, Mr Hickey and the second-named defendant, the Minister for Education. On normal principles, the State has no vicarious liability for the acts of a teacher appointed by the manager of a national school, and there was no legal basis for the imposition on the State of vicarious liability in this case.

Strict Liability

Strict liability is the imposition of liability without the finding of fault. A defendant may not have acted negligently or with intent to be found strictly liable. The plaintiff need only show that the tort happened and that the defendant is responsible. Strict liability is usually statutory in origin. The principle is illustrated by the 'Rule in *Rylands v. Fletcher*', which originated from the case of *Rylands v. Fletcher* (1868). In this case, the defendant built a reservoir on his land. It escaped through an open channel of which he had no knowledge and flooded the defendant's land. **Held**: the doctrine of strict liability was applied. The court **held** that "when a man brings or uses a thing of dangerous character on his own land, he must keep it at his own peril and is liable for the consequences if it escapes and does injury to a neighbour".

Liability for Defective Products

An example of strict liability that was given a statutory effect is liability for defective products as legislated for in the Liability for Defective Products Act 1991. The basic principle of liability under the Act is that "the producer shall be liable in damages in tort for damage caused wholly or partly by a defect in his product". Proof that the defect in the product caused the plaintiff injury is enough; it is not necessary for the defendant to have acted wrongfully.

The 1991 Act defines the consumer broadly as being an injured party. This includes not just someone who suffers damage because of a defect in a product, but also, on their death, their personal representatives or dependants.

The Act goes on to define 'product' as "all moveables except primary agricultural products". The term 'product' does not exclude agricultural produce that has undergone 'initial processing'.

Similarly, the term 'producer' is defined as the manufacturer or producer of a finished product, raw material or of a component part of a product and produce of the soil, farming stock and game where these have undergone initial processing. The term 'producer' includes the person who carries out such processing. The term is also applied to any person who puts his or her name to any distinguishing feature of the product or who holds himself or herself out as a producer. Furthermore, the term also includes any person who imports a product into the EU in the course of business for supply to another.

Under the 1991 Act, plaintiffs do not need to prove fault. They must only prove the existence of the defect and the damage caused by the defect. Damage is defined as death or personal injuries and damage to or destruction of property other than the product itself. Damage is limited to private use or consumption. Thus, the 1991 Act is not designed to compensate for damage to property in a trade or profession. Personal injury is defined in section 1(1) as any disease or impairment of a person's physical or mental conduct. The Act is silent on the question of recovery for pain and suffering.

Defective Product Section 5 of the Liability for Defective Products Act 1991 stipulates that a defective product is one that does not provide the safety which a person is entitled to expect, taking all the circumstances into account, including:

1. the presentation of the product;
2. the use to which it could reasonably be expected the product could be put; and
3. the time when the product was put into circulation.

In addition, a producer ceases to have any liability in respect of a product on the expiration of 10 years after it was put into circulation (except if legal proceedings have been commenced before the 10-year period.)

Defences under the 1991 Act Section 6(e) of the Liability for Defective Products Act 1991 provides that producer is not liable if he proves that "the state of scientific and technical knowledge at the time when he put the product into circulation was not such as to enable the existence of the defect to be discovered".

If a producer can prove that he did not put the product into circulation, or that the defect came into existence after he did so, or that the product was not supplied in the course of a business then he will not be liable under the Act.

Section 9 of the Act makes provision for a reduction of the plaintiff's award where he or she was guilty of contributory negligence.

Furthermore, a manufacturer of a component can rely on the fact that the defect was attributable to the design of the product into which the component was fitted.

Section 7 of the Act provides that the limitation period shall be three years from the date the plaintiff became aware or should reasonably have become aware of:

1. the injury or damage;
2. the defect; and
3. the identity of the producer.

Section 10 of the Act prohibits any contracting out of the Act's provisions. Section 11 provides that the common law and other statutory rights, e.g. Sale of Goods Act 1898, remain unaffected by the Act.

The illustrative cases in this area tend to be English cases, because in Ireland most litigants still prefer to sue in negligence rather than under statute law. For example, in *Richardson v. LRC Products Limited* (2000), the plaintiff become pregnant as a result of a failure of a contraceptive device (a condom) that the defendant manufactured. She sued under the UK equivalent of the 1991 Act claiming damages including the cost of the child's upbringing. The plaintiff alleged that the device was defective by reason of the fact that it had failed. This was due, she claimed, first to ozone damage that had occurred to the condom during the manufacturing process; and, secondly, the fact that the condom broke during use demonstrated that it was defective. Expert evidence was unable to provide an explanation for the failure of the device. However, it appears that the trial judge was persuaded by the defendant's scientific evidence that the condom had not been affected by ozone damage during the manufacturing process. The trial judge drew attention to the fact that the (UK equivalent to the 1991) Act defined defectiveness as meaning that the safety of the product is not "such as persons generally are entitled to expect" taking into account the way it has been marketed, its get-up and warnings among other factors. The manufacturers had never claimed that their product was 100% effective and it was manufactured to a standard exceeding the relevant British standard. **Held**: the plaintiff was required for the purposes of the Act to prove the cause of the failure, which she had not successfully proved. Therefore, her action failed.

Another illustration of the use of defective product legislation in England is the case of *Worsley v. Tambrands Limited* (1999), in which the plaintiff suffered toxic shock syndrome (TSS) as a result of her use of the defendant's product. The plaintiff had used the defendant's product for many years. On occasion, she read some of the instructions and warnings that accompanied the product and modified her behaviour according to the advice contained in those documents. A leaflet in the packaging of the product warned, in some detail, of the risk of TSS and included advice about seeking urgent medical advice if certain symptoms were experienced. In addition to the words of warning, the risks of TSS were printed on the product's packaging. The plaintiff developed TSS and became very ill. Upon her recovery she commenced proceedings against the defendant, alleging that the defendant had been negligent in failing to warn her adequately of the risk of TSS. She also claimed that the defendant's product was defective due to inadequate warnings and claimed damages under the UK equivalent of the 1991 Act. **Held**: the court found that adequate warning on the box and explanation leaflet was what was required to warn the consumer. The court was satisfied that the defendant's leaflet met these requirements.

Concurrent Wrongdoers

Parties to Tort Actions

Where multiple persons are responsible for the harm to the plaintiff, they are known as *concurrent wrongdoers*. All matters relating to the plaintiff's injuries should, as far as possible, be litigated in the same proceedings. Part III of the Civil Liability Act 1961 governs the area of concurrent wrongdoers. Section 11(1) provides that "two or more persons are concurrent wrongdoers when both or all are responsible to a third person for the same damage". The Act provides that each wrongdoer is fully liable for the whole of the plaintiff's loss (the principle of *full responsibility*) and:

- a court can give judgment against concurrent wrongdoers who are sued together jointly/separately; and
- if the judgment is given jointly, it has the effect of being separate.

This is significant, as the plaintiff is entitled to receive damages in full from any defendant (usually the one with the 'deep pockets', i.e. usually the defendant that will be most likely to have the financial means to meet the damages) and that defendant is then forced to seek a contribution from the other defendant(s) in a separate application under section 21 of the Act.

Contribution

Section 21 provides that the contribution is "intended to be just and equitable having regard to the degree of the contributor's fault". This contribution is only attainable after damages have been paid over to the plaintiff (section 23).

The case of *Iarnród Éireann v. AG Gaspari* (1993) involved a constitutional challenge to the legality of section 14 of the Civil Liability Act 1961, which gives the right to the plaintiff in proceedings to obtain the judgment from any one of the concurrent wrongdoers. Earlier proceedings had found Iarnród Éireann 30% liable, and a cattle dealer 70% liable, for the injury caused to the plaintiff (the case involved a collision between a train and some cattle). The plaintiff had elected to extract the full judgment from Iarnród Éireann. Iarnród Éireann's rights under section 21 to seek a contribution from the cattle dealer were rendered near worthless, as the cattle dealer was uninsured. **Held**: the court upheld the constitutionality of the statutory provision (section 14), and also rejected Iarnród Éireann's submission that in such circumstances damages be reduced.

GENERAL DEFENCES IN TORT

Defendants may try to refute an allegation that they have committed a tort. They need only argue a defence once the plaintiff has established the basic requirements of the tort. A successful defence will act to absolve the defendant of liability. There are a number of general defences in tort. These include:

(a) inevitable accident;
(b) necessity;
(c) statutory authority;
(d) limitation of actions;
(e) contributory negligence;
(f) failure to mitigate loss; and
(g) waiver.

(a) Inevitable Accident

Injury that could not be avoided by taking ordinary and reasonable precautions is not actionable. The defendant need only show that no reasonable precaution would have prevented the occurrence of an accident. The circumstances of the case will determine what is 'reasonable'.

In *Counihan v. Bus Átha Cliath/Dublin Bus and Arthur Ebbs* (2005) the plaintiffs, husband and wife, were struck by a tour bus after it crossed a number of lanes and mounted a footpath, causing significant injuries. On the basis of an undisputed medical report, the High Court concluded that the driver of the bus suffered from a latent heart condition, which led to a "profound blackout". There was no preliminary warning of the condition that would have led the driver to be concerned as to his ability to drive and no reasonable test could have disgnosed this condition. The High Court added that the driver remained under a duty of care, after the onset of symptoms, to do his best to control the difficult situation in which he found himself, but that there was no evidence that the driver in question had failed to so. There was a total destruction of the driver's control due to the latent heart defect and liability was not imposed.

(b) Necessity

The defence of necessity arises where an act that would normally be described as tortious is carried out in circumstances where there is no alternative and is done with the intention of preventing a greater evil. The defence is of little practical relevance and is not pleaded in many cases, owing probably to the difficulties in proving the defence.

(c) Statutory Authority

If a statute requires something be done and it would otherwise be unlawful and actionable, then there is no liability. An example is the case of *Smith v. Wexford County Council* (1953) in which the defendant had a duty to keep the rivers clean. Thus, they cleaned out the river adjoining the plaintiff's land and placed all the waste on the land. The plaintiff's cattle ate the waste and died. He sued the defendants. **Held**: the defendants were not liable, as their defence was that they had statutory authority to clean the river.

(d) Limitation of Actions

The plaintiff may not be able to bring proceedings against the defendant if the proceedings are barred by the Statute of Limitations Act 1957. The limitation period for commencing an action are:

- two years for an action caused by negligence;
- one year for defamation (although there is a discretion to extend this to two years in the interest of justice); or
- six years for all other torts.

If plaintiffs are under a disability (minors), time only runs from when they are no longer under a disability.

In *Cunningham v. Neary* (2004) the plaintiff brought proceedings in March 2002 alleging that the defendant, a consultant obstetrician and gynaecologist, had unnecessarily removed her ovary in 1991. In 1998, she had a hysterectomy undertaken and spoke to a nurse about her experiences with Dr Neary. The nurse encouraged her to complain about him. On 19 December 1998, she made a complaint to the Medical Council about the defendant; subsequent to this, she heard media reports about the defendant concerning his medical conduct. The plaintiff contacted a solicitor in 2000 but did not institute proceedings until 2002 after an independent expert obstetrician provided a report in April 2001 in which he advised that the removal of the plaintiff's ovary had been unnecessary and represented incompetent medical practice.

The Supreme Court **held** that the plaintiff's claim was statute barred. They found that the plaintiff's 'date of knowledge' began to run on 19 December 1998 and stopped running on 19 December 2001. Section 2(a) of the Statute of Limitations provides that

> "a person's knowledge includes knowledge which he might reasonably have been expected to acquire from facts ascertainable by him with the help of medical or other appropriate expert advice which it is reasonable for him to seek".

The Court **held** that, at the point of the plaintiff's complaint to the Medical Council, it would have been reasonable of her to seek help from a lawyer and a medical expert.

(e) Contributory Negligence

Contributory negligence is where plaintiffs are found to have contributed to their injuries/damage through their own negligence, and the damages awarded will be reduced accordingly. The case of *CT (a minor) v. Bus Átha Cliath/Dublin Bus* (2013) involved a personal injuries claim by a 12-year-old student hit by a bus. The court determined that the driver was negligent but that there was 30% contributory negligence by the student as he had run out in the path of the bus.

Section 34(1) of the Civil Liability Act 1961 governs the area:

> "Where, in any action brought by one person in respect of a wrong committed by any other person, it is proved that the damage suffered by the plaintiff was caused partly by the negligence or want of care of the plaintiff or of one for whose acts he is responsible (in this Part called contributory negligence) and partly by the wrong of the defendant, the damages recoverable in respect of the said wrong shall be reduced by such amount as the court thinks just and equitable having regard to the degrees of fault of the plaintiff and defendant".

The defence is subject to three exceptions:

1. where it is not possible to establish the different degrees of fault, liability is to be apportioned equally;
2. where the plaintiff has voluntarily waived his or her rights with respect to the acts complained of, the defendant is not liable; and
3. where contract or statute expressly sets a limit to liability, the plaintiff cannot receive more than the limit.

Section 35(1) lists situations in which the plaintiff is deemed to be contributory negligent because contributory negligence is imputed to the plaintiff. These include:

- cases of vicarious liability;
- where the plaintiff is not the immediate victim of the wrong; and
- where the plaintiff is a concurrent wrongdoer.

In *Jones v. Livox Quarries* (1952), Jones worked in Livux quarries. One lunch break, he hitched a lift by standing on the tow-bar of a traxcavator. It was against the company rules to stand on a traxcavator's tow-bar; furthermore, the driver was unaware that Jones had jumped on the back of it. Another vehicle, which was driven by another employee, ran into the back of the traxcavator crushing Jones's legs, which ultimately had to be amputated. **Held**: the defendant was liable but Jones had contributed to the negligence and the courts **held** that he was one fifth to blame. Lord Denning (MR) stated in the case: "Just as actionable negligence requires the foreseeability of harm to others, so contributory negligence requires the foreseeability of harm to oneself. A person is guilty of contributory negligence if he ought reasonably to have foreseen that, if he did not act as a reasonable, prudent man, he might be hurt himself; and in his reckonings he must take into account the possibility of others being careless."

In *Froom v. Butcher* (1976) the plaintiff was injured in a car accident owing to the defendant's negligent driving. However, as he had not worn a seat belt his injuries were more severe than they otherwise would have been. Not wearing a seat belt in a car amounts to contributory negligence and the damages awarded to him were reduced on this basis.

(f) Failure to Mitigate Loss

There is a duty under section 34(2)(b) of the Civil Liability Act 1961 on the plaintiff to mitigate the loss; this is to say that the plaintiff ought to take reasonable steps and opportunity to minimise the harm/damage.

(g) Waiver (formerly defence of voluntary assumption of risk)

If the plaintiff has waived the legal right to sue with an agreement, then under section 34(1)(b) of the Civil Liability Act 1961 the defendant has an absolute defence to the action.

In *Anderson v. Cooke* (2005), the plaintiff passenger suffered injuries in a road traffic accident. In support of the waiver defence, the defendant alleged that both men had planned a challenge to drive at 120mph so that the plaintiff could take a photo to post on the Internet. It was **held** by the court that, despite the mutuality of the agreement, a waiver had not been established. There was no prior discussion of waiver and no express agreement between the parties.

DAMAGES

Damages are the most common remedy for civil wrongs. The primary aim is to put the plaintiff back in the position he or she would have been in had the torts not occurred. Damages may be:

- ordinary;
- aggravated;
- punitive/exemplary;
- contemptuous; or
- nominal.

Ordinary Compensatory Damages

Ordinary damages are divided into two categories that compensate for the different types of loss that an injured party may suffer:

- general damages for personal losses, such as damages for pain and suffering, past and future; and
- special damages – quantifiable out-of-pocket losses, such as medical expenses.

Aggravated Damages

These are awarded when the behaviour of the defendant aggravates the injury to the plaintiff.

Punitive/Exemplary Damages

Punitive damages arise where the extent of the wrong committed or the manner of its commission is such that the court wishes to express its particular disapproval of the defendant or the court wishes to be seen publicly to have punished the defendant or have made an example of him or her.

Contemptuous Damages

These damages are awarded when the court has formed a very low opinion of the plaintiff's bare legal claim, or that the conduct was such that he or she deserved, at any rate morally, what the defendant did to him or her. In *Reynolds Ltd v. Times Newspapers* (1998), former Taoiseach Albert Reynolds brought a successful action in defamation against the defendant newspaper. He was awarded the nominal sum of one penny as the judgment alone was seen by the courts as enough to vindicate his reputation.

Nominal Damages

Nominal damages are awarded in recognition of the fact that the plaintiff has had his or her legal rights infringed where such infringement caused no actual damage. They are often awarded in trespass cases where the plaintiff's only injury is to their dignity.

The Civil Liability and Courts Act 2004

The Civil Liability and Courts Act 2004 introduced a number of procedural changes into how personal injury cases are governed, placing a burden on the plaintiff to inform the defendant of the action within a specified timeframe. Some of the changes introduced by the Act are as follows:

Letter of Claim

Section 8 of the Act provides that a plaintiff who intends to take an action for damages for personal injuries must now serve a letter of claim upon the alleged wrongdoer(s) within two months of the date of the cause of action, or as soon as practicable thereafter. The term 'date of the cause of action' is defined in the Act to mean either the date of accrual of the action or the date of knowledge (if later).

Mediation

Section 15 of the Act provides for the process of mediation in personal injuries cases. It provides that a court may, at the request of a party to a personal injuries action, direct the parties to take part in a mediation conference.

The Injuries Board

The Injuries Board was introduced to reduce the legal costs and delays associated with court actions. The Injuries Board is a statutory body governed by the Personal Injuries Assessment Board Acts 2003 and 2007. Its function is to provide independent assessment of personal injury claims and compensation for victims of workplace, motor and public liability accidents. The Board does not deal with personal injury actions arising out of medical negligence or those involving psychological injuries. It aims to reduce the both the cost and length of time involved to settle a claim. The Injuries Board, on average, resolves a claim within nine months (compared to 36 months through the courts system). If the plaintiff/defendant does not accept the assessment issued, the board will issue an authorisation which allows the plaintiff to pursue the action through the courts system.

REVIEW QUESTIONS

(See Solutions to Review Questions at the end of this text.)

Question 2.1

Martin has been the auditor to Acme Enterprises Ltd for the past 15 years. In the past five years, he has failed to attend the company's stocktake, although he has continued to sign a 'clean' audit report on the company's accounts. It has recently been discovered that the directors have been falsifying the stock figures to make the company appear more profitable and that Martin has been inadvertently signing a 'clean' audit report on these falsified accounts.

Requirement Discuss the law in relation to negligence by explaining duty of care, standard of care, causation, remoteness and damages, and determine whether Martin is liable for any loss sustained by the company.

Question 2.2

Six months ago, the Health Service Executive (HSE) put its waste management contract out to tender and Premier decided to put in a bid for this lucrative contract. As Premier had never been involved in the disposal of medical waste before, it hired an independent consultant, Matt, to advise it on the various costs that it would incur to safely dispose of this waste. Based on Matt's figures, Premier submitted its tender to the HSE. Premier's bid was accepted and it was awarded the contract. However, Premier's accountant has recently informed it that the costs relating to the disposal of this medical waste are significantly higher than Matt originally estimated. Consequently, this additional cost has reduced Premier's estimated profit on the contract by 23%. Premier is now considering suing Matt for negligence.

Requirement Pursuant to the law on negligence, discuss the current test that the Court will apply to determine whether Matt owed Premier a duty to take reasonable care.

(Based on Chartered Accountants Ireland, CAP 1 Law for Accountants, Autumn 2013, Question 3(b))

Question 2.3

ABC employs a warehouse manager, Peter Murphy. Last week, an accident occurred in the warehouse when a chemical drum was overturned. This resulted in a spillage all over the warehouse floor, as the lid of the drum was not properly sealed. Peter, who had been on the warehouse floor at the time of the spillage, incurred serious third degree burns to both feet as the liquid burned through the soles of his shoes. At the time of the incident, Peter was not wearing his regulation work boots, as required by health and safety law.

ABC has recently been contacted by Peter's solicitor informing them that he intends to sue them in negligence for his injuries. ABC's solicitors have advised them that they should defend this claim on the grounds of 'contributory negligence'.

Requirement Outline the nature of the defence of 'contributory negligence' and assess whether this defence can be successfully raised on this occasion.

(Based on Chartered Accountants Ireland, CAP 1 Law for Accountants, Summer 2013, Question 1(b)(i))

Question 2.4

While carrying out the audit, you note that Bluesky Ltd has made a provision for damages in relation to pending court proceedings. The office manager explains to you that last April, Denis, the store manager, was supervising the delivery of a number of new computers when a printer fell on him from an overhead shelf. As a consequence of this incident, Denis broke his arm in three different places and required surgery. Since the accident, Denis has been unable to work.

Requirement In the context of the law of negligence, discuss the concept of 'remoteness of damages'. Your answer should include an assessment of whether the company is obliged to compensate Denis for his injuries.

(Based on Chartered Accountants Ireland, CAP 1 Law for Accountants, Autumn 2012, Question 2(c))

Question 2.5

Florence and Theodore have been operating a jewellery design business, Little Gems ('Little Gems'), in partnership for the past fifteen years. Both Florence and Theodore are active partners in the business, and Florence's father, Ralph, is their silent partner. When the partnership was established, Ralph invested 75% of the venture capital; the balance was invested equally by Florence and Theodore.

Stella is head of sales of Little Gems jewellery. Last month Stella approached the company's financial controller, Myles, to inform him that she was attending a sales conference in Milan and that she was intending to take numerous samples of Little Gem's jewellery to the conference in order to solicit orders.

She told Myles that the consignment of sample jewellery she was taking with her was valued at €500,000 and she asked him to arrange the appropriate insurance for this trip. However, while in Milan there was a robbery of the conference centre's secure vault and the case with the Little Gems jewellery samples was one of the many stolen. Little Gems has filed a claim for the stolen jewellery from their insurance company, but discovered that an error by the financial controller means that the amount insured was actually €50,000 and not €500,000. As a consequence of this loss Little Gems is now operating at a loss and Florence and Theodore have decided to dissolve the partnership.

Requirement Little Gems is considering suing their financial controller for negligence. Outline the factors that the court could take into consideration in determining whether there has been a breach of the standard of care and assess whether the financial controller could be liable for his negligence.

(Based on Chartered Accountants Ireland, CAP 1 Law for Accountants, Summer 2010, Question 4(a)(iii))

Chapter 3

THE LAW OF CONTRACT

A contract is defined as a legally binding agreement.

A **speciality contract** is one that is in writing and is signed and delivered; it is also known as a 'deed' or a 'contract under seal'.

A **simple contract** is one that is not made under seal; all simple contracts require consideration to support them. They can be either oral or in writing, and require no special form.

Finally, there are contracts that must be evidenced in writing where no formal document is necessary. All that is required is some written evidence to prove that a contract was entered into, e.g. a letter or a receipt.

In general, for a contract to be valid and legally enforceable there must be:
1. an offer;
2. an unqualified acceptance;
3. an intention to create legal relations;
4. consideration; and
5. capacity to contract.

OFFER AND ACCEPTANCE

Offer

An **offer** can be defined as a 'clear and unambiguous statement of the terms upon which the offeror is willing to contract'.

The offer must be clear, complete and final. In *White v. Bluett* (1853), a father promised to release his son from an obligation to pay on a promissory note "if the son would stop complaining". **Held**: there was no enforceable contract because the son's promise was too vague. Also, in *Guthing v. Lynn* (1831), Lynn bought a horse from Guthing on the terms that, if the horse were lucky, Lynn would pay £5 more. **Held**: the contract was unenforceable because the term was too vague.

Invitation to Treat

An offer must be distinguished from an invitation to treat An invitation to treat has no legal effect. It is a mere offer to receive offers. It is the first step in negotiations, which may or may not result in the making of a firm offer.

Examples of Invitations to Treat

Items for Sale in Shop Windows In *Fisher v. Bell* (1961) the defendant displayed a flick knife in his window, and was charged with "offering for sale a flick knife in their window" contrary to the Restriction of Offensive Weapons Act 1959. The court **held** that displaying of goods is an invitation to treat, not an offer.

In *Pharmaceutical Society of Great Britain v. Boots Cash Chemists* (1953) certain drugs containing poisons could only be sold under the supervision of a pharmacist. It was alleged by the Pharmaceutical Society that placing the drugs on the shelves in a self-service shop constituted an offer. **Held**: the court agreed with Boots' contention that displaying the goods was an invitation to treat. There was no sale until the customer brought the drugs to the cash desk where the pharmacist was stationed and offered to buy them. The court commented that if it were true that a customer accepted an offer by removing the goods from the shelf then they would not be able to change their mind and put them back because it would be a breach of contract. Clearly, neither Boots nor their customers intended such a result.

In *Minister for Industry and Commerce v. Pim Bros Ltd* (1966) the defendant company was prosecuted for the offence of 'offering for sale' goods on credit terms without specifically stating the terms for credit. The company displayed goods in a window with a price tag attached, which did not state the credit terms. **Held**: the price tag was an invitation to treat and not an offer for sale.

Tenders The mere advertisement of a tender constitutes an invitation to treat. When another party puts in a bid in response this constitutes an offer capable of acceptance.

In *Great Northern Railway v. Witham* (1873) the defendant successfully tendered for the supply of stores to GNR over a period of one year. In his tender he "undertook to supply . . . such quantities as the company may order from time to time". The defendant made some deliveries and then refused to fulfil an order that GNR had given. The court **held** that by refusing to fulfil the order, the defendant was in breach of contract but could revoke his tender and need not fulfil any further orders given within the remainder of the 12-month period.

In *Harvela Investments Ltd v. Royal Trust Company of Canada (CI)* (1986) the first defendant was the registered owner of shares in a company. They invited the plaintiff and the second defendant to submit offers by sealed tender or confidential telex to their solicitors. This was to be the single offer for all shares held and the defendants bound themselves to accepting the highest bid. The plaintiff offered $2.175 million and the second defendant made a lower bid of $2.1 million or $101,000 in excess of any other offer received (referential bid). The House of Lords **held** that the first defendant was not allowed to accept the bid of the second defendant. He had an obligation to sell to the highest *bona fide* bidder, which in this case was the plaintiff. This unilateral contract was to invite fixed bids rather than an auction type sale. This type of sale precluded the first defendant from accepting the referential bid.

Auctions Advertising an auction does not amount to an offer. In *Harris v. Nickerson* (1873) the defendant, an auctioneer, advertised a sale by auction of certain lots including office furniture on a certain day and the two following days. The sale on the third day was withdrawn. The plaintiff attended the sale and claimed against the defendant for breach of contract in not holding the sale, seeking to recover his expenses in attending. **Held**: the court rejected the plaintiff's claim:

> "It amounts to saying that anyone who advertises a sale by publishing an advertisement becomes responsible to everybody who attends the sale for his cab hire or travelling expenses."

Advertisements The general rule is that an advertisement is an invitation to treat and not an offer for sale. In *Partridge v. Crittenden* (1969) an advertisement placed by Partridge in *Cage and Aviary Birds*, under the general heading 'Classified Advertisements', which contained, among others, the words "Quality British A.B.C.R... Bramblefinch cocks, Bramblefinch hens 25s each". There was no use of the words "offer for sale". Partridge was prosecuted for offering for sale a wild bird and the court had to consider if this constituted an offer or an invitation to treat. The court considered this situation to be akin to *Fisher v. Bell* (see above) and **held** that:

> "the insertion of an advertisement in the form adopted here under the title 'Classified Advertisements' is simply an invitation to treat."

However, the rule that an advertisement is an invitation to treat is open to exceptions. An offer may only be accepted by a person to whom the offer has been made, but it is possible to make an offer to an individual or to the world at large. In the case of *Carlill v. Carbolic Smoke Ball Company* (1893) the Carbolic Smoke Ball was a medicine that was designed to "prevent flu," and was manufactured and marketed by the defendants. They published an advertisement by which they undertook to pay a £100 reward to any person who contracted flu having used the smoke ball three times weekly for two weeks, and added that £1,000 had been deposited in a bank "showing our sincerity in this matter".

Billings v. Arnott (1945): in order to encourage their employees to join the Defence Forces, the defendants posted a notice and offered their employees who joined up half their salaries, up to two pounds a week. The plaintiff decided to accept the offer and informed the defendant. He was told that as another person in his department had signed up, he could not be spared from the business. The plaintiff signed up anyway and later sued for half his salary. The High Court examined the circumstances and **held** that the notice went beyond a statement of intention. It constituted a unilateral offer, in that it was clear and left nothing open to negotiation and the plaintiff had complied with it by performance of the conditions of the offer. The plaintiff, having seen the advertisement, bought the smoke ball. She contracted flu, having used the product as instructed, and sought to claim the £100. The defendant company argued that the advert was too vague to constitute an offer. It was mere 'puff' or sales promotion. It also argued that an offer could not be made to the world at large. **Held**: in this instance the advert constituted an offer to the world at large and not an invitation to treat.

1. The terms of the offer were sufficiently clear.
2. The advert required the offeree to do something to avail of the offer, i.e. purchase the smoke ball.
3. Depositing £1,000 in a bank was proof of the intention to create legal relations.
4. It is not necessary to know the identity or quantity of the offerees; offers can be made to the world at large.

Statements of Interest

An offer for sale must also be distinguished from a statement of interest. This is usually a declaration of intention to make an offer and, as such, is not an offer.

A mere statement of price will also not be construed as an offer to sell. In *Harvey v. Facey* (1893) the plaintiff telegraphed the defendant asking: "Will you sell Bumper Hall Pen? Telegraph lowest cash price". The defendant replied that the lowest cash price was £900. The plaintiff replied: "we agree to buy". The defendant made no further reply. **Held**: no contract had been made, as the second telegraph was a statement of price and not an offer.

Termination of an Offer

There are four ways by which an offer may be terminated:

- rejection;
- lapse of time;
- death; or
- revocation.

Rejection

When the offer is rejected, it is terminated and cannot subsequently be accepted. In *Hyde v. Wrench* (1840), the defendant offered to sell his farm for £1,000. The plaintiff made a counter offer of £950, which the defendant rejected three weeks later. The plaintiff then sought to accept the original offer of £1,000. The court **held** that a counter offer is viewed as a rejection of the original offer.

In *Stevenson v. McLean* (1880) the defendant offered to sell the plaintiff an amount of iron for £40 in cash, indicating that the offer would remain open until the following Monday. On Monday at 9:42am, the plaintiff sent the defendant a telegram sounding out what flexibility there might be to negotiate before the day's trading began: "Please wire whether you would accept 40 for delivery over 2 months, if not, longest time limit." There was no response from the defendant and the plaintiff then purported to accept the original offer. The defendant claimed that the telegram had constituted a counter offer, so his acceptance was invalid. The court **held** that the telegram was not a counter offer, but a mere inquiry "which should have been answered". Once the offer was made, it is taken to be continuing until accepted, rejected or revoked. There was no notice of revoking this offer, therefore it was still good and the plaintiff was entitled to accept it.

Lapse of Time

In circumstances where a time limit is not set for acceptance of the offer, it will remain open for a reasonable time only. What is a 'reasonable time' will depend upon the circumstances of the case. In the case of *Ramsgate Victoria Hotel Co v. Montefiore* (1866) the defendant applied in June for shares and paid a deposit to the company's bank. Five months later the company sent him an acceptance by issue of a letter of allotment. The defendant contended that his offer had expired and could no longer be accepted. **Held**: the defendant's offer was for a reasonable time only. The offer had lapsed after five months which was an unreasonable time in the circumstances, as share prices fluctuate regularly.

Death

If the contract is for personal services, the death of the party to the contract who was to perfom these services results in the contract being terminated.

Revocation

The general rule is that the offeror may revoke their offer at any time before acceptance. If the offeror undertakes that the offer shall remain open for acceptance for a specified time, they may, nonetheless, revoke it within that time, unless by a separate contract (an option agreement) they have bound themselves to keep it open for the whole of the specified period.

In *Routledge v. Grant* (1828) Grant offered to buy Routledge's horse, acceptance to be made within six weeks. Within the six weeks, Routledge withdrew his offer. The court **held** that, as there was no option agreement (for which consideration must be given), Routledge could revoke his offer at any time up to acceptance.

Provisos to the General Rule regarding Revocation

1. Revocation is, however, legally effective only when communication of it reaches the offeree. This applies even when the revocation is posted (and as such is an exception to the normal postal acceptance rule). The revocation may be communicated by the offeror or by a third party. In *Byrne v. Van Tienhoven* (1880), the offeror was in Cardiff and the offeree was in New York.
   - On 1 October – a letter is posted in Cardiff offering to sell tin.
   - On 8 October – a letter of revocation is posted in Cardiff.
   - On 11 October – letter of offer is received in New York and a telegram of acceptance sent. This is confirmed in a letter posted on the 15 October.
   - 20 October – the letter of revocation arrives in New York. The offeree had meanwhile re-sold the contract goods.

   Held: the letter of revocation could not take effect until it is received. It could not revoke the contract made by acceptance of the offer on 11 October. Simply posting a letter does not revoke the offer until it is received.

   In *Dickinson v. Dodds* (1876), on 10 June, A wrote to B offering to sell B property for £800 stating that the offer would remain open until 9am on Friday 12 June. On the Thursday, the plaintiff was informed by the intermediary, C, that the property was sold. The plaintiff then handed in a letter of acceptance before 9 am on 12 June. **Held**: A was free to revoke his offer and had done so by sale to a third party. B could not accept the offer after he had learnt from a reliable informant (C) of A's revocation of the offer to B.

2. *Revocation and Unilateral Contracts* In the English Court of Appeal decision *Daulia v. Four Millbank Nominees* (1978) it was **held** that, in such a situation, the offer becomes irrevocable once the offeree has embarked on performance of the offer. (There is no Irish precedent directly on this point.)

Acceptance

Acceptance is defined as the final, unconditional and certain indication of agreement to all the terms of an offer, communicated to the offeror, with the intention of accepting the offer.

The general rule is that acceptance must be communicated to the offeror.

Furthermore, it is not open to the offeror to state that silence will be taken as acceptance. In *Felthouse v. Bindley* (1863), an uncle wanted to purchase his nephew's horse. After a letter from his nephew regarding previous discussions to buy the horse, he replied: "If I hear no more about him, I consider the horse mine at £30 and 15 shillings." The court **held** that acceptance must be communicated clearly and cannot be imposed due to the silence of one of the parties.

Exceptions to the Rule

Exceptions to the general rule (that acceptance must be communicated to the offeror) are:

Performance constitutes acceptance (see *Carlill v. Carbolic Smoke Ball Company*, above). Once the offeree does whatever act is required of him or her according to the terms of the offer, there is no need for communication.

When acceptance is made by post (the "postal rule") Once a letter is posted, acceptance is complete. This is so even if the letter is lost in the post and never reaches the offeror, once it is properly addressed and stamped.

The classic authority in this area is *Adams v. Lindsell* (1818). The defendant wrote to the plaintiff on 2 September offering to sell wool at a price and requesting an answer in the course of the post. The letter was wrongly addressed and it only reached the plaintiff on 7 September. On that same day, the plaintiff posted a letter of acceptance and it only reached the defendant on 9 September. At this point the defendant had sold the wool on the previous day. **Held**: in the circumstances a contract had come into existence on 7 September when the letter of acceptance was posted. To have been an effective acceptance the letter must be:

- properly stamped;
- properly addressed; and
- properly posted.

The postal rule was set forth in the case of *Household Fire & Carriage Insurance Co v. Grant* (1879). Grant applied for shares in the plaintiff company. A letter allotting him shares was lost in the post. When the company went into liquidation, he was sued for the balance outstanding on the shares. **Held**: Grant was liable as there had been a valid acceptance effective since posting.

The courts have taken the view that, where an acceptance is communicated by way of an instantaneous means of communication (e.g. fax, telephone or email), then the general rule applies that acceptance becomes effective only when it is received by the offeror. In *Entores v. Miles Far East Corporation* (1955) the plaintiffs sent a message by telex from London to the defendants in Amsterdam offering to purchase a certain quantity of steel cathodes. The defendant accepted this offer by telex from Amsterdam. The court **held** that the rule about instantaneous communications differs from the postal rule. The contract is only complete when the acceptance is received by the offeror. (See the section on electronic contracts below for the position of e-mail communication.)

In *Holwell Securities v. Hughes* (1974) Hughes granted to the plaintiff an option to purchase land to be exercised "by notice in writing". A letter giving notice of the exercise of the option was lost in the post. It was **held** that the words "notice in writing" must mean notice received by the vendor; hence notice had not been given to accept the offer.

Agreements Entered into 'Subject to Contract'

It is possible to respond to an offer without accepting or rejecting it either by a request for more information or by acceptance *subject to contract.* This type of acceptance means that the offeree is agreeable to the terms of the offer, but suggests that the parties should negotiate a formal (usually written) contract on the basis of the offer. Neither party is bound until and unless the formal contract is made between the parties.

In *Jodifren v Fitzgerald* (2000), written agreements concerning the sale of a property were executed. However, correspondence between the parties' solicitors that followed was headed "subject to contract/contract denied". **Held**: the expression "subject to contract" when placed at the head of a letter is effective to deny a contract. If it is contained in the body of the text, it is a matter of construction of the writing as a whole whether it is intended to deny the existence of a contract.

Electronic Contracts

It should be noted that section 19 of the Electronic Commerce Act 2000 provides that acceptance of an offer or any related communication (including any subsequent amendment, cancellation, revocation or acceptance of an offer) may, unless otherwise agreed by the parties, be communicated by means of an electronic communication.

The Act does not indicate when this communication becomes effective and in the absence of any other guidance, it should be assumed that the same principle applies as to other instantaneous communication, whereby the acceptance is effective when received by the offeror.

There has been a UK case on this issue, *Thomas v. BPE* Solicitors (2010) where the court found that the timing of receipt by the offeror was dependent on the expectations of the parties. In this case, the court **held** that, where the parties were in the throes of negotiating a share purchase and the deal was expected to close that day, then it could reasonably be expected that the offeror would be at their office at 6 pm, when the e-mail was delivered. (As this is a UK case, it will only be of persuasive value in this jurisdiction.)

INTENTION TO CREATE LEGAL RELATIONS

Not all social arrangements that are made constitute contracts. There must be an intention (express or implied) to create a relationship in a contract. Due to the requirement to have an intention to create legal relations, social communications do not create a contractual relationship between persons. In contrast, there is an automatic assumption of this intention for commercial relations, unless expressly indicated otherwise.

Express Statements

There can be no intention to be legally bound if this is expressly stated by the parties. In *Rose & Frank Co v. Crompton Bros* (1923), a commercial agreement was expressed to be "not subject to legal jurisdiction in the law courts". There was a breach of contract and the plaintiffs sued. The court **held** that there was an express statement rebutting the presumption to create legal relations and there was, therefore, no binding contract.

Implied Intention

Where there is no express statement, as is the case in the majority of contracts, the courts apply two presumptions:

- in social and family arrangements, the presumption is that there is no intention to create legal relations; and
- in commercial and business arrangements, there is a presumption of an intention to create legal relations.

Domestic Arrangements

The presumption that there is no intention to create legal relations may be rebutted by evidence to the contrary. In *Balfour v. Balfour* (1919) a man working in Ceylon returned with his wife to the UK on leave. It was agreed that for health reasons, the wife would not return to Ceylon. The husband promised to pay her £30 per month as maintenance. The marriage later ended in divorce and the wife sued for the monthly allowance, which the husband no longer paid. **Held**: an informal agreement of an indefinite period made between husband and wife whose marriage was intact was not intended to be legally binding.

In *Merritt v. Merritt* (1970), a husband left the family home, which was owned by him, to live with another woman. The spouses met in the husband's car, where the husband agreed to pay the wife £40 per month, out of which she would pay the mortgage on their house. The wife refused to leave the car until the husband signed a note agreeing to these terms and an undertaking to transfer the house into her sole name when the mortgage was paid off. The wife paid off the mortgage but the husband refused to transfer the house to her. **Held**: in these circumstances an intention to create legal relations could be inferred and the wife could sue her husband for breach of contract.

In *Simpkins v. Pays* (1955), A, her granddaughter and a paying boarder took part in weekly competitions organised by a Sunday newspaper. Entrants were made in A's name and there were informal arrangements about postage, etc. Then, one week they won £750. The paying boarder was denied a share by the other two. **Held**: there was a "mutuality of agreement" among the parties, amounting to a joint enterprise. It was not a "friendly adventure", as A had claimed, but a contract.

Commercial Agreements

When business people enter into commercial agreements it is presumed that there is an intention to create legal relations, as was seen in the case of *Edwards v. Skyways* (1964). There, in negotiations over redundancy terms with an employee, the employer undertook to make an *ex gratia* payment to him, which it then reneged upon (an *ex gratia* payment is a payment without admission of previous liability). **Held**: the agreement was made in a business context and therefore there was a presumption that the agreed terms were intended to be legally binding.

In *Rose & Frank Co v. Crompton Bros* (1924) the plaintiff entered into an agreement with the defendant whereby they were appointed the defendant's agents in the United States. The agreement stated that "this agreement is not entered into nor is this memorandum written as a formal or legal agreement and it shall not be subject to legal jurisdiction in the Courts of the US or England". The courts **held** that they would respect the intention of the parties that the agreement was not to be legally binding, even though it would be classified as a commercial agreement.

Collective Agreements

There is a legal presumption that collective agreements between trade unions and employers' associations/individual employers are not intended to be legally binding. The courts have often been willing to hold that collective agreements are nothing more than a 'peace treaty' and cannot be considered as legally enforceable. This view was reinforced by the *Report of the Commission of Inquiry on Industrial Relations* (1981), which found that both trade unions and employers' associations/employers were generally against the legal enforcement of collective agreements and recommended that collective agreements should not be legally binding.

However, this presumption may be rebutted, as illustrated in *O'Rourke v. Talbot (IR) Ltd* (1983). In this case the plaintiffs were foremen employed by a motor assembly company. Their trade union had made collective agreements regarding pay with the company. However, the plaintiffs also formed a committee that discussed particular matters of interest between them and the company. The committee also wanted an agreement that, following redeployment, they would not be made redundant for at least five years. The company produced a document giving its **assurance** on this point, but the foremen wanted this word changed to "guarantee". The company agreed to change the wording. Later, the company made the plaintiffs redundant before the five-year period had elapsed and the plaintiffs sued. The company's defence was that it had never intended that the agreement with the foremen would be legally enforceable. However, the court ruled in favour of the plaintiffs.

CONSIDERATION

Consideration is a requirement of a valid contract, and is something of value in the eyes of the law.

Consideration was defined in *Currie v. Misa* (1875) as follows:

> "A valuable consideration, in the sense of the law, may consist either in some right, interest, profit, or benefit accruing to the one party, or some forbearance, detriment, loss, or responsibility, given, suffered, or undertaken by the other."

Another definition was provided by the House of Lords in *Dunlop v. Selfridge* (1915):

> "[consideration is] an act or forebearance of one party, or the promise thereof, is the price for which the promise of the other is bought and the promise thus given for value is enforceable".

Consideration may be:

- executory – a promise in return for a future action; or
- executed – an act in return for a promise.

Past Consideration

Past consideration cannot support a promise, since the act was performed before the other party's promise was made – the benefit had already been received.

In *Roscorla v. Thomas* (1842) the plaintiff agreed to buy a horse from the defendant. Following the sale, the defendant told the plaintiff that the horse was healthy. The plaintiff took the horse home and found it to be in bad health. **Held**: the promise was only made after the sale; past consideration is insufficient. The contract was fully concluded following the payment of the money for the horse. There was no new consideration for the promise that the horse was in good health.

In *Re McArdle* (1951) a mother left her home to her children in her will. In the mother's lifetime, one of her children and his wife lived with her at her house. The wife carried out improvements to the house. The other children later agreed in writing to pay her for the cost of these improvements. After the mother's death, they refused to do so. **Held**: at the time of the promise by the testatrix's (the mother's) children, the improvements were past consideration, and therefore the promise was not binding.

Exception to the Rule that Past Consideration is Invalid

There is an exception where past consideration will be binding, where two conditions are met:
1. where the act was done at the request of the promisor; **and**
2. where the parties contemplated that payment would be made.

An example that illustrates this point is *Lampleigh v. Braithwait* (1615) in which the defendant pleaded for the plaintiff to organise a royal pardon sparing his life. The plaintiff obtained the pardon and afterwards the defendant agreed to pay the plaintiff £100 for his services. **Held**: the promise was legally enforceable: there was an implied promise by the defendant to pay for the service which he had requested.

Rules of Consideration

There are a number of rules that govern consideration.

Consideration need not be Adequate but must be Sufficient

This maxim is shorthand for two rules of law:
1. *Consideration must be sufficient* This means that, provided that it has some economic value, the consideration need not be adequate. If I sold a brand new bicycle for €1, the courts are not going to interfere in my freedom to contract just because it appears unfair. This is based on the rationale that the best person to judge one's financial interests is oneself.

In *O'Neill v. Murphy* (1936), a builder worked for a neighbouring parish in exchange for prayers being said for his family. **Held**: prayers were not sufficient consideration in the eyes of the law.

In *Chappell v. Nestlé* (1960), as part of a promotion, Nestlé offered a record for sale for 7p and three chocolate bar wrappers. In a dispute over royalties, the issue was whether the wrappers, which were thrown away upon receipt, were capable of constituting consideration. **Held**: the wrappers were adequate consideration, as they had a commercial value.

2. *Consideration need not be adequate* In *Glasbrook Bros v. Glamorgan County Council* (1925), at a time of industrial unrest, mine owners asked for and agreed to pay for special police guard at a mine. They later repudiated liability saying that it was the duty of the police to promote public order. **Held**: the extra services by the police were consideration for the promise to pay.

   In the case of *Ward v. Byham* (1956), the father of an illegitimate child wrote to the child's mother and agreed to pay her £1 a week for maintenance, "providing you can prove that (the child) will be well looked after and happy". The father made payments until the child's mother married, and then he refused to continue. The mother sued for breach of contract. The father claimed that there was no consideration to the agreement, as the mother was legally obligated to care for the child. **Held**: an offer to perform a legal obligation (caring for her child) is not consideration, but doing it in a certain way (ensuring that the child was well looked after and happy) in accordance with the wishes of her father was sufficient to amount to consideration.

Where the Plaintiff is Bound by an Existing Contractual Duty to the Defendant, this will not amount to Consideration

If the plaintiff has already contractually agreed to carry out certain works, performance of this obligation will not be sufficient to amount to a new consideration giving rise to a new contract. This is best illustrated by the old case of *Stilk v. Myrick* (1809), which concerned a return sea voyage from London to the Baltic. Two sailors deserted halfway through the voyage and could not be replaced. The captain of the ship could not find replacements and offered to share the deserters' wages among the remaining crew if they would complete the voyage home. Upon return, the captain refused to pay up. The court **held** that the sailors provided no additional consideration; they were under an existing duty to do the work, and so their claim failed.

But, in *Hartley v. Ponsonby* (1857), deserters reduced a ship's crew below the workable minimum and the crew were **held** to have provided consideration by working above and beyond their contractual duties.

In *Williams v Roffey Bros & Nicholls (Contractors) Ltd* (1990) the plaintiffs contracted with the defendants to carry out work on a construction project. There was a penalty clause for non-completion by the agreed date. The defendants subcontracted this job to another company, which subsequently experienced financial difficulty. The subcontractors agreed to complete the job for extra money. When the job was completed on time the defendants refused to pay the additional amount of money. **Held**: this was legally enforceable because the defendants received an extra benefit in avoiding the penalties.

This decision has not been followed in Ireland due to the fact that it may be considered unfair as the stronger party could take advantage of the vulnerability of the weaker party.

Payment of a Lesser Sum than that Due Does Not Amount to Consideration

The general rule is that the payment of a lesser sum than that due to a creditor is not sufficient consideration in law for the full debt, even where the creditor has agreed that part payment will discharge the entire debt. This is known as *the rule in Pinnel's case*. In *Pinnel's* case (1602), Pinnel brought an action against Cole for payment of a debt of £8 10s due on 11 November 1600. The defendant pleaded that, at the suggestion of the plaintiff, he had paid £5 2s on 1 October 1600, and that the plaintiff had accepted it in full satisfaction of the debt. **Held**: the court ruled in favour of the plaintiff and stated that

> "payment of a lesser sum on the day in satisfaction of a greater, cannot be any satisfaction for the whole, because it appears to the Judges that by no possibility, a lesser sum can be a satisfaction to the plaintiff for a greater sum: but the gift of a horse, hawk, or robe, etc. in satisfaction is good . . . [as] more beneficial to the plaintiff than the money".

This rule was reiterated in the case of *Foakes v. Beer* (1884). Foakes owed Beer £2,090 19s. Beer agreed that she would not take any action against Foakes for the amount owed if he would sign an agreement promising to pay an initial sum of £500 and pay £150 twice yearly until the whole amount was paid back. Foakes was in financial difficulty, and so Beer waived any interest on the amount owed. Foakes made the payments as agreed without any interest. Beer then sued for the interest. **Held**: Beer was successful in her claim. Although the agreement did not contemplate the interest owed, it could still be implied. However, the promise to pay a debt was deemed not to be sufficient consideration as there was no additional benefit moving from Foakes to Beer.

However, there are exceptions to the rule in *Pinnel's* case when:

- the person who owes the money pays it before the date due at the creditor's request;
- the method of making payment is altered or in a different place at the creditor's request;
- there is payment of a lesser sum plus a chattel;
- there is partial payment of the debt from a third party in full settlement.

An example of the last exception listed above was in *Welby v. Drake* (1825) where the defendant owed £18 to the plaintiff, who accepted £9 from the defendant's father in "full settlement of the debt". The plaintiff later sued for the balance outstanding. The court ruled that the debt was discharged by the father's actions and that the plaintiff was not entitled to recover the balance due.

Equitable Doctrine of Promissory Estoppel

The doctrine of promissory estoppel provides that, where a promise is made and there is reliance on it, not to enforce it would lead to unfairness.

In *Central London Properties Trust v. High Trees House Ltd* (1947) prior to the Second World War, the defendant leased a block of flats at a rate of £2,500 per annum from the plaintiff. An agreement was formulated during the war that the defendant would pay a reduced rate. After the war, the plaintiff sued for back rent. **Held**: the plaintiff was estopped from reneging on the promise and the court did not allow the plaintiff to claim back rent for the war years.

The doctrine is of limited application in that it requires:

1. a pre-existing contractual relationship;
2. reliance by the person to whom the promise is made to their detriment or, if there is no detriment, he or she alters his or her position in reliance on that promise; and
3. that it is inequitable for the promisor to go back on their promise (that to do so would lead to injustice).

Consideration must move from the Promisee to the Promisor

The general rule is that the promisee must provide the consideration.

In *Tweddle v. Atkinson* (1861) a groom's father agreed with the bride's father to pay the groom a sum of money. The father-in-law failed to make this payment after the wedding. The groom sued the father-in-law's estate. **Held**: consideration must move from the promisee and the groom was not privy to the contract.

PRIVITY OF CONTRACT

The Privity of Contract Rule

The privity of contract rule provides that a contract does not confer rights or impose obligations arising under it on any person except the parties to that contract. (See *Tweddle v. Atkinson*, outlined above.)

The general rule is that only a person who is party to the contract has enforceable rights or obligations under it. In *Dunlop v. Selfridge* (1915), Dunlop, a tyre manufacturer, sold tyres to X, a distributor, on terms that X would not re-sell the tyres at less than the retail price. If X sold on the tyres to the trade, he must impose a similar condition on those buyers to observe the minimum retail prices. X resold tyres on these conditions to S. Under the terms of contract between X and S, S was to pay Dunlop £5 per tyre if it sold tyres to customers below the minimum retail prices. S sold two tyres to customers below this minimum and Dunlop sued S seeking to recover £5 per tyre. **Held**: Dunlop could not recover damages under a contract between X and S to which Dunlop was not a party.

Exceptions to the Privity of Contract Rule

There are a number of exceptions to the privity of contract rule. These include:

Executor or Administrator of a Deceased's Estate

A person legally appointed to administer the estate of an original party to a contract acquires the power to enforce it. This occurs in contracts that are not contracts for personal services.

Collateral Contract

A collateral contract is where X promises something to Y on the condition that they enter into a contract with Z. An illustration of this in practice is *Shanklin Pier v. Detel Products* (1951). In this case, the plaintiff hired a contractor to paint Shanklin Pier. The plaintiffs spoke to the defendant about whether a particular paint was suitable. The defendant assured them that it was, and that it would last for at least seven years. On the basis of this conversation, the plaintiff instructed the contractors to use that particular paint, which they did. The paint started to peel after three months and the plaintiff sought compensation from the defendant. There was no direct contract between the parties as the contractors had bought the paint from the defendant. **Held**: The court found a collateral contract to exist. In addition to the contract for sale of the paint, there was a second collateral contract between the defendant and the plaintiff by virtue of the guarantee of the paint's suitability in return for the pier company specifying that the contractors use it.

Valid Assignment of the Benefit of the Contract

A party can transfer the benefit under a contract to a third party through a written assignment.

Where it is foreseeable that Damage caused by Breach of Contract will cause a Loss to a Third Party

This exception is illustrated in the Court of Appeal decision of *Darlington Borough Council v. Wiltshire Northern Ltd* (1994). The plaintiff local authority wished to create a recreational centre on land that it owned. For funding reasons, the plaintiff arranged a contract between the building contractors, Wiltshire Northern Ltd, and a third party, Morgan Grenfell Ltd. There was no contract between the plaintiff and the building contractors. The building work was defective and the local authorities suffered a loss. However, the party in a contractual relationship with Wiltshire had suffered no loss and could transfer no claim for substantial damages. On the other hand, the council which suffered the loss was precluded by the privity rule from claiming the damages which it had suffered. **Held**: the Court of Appeal found in the council's favour.

The principle in this case is akin to the Irish Law Reform Commission recommendation that, subject to certain limitations, the rule should be changed so that, where the contracting parties have clearly intended a third party to benefit from the contract, that third party may sue if the contract is not carried out properly.

Statutory Exceptions to the Privity of Contract Rule

There are a number of statutory exceptions to the rule, including section 14 of the Sale of Goods and Supply of Services Act 1980, which provides that, if a consumer buys a car on a finance deal and the car turns out to be defective, the consumer may sue either the dealer or the finance company, despite the fact that the actual sale might be between the dealer and the finance company. Another exception is provided for by section 11(6) of the Data Protection Acts 1988 and 2003, which stipulates that a data subject may enforce rights under a data export agreement which is made between the data exporter and the data importer and not the data subject.

LEGISLATION REGULATING THE CONTENTS OF CONTRACTS

Legislation regulating the contents of contracts includes the:

- Sale of Goods and Supply of Services Acts 1893 and 1980.

- Unfair Terms in Consumer Contracts Regulations 1995 (S.I. No. 27 of 1995) as amended by the Unfair Terms in Consumer Contracts (Amendment) Regulations 2000 (S.I. No. 307 of 2000).
- E-Commerce: The Distance Contracts Regulations 2001 (S.I. No. 207 of 2001).
- E-Commerce: The European Communities (Directive 2000/31/EC) Regulations 2003 (the E-Commerce Regulations) (S.I. No. 68 of 2003).
- EU (Consumer Information, Cancellation and Other Rights) Regulations 2013 (S.I. No. 484 of 2013).
- EU (Certain Aspects of the Sale of Consumer Goods and Associated Guarantees) Regulations 2003 (S.I. No. 11 of 2003).

Sale of Goods and Supply of Services Acts 1893 and 1980

The law relating to the sale of goods (as distinct from the sale of land) is contained in the Sale of Goods Act 1893 and the Sale of Goods and Supply of Services Act 1980. Since the sale of goods is based on contract, the normal rules of contract law apply.

Definition

Section 1 of the 1893 Act defines a contract for the sale of goods as a contract whereby the seller transfers or agrees to transfer the property in goods to the buyer for a money consideration called the **price**.

Terms of the Contract

Section 11 of the 1893 Act provides that the right to repudiate a contract for breach of condition is replaced by a right to damages for breach of warranty where:

- the buyer waives the condition entirely or elects to treat the breach of condition as a breach of warranty and sues for damages; or
- where the buyer has accepted part of all of the goods and the contract is not severable.

A person buys as a consumer when not buying "in the course of [a] business [and] the goods are of a type ordinarily supplied for consumption or private use".

When the buyer is not dealing as a consumer, then all the implied conditions and warranties may be excluded by agreement, with the exception of those implied by section 12, but only when to do so is fair and reasonable.

Sections 11, 12, 13, 14 and 15 of the 1893 Act have been incorporated into section 10 of the 1980 Act.

Seller's Title (Section 12)

There is an implied condition that the seller has the right to sell the goods at the time when the property in the goods is to pass to the buyer under the contract.

In *Rowland v. Divall* (1923) the defendant sold a stolen car to the plaintiff. The plaintiff then sold it to a third party. The original owner reclaimed the car. The plaintiff sued the defendant for the price he had paid for the car. **Held**: the plaintiff was successful and entitled to the full purchase price of the car. The plaintiff had contracted under the belief that the defendant had good title to the car.

The right to quiet enjoyment is an implied warranty in a contract.

Goods to Correspond with their Description (Section 13)

Section 13 of the Act provides that, where a contract for sale of goods is by description, there is an implied condition that the goods will correspond with that description.

In *T. O'Regan & Sons Ltd v. Micro-Bio (Ireland) Ltd* (1980) the defendant was told by the plaintiff that they required a specific vaccination for young chickens. The plaintiffs were given the wrong vaccination and, unfortunately, a large number of their chickens died. **Held**: there was a breach of condition as to the description, as the vaccine did not correspond with the description requested by the plaintiffs.

A sale will be a sale by description even though the buyer may have inspected the goods. In *Beale v. Taylor* (1967), a car had been advertised as a 1961 Triumph Herald 1200. The buyer came to see the car and noted the metal disc on the rear showing "1200". It transpired after he purchased the car that only the rear met with this description – two different, separate models of the Herald car had been welded together. The seller argued that it had not been a sale by description and tried to rely on the buyer's inspection of the car. **Held**: the advertisement and the metal disc indicated that the car was a 1200. It was a sale by description, despite the buyer's inspection of the car. The buyer had relied to some extent on the description contained in the advertisement. He was entitled to damages for breach of section 13. In contrast, if the purchaser does not rely on the description offered by the vendor, then there will be no remedy for a breach of section 13.

Quality and Fitness

In *Egan v. McSweeney* (1956), coal was purchased by the plaintiff for domestic purposes. When lit, the coal exploded and caused the plaintiff injury. The coal was not of merchantable quality – the product was prejudiced. A good is not of merchantable quality where the performance of the product is prejudiced and the defect cannot be easily remedied or repaired without expense or taking some time to perform. There are exceptions, such as defects brought to the attention of the buyer before the contract is made and defects obvious to a reasonable person.

Section 14(2) of the 1893 Act provides that, where a seller sells goods in the course of a business, the goods must be of merchantable quality. The 1980 Act defines "merchantable quality" as being "fit for the purpose for which goods of that kind are normally supplied and as durable as it is reasonable to expect having regard to any description applied to them, the price if relevant and all the other circumstances".

Cehave v. Bremer (1975) involved a contract to sell citrus pulp pellets. The contract said that the shipment was to be in "good condition". On arrival, there was major damage to 1260 metric tons of the shipment and minor damage to a further 2053 tons. The buyers rejected the shipment claiming return of purchase price, which had already been paid. The seller sold the pellets onto a third party for £33,000 and they were then resold to the original buyers for the same price. They were consequently used for cattle feed. The contract price was £100,000 and market value £86,000. Lord Justice Denning **held** that the buyer was not entitled to refuse the goods as they could not be so bad if they were used for the original intended purpose.

Section 14(3) provides that "where the seller sells goods in the course of a business and the buyer, expressly or by implication, makes known to the seller any particular purpose for which the goods are being bought, there is an implied condition that the goods will be fit for that purpose" (see also the *O'Regan* case above).

In *Priest v. Last* (1903), the plaintiff purchased a hot water bottle for his wife from the defendant and did not state the purpose for which it would be used. On the fifth time of using the bottle, it burst, injuring his wife. The defendant argued that the buyer had not made known the purpose for which he would be using the hot water bottle. **Held**: a hot water bottle is a product with one purpose. In a situation such as this, where there is only one purpose for a particular good, that purpose is disclosed by buying the good i.e. when buying a hot water bottle, its purpose is obvious. Because it was not an effective hot water bottle, the implied condition in section 14(3) had been breached.

Sale by Sample

Section 15 of the 1893 Act as inserted into section 10 of the 1980 Act provides that, in cases of sale by sample, there is an implied condition that:

- the bulk will correspond with the sample;

- the buyer is to have reasonable opportunity of comparing the bulk with the sample; and
- the goods shall be free of any defect rendering them unmarketable, which would not be apparent on a reasonable examination of the sample.

Supply of Services

Section 39 of the 1980 Act implies certain terms into a contract where the supplier is acting in the course of his or her business (e.g. providing a service such as hairdressing) that:

- the supplier has the necessary skill to provide the service;
- the service will be provided with due skill, care and diligence;
- materials used will be sound and reasonably fit for the purpose for which they are required; and
- where goods are supplied under the contract, they will be of merchantable (sellable) quality.

Contracting out of the Terms implied by the Sale of Goods Acts

The only term that may be excluded in a contract is a term as to the necessary skill, due care and diligence implied into a contract for services.

Exclusion Clauses relating to Implied Terms

Section 55 of 1893 Act as amended by the 1980 Act states that it is no longer possible for a seller of goods to exclude the statutory terms totally from a sale of goods contract. Thus:

- a term that purports to exempt a party from section 12 of the Act concerning the seller's title is void; and
- any term that purports to exempt a party from the provisions of sections 13, 14 or 15 of the Act, as amended, which concern implied terms as to the quality and fitness of goods are void where the buyer is a consumer. In cases where the buyer is acting other than as a consumer, terms exempting the seller from these implied conditions must be fair and reasonable.

For the purposes of 'acting as a consumer':

- the buyer is not acting in the course of business, while the seller is; and
- the goods or services supplied are the type ordinarily used for private consumption.

Contracts for the Sale of Motor Vehicles

Where the seller of a motor vehicle is a motor dealer, he or she is obliged by section 13(4) of the Sales of Goods and Supply of Services Act 1980 to provide a certificate in writing to the buyer which states that the vehicle is, at the time of delivery, free from any defect that would render it a danger to the public.

Section 13(2) provides that there is implied condition in contracts involving consumers with regard to all motor vehicles that, at the time of delivery, they are free from any defect that renders them a danger to the public, including passengers in the vehicle. This applies to all situations where the buyer is a consumer, including instances where the seller is not selling in the course of business.

These terms are not implied where it has been agreed between the two parties that the vehicle is not intended for use in its present condition.

'Motor vehicles' are mechanically operated vehicles such as cars, tractors, etc. Importantly, this section of the Act makes no distinction between new and second hand vehicles.

Warranties

In addition to a consumer's statutory rights, when certain items (usually electrical goods) are purchased, the manufacturer may also include a warranty. Manufacturers do this to promote trust in their products, in that they are willing to stand over them for a certain length of time. A manufacturer's warranty is an agreement to provide some remedies if a defect in the product occurs. The majority of standard manufacturers' warranties last six months to one year.

Retention of Title Clauses

A retention of title clause (also known as a '*Romalpa* clause') is a clause in a contract which provides that ownership remains with the seller until certain conditions are met, such as the payment of money. This means that one party gets possession of the goods while the other person still retains legal title to those goods. Thus, in the event of the purchaser going into liquidation, for example, the person who has retained title can simply reclaim the goods to which he or she has title.

As mentioned above, reservation of title clauses are also known as 'Romalpa' clauses after a leading case in this area. In *Aluminium Industrie Vaassen v. Romalpa Aluminium Ltd* (1976) a contract for aluminium foil contained a detailed retention of title clause stipulating that ownership would only pass to the buyer upon full payment. The defendants subsequently sold on some of the foil, and then later went into liquidation. The plaintiffs, who had not received the purchase price, sought to enforce the retention of title clause in order to secure payment before distribution of the defendants' assets. **Held**: the plaintiffs were entitled to trace and recover the proceeds of the subsequent sale of the foil.

There are many types of retention of title clauses, which include:

Simple Retention of Title Clauses

Title in specific goods will not pass until the full purchase price of the goods has been paid.

Aggregated Retention of Title Clauses

With an aggregated reservation of title clause, until the goods are paid for, not only will the title in the goods remain with the seller, but title in any goods manufactured from the supplied goods will also be subject to the reservation of title clause. It is necessary to distinguish between cases where:

(a) the supplied goods are irreversibly mixed – if so, title is extinguished and a charge has been created (see discussion of charges below); and

(b) where the supplied goods remain readily identifiable – here title is reserved and no charge is created.

A 'Tracing' or Proceeds of Sale Clause

This clause allows the purchaser to sell the goods on, with the proceeds of such sale being held in trust for the vendor.

Current Account Clauses

A current account clause provides that the title to the goods shall not pass until all sums due to the seller by the purchaser are paid. This is also called an 'all sums due clause'.

Creation of a 'Charge'

The important distinction between 'charges' and retention of title clauses is that charges require registration within 21 days of their creation (as discussed under registration of charges in Chapter 14). Failure to register a charge will render that charge void as against the liquidator and any creditor of the company. Simple retention of title clauses are not held to constitute charges, as the seller has retained legal title to the property in the form in which it was sold.

In the case of mixed goods, if the court finds that the goods remain identifiable, it will deem that an aggregate reservation of title clause exists. However, if the courts find that the goods are irreversably mixed, a charge will be created.

This can be seen in the case of *Re Bond Worth Ltd* (1980). In this case, a carpet company had taken delivery of a consignment of fibres from another company and used them to manufacture carpets. Both companies then went out of business and the receivers went to court over who owned the title to the fibres. The court **held** that the clause that the fibre company receivers sought to rely on was a charge. Reservation of legal title over mixed goods that lose their identity will result in the creation of a charge requiring registration. As the charge in this case was unregistered, it was therefore unenforceable.

The rules regarding reservation of title were further refined in the case of *Hendy Lennox (Industrial Engines) Ltd v. Grahame Puttick Ltd* (1984). A contract for supply of diesel engines contained a reservation of title clause. **Held**: the fact that the engines were incorporated into a generating set did not negate the clause. The incorporation was reversible without damage to either product and the clause was upheld. Staughton LJ distinguished some of the above cases stating that, in this case, "it was a question of doing up bolts and other connections which could later be undone". He clarified the law in stating that:

> "[T]he proprietary rights of the sellers in the engines were not affected when the engines were wholly or partly incorporated into generator sets. They were not like the fibres in *Re Bond Worth* which became yarn and then carpet, or the resin which became chipboard in *Borden* or the leather which became handbags in *Peachdart*. They just remained engines, albeit connected to other things."

The sellers retained title to the engines which had been incorporated into generating sets, as they could easily be removed.

In *Clough Mill Ltd v. Martin* (1985), the plaintiff had sold yarn to the buyer who intended to make fabric from it. The contract of sale provided that the title (or property) in the yarn remained with the seller until paid for; however, the buyer was permitted to use the yarn in its manufacturing process and the seller was accordingly to become the owner of any product made from yarn supplied by them. **Held**: the plaintiff's goods remained identifiable and, in the absence of payment, the seller was entitled to claim back the goods which he had sold. This can be distinguished from the *Re Bond Worth* case: full legal title did not leave the seller; therefore, there was no need to register a charge.

Proceeds of Sale Clauses

If the proceeds are to be held in trust for the vendor, it has been held by the court that such reservation of title clauses can create a charge. However, it depends on the circumstances of each case. This was seen in the case of *Aluminium Industrie Vaassen v. Romalpa Aluminium Ltd* (1976) as discussed previously.

Unfair Terms in Consumer Contracts

The EC (Unfair Terms in Consumer Contracts) Regulations 1995 (S.I. No. 312 of 1995) and 2000 (S.I. No. 37 of 2000) give effect to an EC Directive on unfair terms in consumer contracts 93/13/EEC. EU legislation only applies to **standard form contracts** (contracts that have not been individually negotiated). The idea behind this is that in terms that have not been individually negotiated the consumer is the weaker party and the Regulations are designed to protect the consumer from unscrupulous sellers. However, the onus is on the seller or supplier to show that a specific term was individually negotiated, which makes the regulation not apply to the contract. The legislation, however, does not apply to employment contracts.

Article 2 defines the key words used in the regulations:

> "Consumer" – natural person who is acting for purposes which are outside his or her business.
>
> "Seller" – person acting for purposes related to his or her business who sells goods.
>
> "Supplier" – person acting for purposes related to his or her business who supplies services.

Article 3(2) of the regulations provides that a contractual term shall be regarded as unfair if it causes a significant imbalance in the parties' rights and obligations under the contract, to the detriment of the consumer, contrary to the argument of good faith.

In deciding if 'good faith' has been breached, the following must be considered:

- strength of bargaining power of the parties;
- whether the consumer had an inducement to agree to the term;
- whether the goods or services were sold or supplied to the special order of the consumer; and
- extent to which the supplier or seller has dealt fairly with the consumer whose legitimate interest he or she has to take into account.

Schedule 3 of the regulations contains a list of terms in contracts that are automatically unfair:

- excluding legal liability for death or injury;
- inappropriately excluding or limiting liability for total or partial non-performance of the contract on the part of the seller;
- permitting the seller to retain sums paid by the consumer where the latter decides not to conclude the contract without providing for the consumer to

receive compensation of an equivalent amount from the seller or supplier where the latter is the party cancelling the contract;
- requiring a consumer who fails in his or her obligation to pay a disproportionately high sum in compensation;
- making an agreement binding on the consumer but giving the seller an option regarding performance; and
- enabling the seller to terminate a contract of indefinite duration without first giving reasonable notice.

Online and Distance Contracts

Consumer and shopping habits have evolved considerably in recent years. Contracts are increasingly entered into by consumers shopping online and over the telephone, and away from traditional 'bricks and mortar' shop premises. Special protections are afforded to consumers in these circumstances when they contract with a trader within the EU. The European Union (Consumer Information, Cancellation and Other Rights) Regulations 2013 (S.I. No. 484 of 2013) came into effect on 13 June 2014 implementing EU Directive 2011/83/EC, and consumers now benefit from increased protection and up-to-date rules replacing previous directives in the area.

The regulations govern rules that apply to distance and off-premises contracts. '*Distance contract*' is defined as a contract concluded between a trader and consumer under an organised distance sales or service-provision scheme, using one or more means of distance communication. An 'off-premises contract' refers to contracts concluded (or where an offer has been made by a consumer) away from the trader's premises, such as in the consumer's home, workplace or on an excursion organised by the trader. A 'consumer' for the purposes of the regulations is a "natural person who is acting for purposes which are outside the person's trade, business, craft or profession". A 'trader' is a person or company acting in the course of trade or business.

There are certain contracts which are specifically excluded from the regulations such as:
- social services and healthcare contracts;
- gambling contracts;
- contracts for financial services like insurance or banking;
- contracts for the sale of land;
- contracts for the construction of new buildings or substantial conversions;
- residential accommodation rental contracts;
- package holiday contracts;

- timeshares and long-term holiday product contracts;
- contracts for food and drink delivered to the consumer by regular roundsmen (for example, milkmen). However, once-off transactions are covered;
- contracts concluded by means of automatic vending machines or automated commercial premises; and
- contracts concluded with telecommunications operators through the use of public payphones.

The regulations provide consumers with the following rights and protections with regard to online/distance selling contracts:

1. Right to Cancel

Consumers who enter into an online contract are entitled to a 14-day 'cooling-off' period during which they can withdraw from the contract and return the goods to the seller, who must refund in turn the consumer within 14 days. The consumer is not required to provide a reason for the return.

> "[T]he consumer may, at any time prior to the expiry of the cancellation period … cancel a distance contract or an off-premises contract without giving any reason for the cancellation." (Reg. 14)

Certain goods and services are excluded from this right to cancel and the cooling-off period. Examples include:

(a) service contracts, after the service has been fully performed;
(b) digital content not supplied on a tangible medium; (exceptions (a) and (b) require the consumer's prior express consent and acknowledgement at point of contract that he or she would thereby lose the right to cancel);
(c) bespoke goods made on the basis of the consumer's individual choice;
(d) goods that are clearly personalised (e.g. a tee shirt with consumer's name);
(e) sealed audio or sealed video recordings or sealed computer software that were unsealed after delivery.

2. Right to Provision of Clear Information

Online traders must provide consumers with detailed information, including their contact details, the main characteristics of the product or service and its total cost, including all taxes and delivery charges. Before a contract is formed, the trader must provide the following information in a "clear and comprehensible manner".

- The name and address of the supplier.
- The main characteristics of the good/service.
- The price including taxes and delivery costs and how payment is to be made.
- How the goods are to be delivered or how the service will be performed.

- That a right to cancel exists.
- The minimum duration of the contract.
- How long it will be open to the consumer to enter into the contract on these terms.
- The cost of the communication between the parties if it is above a basic rate.
- How the contract may be cancelled.
- Any guarantees and after-sales services available.
- The conditions for terminating the contract if it is of unlimited duration or for longer than one year.

(Source: European Consumer Centre Ireland)

3. Right to Cancellation for Delayed Delivery

The trader is obliged to deliver goods within 30 days unless expressly agreed between the parties. If the trader fails to do so, the consumer can contact the trader and make arrangements for a mutually convenient delivery date, and if this is then not adhered to, then the consumer is entitled to a full refund within 14 days. The consumer may cancel the contract after the 30-day period if delivery within the timeframe was essential, e.g. the delivery of a St Valentine's Day gift.

4. Right to Redress in the Case of Faulty Goods

Under EU law a fault is presumed to have existed at the time of delivery if that fault is discovered within six months after purchase. If this is the case, the consumer may be offered a repair or replacement or, if neither of these are possible or sufficient, a full refund. The trader must refund the consumer within 30 days. Furthermore, for two years after purchase, the trader remains accountable to the consumer for any faults that may be discovered, though a consumer could be asked to prove that a fault that occurred after the initial six-month period was not caused by misuse.

CONTENTS OF A CONTRACT

A contract can be oral or in writing, but there are occasions where the law requires that certain contracts be in a certain format. They are:

Contracts that must be Evidenced in Writing

Under section 2 of the Statute of Frauds (Ireland) Act 1695, the following contracts must be evidenced in writing:

- contracts for the sale of *land*, or any interest therein;
- contracts to pay for the debts of another (*contracts of guarantee*);

- agreements made in consideration of marriage; and
- contracts not to be performed within one year.

Contracts that must be in Writing

Some statutes require that contracts must be made in writing. Examples of these are as follows.

- The Consumer Credit Act 1995, which requires that all consumer credit contracts must be in writing in order to be enforceable, e.g. hire purchase, credit sales, lease agreements, etc.
- The Bills of Exchange Act 1882, which requires that all promissory notes, bills of exchange and cheques are in writing.
- Leases of land for more than one year.

Contracts by Deed

The following contracts must be encompassed in the form of a deed to be enforceable:

- contracts not supported by consideration; and
- conveyances (transfers) of title to land.

Contractual Terms

The stipulations contained in any contract are called the terms of the contract and these regulate the rights, rules and obligations which the parties have bound themselves to in any agreement.

Contractual terms can arise from two sources:

Express terms – those which the parties have agreed between themselves. The words used by the parties when making the contract (whether written or oral) become the express terms of the contract.

Implied terms – those which are implied by law to give effect to the presumed intentions of the parties; for example, where a term is implied on the grounds of a trade or professional custom, or in accordance with a statute.

It is important to understand the meaning of the following terms (as in words and phrases):

- void,
- voidable,
- express terms,
    - conditions;

  - warranties;
  - innominate terms.

Void

Void means 'null' or invalid and therefore not binding in law. A void contract does not give rise to rights or liabilities. Such contracts have no legal effect whatsoever.

Voidable

In contract law, **voidable** means valid and enforceable until avoided by the innocent party. Here it rests with the injured party elect to either declare the contract void or to affirm it.

The terms of a contract must be distinguished from **representations**, which are not intended to be part of the contract. The courts use the **objective test** ('what would the reasonable person think?') in deciding whether a statement is a term or a non-contractual representation. The importance of knowing the distinction is that, if something said in pre-contract negotiations proves to be untrue, the party misled can only claim for breach of contract **if it was a term of the contract**. If the party who makes the statement has special knowledge of its subject, the statement is more likely to be treated as a term.

In *Oscar Chess v. Williams* (1959), a private motorist agreed to sell an old car to motor dealers in part exchange for a new car. The seller honestly believed that the car was a 1948 model, as was stated in the registration book. In fact it turned out to be a 1939 model (the registration book having been altered by a previous owner). It was **held** that the statement was not a term of the contract but a mere misrepresentation. The seller was not an expert and the buyer had better means of knowing the truth.

Express Terms

Express terms are either written or oral words used by the parties. The terms of a contract are usually classified by their relative importance:

- **Conditions** – these are the major terms, breach of which entitles the innocent party to repudiate the contract and sue for damages. The major terms of a contract are vital or prime – they go to the root of the contract, they are responsible for enticing a party to create the contract.

  In *Poussard v. Spiers and Pond* (1876), the defendant engaged the plaintiff to sing and play the principal part in an opera. A few days before the opera was due to open, the plaintiff became ill. The plaintiff recovered and sought to take up her lead role. The defendant refused because he had engaged someone else. She sued for breach of contract. **Held**: the opening night was of high importance; the plaintiff's failure to be available on the first night was the very basis of the contract. The obligation to perform on the first night was considered a condition and a failure of this entitled the defendant to repudiate the contract.

Re Moore & Co Ltd and Landauer & Co (1921): a contract for the sale of 3,100 tins of peaches described the tins as being packed in cases of 30. When they arrived the tins were packed in cases of 24. Although the agreed overall number of tins was supplied, the goods were rejected. The court was influenced by the fact that the cases may have been brought for subsequent resale, which would have involved repacking to obtain the correct number of tins and **held** that the purchaser was entitled to reject the goods as they were not as described.

- **Warranties** – warranty is a less important term of a contract. Breach of a warranty merely entitles the injured party to claim damages. Less important terms of a contract are not the basis of the contract, but are peripheral to the overall agreement.

  In *Bettini v. Gye* (1876), Bettini, an opera singer, was engaged by Gye to perform in a number of concerts. Bettini undertook to be in London six days prior to the start of the concert. He arrived three days late. Gye repudiated his services. **Held**: the plaintiff had been engaged for a 15-week season and failing to attend for three days' rehearsal involved a less important term. The defendant could claim compensation for a breach of warranty, but could not repudiate the contract.

- **Innominate Terms** – these are terms that are neither conditions nor warranties. An innominate term is an unclassified term: it depends on the nature and consequences of the breach, and is determined by the facts of the case.

  The concept of the innominate term was established in the case of *Hong Kong Fir Shipping Co Ltd v. Kawasaki Kaisha Ltd* (1962). The English Court of Appeal refused to adopt the traditional classification of 'condition' and 'warranty', and instead the Lord Justices concentrated on the gravity of the harm resulting from the breach of the clause in question. If the harm was serious, the court would be more likely to categorise the clause as a condition. If only trivial loss was caused by the breach, the clause in question would undoubtedly be regarded as a warranty.

  In this case, the defendants had chartered a ship from the plaintiffs for two years. Elderly engines and an inadequate and incompetent staff resulted in a total of 20 weeks of charter being lost to breakdowns and repairs. The agreement between the parties contained a clause that stated that the ship was "in every way fitted for ordinary cargo service". Although the defendants were entitled to bring an action for damages for breach of contract, the defendants actually terminated the contract based on the breach. The plaintiffs then brought an action for the wrongful termination of the contract based on their assumption that the broken term was a warranty and not a condition. The Court of Appeal agreed with the plaintiffs and deemed the term a warranty, based on the fact that the breach did not deprive the defendants of the whole of the benefit that they were entitled to under the contract. Thus, the termination of the contract was not justified.

Oral Evidence Relating to Contracts in Writing

It is a general rule (the **parol evidence rule**) that a contract, which is or includes a written document, may not be added to, varied or contradicted by way of oral evidence.

However there are numerous exceptions to this rule:

- oral evidence may be given of trade practice or custom;
- evidence may be given to show that the parties agreed orally that the written contract should not take effect until a 'condition precedent' had been satisfied, e.g. a written contract to buy a house subject to an oral agreement that it would take effect only if the architect's report was good;
- oral evidence may be given as an addition to a written contract if it can be shown that the written document, such as the printed conditions of sale, was not intended to comprise all the agreed terms;
- oral evidence may be given to correct a written agreement drawn up subsequently which contains a mistake;
- oral evidence may be given to establish consideration; and
- oral evidence may be given to explain the subject matter of the contract.

Implied Terms

Terms Implied by the Courts

In certain circumstances the terms of a contract may be implied by the courts:

- a term may be implied **by reason of the conduct of the parties** – where the court concludes that the parties intended a term to apply but did not express it because it was taken for granted; and
- a term may be implied **to give a contract business efficacy**. In such cases, the **officious bystander** test is used. The test is, if an officious bystander had intervened to remind the parties that, in formulating the contract,

they had failed to mention a particular point, they would have replied "of course it is included". In the case of *The Moorcock* (1889), the owners of a wharf agreed that the vessel *Moorcock* could be unloaded at its wharf. When the tide went out, the boat was grounded and damaged and the owners brought an action. It was **held** that there was an implied term that the defendants would take reasonable care to see that the wharf was safe as both parties knew that the ship would be damaged if it was not.

Terms Implied by Statute

Statutory implied terms operate irrespective of the intentions of the parties, in the absence of a valid exclusion clause. In some statutes, the implied terms are obligatory and the parties cannot exclude them, e.g. under the Sale of Goods and Supply of Services Act 1980, the Organisation of Working Time Act 1997, etc.

Terms Implied on the grounds of Trade or Professional Custom

A party to a contract may be able to show an implied term to be bound by custom. However, any express term overrides a term that may be implied by custom.

In *O'Reilly v. Irish Press* (1937), a chief sub-editor was dismissed from his post. He claimed that, as he was a senior journalist, it was a custom that he be given six months' notice. **Held**: O'Reilly had failed to show any such notoriety for this custom.

Terms may be implied by the Constitution of Ireland

The Irish Constitution safeguards and protects individual rights:

Right of Association In *Meskell v. CIÉ* (1973) the plaintiff, upon commencing employment with the defendant, was told that he was obliged to join a trade union. The plaintiff refused and was accordingly dismissed from his position. The plaintiff then sued and the court **held** that, as the Constitution recognises the right to form associations and unions, subject to public order and morality, it would also recognise the right of any individual to refuse to become a member of any group or association. Therefore the court implied the right of dissociation into Meskell's contract and accordingly found the actions of CIÉ to be in breach of that contract. Therefore the plaintiff was entitled to damages.

Right to Equality Under the Constitution and equality legislation, any contract that purports to treat a person in a prejudicial or disadvantageous manner because of their gender, marital status, family status, sexual orientation, religion, age, disability, race or membership of the Traveller Community will be automatically invalidated by the court. The courts will imply a term guaranteeing a right to equality into every contract.

Exclusion Clauses

An exemption or exclusion clause is a clause that limits or excludes the liability of a party to a contract. The law does not look with favour on these clauses and the courts have accordingly imposed certain conditions.

There are a number of rules governing exclusion clauses:

Incorporation of a Clause into a Contract

Signature A clause that is contained in a signed document cannot usually be disputed.

In *L'Estrange v. Graucob* (1934) the plaintiff purchased a vending machine on terms set out in the sales agreement. These terms excluded the plaintiff's normal rights under the Sale of Goods Act 1893. A number of these terms were set out in legible but very small print. The plaintiff had not read the agreement prior to signing it. **Held**: the plaintiff was bound by the agreement regardless of whether she had read it or not.

An exception will apply where a party has signed an agreement as a result of misrepresentation or fraud.

In *Curtis v. Chemical Cleaning & Dyeing Co* (1951), the plaintiff took her wedding dress to a dry cleaners where she was asked to sign a receipt which she was told disclaimed liability for damage to the beads or sequins. In fact, the receipt disclaimed liability for any damage to the dress. The fabric of the dress was badly stained as a result of the defendant's negligence during the cleaning process. The court **held** that the cleaners could not rely on the disclaimer as they had misled the plaintiff as to the effect of the document.

Notice An exclusion clause must be brought to the attention of the party before the contract is made if it is made orally or in the form of an unsigned document.

In *Olley v. Marlborough Court Hotel Ltd* (1949) a husband and wife arrived at a hotel, where they paid for their room in advance. In their bedroom they later noticed a sign that disclaimed liability for loss of valuables. The wife locked the room and handed the key into the reception. The key was later stolen and her fur coat was stolen from the room. **Held**: the disclaimer was too late. The hotel could not rely on the disclaimer since the contract had been concluded prior to it being brought to the attention of the customers.

The exemption clause must be an integral part of the contract and the party must have received adequate notice of it at the time it was 'accepted'. If the injured party was not actually aware of the exclusion clause, it must then be asked whether the party relying on the clause made reasonable efforts to bring the clause to the attention of the other party.

In *Interfoto Picture Library v. Stiletto Visual Programmes* (1988), Stiletto telephoned Interfoto on 5 March 1984 to enquire if they had certain photos from the 1950s that might be suitable for a presentation they were doing. Interfoto had not dealt with Stiletto before. The same day, 47 transparencies, together with a delivery note, were dispatched to the defendant. The transparencies were not returned until 2 April. A condition on the delivery note required that they be returned within 14 days or a "holding fee of £5.00 plus VAT per day will be charged for each transparency which is retained by you longer than the said period". The conditions were supposed to be the conditions of bailment (a situation where the physical control over the goods is given over to someone else for safekeeping). If Stiletto wished to use the transparencies, a fresh contract had to be agreed. The plaintiff sued the defendant for the amount of £3,783.50. **Held**: Interfoto did not take reasonable steps to bring this clause to Stiletto's attention. The clause in question was very onerous and Stiletto could not have known of the holding fee at such an "extortionate" rate. This condition did not become part of the contract between the two.

The case of *Chapleton v. Barry UDC* (1940) involved deckchairs advertised for hire for "2d per session of 3 hours". The plaintiff took two chairs, paid for them and put the receipt in his pocket. One of the chairs collapsed and injured him. The defendant attempted to rely on a notice on the back of the ticket which disclaimed liability for injury. **Held**: The disclaimer was not binding on the plaintiff. The advertisement gave no notice of limiting conditions and it was not reasonable in the circumstances to communicate them on the back of the receipt.

Previous dealings If the parties have had previous dealings with each other, then a party may be bound by an exemption clause on the basis of these dealings.

In *Spurling v. Bradshaw* (1956), the defendant stored goods in the plaintiff's warehouse over several years. On this occasion, he deposited some barrels for storage and later received his receipt containing a clause excluding liability for negligence. On collection of the barrels, they were found to be empty and the defendant refused to pay. He admitted that, in previous dealings, he had received this receipt but had never read it. The exclusion clause was upheld by the court as it had been present in the course of previous dealings between the pair.

Interpretation of Exclusion Clauses

The courts have adopted principles in dealing with exclusion clauses in contracts, which we will now examine.

Contra Proferentem Rule It is a general rule that all ambiguities in exclusion clauses will be construed against the party seeking to rely on them (*contra proferentem*).

For example, in *Walls, Son & Wells v. Pratt* (1910) a clause that excluded liability for "breach of warranty" was **held** not to cover "breach of condition". It is, however, possible to defeat the rule by careful and exhaustive drafting.

Article 5 of the EC (Unfair Terms in Consumer Contracts) Regulations 1995 and 2000 (see above, where these are discussed) introduces the *contra proferentem* rule into legislative format by providing in the case of standard form contracts that the meaning most favourable to the consumer shall be applied in cases of doubt as to the meaning of a term.

Exemption Clauses and Fundamental Breach of Contract The principle of fundamental breach is based on the notion that every contract has a central core, i.e. one basic obligation so fundamental that any attempt to exclude it would destroy the whole object of the contract.

The status of this principle in Irish law is, at the moment, somewhat uncertain. The leading Irish case is the Supreme Court decision in *Clayton Love & Sons (Dublin) Ltd v. B & I Steam Packet Co.* (1970). Here the plaintiff had a contract with B & I to ship a consignment of scampi from Dublin to Liverpool. It was a term of the contract that the goods would be loaded under refrigerated conditions. This was not done. The scampi was left on the quayside and rotted. The defendants, when sued, sought to rely on an exemption clause in the contract. The plaintiff challenged the operation of these clauses and was successful in the Supreme Court. Therefore, in this jurisdiction, it seems to be a rule of law that a party may not exclude liability for a fundamental breach of contract by incorporating an exclusion clause into the contract.

In *Photo Productions v. Securicor Transport* (1980), Securicor had agreed to provide security for the plaintiff's factory. There was an exemption clause in the contract, which exempted Securicor from liability for damage caused by any of their employees. A guard deliberately started a fire (to keep warm) which got out of control, and the plaintiff sued for the damage caused. It was **held** (by the House of Lords) that there is no principle that total failure to perform a contract deprives the party at fault from relying on an exemption clause. It is a question of interpretation of the exemption clause whether it is widely enough drafted to cover the damage done. In the present case, the exemption clause was wide enough to cover the damage that had occurred.

Statute Law

The legislature has responded by enacting statute law to restrict the use of exclusion or exemption clauses. The purpose of this is to protect the consumer.

Under the Sale of Goods and Supply of Services Act 1980, it is no longer possible for the seller of goods to exclude the statutory implied terms of sections 13 to 15 when the purchaser is a consumer. Furthermore, all exclusion clauses are subject to the test of reasonableness.

Section 200 of the Companies Act 1963 provides that the Articles of Association of a company cannot exclude liability of its directors, secretary or auditors for negligence.

The European Communities (Unfair Terms in Consumer Contracts) Regulations 1995 and 2000 limit the use of certain terminology between consumers and businesses. These apply to contracts that are not 'individually negotiated', i.e. the regulation protects consumers who have to accept standard form contracts.

Restraint of Trade Clauses

A restraint of trade clause restricts a person's freedom in the marketplace. For example, it restricts a person's ability to do business. Restraint of trade clauses are usually contractual where, for instance, a purchaser of the business wishes to restrict the vendor's ability to do business of the same type in the same geographical area. All restraints of trade, in the absence of special justifying circumstances, will be invalid. The court may decide to enforce such a clause that is considered reasonable in the interests of both parties. The reasonableness of the clause will be examined in determining if it is justified.

Factors Governing the Enforceability of Restrictive Covenants

A restraint of trade clause should serve to protect a legitimate business interest and go no further than to protect that interest. The burden of proof falls on the party seeking to rely on the clause.

In particular, the court will examine the following.

- **Time limits** for the enforceability of the clause. The more limited the temporal scope of the clause, the more it will appear reasonable to the courts. What is deemed reasonable depends on the purpose of the clause and the industry in question.

- **Geographical scope** should be limited to the area were the trade was carried out. An example of this can be seen in a 2003 determination of the Competition Authority involving Musgrave/Express Check-out (M/03/001). When Musgrave acquired Express Check-out, it found that there was a restriction on the vendor competing with the purchaser "anywhere in the island of Ireland" for two years. This was **held** to be too broad and the restriction was limited to narrower geographical areas. This decision is also an example of the consideration of the **anti-competitive** effect of a clause.
- **Scope** of the protection should not be any wider than necessary. For instance, would a non-solicitation clause whereby a vendor/employee would agree not to poach current customers be more a reasonable arrangement? In the *Murgitroyd* case set out below, the court suggested that the use of such a clause would be more appropriate than a restraint on soliciting actual and prospective customers.
- **Legitimate business interest served.**

Restraints on Employees

The employer must establish a trade secret/trade connection in order to prove that the restraint of trade clause serves a legitimate interest. In *Murgitroyd & Company v. Purdy* (2005), a patent agent worked out of the plaintiff's office and subsequently commenced trading as 'Purdy and Associates'. **Held**: a service agreement between the parties and the 'restraint of trade' clause contained therein was operative at the time the defendant terminated his employment. Mr Justice Clarke **held** that, on the facts of this particular case:

1. a geographical restriction based on the territory of the Irish State was reasonable;
2. a period of 12 months was not unreasonable; and
3. the prohibition on dealing with potential, as opposed to actual customers of the plaintiff (non-competition clause) was too wide.

Levinwick Limited v. Hollingsworth (2014)

The clause must be for the purpose of protecting the goodwill of the business. In the case of *Levinwick Limited v. Hollingsworth* (2014) the defendant former employee, a pharmacist, had left a pharmacy in Celbridge, County Kildare, and took up a job in a competing pharmacy, also in Celbridge. The employer sought to rely on a non-compete clause in the employee's contract of employment but the court refused to enforce the clause because the nature and extent of the restriction was more than was reasonably necessary to protect the goodwill of the employer's business.

Generally, these types of covenants against competition from former employees are rarely enforceable, only being upheld where the employee has any influence or direct personal knowledge of the employer's customers. When the employee has this influence or personal knowledge the provisions of the clause will be examined to ensure that they are reasonable in extent and duration.

Restraints on Businesses

A restraint on business clause seeks to protect the goodwill that comes with a business. It is used to prevent the previous owner of a business from usurping the goodwill that is attached to the business.

In *Nordenfelt v. Maxim Nordenfelt* (1894), the plaintiff traded in arms and munitions. **Held**: given the worldwide and limited nature of trade in this category, a restraint of trade clause in relation to the whole world was held to be legitimate.

*Restraints on Distributors/*Solus *Agreements*

A *solus* agreement is a requirement contract whereby the retailer will only sell or buy the supplier's products for a number of years.

Esso Petroleum v. Harpers Garage (1968) concerned a *solus* agreement whereby the two garages agreed to take all petrol supplies etc., from a particular distributor for a period of four and a half years and 21 years respectively. **Held**: such an agreement is acceptable as long as it is of a limited timeframe. A *solus* agreement for a 21-year period was unreasonable and void.

VITIATING FACTORS

As discussed previously, a contract is *prima facie* valid if all of the elements of a contract are present. A 'vitiating factor' (i.e. one of a number of circumstances that will invalidate the contract) can render a contract void or voidable.

These vitiating factors are:
1. mistake;
2. misrepresentation;
3. duress and undue influence;
4. contracts that are illegal or void; and
5. lack of capacity to contract.

1. Mistake

Where one or both of the parties to a contract have entered into that contract based on a mistaken belief, it may not be enforceable. There are two categories of mistake:

- bilateral mistake; and
- unilateral mistake.

Bilateral Mistake

A bilateral mistake is when both parties are mistaken as to the terms or subject matter of the contract. There are two types of bilateral mistake:

- common mistake; and
- mutual mistake.

Common Mistake In a common mistake, parties are labouring under the same common mistake and, though in complete agreement, are mistaken on a fundamental point that goes to the root of the contract.

In the case of *Cooper v. Phibbs* (1865), the plaintiff purchaser took a lease of a fishery from the defendant. It transpired (unknown to either party) that the plaintiff was the true owner and the contract was **held** to be void on this basis.

In *Couturier v. Hastie* (1872), corn was sold while in transit by sea from Salonica in Greece to England. It later transpired, unknown to either party, that before the contract had been formed, the ship's master had in fact disposed of the corn at Tunis as it had begun to rot. The contract was void due to mistake as to the subject matter of the contract.

Mutual Mistake A mutual mistake is where the parties are at cross-purposes and neither party is aware of the other's different view.

In *Raffles v. Wichelhaus* (1864), the plaintiff entered into a contract to sell 125 bales of Surat cotton. The contract specified that the cotton would be arriving into Liverpool on the ship *Peerless* from Bombay ("to arrive ex Peerless from Bombay"). There were in fact two ships named *Peerless* arriving in Liverpool from Bombay: one departing in October and another departing in December. The defendant thought the contract was for cotton on the October ship while the plaintiff thought the contract was for the cotton on the December ship. **Held**: the contract was void for mutual mistake.

In *Leaf v. International Galleries* (1950), a picture believed by both parties to be by Constable was sold by the one to the other. Several years later, it was discovered not to be a Constable and the buyer sued for rescission on the grounds of misrepresentation (see below). The court approved this course of action and intimated that the mistake was not one which would avoid the contract.

Unilateral Mistake A unilateral mistake is where only one party to a contract is mistaken as to the terms or subject-matter of the contract.

In *Cundy v. Lindsay* (1878), Lindsay & Co were manufacturers of linen handkerchiefs. They received correspondence from a rogue named 'Blenkarn', who purported to be 'Blenkarn & Co', with premises on 37 Wood Street. Lindsay & Co knew of a reputable business named as Blenkiron & Co on the same road. Under this guise, and the rogue's signing of his letters as 'Blenkiron & Co', Lindsay & Co sold the rogue a large order of handkerchiefs. Blenkarn then sold the goods (250 dozen linen handkerchiefs) to an innocent third party, Cundy, whom Lindsay & Co sued. The contract was **held** to be void.

The courts seem to create an artificial distinction between this situation and cases that are concluded face to face. This distinction can be seen in the case of *Phillips v. Brooks* (1919) in which the plaintiff jeweller sold various items of jewellery to a rogue. The rogue entered the jeweller's premises and selected various items and proposed to pay by cheque. He said: "You see who I am, I am Sir George Bullough." The jeweller checked that Sir George Bullough lived at the address given by the rogue. The rogue then asked if he could take a ring away with him which he later pawned and the jeweller sought to recover the ring from the pawnbroker. **Held**: The courts concluded that the jeweller had intended to deal with the person in front of him whoever he was. He had agreed to accept a cheque payment before the swindler revealed his false identity. Thus, as he was dealing with the person in front of him, the jeweller was not entitled to recover the ring.

2. Misrepresentation

A representation is a statement of fact made by one party to another in the course of negotiations, with a view to inducing one party to enter into a contract. A false representation is a misrepresentation.

The requirements to show misrepresentation are:

- the false statement is one of fact and not mere 'sales puff';
- the statement was directed at the party who is taking the action; and
- the statement was relied upon and induced the plaintiff to enter the contract.

In the case of *With v. O'Flanagan* (1936) the plaintiff entered into a contract to purchase a medical practice. The defendant during negotiations said that the practice produced an income of £2,000 per year. The practice took a downward turn and lost a significant amount of value before the contract was signed. The plaintiff discovered this after the contract was concluded and sued. The court **held** that a representation made as a matter of inducement to enter into a contract is to be treated as a continuing representation. The plaintiff's action was successful as this was a material fact which induced him to enter the contract.

Types of Misrepresentation

There are three main types of misrepresentation:

1. fraudulent misrepresentation;
2. negligent misrepresentation; and
3. innocent misrepresentation.

Fraudulent Misrepresentation Fraudulent misrepresentation is when a statement is made with the intention of deceiving and with the knowledge that it is false. The misled party may rescind, refuse to perform and/or recover damages. Fraudulent misrepresentation is also an action in the tort of deceit.

In the case of *Derry v. Peek* (1889), the directors of a company issued a prospectus stating that the company was empowered to run steam trams in Plymouth. This was not true, as authorisation had to be obtained from the Board of Trade. **Held**: the directors honestly believed that the statement in the prospectus was true. The court concluded that the promoters were not liable in tort for their non-fraudulent misrepresentation and held that it was necessary to show a party made a false statement knowing it to be false, believing it to be false or acting recklessly as to whether the statement was true or false.

Negligent Misrepresentation Negligent misrepresentation is when a statement is made in the belief that it is true but without reasonable grounds for such a belief. In this type of misrepresentation, a 'special relationship' must exist between the parties. The principle of negligent misrepresentation was born out of the case of *Hedley Byrne & Co Ltd v. Heller and Partners Ltd* (1964) (which was discussed in **Chapter 2**, on tort). A 'special relationship', the courts **held**, is one of trust and advice, usually given in a professional capacity.

Innocent Misrepresentation An innocent misrepresentation is when a statement is made in the belief that it is true and with reasonable grounds for this belief. The misled party may rescind the contract subject to being awarded damages in lieu of rescission. Innocent misrepresentation occurs in an 'honest mistake' type situation.

3. Duress and Undue Influence

Duress and undue influence are forms of coercion that negate a person's free-will to enter a contract. The court may set aside a contract when it is satisfied that the parties did not meet as equals and that one party has induced the other to enter a contract through coercion.

Duress

Duress is the more severe form of coercion. Parties enter a contract under duress where they are forced by actual violence or threats of violence. In *Griffith v. Griffith* (1944), a young woman became pregnant and it was alleged that the plaintiff was the father. He was subjected to extreme duress and was forced to go through a marriage ceremony by her mother, his own father and the local priest. It later transpired that he was not the father and he successfully challenged the marriage contract on the grounds of duress.

Undue Influence

Undue influence is a more subtle form of coercion which falls short of duress. The doctrine allows the court to set aside contracts where the weaker party did not exercise his free will to enter the contract due to the pressure exerted by the stronger party to the contract.

Undue influence takes two forms:

1. presumed undue influence; and
2. actual undue influence.

1. Presumed Undue Influence There are certain categories of relationship that give rise to an automatic presumption of undue influence. This presumption places a burden on the party acquiring the benefit from the contract to show that, in fact, undue influence was not exerted. Examples include a doctor-patient relationship and a solicitor-client relationship.

2. Actual Undue Influence Actual undue influence is where the party seeking to have the contract put aside must prove that actual undue influence was exerted which compromised the free will to negotiate the contract.

In the case of *Smelter Corporation v. O'Driscoll* (1977), the defendant contracted to sell her lands to the plaintiffs but later refused to complete the sale. The plaintiff sought an order of specific performance, which would oblige the defendant to complete the sale. The defendant told the court that an agent of the company visited her home and told her "If you don't consent, the local authority will compulsorily acquire the land and you will get less money for it." A group of senior officials also visited her and mentioned "compulsory purchase". There were, in fact, no plans for compulsory purchase of the property. **Held**: the court refused to grant an order for specific performance as the defendants and their agents had placed the defendant under a manifest disadvantage in leading her to believe one way or another she would lose her land.

The more recent case of *Ó Siodháchain v. O'Mahony* (2002) provides further illustration of undue influence. This "sorry saga" began with the desire of the defendant couple to sell their farm and farmhouse. The plaintiff befriended the defendants after viewing their property and later moved into the house and continually promised to complete the sale. Evidence established that he was at no time in a financial position to purchase the property and additionally borrowed £35,000 from the defendants. **Held**: the court ordered the plaintiff who had paid no rent on the property to return it to its owners and was satisfied that undue influence existed in this case. The evidence established that the plaintiff endeavoured to make them more malleable as to the terms they would accept for the property. The defendant was clearly very much under the influence of his parents and acted, in the words of the plaintiff, like a 15-year-old. The parties had not met as equals and the conduct of the plaintiff further exacerbated this. The court was satisfied that the plaintiff had "intervened in the lives of this young couple in a manner totally inappropriate for persons who had in mind purchasing the O'Mahonys' property".

4. Contracts that are Illegal *or* Void

Illegal Contracts

Contracts may be illegal at common law or by statute. Illegality means that the contract is injurious to society and the public interest, though no element of criminality need be involved. Collateral contracts depending on an illegal contract are unenforceable.

Examples of contracts illegal at common law include the following.

(a) Contracts whose object is the commission of a crime or a civil wrong, e.g. a contract to murder somebody (a crime), or to defame someone (a tort).

(b) Contracts with a sexually exploitative element, e.g. a contract of prostitution.

(c) Contracts against public policy such as:

  (i) contracts interfering with marital duties;

  (ii) contracts leading to corruption in public affairs;

  (iii) contracts to defraud the revenue;

  (iv) contracts which interfere with the course of justice; and

  (v) contracts to commit a crime or a tort.

Examples of contracts illegal by statute include the following.

(a) Wagering contracts under the Gaming and Lotteries Acts 1956–1986: all contracts for gaming or wagering are void and are only enforceable when a licence has been obtained.

(b) Contracts of insurance under the Insurance Acts 1936–1986 and the European Communities Framework Regulations which fail to disclose an insurable interest are void.

(c) Under the Family Home Protection Act 1976, the conveyance of a family home without the prior consent in writing of the other spouse is void.

Consequences of Illegality In general, no court will enforce a contract which is either illegal in its entirety or which contains an illegal clause or purports to carry out an illegal act. However, the courts will occasionally, where one party is clearly innocent of the illegality and did not intend to perform the contract in an illegal way, enforce the contract and sever the illegal part.

Void Contracts

In general, a void contract is not enforceable in a court of law. However, in practice, the courts will usually sever a void clause, or may amend the clause and may delete the offending part. If the contract is void for reasons of public policy, the courts will not enforce it so as to discourage this type of contract.

Types of void contracts are:

- contracts to oust the jurisdiction of the courts;
- contracts void at common law due to operative mistake or incapacity; and
- contracts prejudicial to marriage (any agreement which restricts a person's freedom to marry).

5. Lack of Capacity to Contract

The term *capacity* refers to a person's ability to enter into contractual relations. The general rule is one of ability to enter into contracts. However, particular categories of persons have either a limited ability to enter into contracts, or have additional protections available to them once they have entered into a contract, on the basis that, as a matter of policy, they should not be allowed to contract, or that they are in need of additional protection when they do so.

Minors

Minors do not have any contractual capacity to enter into certain contracts. A minor is defined under the Age of Majority Act 1985 as any person under the age of 18 years and who is not or has never been married. Contracts entered into by minors may be divided into:

1. valid contracts;
2. voidable contracts; and
3. void contracts.

Minors: Valid Contracts

(a) Contracts for necessaries Where a minor enters into a contract for necessaries, then he or she is bound by that contract as an adult would be. 'Necessaries' are defined in section 2 of the Sale of Goods Act 1893 as those goods that are necessary to **support** the minor's way of life. The definition has been extended to include goods that are necessary to **maintain** the minor's way of life also. The definition does not include goods that may be deemed luxuries.

In *Nash v. Inman* (1908) it was **held** that the purchase of a waistcoat was considered to be a luxury purchase where the minor in question was already more than adequately supplied with such apparel.

Skrine v. Gordon (1875) involved an action for the price of a horse purchased by a minor on credit. **Held**: the action was dismissed as the court deemed that the purchase of a horse for hunting was not a contract for necessaries and was, therefore, unenforceable.

In *Soon v. Wilson* (1962) it was **held** that a contract for the purchase of books by a minor was valid. The books were necessary to support the minor's studies.

(b) Beneficial contracts of service Closely linked to contracts for necessaries are beneficial contracts of service, such as apprenticeships. Such contracts, as long as they are to the benefit of the minor, are enforceable.

In *Doyle v. White City Stadium* (1935), under British Boxing Board of Control Rules, the plaintiff (a minor) was obliged to return the prize money for punching below the belt. He argued that he was not bound by the rules of the board as he was a minor and the contract was not to his benefit. **Held**: the minor was bound by the rules of the board. The rule existed for his benefit (boxing fairly).

In *Shears v. Mendeloff* (1914) it was **held** that the a minor boxer was not bound by the contract with his manager as it conferred no substantial benefit upon him and the terms of the contract were in fact heavily weighted in favour of his manager. The terms of the contract provided (1) the manager was under no obligation to arrange matches for the boxer, (2) the boxer had to cover his own expenses, (3) 25% of any fees earned by the minor had to be paid over to the manager.

Minors: Voidable Contracts

If a contract is not for the supply of necessaries or a beneficial contract of service, it is voidable at the option of the minor. Such contracts may be further divided as follows:

Recurring obligations Where the contract contains recurring obligations, i.e. company shares, insurance, etc., then these can be avoided by the minor, but the courts require the minor to reject the contract by some positive act before coming of age or within a reasonable time thereafter.

All other contracts These contracts are enforceable by the minor, but not against him or her, unless the minor positively affirms the contract within a reasonable time after coming of age.

Minors: Void Contracts

The Infant Relief Act 1874 provides that, where an infant enters into a contract to purchase goods (other than necessaries) or receive a loan, such contracts are absolutely void. Therefore, such contracts are unenforceable against the minor and unenforceable by him or her.

Capacity of Married Women

Until 1957, married women's capacity to contract was restricted in regard to entering into contracts and the holding of property. The Married Women's Status Act 1957 finally dragged this particular area of the law into the twentieth century, and the capacity of a woman to enter contracts is now unaffected by marriage.

Capacity of Convicts

Until recently, convicts (persons convicted of treason or felony) could not enter a contract under the Forfeiture Act 1870. Once they had served their sentence, they were restored to their rights. However, the Criminal Law Act 1997 has removed this disability of convicts.

Capacity of the Mentally Ill

The rule here is that a contract is valid unless:

(a) the mental illness was such as to prevent the sufferer from knowing the nature of the actions; and
(b) the other party was aware of that mental illness.

This rule appears to be based on requirements of commercial certainty and, at first glance, seems quite harsh. However, it should be noted that some protections are available. The requirement that the other party should be aware of the mental illness means that exploitative contracts made in this knowledge will be void; if the other party is genuinely unaware of the mental illness, then the equitable doctrine of unconscionable bargain may apply if the contract is so unfair as to justify intervention. Contracts for necessaries are enforceable at a reasonable price even if the other party knew of the mental illness.

Capacity of Drunks

The position of drunks is similar to that of the mentally ill. Before any question of unenforceability arises, the party must be so drunk as not to know the nature of his or her actions: mild inebriation will not suffice. Once this is established, then if the contract concerns necessaries, the party will be bound to pay a reasonable price, even if the other party knew of their drunkenness. In the case of non-necessaries, the party will be bound unless they can establish that the other party was aware of the intoxication at the time of the making of the contract. Once this is established, the party may elect to affirm or reject the contract on sobering up.

In *White v. McCooey* (1976) a person challenged a contract made while drunk. His challenge was, however, rejected on the basis that, while his inhibitions were undoubtedly lowered, he was not so drunk as not to understand what he was doing. **Held**: the contract was so one-sided as to justify its rejection on the grounds of unconscionability.

DISCHARGE OF CONTRACTS

There is a variety of ways in which contractual relations between two parties may come to an end. The rights and obligations arising under a contract may be discharged in any of the following ways:

1. performance;
2. agreement;
3. breach; and
4. frustration.

Discharge by Performance

This is the usual method of discharge. The general rule is that contractual obligations are discharged only by complete and exact performance.

In *Cutter v. Powell* (1795), the plaintiff was the legal representative of the estate of her deceased husband. Her husband had been employed on a ship sailing from Jamaica to Liverpool and the wage was for the complete voyage. The husband died three-quarters way through the journey and she sued for a proportion of the wages. It was **held** that the plaintiff was not entitled to any money, as the husband had not completed the voyage.

If time is not of the essence of a contract, then a party may perform it late. However, if time is of the essence and prompt performance is a condition, conclusive, and late performance will not discharge the obligations. If time was not originally of the essence, either party may make it so by serving on the other a notice to complete within a reasonable time. In *Richards v. Oppenheim* (1950) the original contract between the parties required the building of a Rolls Royce chassis within seven months. It was not done and the purchaser agreed to wait longer. When it was not built within the specified time, he served a notice requiring completion within four weeks, otherwise he would cancel the order. He did cancel it but the makers tendered delivery three months later. It was **held** that the contract was discharged as there was no performance within the period of the notice. By serving the notice, he made time of essence to the contract.

There are three important exceptions to the rule in *Cutter v. Powell* (above):

- **divisible contracts** – the contract may provide for performance by instalments, i.e. each contract is independent of the other.
- **partial performance** – this arises where a contracting party has partially done what he has promised to do and is entitled to sue on the contract.
- **prevention of performance** – one party may prevent performance and the party prevented from completing is entitled to be paid for what they have done under the doctrine of *quantum meruit* (see also below under breach of contract).

In *Sumpter v. Hughes* (1898), Sumpter undertook to erect buildings on lands owned by Hughes. Sumpter abandoned the work a little over half way through. Hughes completed the work using materials left by the plaintiff. The plaintiff sued for the price of the materials and the work done. It was **held** that he was entitled to be paid for the materials but not for the work done as it was not a case of substantial performance.

Discharge by Agreement

Just as a contract is formed by agreement, so it may be discharged by agreement in the following ways.

- A contract may include a provision for its own discharge by imposing a **condition precedent,** which prevents the contract from coming into existence unless the condition is satisfied.

- It may impose a **condition subsequent** – a condition that does not prevent a contract from coming into existence but, if the condition is unfulfilled, then the contract can be rescinded.
- **A** contract may be discharged by subsequent agreement, for which there must be some consideration. If the contract remains unperformed by both parties, then each party provides consideration by agreeing to release the other from their obligation (bilateral discharge). But if one party has completely performed his obligations, his agreement to release the other from his obligations (unilateral discharge) requires consideration, such as payment of a cancellation fee called **accord and satisfaction.**
- If the parties enter into a completely new contract. This is called a **novation** contract.

Discharge by Breach

If one party is in breach of a condition, the other party may treat the contract as discharged. The injured party may want to treat the contract as still continuing and merely claim damages for his loss.

Anticipatory Breach

An anticipatory breach will occur where parties declare in advance that they will not perform their obligations under the contract. The innocent party can then immediately sue for damages if they so choose. They are not required to take immediate action and may choose to wait until the actual time the performance is due to take place. An anticipatory breach can be either **express** or **implied**.

1. *Express anticipatory breach* In *Hochster v. De la Tour* (1853) De la Tour agreed to employ Hochster as his courier for three months, from 1 June 1852, to go on a trip around Europe. On 11 May, De la Tour wrote to say that Hochster was no longer needed. On 22 May, Hochster sued for breach of contract. De la Tour argued that Hochster was still under an obligation to stay ready and willing to perform until the day when performance was due, and therefore could commence no action before that. It was **held** that the plaintiff was entitled to sue as soon as the anticipatory breach occurred on 11 May.

   The innocent party may elect to treat a contract as still in force despite the anticipatory breach of the other party; the former may continue with their preparations and recover the agreed price for their services. In *White and Carter (Councils) Ltd v. McGregor* (1961) the defendant entered into an agreement with the plaintiff to advertise his business. He then wrote to cancel the contract but the plaintiff chose to perform its part of the bargain. The council then claimed the agreed payments. It was **held** that the contract continued in force and the plaintiff could recover the agreed price for its services.

2. *Implied anticipatory breach* In *Omnium D'Enterprises v. Sutherland* (1919) the defendant agreed to lease a ship to the plaintiff but, before the time of performance, the defendant sold the ship. **Held**: the sale of the ship amounted to a clear repudiation of the contract and the plaintiff was entitled to bring an action for damages immediately.

Repudiatory Breach

A repudiatory breach occurs where one party does not fulfil the obligations under the contract.

In *Athlone RDC v. Campbell & Son* (1912), contractors were engaged by the council to dig a well. A dispute arose during the work and the contractors wrote to the council indicating that they were willing to complete the work. The council wrote back indicating that they did not want this to be done. **Held**: the reply by the council was a repudiatory breach of the contract.

Discharge by Frustration

The doctrine of frustration differs from the vitiating factors dealt with above: all of these factors take place at the time that a contract is purportedly entered into; frustration takes place only **after** a contract has been entered into, and does not mean that the contract is liable to be set aside, but rather means that the contract ceases to have effect from a particular date. Therefore, the frustrating event must be beyond the control of both parties.

Frustration has been defined as: "external factors, which so radically alter the basic assumptions on which a contract is founded that its performance is impossible or futile" (Raymond J. Friel, *The Law of Contract* (Round Hall Press, 1995) p. 289).

The seminal case of frustration was *Paradine v. Jane* (1647) where the occupancy of a tenant under a lease was interrupted by the fact that his lands were requisitioned by armed forces during the English Civil War. An action against the tenant for arrears of rent was successful, notwithstanding these circumstances, and it was **held** that the tenant should have sought to guard against this contingency by the terms of his lease.

This doctrine was brought to absurd lengths in *Gamble v. Accident Assurance Co* (1869). Here it was a term of an insurance policy that the insured should inform the company of any accident within seven days. The insured died by drowning, and then did not have the good grace to notify the company! The company was not, it was **held**, liable to pay out on the policy of insurance, notwithstanding that it was impossible for the deceased to meet this obligation: he should have, it was **held**, arranged for another person to do so on his behalf in those circumstances.

However due to the absurdity of this doctrine's application, the courts curtailed its use.

Where the Doctrine of Frustration may Arise

The doctrine of frustration may arise in the following situations:

Destruction of the subject matter of the contract In *Taylor v. Caldwell* (1863) the plaintiff entered into a contract with the defendant to rent his hall for four days for a series of concerts. Before the first concert took place, the hall was destroyed by fire. The plaintiff sued the hall owner for damages. **Held**: the destruction of the subject-matter rendered the contract impossible to perform and discharged the contract.

Death and personal incapacity to perform a contract of personal service In *Shepherd & Co Ltd v. Jerrom* (1986), J entered into a contract of apprenticeship with Shepherd & Co. Subsequently, he was sentenced to 39 weeks in Borstal following a conviction for assault. **Held**: the contract was frustrated by his sentence in Borstal.

In *Flynn v. Great Northern Railway Company* (1953), an employment contract was **held** to be frustrated as medical evidence established that a van driver was unable to return to work.

Government intervention A contract may be frustrated if there is a change in the law where the contract becomes illegal or where a government declares that its performance will be void.

Ross v. Shaw (1917) concerned a contract that was impeded by the outbreak of World War I. A contract for purchase of yarn could not be lawfully performed owing to the occupation of the mill by German troops, which was **held** to be a frustrating event and the contract was discharged.

Non-occurrence of an event fundamental to the contract In *Krell v. Henry* (1903), the defendant paid a deposit to hire a room from which to view the coronation procession of Edward VII. The procession was called off because of the King's illness and the defendant was sued for the balance. **Held**: the contract was made for the *sole purpose* of viewing the coronation and, as this did not occur, the contract was frustrated. However, the defendant could not get his deposit back because **the rights and liabilities of the contracting parties are fixed at the moment of the frustrating event**. Therefore, the plaintiff could keep the deposit but was not entitled to the balance.

In *Herne Bay Steam Boat Co. v. Hutton* (1903) a steamboat was hired to carry passengers round the naval review which had been arranged as part of the coronation celebrations. The review was cancelled and the hirers refused to take the boat. It was **held** that as the royal review was not the sole purpose for hiring the boat (the boat could be used for pleasure), there was no discharge by frustration. The owner of the boat was entitled to the agreed hire price.

A contract will not be discharged by frustration in the following circumstances:

- if an alternative mode of performance is still possible;
- if performance suddenly becomes more expensive;
- if one party is deemed to have accepted the risk that they will be unable to perform; and
- if one party to the contract has induced the frustration.

In *Maritime National Fish v. Ocean Trawlers* (1935), the parties contracted to rent a trawler for use in otter fishing. The hirers had four other trawlers and they applied to the Canadian Government for licences for five boats but were granted only three licences. They allotted these to three of their own trawlers and argued that the contract for hire of the trawler was frustrated since it could not lawfully be used. **Held**: the only reason the trawler could not be used was as a result of the choice made by the hirers in allotting the licences. There was no frustration of the contract.

Effect of Frustration on a Contract

If a contract is found to be frustrated, it ceases to have effect from the date of the frustrating event only. Neither party is liable to perform obligations after the frustrating event. However, any rights and obligations before the event remain in place. The practical effect is that 'the loss lies where it falls', except if there is a total failure of consideration, i.e. any money paid prior to the frustration cannot be reclaimed.

BREACH OF CONTRACT

When a contract is broken/breached by one of the parties, the other party will seek a remedy from the court for a breach of contract.

The remedies for breach of contract are:

- damages;
- rescission (where the contract is cancelled, and the parties put back in the position they were in prior to the contract being made);
- specific performance;
- injunction; and
- rectification.

Damages

A party may sue for damages as compensation for the loss caused by the breach, the idea being to restore the parties who have suffered loss to the same position they would have been in **had the contract been performed**.

Remoteness of Damage

In determining whether the loss arising from a breach of contract is too remote, and therefore not compensatable, the courts will apply the rule in *Hadley v. Baxendale* (1854). Under this rule, damages may only be awarded:

- in respect of loss which either arises naturally, according to the usual course of things, from the breach; or
- in respect of loss which the parties may reasonably be supposed to have contemplated as the probable result of the breach of the contract.

In *Hadley v. Baxendale* the plaintiff owned a mill which ceased to operate because the main drive-shaft had broken. He contracted with the defendant, a carrier, to transport the broken shaft to the makers who would use it as a pattern for making a new one. Owing to Baxendale's neglect delivery was delayed and the mill was out of action for longer than was necessary. Baxendale did not know that his delay would cause the mill to be idle. The plaintiff claimed for loss of profits.

However, it was **held** that his claim must fail. The defendant did not know the mill would be idle owing to his neglect and, furthermore, the loss was outside the natural course of events. It was not a natural consequence of delay in transport of a broken shaft.

In *Victoria Laundry (Windsor) v. Newman Industries* (1949) the defendant contracted to sell a boiler to the plaintiff for immediate use. Delivery was delayed by 20 weeks. The plaintiff claimed damages for:

1. normal loss of profits; and
2. loss of abnormal profits which would have been earned on completion of highly lucrative dyeing contracts.

Held: while damages for loss of normal profits was recoverable, the claim for loss of special profits had to fail. The defendant had no knowledge of the dyeing contracts, and the loss of profits did not arise naturally according to the ordinary course of things.

Measure of Damages

In general, damages can be measured under the following headings:

Non-financial loss As a general rule, the amount of damages awarded is what is needed to put the plaintiff in the position they would have achieved if the contract had been performed. At one time damages could not be recovered for any non-financial loss arising from breach of contract. However damages have been recovered for mental distress where this is the main consequence of the breach.

In *Jarvis v. Swan Tours* (1973), the plaintiff solicitor took a two-week ski holiday in Switzerland based on the brochure description. The brochure stated that the owner of the accommodation had excellent English, that there was a bar on the premises and regular entertainment. What was provided was inferior to the description. Damages on the basis of financial loss were assessed at £32. The plaintiff sought additional damages for loss of enjoyment. **Held**: damages of £125 were awarded to compensate for disappointment and distress.

Liquidated damages (capable of calculation) i.e. the sum that becomes payable in the event of a breach.

Unliquidated damages Here the amount is decided by the court. The following will be taken into consideration:

- the **expectation loss** arising out of the breach of contract, i.e. the difference between the contract price and the price of substitute goods purchased at a later date (date of breach);
- the **reliance loss** arising out of the breach of contract, i.e. relying on the services of third parties;
- the **restitution loss** arising out of the breach of contract, i.e. the cost of replacing the goods and services originally contracted for;
- the **consequential loss** arising out of the breach of contract, i.e. all ancillary losses arising out of the original breach; and

- the **incidental loss** arising out of the breach of contract, i.e. all incidental losses arising out of the original breach, e.g. loss of trade, customers or future business.

Nominal damages A token award where there has been a contractual breach but little actual loss.

Punitive/Exemplary damages These are designed to punish the party who deliberately breaches a contract.

Quantum Meruit

If the party incurring loss has performed work as a result of the obligations under the contract and the contract is discharged by breach of the other party, the injured party may claim for the **value of the work**. The aim of such an award is to restore the plaintiff to the position he or she would have been in if the contract had never been made.

In *Folens v. Minister for Education* (1984), the plaintiff publisher had carried out preparatory work on a children's text at the request of the defendant, who ultimately decided not to go ahead with the project. The defendant had not benefited from the work, but the plaintiff had suffered loss thereby. It was **held** that the plaintiff could recover in *quantum meruit*.

Mitigation of Damages

The innocent party has a duty to reduce/mitigate/minimise the losses. In *Bord Iascaigh Mhara v. Scallan* (1973), the defendant hired a boat and abandoned it. The owners, BIM, left it to deteriorate and later attempted to recover for the physical damage that had resulted. **Held**: BIM had a duty to mitigate its losses by removing the boat from the water.

Rescission

The remedy of rescission aims to restore the parties to the position they were in prior to the contract being formed. There are limited grounds on which a court will agree to order rescission, such as where the contract has been entered into as a result of fraud or undue influence exercised by one of the parties.

The remedy of rescission may be lost for a variety of reasons:

- if the parties cannot be returned to their pre-contractual position; or
- if there is delay in seeking relief.

Specific Performance

An order for specific performance directs a party to perform his or her obligations under a contract. This order will not be granted to enforce contracts of personal service. The remedy of specific performance, in common with all other equitable remedies, is discretionary in nature. It will not be ordered where damages are an adequate remedy.

Specific performance will not be awarded:

- for contracts for personal services;
- for contracts to advance money;
- where constant supervision by a court is required;
- where one of the parties is an infant/minor; or
- where the contract is neither fair nor equitable.

Specific performance will be awarded for:

- the sale of land; and
- the sale of unique goods.

Co-operative Insurance Society Ltd v. Argyll Stores (Holdings) Ltd (1998)

In this case, the defendants were given a lease by the plaintiffs for one of the units in a shopping centre in Hillsborough in Northern Ireland for a period of 35 years. This unit was used to operate "Safeway", a supermarket, and became the key unit in the shopping centre complex, and generated footfall to the benefit of other tenants. The defendant supermarket group decided to close 27 stores across the UK, which were either making a loss or were less profitable, including this one.

An action for specific performance was brought seeking to force the operation of the supermarket and the case went all the way to the House of Lords. However, the action was dismissed.

The House of Lords gave a number of reasons for the refusal, namely the "difficulty of supervision, the heavy-handed nature of the enforcement mechanism and that the carrying on of business under a potential threat of contempt is oppressive". They also claimed that damages were a suitable alternative.

Aranbel Ltd v. Darcy & Ors (2010)

This case was taken by a developer against a party with whom it had entered into binding contracts to sell an apartment "off the plans" just prior to the financial collapse of the property market. The defendant refused to complete the sale and an action of specific performance was taken seeking to force him to honour the contract entered into and complete the purchase. He admitted that he was bound to complete, but said that such an order should not be made owing to the financial impossibility of him being able to comply as a result of his changed financial position. The court stressed that the defence here was 'impossibility' as opposed to 'impracticability'. The position was such that, even if the defendant had sold his own properties, he would not be in a position to finance the purchase of the property. Equity does not act in vain. The action for specific performance was dismissed and instead damages were assessed.

Injunction

An injunction is an order of the court requiring a party to do or refrain from doing a particular act. Injunctions can be mandatory, prohibitory, or *quia timet* (granted 'in fear of' a wrong being committed) in nature. Some injunctions are of perpetual duration, while others are granted on an interlocutory or interim basis.

A **mandatory injunction** requires an individual to carry out a positive act at the direction of the court. An injunction may be granted compelling the defendant to carry out what he or she has contracted to do, such as the delivery of goods by a courier company, or an injunction to remove something that is causing a nuisance to the neighbours' property.

A **prohibitory injunction** is preventative in nature. It forbids or bans a certain action, such as playing music at certain times in a residential neighbourhood or the publication of a newspaper article.

In contract law, an injunction is only granted where monetary compensation would be an inadequate remedy.

Types of Injunction Granted by the Courts

- An **interim injunction** lasts only until the next sitting of the court.
- An **interlocutory injunction** lasts from the application until the court hearing months later.
- A **perpetual injunction** lasts forever.
- A **Mareva injunction** is a form of injunction which stops the defendant dissipating his or her assets.

Rectification

An order of rectification is made to amend a written instrument so that it accords with the true agreement reached by the parties.

REVIEW QUESTIONS

(See Solutions to Review Questions at the end of this text.)

Question 3.1

A client has come to you and stated that she has offered her friend €100,000 to purchase her business and that her friend has accepted this offer; however, no monies have changed hands yet.

Requirement List and describe briefly the main legal elements of a contract.

Question 3.2

Anton and Aaron are two friends, both 16 years old. Both are avid computer programmers and have recently developed their own computer game called 'Astroid Fighters'. Bridgewater Computer Gaming Ltd ('BCG') is a Cork-based private company specialising in computer games. Anton and Aaron have approached the owners of BCG offering them the opportunity to purchase the rights to Astroid Fighters. BCG is keen to do so and has approached you to draft the contract for purchasing the rights to the game. However, you explain to BCG that Anton and Aaron have no contractual capacity to enter into a contract.

Requirement:

(a) In relation to the law of contract, explain the concept of contractual capacity in the context of minors **and** outline the type of contracts that are presumed to be valid.

(b) Assess whether Anton and Aaron have the capacity to enter into a contract with BCG Ltd.

(Based on Chartered Accountants Ireland, CAP 1 Law for Accountants, Autumn 2014, Question 2(a))

Question 3.3

BCG is expanding its business and has decided to purchase land in Waterford from Mr Elis. BCG has agreed a purchase price of €100,000 with Mr Elis and it is the intention of BCG to build the company premises on the land. Contracts have been signed between Mr Elis and BCG and a completion date has been finalised for the transfer of the land and monies to be exchanged. However, Mr Elis has recently been told that he could have received twice the price for the land and has just phoned his solicitor to say that he no longer wishes to sell the land and is refusing to complete the transfer document.

Requirement In relation to the law of contract formation, list and describe briefly the main elements of a contract **and** state with reasons, whether or not a valid contract was entered into between Mr Elis and BCG Ltd.

(Based on Chartered Accountants Ireland, CAP 1 Law for Accountants, Autumn 2014, Question 2(b))

Question 3.4

Last year Bella was made redundant from her job as a chartered accountant. Following this redundancy Bella decided to change her career path and pursue her lifetime ambition of opening a bakery. She signed a lease on commercial premises for a period of 12 months and then set about re-fitting these premises to become an operational bakery. Prior to opening, the business premises were inspected by the Fire Safety Authority for the purpose of obtaining a fire safety certificate. Unfortunately, the premises failed the inspection due to a lack of fire retardant ceiling tiles, an improper swing of the exit door, and the fact that the cooking ventilation system was not fire compliant and needed updating. Following this inspection, Bella contacted the landlord, Alliance Realty ('Alliance'), requesting that they make the required alterations to the property as specified in the inspection report. Alliance is refusing to undertake the alterations as they consider the premises fire compliant. Bella is now considering terminating the lease with Alliance and seeks your advice.

Requirement:
(a) Discuss any **four** methods by which a contract can be discharged.
(b) Advise Bella of the most appropriate method of contractual discharge in these circumstances, commenting also on the legal consequences for Bella of this discharge.

(Based on Chartered Accountants Ireland, CAP 1 Law for Accountants, Summer 2014, Question 1(a))

Question 3.5

Last year, Dylan Accounting College ('Dylan') experienced a 20% drop in student numbers and, in an attempt to stem this decline, Dylan called a meeting with all 20 of their lecturing staff to discuss what could be done to increase student numbers. Following this meeting, Dylan's CEO sent an email to all lecturers stating that he had decided to offer a €5,000 bonus to any lecturer who developed and marketed a new course that generated in excess of 50 student applications.

For the next nine months one of the lecturers, Anne, devoted all of her free time to developing and marketing a course leading to the award of a Masters in Corporate Governance and Ethics. As a result of Anne's work, Dylan secured applications from 72 students for entry onto the Masters programme.

In addition, the college's registrar (who is not part of the lecturing team), Frank, developed a Diploma in Advanced Auditing Practice. Two weeks ago the marketing department informed Frank that, to date, they had received 53 applications for entry onto the diploma course.

Last week, the CEO called a meeting with both Anne and Frank and informed them that Dylan did **not** intend to run either of their new proposed courses, as another new course had generated over 100 student applications and would generate more income than either Anne's or Frank's courses. When Anne and Frank queried whether or not they would be receiving the €5,000 bonus, the CEO told them that they were not entitled to it as they had no contract with Dylan. Anne and Frank believe that there is a contract and are considering suing Dylan for breach of contract.

Requirement By discussing the law regarding 'offer and acceptance', assess whether a valid contract has been formed between:

- Dylan and Anne; and
- Dylan and Frank.

(Based on Chartered Accountants Ireland, CAP 1 Law for Accountants, Autumn 2013, Question 1(a))

Question 3.6

ABC Pharmaceuticals ('ABC') has had a contract with Rossmore Medical ('Rossmore') for the past three years for the supply of drugs to treat clinical depression. The contract term agreed between the parties was five years, but last month Rossmore contacted ABC to inform them that they would be cancelling the contract with immediate effect, as a government order recently enacted in the country in which Rossmore is located has put a ban on the importation of this drug.

ABC is considering suing Rossmore for breach of contract but its solicitor has advised that it is unlikely to be successful, as the contract is frustrated.

Requirement:

(a) Define 'frustration' and explain any three grounds upon which a contract can be deemed to be frustrated.

(b) State, with a reason, whether the contract between ABC and Rossmore is frustrated.

(Based on Chartered Accountants Ireland, CAP 1 Law for Accountants, Summer 2013, Question 1(a))

Question 3.7

Jim has worked for Purity for the last 10 years as a research scientist. Prior to joining the company, Jim signed a contract that contained a restraint of trade clause, which stated that he was prohibited from working for a competitor of Purity within the Republic of Ireland for six months after the termination of his contract. He has recently resigned and is now taking up employment with Purity's main rival company.

Requirement:
(a) Explain the nature of a restraint of trade clause, and give **two** examples of such clauses.
(b) Outline whether you consider the clause in Jim's contract is likely to be classified as valid or invalid, providing **one** reason for your answer.
(c) On the assumption that the clause is valid, Purity are considering applying for an injunction to restrain Jim taking up employment. Explain the purpose of an injunction.

(Based on Chartered Accountants Ireland, CAP 1 Law for Accountants, Summer 2012, Question 4(b))

Question 3.8

Adam has taken over the position of financial accountant from Gabriel, whose contract with the company was terminated as a consequence of contractual frustration resulting from his permanent incapacity.

Requirement Define the concept of 'contractual frustration', and list any other **four** situations where the court is likely to uphold a claim of frustration.

(Based on Chartered Accountants Ireland, CAP 1 Law for Accountants, Summer 2011, Question 2(b))

Question 3.9

As Adam has regular access to confidential company information and trade secrets in his employment, Downey Investment Advisors have included a restraint of trade clause in Adam's employment contract to the effect that should he leave their employment, he is restrained from working for a competitor or setting up a business in competition with Downey Investment Advisors for a period of six months, and within a 50-kilometre radius of Downey's offices in Galway and Limerick.

Requirement:

(a) Define a restraint of trade clause.

(b) Outline the **three** main factors that a court will take into consideration in determining the validity of restraint of trade clauses.

(c) Determine whether the court would consider the clause in Adam's contract valid or invalid.

(Based on Chartered Accountants Ireland, CAP 1 Law for Accountants, Summer 2011, Question 2(c))

Question 3.10

Explain the distinction between a contractual condition and a contractual warranty.

(Based on Chartered Accountants Ireland, CAP 1 Law for Accountants, Summer 2011, Question 3(a))

Question 3.11

ABC Ltd has encountered a problem with one of its suppliers. The supplier signed a contract with ABC Ltd for the supply of component parts at a price of €85 per unit, with the requirement that 200 units are delivered on a monthly basis. Last month, the supplier notified ABC Ltd that they would no longer be able to supply the components at the agreed price. ABC Ltd is outraged and is considering asking the court for an order for specific performance of the contract.

Requirement Explain the nature of an order for specific performance, referring specifically to the various grounds when this order will not be granted, and review the likelihood of the court granting ABC Ltd the order in these circumstances.

(Based on Chartered Accountants Ireland, CAP 1 Law for Accountants, Autumn 2011, Question 4(b))

Question 3.12

Discuss the requirements of a valid contract.

(Based on Chartered Accountants Ireland, CAP 1 Law for Accountants, Autumn 2010, Question 2(a))

Question 3.13

Run Ltd ('Run') is a company based in Galway specialising in selling sportswear. This business is managed by Gerry. Mark, in Salthill, wishes to purchase running shoes, in a size 9, and has asked the manager to let him know when his size becomes available in stock. On 8 January, Gerry emailed Mark to let him know that one pair of shoes was in stock. Mark posted a cheque for €70 that evening to Gerry saying:

"Many thanks for your email of 8 January. I enclose a cheque, in the sum of €70, and look forward to receipt of shoes."

A postal strike took place from 8 to 13 January and Mark's cheque did not arrive until 15 January. By this stage, Gerry had sold the running shoes requested by Mark, to another customer.

Requirement Discuss the effect of the postal rule on the contract and assess whether a valid contract exists between Mark and the company.

(Based on Chartered Accountants Ireland, CAP 1 Law for Accountants, Autumn 2010, Question 2 (b))

CHAPTER 4

PLANNING AND DEVELOPMENT LAW

Introduction

The Planning and Development Act 2000 created a statutory framework for modern planning law in Ireland. It has since been amended by the Planning and Development Regulations 2001, the Planning and Development Regulations 2002 (S.I. No. 70 of 2002) and the Planning and Development (Amendment) Act 2002.

Section 3(1) of the Act defines 'development' as:

> "save where the context otherwise requires, the carrying out of works on, in, over or under land or the making of any material change in the use of any structures or other land".

Planning permission should be sought before any development on land has begun, although certain categories are 'exempted' by the 2000 Act, which we shall examine later in this chapter.

Requirement for Planning Permission

Planning permission is required for:

- new buildings;
- extensions (subject to certain exemptions for certain extensions to houses);
- material change of use;
- demolitions; and
- exempted development.

Material Change of Use

'Change of use' is the term used to describe the situation where the use of land and the former use for which it has been granted planning permission are substantially different in planning and development terms. If a change of use is material, it requires planning permission. Whether a change of use is material is decided by a number of factors.

In *Dublin Corporation v. Bentham* (1993), Bentham was the owner-occupier of 8, 9 and 10 Belgrave Square in Dublin. The premises had previously been used as a bedsit, and a planning injunction was sought against Bentham for the unauthorised use of the premises as a guest house. The court concluded that there was a clear distinction between the features of a bedsit and a guest house and that this was a material change of use requiring planning permission.

Intensification of an existing use can also constitute a material change of use. In *Readymix (Eire) Ltd v. Dublin City Council* (1978) Mr Justice Griffin cited the substantial traffic increase as a factor that could indicate a material change of use.

Demolitions

Planning permission is required to demolish a protected structure or a proposed protected structure. It is also required where the building was last used as a residence, or where it is attached to a property owned by someone else.

Exempted Development

Planning law exempts certain types of development from the planning permission process. The purpose of exemption is to avoid controls on developments of minor nature. Exempted developments include:

- any work that is carried out to change the inside of the structure;
- incidental use of land within the garden of the house (e.g. erecting a shed);
- building an extension to the rear or side of the house (subject to conditions and limitations); and
- developing the use of land for the purposes of a casual trading area.

The Planning Process

Notice

Planning regulations require the publication of the notice of intention to apply for planning permission before you make an application for planning permission. The application for planning permission must be made within two weeks of the publication of the notice. Publication is required in two ways:

1. an advertisement conforming to the regulations in a newspaper circulating in the district; and
2. by the erection or fixing of a notice on the land or structure.

The notice should be securely erected and fixed in a conspicuous position, easily visible and legible by a person using a public road and should be in place and maintained for five weeks from the date of application.

Application

The planning application must be submitted to the relevant planning authority. The applicant should also submit copies of the public notices as well as the necessary documents, particulars, plans, drawings and maps.

The planning application must state whether the application is for permission for development, permission for retention of development, outline permission for development or permission consequent on the grant of outline permission.

Types of planning permission:
1. permission (commonly known as full planning permission);
2. outline permission; and
3. retention permission.

Permission

This is applied for prior to engaging in an activity on the land which requires planning permission, such as building a house.

Outline Permission

Outline permission is planning permission that is granted in principle for the development of land that is subject to a subsequent detailed application. It enables an applicant to gauge whether a proposed development would be acceptable to a planning authority.

Retention Permission

Retention permission is applied for in circumstances where an unauthorised use or works has already been carried out on the land. An example is where someone builds a structure, such as a house, without first applying for planning permission. The applicant, in making an application for retention permission, is subject to a high fee and will face enforcement proceedings should retention permission be denied.

Inspection

The relevant planning authority shall, on inspection of the land, consider whether the requirements of the regulations relating to the site notice have been complied with.

Public Participation

Any person or body upon payment of a fee may make a submission or observation in writing to the planning authority on an application within five weeks beginning on the date that the application is received. Only a person or body that has done so may appeal against the grant of a planning permission. A member of the public may also apply for a planning injunction.

Notice of Decision

The planning authority must give its decision within eight weeks of the submission of a valid planning application (although it may not make its decision within the first five weeks). If the applicant does not receive a notice of decision within the appropriate period, a default permission may arise. This eight-week period may be extended where the planning authority makes a request for additional information.

The planning authority may decide to grant planning permission, which is normally subject to a number of conditions that must be complied with. Planning permission is generally valid for five years.

An applicant for planning permission may appeal the decision to An Bord Pleanála, which is generally required to consider the appeal *de novo* (as if the application has been made for the first time). Members of the public who participated in the submission process may also appeal against the grant of a permission. The board can either grant permission/outline permission with or without conditions, or refuse permission.

Enforcement and Compliance

Where a person has not complied with planning law, the following consequences may arise.

Enforcement Notice

Enforcement notices are the most commonly used tool in enforcing planning law. Where an unauthorised development comes to the attention of a planning authority, an enforcement inspector will carry out an inspection and will recommend in his or her report the enforcement action that is deemed necessary. This can be the issuing of a warning letter or an enforcement notice.

- **A warning letter** – warns the developer against the unauthorised use of the land and allows him or her to make a written submission.

- **Enforcement notice** – if the warning letter is not complied with an enforcement notice will be issued. An enforcement notice sets out times and methods whereby the developer must discontinue the unauthorised use of the land.

Planning Injunction

Section 160 of the Planning and Development Act 2000 governs the use of a planning injunction. A planning injunction is a powerful tool in ensuring that planning law is complied with. An application may be brought by any member of the public or planning authority, and unauthorised development can be pre-empted, in that section 160 provides that an application may be brought:

> "where an unauthorised development has been, is being or is likely to be carried out."

The High Court or the Circuit Court may make an order to ensure that an unauthorised development does not commence or continue, and may also order that the land, as far as is practicable, be restored to its condition prior to unauthorised development.

Time Limits on Enforcement

An enforcement proceeding has a time limit of seven years from the date of commencement of the development (section 57 Planning and Development Act 2000).

REVIEW QUESTIONS

(See Solutions to Review Questions at the end of this text.)

Question 4.1

(a) Mary has bought a site and wishes to build a house on it.

Requirement Prepare a brief memo outlining the steps Mary should take when she is making her application.

(b) Jim built a house last year without seeking planning permission; he is now worried and wishes to seek planning permission.

Requirement Briefly describe the type of planning permission he should apply for.

Question 4.2

Identify any **three** steps involved in the application process for planning permission and name any **two** consequence of proceeding without planning permission.

(Based on Chartered Accountants Ireland, CAP 1 Law for Accountants, Autumn 2012, Question 3(b)(i))

Chapter 5

LANDLORD AND TENANT LAW

Introduction

The Landlord and Tenant Law (Amendment) Act 1860, more commonly known as 'Deasy's Act', is the basis of the relationship between landlords and tenants.

Section 3 of Deasy's Act states that the relationship of landlord and tenant is deemed to be founded on the expressed or implied contract of the parties.

Section 4 of the Act requires that leases for a fixed term of more than one year be in writing and that they must be signed by the landlord. (Leases for lesser periods have no formalities and may be made orally.)

Leases

A lease is defined by Deasy's Act as "any instrument in writing, whether under seal or not, containing a contract of tenancy in respect of any lands, in consideration of a rent or return". A lease is a property interest that gives the holder exclusive possession of the land. A lease determines the relationship between landlord and tenant.

There are different forms of leases, the most common being as follows.

Fixed-Term Lease

A fixed-term lease is a contract that is used to bind a landlord and tenant for a fixed period, such as one year. On expiration, the possession of the premises reverts to the landlord.

Tenancy at Sufferance

This type of tenancy arises when the fixed-term lease ends and the tenant stops paying rent, but does not vacate the premises.

Periodic Tenancy

A periodic tenancy is not for a fixed period of time. This depends on the agreement of when the rent is paid. The tenancy is automatically renewed at the end of such period and is terminable by notice (**notice to quit**).

Statutory Tenancies

A number of statutes create implied tenancies. An example of this is section 40 of the Landlord and Tenant Act 1980 which provides that a tenant who is entitled to a new lease at the end of the present tenancy may remain in possession until the application has been decided.

Tenancy at Will

A tenancy at will is a type of tenancy that does not involve the payment of rent, but where the tenant is in possession of the land for an indefinite period of time with the consent of the landowner. The agreement, therefore, exists at the 'will' of tenant and landowner. It is a concept that has declined in importance. A tenancy at will may be terminated by either party at any time. Section 17 of the Statute of Limitations Act 1957 provides that a tenancy at will is deemed to end one year after it begins, unless previously determined.

Tenancy by Estoppel

Tenancy by estoppel arises where the requirements of a valid lease were not complied with, but both parties have carried out their business as if it were. In such circumstances, the parties are subject to the same rights and obligations as if a valid lease had existed.

Licences

A licence can be distinguished from a lease in that a licence does not confer a property right on the holder. At its simplest, a licence is a permission to do something that otherwise would be unauthorised. There are different forms of licence.

Bare Licence

A bare licence is the simplest form of licence. It is where the landowner invites someone onto his or her land.

Licence Coupled with an Interest

A licence coupled with an interest is a licence that bestows an extra interest in the land. A simple example is when someone has the right to fish from a river on another's property.

Contractual Licence

This is a licence created by contract, e.g. the right that attaches to your ticket to enter a football stadium to watch a match.

Contents of a Lease

The following is normally included in a lease:

- the names and addresses of parties to the lease;
- the date the lease commences;
- a description of the premises;
- the amount of rent payable;
- the period of the lease;
- a clause outlining consequences of breach of the lease; and
- covenants (as explained below).

Covenants

A covenant is an obligation to do or to refrain from doing something. A lease generally contains several covenants outlining the respective obligations of landlord and tenant.

Covenants that bind the landlord include:

- covenant to allow the tenant quiet enjoyment of the premises (implied by law);
- covenant that the landlord has the right to let the premises (implied by law); and
- covenant to maintain and repair the structure.

Covenants that bind the tenant include covenants to:

- pay the rent on time and in full (unless agreed otherwise);
- keep the property in good order;
- inform the landlord if repairs are needed and give the landlord access to the property to carry out repairs;
- give the landlord access (by appointment) for routine inspection;
- deliver possession to the landlord peaceably at the end of the tenancy;
- pay service charges; and
- refrain from assigning, sub-letting or sharing the premises without the landlord's consent.

Forfeiture

The landlord may be entitled to bring the lease to an end earlier than the agreed time if the tenant breaches a covenant. This is known as **forfeiture**.

Forfeiture may be allowed:

- if the tenant claimed to be the legal owner of the property and issued legal proceedings;
- if a tenant does not comply with the covenants in the lease and there is an express term of forfeiture; and
- in circumstances where the tenant does not comply with covenants and there is no express term allowing for forfeiture. The courts will have to determine if the term is a condition or a warranty.

Right to a New Tenancy: Business Premises

Situations giving rise to a right to a new tenancy after the original tenancy comes to an end are known as 'equities' and include:

- business equity;
- long occupation equity; and
- improvements equity.

Business Equity

The Landlord and Tenant Act 1980, as amended by the Landlord and Tenant (Amendment) Act 1994, states that a tenant may be entitled to a new tenancy for business tenants if he or she has been in continuous occupation of the premises for five years.

The Civil Law (Miscellaneous Provisions Act) 2008 was introduced to remedy the situation whereby it was not possible for business premises to contract out of their right to renew their tenancy after five years unless the business premises was an office. Section 43 of the Act now provides that a tenant may contract out of the rights to a new tenancy to all commercial premises. The wording of this Act appears to imply that the tenant may do this at any stage during the existing tenancy. In order for this renunciation to be valid, it must be in writing and the tenant must have received independent legal advice in respect of the renunciation.

Long Occupation Tenancies

Section 13(1)(b) of the Landlord and Tenant Act created what is known as a 'long occupation' tenancy. The tenant must have been in occupation for 20 continuous years and is entitled to a new tenancy on the termination of the old one. The position on long occupation tenancies has been modified in relation to residential tenancies. The Residential Tenancies Act 2004 abolishes this provision in relation to residential tenancies from 1 September 2009 (i.e. if a tenant's right to a long occupation equity arises before 1 September 2009, the right is unaffected).

The long occupation equity will continue to exist in respect of business premises and is unaffected by its abolition in respect of residential tenancies.

Improvements Equity

'Improvements equity' applies to both business and residential tenancies. Section 13(1)(c) of the Landlord and Tenant Act 1980 provides a right to renewal where the tenant would otherwise be entitled to compensation for improvements. These improvements must amount to at least half of the letting value of the property. Under section 45 of the Act, 'improvement' means an addition or alteration to the building including the installation of water, gas or electricity, but excludes redecoration or repair.

Terms of a New Tenancy

Notice of Intention to Claim Relief

In order for tenants to benefit from one of the equities, they must apply to the landlord with a document known as a *Notice of Intention to Claim Relief*. The terms of the new tenancy may then be agreed between the landlord and tenant. They can apply to the court for a rent review after five years. If the landlord and tenant are unable to agree on terms, they may apply to the court.

Length of New Tenancy

Business equity The maximum length of a new tenancy that arises under business equity is 20 years but no less than five years (unless the landlord agrees to a lesser term).

Long-term occupation equity and improvements equity The maximum length of a new tenancy in respect of these two equities is 35 years.

Commercial Leases and Residential Tenancies

Commercial Leases

Short-term commercial leases typically run for a period of less than five years, while long-term leases tend to run for 20–25 years.

Full Repairing and Insuring (FRI) Lease

Most commercial leases are on a 'full repairing and insuring' basis. FRI leases are generally for 20 years, but may be longer, depending on the circumstances. In the case of an FRI lease, the tenant is responsible for all repairs, insurance and outgoings on the building. It is normal that the landlord remains responsible for the structure of the building. Rent reviews are usually every five years. There is a statutory ban on upward-only rent review clauses in leases entered into after 28 February 2010.

Subject to limited exceptions, a commercial tenant who has been in continuous occupation for business purposes for a minimum of five years has a statutory right to renew that tenancy, or to obtain compensation from the landlord if the landlord does not wish to renew the tenancy. Following the Civil Law (Miscellaneous Provisions Act) 2008, all commercial tenants (and not just office tenants, as was previously the case) may now opt out of their entitlement to a new tenancy after five years.

The contents of the lease will vary, depending on whether the premises are a stand-alone unit or a unit in part of a larger building with shared common areas. Leases for tenants in supermarket complexes, for example, tend to include a number of quite specific provisions, such as minimum trading hours, non-permissible uses and regulations concerning window displays and shop fronts, etc.

Common Terms in Commercial Leases

Some terms are common to most commercial leases. These include:

Rent review clauses The form of commercial lease found over the last 25 years is almost invariably an upwards only market rent lease with five yearly rent reviews. However, Section 132 of the Land and Conveyancing Law Reform Act 2009 prohibits the provision for upward only rent review clauses. It applies to all new commercial leases granted on or after 28 February 2010. Therefore, from this date forward, all new commercial leases allow for a rent review to be greater, less or equal to the then passing rent notwithstanding the wording in the lease. Existing commercial leases are not subject to this legislation.

Service charge clauses In situations where a tenant is leasing a unit in a larger building, a service charge clause is commonly included to deal with charges to maintain common areas. Service charges are usually payable quarterly in advance, based on estimates previously provided by the landlord's managing agents, and are paid into a communal fund. At the end of each financial year, the managing agents prepare a final service charge statement detailing the amounts actually incurred. If the tenant has made an overpayment during that year, it is usually credited against the next service charge year. If there has been any underpayment, then the tenant will have to settle that underpayment.

Alienation is the legal term used for an assignment (transfer) or subletting by the tenant of the lease to a third party. The standard FRI lease contains a covenant preventing the tenant from assigning or sub-letting without the consent of the landlord.

Residential Tenancies

The Residential Tenancies Act 2004 regulates residential tenancies. This Act does not apply to any of the following:

- public authority housing;
- holiday homes lettings;
- business premises lettings;
- landlord occupied lettings; and
- 'rent a room' scheme.

Tenant's Obligations

The tenant's main obligations are to:

- pay the rent;
- keep the premises in good repair;
- not involve themselves in antisocial behaviour; and
- provide information to the landlord about who is living in the property.

Landlord's Obligations

The landlord's main obligations are to:

- allow the tenant of the property to enjoy peaceful and exclusive occupation;
- carry out to the structure all such repairs as are, from time to time, necessary;
- provide the tenant with their contact details; and
- maintain a policy of insurance in respect of the structure of the property.

Rents

Rents are dealt with by Part 3 of the Residential Tenancies Act 2004. The key provisions of this section are:

- rent must not be above market rate;
- rent may be reviewed once a year (unless there is a substantial change to the property);
- notice of 28 days must be given to tenants of new rents; and
- disputes may be referred to the Private Residential Tenancies Board (PRTB): www.prtb.ie.

Security of Tenure

Section 4 of the 2004 Act introduces some security of tenure based on the concept of a four-year tenancy. Landlords may only terminate a lease without specific grounds within the first six months of the tenancy. After this six-month period, they will only be able to terminate the lease if one of the following can be shown:

- non-compliance with tenancy agreement;
- property is no longer suited to the tenant's needs;
- landlord is selling the property within three months;
- landlord/family member wishes to occupy the property;
- landlord intends to remodel the property; or
- landlord intends to alter the business use of the property.

This cycle is repeated after four years.

Termination

Tenancies are to be terminated by means of a **notice of termination**, regardless of why the termination is happening. The notice period to be given depends on the length of the tenancy – see **Table 5.1**.

Table 5.1 Duration of Tenancy and Notice Periods

Duration of Tenancy	*Notice by the Landlord*	*Notice by the Tenant*
Less than six months	28 days	28 days
Six or more months but less than one year	35 days	35 days
One year or more but less than two years	42 days	42 days
Two years or more but less than three years	56 days	56 days
Three years or more but less than four years	84 days	56 days
Four or more years	112 days	112 days

In a situation where a landlord refuses consent to assign or sub-let a fixed-term tenancy, the tenant may terminate the tenancy before the expiry of the fixed term.

Dispute Resolution under Part 6 of the 2004 Act

Disputes must be referred to the Private Residential Tenancies Board (PRTB), and not to the courts. Examples of disputes that will be dealt with by the PRTB include:

- issues relating to deposit refunds;
- breaches of tenancy obligations;
- lease terms;
- termination of tenancies;
- rent arrears; and
- complaints by neighbours regarding tenant behaviour, etc.

Dispute Resolution Process by the PRTB - This may consist of two stages:
1. mediation or adjudication; and/or
2. public hearing by a three-way panel.

Parties are invited to elect to resolve their dispute through either **mediation** (where a neutral party assists them to find a mutually agreeable solution) or by **adjudication** (where details are provided to a decision maker who will issue a determination). Parties have 21 days from a failed mediation or the decision of an adjudicator to appeal to the tribunal or a determination order is issued by the PRTB. If an appeal is made, an order will be issued by the panel subsequent to the public hearing. A tribunal hearing determination is binding if not appealed to the High Court within 21 days. A determination order sets out the terms to be complied with, including any payments owing, and the length of time a party has to comply. If a determination order is not complied with, enforcement may be sought through the courts.

The PRTB may award damages of up to €20,000 and arrears of rent of up to €20,000, or twice the annual rent, whichever is greater (though a maximum of €60,000 applies to rent arrears awards). Cases involving amounts greater than these will have to be taken through the courts.

Registration of Tenancies

Landlords have to register a tenancy within one month of the tenancy commencing for a fee, currently €90. If they do not register on time they are also subject to a late fee, currently €180. Landlords must be registered with the PRTB to avail of the dispute resolution service. Tenants, however, have access to the dispute resolution service irrespective of whether the landlord has registered the tenancy or not. The PTRB will pursue compliance by landlords with the registration requirement. Failure to register is an offence and the penalty on conviction is a fine of up to €3,000 or up to six months' imprisonment, or both.

Accommodation Standards and Rent Books

Landlords are legally obliged to provide a tenant with a rent book or another appropriate document to comply with the Housing (Rent Books)

Regulations 1993. Failure to do so may result in a fine of up to €3,000 and/or imprisonment for up to six months. The rent book must contain:

- specific information on the tenancy;
- a record of all payments made by the tenant; and
- a statement of information on the rights and responsibilities of landlords and tenants.

There are also certain minimum standards of quality for any private rental accommodation. Local authorities have responsibility for enforcement under the Act.

REVIEW QUESTIONS

(See Solutions to Review Questions at the end of this text.)

Question 5.1

Your client has recently purchased a house which she is keen to lease out. She seeks your advice on what information should be contained in a lease.

Requirement:

(a) Advise your client on **any five** pieces of information/contract terms typically contained in a lease.

(b) Explain briefly **any three** of the typical covenants of the tenant to the landlord and **any three** covenants of the landlord to the tenant.

Question 5.2

Michael and Joseph are brothers who were left land, in equal shares, by their father in his will. They are considering building a restaurant on this land.

If the brothers are unsuccessful in obtaining planning permission, they plan to lease commercial premises.

Requirement List any **five** terms that are normally contained in a commercial lease.

(Based on Chartered Accountants Ireland, CAP 1 Law for Accountants, Autumn 2012, Question 3(b)(ii))

Question 5.3

Explain the significance of a rent review clause in a commercial lease.

(Based on Chartered Accountants Ireland, CAP 1 Law for Accountants, Summer 2011, Question 4(c))

Chapter 6

COMMERCIAL LAW

SALE OF GOODS

The law relating to the sale of goods (as distinct from land) is contained in the Sale of Goods Act 1893 and the Sale of Goods and Supply of Services Act 1980. Since the sale of goods is based on contract, the normal rules of contract law apply. (See **Chapter 3** where legislation regulating the contents of contracts is discussed.)

Definition

Section 1 of the 1893 Act defines a contract for the sale of goods as a contract whereby the seller transfers or agrees to transfer the property in goods to the buyer for a money consideration, called the **price**.

Terms of the Contract

There are certain sections that have been incorporated into the Sale of Goods Act 1893 to ensure that consumers especially are protected. The sections are as follows:

Section 11 of the 1893 Act, as amended by the 1980 Act, provides that the right to repudiate a contract for breach of condition is replaced by a right to damages for breach of warranty where:

- the buyer waives the condition entirely or elects to treat the breach of condition as a breach of warranty and sues for damages; or
- where the buyer has accepted part of all of the goods and the contract is not severable.

A person buys as a consumer when not buying "in the course of [a] business [and] the goods are of a type ordinarily supplied for consumption or private use".

When the buyer is not dealing as a consumer, then all the implied conditions and warranties may be excluded by agreement, with the exception of those implied by section 12 of the 1893 Act, but only when to do so would be fair and reasonable.

Seller's Title (Section 12)

There is an implied condition that the seller has the right to sell the goods at the time that they are being sold.

In *Rowland v. Divall* (1923) the defendant sold a stolen car to the plaintiff. The plaintiff then sold it to a third party. The original owner reclaimed the car. The plaintiff sued the defendant for the price he had paid for the car. **Held**: the plaintiff was successful and entitled to the full purchase price of the car. The plaintiff had contracted under the belief that the defendant had good title to the car.

Goods to Correspond with their Description (Section 13)

This section provides that, where a contract for sale of goods is by description, there is an implied condition that the goods will correspond with that description.

In *T. O'Regan & Sons Ltd v. Micro-Bio (Ireland) Ltd* (1980) the defendant was told by the plaintiff that they required a specific vaccination for young chickens. The plaintiffs were given the wrong vaccination and, unfortunately, a large number of their chickens died. **Held**: there was a breach of condition as to the description, as the vaccine did not correspond with the description requested by the plaintiffs.

A sale will be a sale by description even though the buyer may have inspected the goods. In *Beale v. Taylor* (1967), a car had been advertised as a 1961 Triumph Herald 1200. The buyer came to see the car and noted the metal disc on the rear showing '1200' It transpired after he purchased the car that only the rear met with this description – two different, separate models of the Herald car had been welded together the seller argued that it had not been a sale by description and tried to rely on the buyer's inspection of the car. **Held**: the advertisement and the metal disc indicated that the car was a 1200. It was a sale by description, despite the buyer's inspection of the car. The buyer had relied to some extent on the description contained in the advertisement. He was entitled to damages for breach of section 13 of the 1893 Act. In contrast, if the purchaser does not rely on the description offered by the vendor, then there will be no remedy for a breach of section 13.

Quality and Fitness (Section 14(2))

Section 14(2) of the 1893 Act provides that, where a seller sells goods in the course of a business, the goods must be of merchantable quality. The 1980 Act defines "merchantable quality" as being "fit for the purpose for which goods of that kind are normally supplied and as durable as it is reasonable to expect having regard to any description applied to them, the price if relevant and all the other circumstances".

Section 14(3) provides that "where the seller sells goods in the course of a business and the buyer, expressly or by implication, makes known to the seller any particular purpose for which the goods are being bought, there is an implied condition that the goods will be fit for that purpose" (see *O'Regan's* case).

In *Priest v. Last* (1903), the plaintiff purchased a hot water bottle for his wife from the defendant and did not state the purpose for which it would be used. On the fifth time of using the bottle, it burst injuring his wife. The defendant argued that the buyer had not made known the purpose for which he would be using the hot water bottle. **Held**: where there is only one purpose for a particular good, that purpose is disclosed by buying the good i.e. when buying a hot water bottle, its purpose is obvious. Because it was not an effective hot water bottle, the implied condition in section 14(3) had been breached.

Sale by Sample (Section 15)

Section 15 of the 1893 Act as inserted into section 10 of the 1980 Act provides that, in cases of sale by sample, there is an implied condition that:

- the bulk will correspond with the sample;
- the buyer is to have reasonable opportunity of comparing the bulk with the sample; and
- the goods shall be free of any defect rendering them unmarketable, which would not be apparent on a reasonable examination of the sample.

SUPPLY OF SERVICES

Section 39 of the Sale of Goods and Supply of Services Act 1980 also affords the consumer protections to ensure that services are provided by individuals who have the appropriate capabilities to do so.

At a minimum, a consumer may expect that:

- the supplier has the necessary skill to provide the service;
- the service will be provided with due skill, care and diligence;
- materials used will be sound and reasonably fit for purpose; and
- any goods supplied with the service will be of merchantable (sellable) quality.

CONSUMER PROTECTION LAW

The Consumer Protection Act 2007

The Consumer Protection Act 2007 was enacted to give effect to the EU Unfair Commercial Practices Directive (Directive 2005/29/EC) and to establish the National Consumer Agency. The Act applies to transactions involving goods and services between traders and consumers. A 'trader' is defined in the Act as "any natural or legal person who is acting for purposes relating to [their] trade, craft, business or profession". The 'average consumer' for the purposes of the Act is a "reasonably well informed and reasonably observant" individual.

According to the Unfair Commercial Practices Directive, a commercial practice is unfair if:

- it is contrary to the requirements of professional diligence; and
- it materially distorts or is likely to distort the economic behaviour with regard to the product of the 'average consumer' whom it reaches or to whom it is addressed, or of the average member of that group when a commercial practice is directed at that group.

The Consumer Protection Act 2007 Act deals with three types of unfair commercial practices namely:

1. misleading practices;
2. aggressive practices; and
3. prohibited practices.

Misleading Practices

A misleading practice involves providing false, misleading and deceptive information that would be likely to cause consumers to make a transaction they would not otherwise make. Misleading advertising, misleading information and withholding material information are considered misleading practices.

Misleading commercial practices are offences under the Consumer Protection Act 2007. Misleading commercial practices involve a trader making a false or misleading claim in relation to any of the following:

- the price of the goods;
- the geographical origin of the product;
- the method of manufacture;
- the quality of the product;
- the product's availability;
- the quantity of the product;

- the expected benefits or fitness for purpose of the product;
- the risks associated with using the product;
- the product's ingredients;
- the provision of components or accessories;
- the after-supply customer care available;
- the legal rights of a consumer; and
- the trader's identity, qualifications or affiliation with others.

Aggressive Practices

Aggressive practices are prohibited by section 52 of the 2007 Act. A commercial practice is aggressive where the harassment, coercion or undue influence used would be likely to:

- cause significant impairment of the *average consumer's* freedom of choice or conduct; and
- cause the *average consumer* to make a decision that he or she would not otherwise make.

Prohibited Practices

The Consumer Protection Act 2007 prohibits 32 commercial practices in all circumstances. Section 55 of the 2007 Act provides a complete list. These include false claims such as

- the trader has the endorsement of a regulatory or approved body;
- the trader is about to cease trading;
- cures for illnesses;
- indicating that a product is "free" when it costs the consumer more than the reasonable costs in responding to the representation or collecting the product or having it delivered;
- limited availability to encourage quick sales;
- running promotions/competitions without awarding the prizes described or reasonable equivalents;
- disguised business sales;
- false invoicing;
- exhortations directed at children; and
- demanding payment for unsolicited goods.

Penalties

A person guilty of an offence under the Consumer Protection Act 2007 is liable on summary conviction (where the act is minor) to the following penalties:

- on a first summary conviction to a fine not exceeding €3,000 or imprisonment for a term not exceeding six months or both;

- on any subsequent summary conviction for the same offence or any other offence under the Act to a fine not exceeding €5,000 or imprisonment for a term not exceeding 12 months or both; and
- if, after being convicted of an offence, the person continues to contravene the requirement or prohibition to which the offence relates, the person is guilty of a further offence, on each day that the contravention continues and for each such offence the person is liable on summary conviction to a fine not exceeding €500.

Civil Proceedings by Consumers

A consumer who has been materially affected by the actions of a trader may apply to the District, Circuit or High Court for damages, including exemplary or punitive damages.

The Competition and Consumer Protection Commission

The Consumer Protection Act 2007 created an independent agency, the National Consumer Agency (NCA), to deal with consumer affairs. The NCA and the Competition Authority were then replaced by the Competition and Consumer Protection Commission (CCPC) under the Competition and Consumer Protection Act 2014. The functions of the two agencies were also taken over by the CCPC.

The functions of the CCPC are:

- investigating and challenging practices that are damaging to consumers and/or the wider economy;
- bringing anti-competitive behaviour and practices that are harmful to consumers to an end, where necessary via court actions;
- providing information to consumers to help them make informed decisions;
- examining certain mergers and acquisitions to ensure that there is not a substantial lessening of competition in Ireland;
- advising policy-makers in relation to consumer protection and competition matters;
- promoting compliance with a new regulatory regime in the grocery sector aimed at ensuring balance and fairness in commercial relationships;
- responsibility for market surveillance in relation to the safety of products covered by a number of EU Directives, including monitoring and processing non-food product recalls in Ireland.

(Source: www.ccpc.ie)

Misleading Advertising

The European Communities (Misleading Advertising) Regulations 1988 provide that it is a criminal offence to make false or misleading claims in advertisements. This constitutes advertising that in anyway deceives or is likely to deceive the person to whom it is addressed and is likely to influence their spending behaviour. This may take the form of an advertisement, label or shop notice. Under the regulations, any person can apply to the High Court for an order forbidding the publication or broadcasting of misleading advertising. The offence is committed when:

1. a claim is false to a material degree; and
2. the person who made it knew it was false, or had no genuine reason to believe it was true.

Prices

Legislation governing the way prices of products and services are displayed to consumers consist of the EC (Requirements to Indicate Product Prices) Regulations 2002 and Orders made under the Prices Acts 1958 to 1972, as well as the Consumer Protection Act 2007. The purpose of these is to make it easy for the consumer to make price comparisons.

Retailers must show the correct selling price in euro, including taxes. They must also clearly display the unit prices for products sold by weight volume or measure. Part 3 of the Consumer Protection Act 2007 provides that retailers commit an offence where they prevent a person from reading the price of products on display.

In order to qualify as a 'sale' item, a product must actually have been on sale in the shop at a higher price for 28 days out of the previous three months.

There are also individual regulations dealing with the display of prices for hairdressers, air fares, concert and theatre tickets, petrol, restaurants, hotels, etc. Hairdressers, for example, are required to post a list of their prices in a prominent position.

Defective Products

Under the Liability for Defective Products Act 1991, a purchaser who has been sold a defective product may, depending on the circumstances, pursue a claim in contract law under the Sale of Goods and Supply of Services Act 1980 (where there is a contract of sale between the parties and the terms have been breached) or in negligence, or under the Liability for Defective Products Act 1991.

The Liability for Defective Products Act 1991 imposes liability on the producer for damage caused by defective products. Though liability under the Act is strict, the Act also provides a number of defences to the producer (see below).

'Damage' is defined by section 1 to include death, personal or mental impairment and certain types of damage to property.

'Producer' is widely defined and includes manufacturers and producers of finished products, component parts or raw materials and processors of agricultural products. Significantly a supplier may constitute a 'producer' in certain circumstances under section 2.

A product is 'defective' where "it fails to provide the safety which a person is entitled to expect, taking all circumstances into account". These circumstances according to section 5 include:

- the presentation of the product;
- the use to which it could reasonably be expected that the product would be put; and
- the time when the product was put into circulation.

Onus of Proof and Defences

Section 4 of the 1991 Act provides that the plaintiff must prove that the damage was caused by a defect in the product concerned.

The Act provides for six defences set out in section 6 which, when successfully pleaded, act as a full bar to liability:

1. that the defendant did not put the product into circulation;
2. having regard to all the circumstances, it is probable that the defect that caused the damage did not exist at the time the product was put into circulation by the defendant or that the defect came into being at some other point;
3. the product was neither manufactured by the defendant for sale or any form of distribution for an economic purpose nor manufactured or distributed by him in the course of his business;
4. the defect arose due to mandatory compliance with EU or national law;
5. the state of scientific and technical knowledge at the time when he put the product into circulation was not such as to enable the existence of the defect to be discovered; and
6. in the case of raw materials, where the raw material has been incorporated into the product or that the defect is attributable entirely to the design of the product in which the component has been fitted.

Food Safety

The Food Safety Association of Ireland has overall coordinating responsibility for all the food safety organisations such as the HSE and Department of Health and Children.

There is a wide range of legislation dealing with food safety. The main EU legislation on food safety is EU Regulation 178/2002, which establishes the European Food Safety Authority and sets out procedures in matters of food safety. The Regulation defines a food business as "any undertaking, whether for profit or not and whether public or private, carrying out any of the activities related to any stage of production, processing and distribution of food".

Other additional pieces of legislation that apply to the food business include:

- European Communities (Hygiene of Foodstuffs) Regulations 2006;
- Regulation 852/2004 HAACP Principles. All food businesses are required to have a food safety management system known as Hazard Analysis and Critical Control Points to ensure that food handlers are properly supervised and trained and are fully aware of the principles of HAACP; and
- Food Hygiene Regulations (1950–1989). These require the food business operator to register with the HSE which undertakes regular inspections of the premises of food businesses.

Enforcement Powers of the Competition and Consumer Protection Commission

Prosecution

The CCPC may prosecute summarily in its own right in the District Court. The maximum penalties on summary conviction comprise a fine not exceeding €3,000 or imprisonment of six months, or both. The CCPC may also refer serious cases for prosecution on indictment to the Director of Public Prosecutions.

Fixed Payment Notices

Under section 85 of the Consumer Protection Act 2007, the CCPC has the power to impose fines (fixed payment notices) of €300, to be paid within 28 days, in person or by post, on traders in breach of price display regulations. Failure to pay will result in prosecution.

Compliance Notices

Under section 75 of the Consumer Protection Act 2007 an officer of the CCPC may issue a compliance notice if he or she is of the opinion that a trader has committed an offence. This notice may be appealed within 14 days. The trader is liable to penalties if he or she fails to comply with the notice requirements.

Undertakings

If the CCPC has reason to believe that a trader is involved in a prohibited practice, the CCPC may seek and obtain a written undertaking that the trader will comply with the Act. An undertaking may also include a commitment to compensate the consumer, including reimbursement, or a commitment to publish at the trader's expense an advertisement containing a corrective statement relating to the prohibited practice. If the trader fails to comply, the CCPC may apply to the Circuit Court or the High Court for a Prohibition Order.

Prohibition Orders

The CCPC may seek an order from the Circuit Court or the High Court. The purpose of this order is to prohibit a trader from committing or engaging in a prohibited act or practice. Failure to comply with the Court Order, without a reasonable excuse, means the trader is guilty of an offence and is liable on conviction to the fines and penalties outlined in the Consumer Protection Act.

Compensation Order

This may be applied for where a consumer is seeking damages after being affected by the wrongful act. The consumer may apply individually or the CCPC may, with his or her permission, take a case on his or her behalf.

REVIEW QUESTIONS

(See Solutions to Review Questions at the end of this text.)

Question 6.1

James purchased a textbook for his accountancy course that was recommended by his college lecturer. When he got home and was flicking through the book, he was shocked to discover that several pages had been torn out and that other pages of text were blank. He took the book back to the store the following day but the store manager refused to replace the book or refund the purchase price, and pointed instead to a notice on the wall behind the cash desk, which read "No returns on books".

Requirement Advise James as to his legal options as a consumer, pursuant to the terms of the Sale of Goods and Supply of Services Act 1980.

Question 6.2

Marcus and Isabella run a furniture shop in Galway, called MI Ltd ('MI'), which stocks sofas, luxury chairs and dining furniture. Last year, MI stocked a number of glider chairs from a producer called Children's Supplies Ltd. However, in recent months, an increasing number of customers are contacting MI complaining that they have fallen off the chairs and suffered injury. MI is now threatening legal action against the producer, Children's Supplies Ltd.

Requirement:
(a) Define a defective product and producer.
(b) Outline any **three** defences that may be raised by a producer where such a defective product claim is made.

(Based on Chartered Accountants Ireland, CAP 1 Law for Accountants, Autumn 2014, Question 4(a))

Question 6.3

In order to establish her bakery, Bella purchased a food processor from Premier Kitchen Supplies ('Premier'). When she was purchasing this item, Bella had a detailed discussion with one of the shop assistants and explained to her the various purposes for which this machine would be used. In particular, she informed the assistant that the food processor was for commercial use and needed to be durable. Bella purchased the Kitchen Ninja 1400, based on the recommendations of the shop assistant. However, within one month of use, a number of issues arose with the machine. In particular, the rotator blade became blunt and the machine stopped mixing at high speeds. When Bella contacted the manufacturers of the Kitchen Ninja 1400, she explained the problems she was encountering with the processor, but they explained to her that this machine was only designed for non-commercial use and was unable to deal with the quantity and frequency of commercial use. Bella then contacted Premier about this issue, but they are refusing to deal with her, stating that the company operates a no-refunds policy. Bella is now considering bringing an action against Premier for breach of the Sale of Goods Acts 1983–1980.

Requirement:

(a) Explain the obligations imposed on a seller by the Sale of Goods legislation in relation to merchantable quality and fitness for purpose.

(b) Advise Bella whether the actions of Premier Kitchen Supplies are in breach of the Sale of Goods legislation, and the remedies available to her, if they are in breach.

(Based on Chartered Accountants Ireland, CAP 1 Law for Accountants, Summer 2014, Question 1(b))

Question 6.4

Regal has been contacted by the Competition and Consumer Protection Commission regarding consumer complaints in relation to a recent advertising campaign. The campaign involved female models dressed as air stewards but wearing very short skirts and very low cut tops. The Competition and Consumer Protection Commission has informed Regal that it will refer these complaints to the Advertising Standards Authority of Ireland unless Regal voluntarily withdraws the advertisement.

Requirement The directors of Regal are unaware of the functions of the CCPC and have asked you to advise them of any **three** functions of this body.

(Based on Chartered Accountants Ireland, CAP 1 Law for Accountants, Autumn 2013, Question 4(c))

CHAPTER 7

EMPLOYMENT LAW

HEALTH AND SAFETY AT WORK

Employers owe both common law and statutory duties to employees in the workplace regarding their health and safety.

Common Law Duties

Every employer has a common law duty to provide a safe workplace, safe equipment and safe system of work for employees. In *Connolly v. Dundalk UDC* (1990), the defendant had piping installed and chlorine gas escaped through a defective joint, injuring the employee. Mr Justice O' Flaherty in the Supreme Court said:

> "The common law duty is to take reasonable steps to provide safe plant and a safe place of work . . . [and] they cannot be delegated to independent contractors so as to avoid the primary liability that falls on employers to make sure that these duties are carried out."

In *Heeney v. Dublin Corporation* (1991), action was taken by the widow of the deceased, who had been employed as a fire brigade station officer. He died in 1985 from inhaling gases while fighting a fire without breathing equipment. Evidence established that the fire authority had begun supplying breathing equipment and training in 1977. By 1984 all the permanent fire brigades had been issued with the equipment, but not all retained brigades (not in use on a full-time basis), such as that which had employed the deceased, had received it **Held**: the fire authority was liable for failing to supply the deceased with breathing equipment, which had been available for seven years.

Health and Safety Legislation

Since the 1980s, these common law duties have been supplemented by legislation. The Safety, Health and Welfare at Work Act 2005 is the main Act in this area. It sets out the rights and obligations of employers and employees, and provides for substantial fines and penalties for breaches of the health and safety legislation. It applies to all employers, employees (including fixed-term and temporary employees) and self-employed people, in their workplaces.

The Safety Health and Welfare at Work Act is supplemented by a number of regulations, the most important being the Safety, Health and Welfare at Work (General Application) Regulations 2007, which consolidate various regulations adopted to implement EU Directives on health and safety into Irish law. In addition, there are 'standalone' regulations affecting individual industries including:

- the Safety, Health and Welfare at Work (Construction) (Amendment) Regulations 2008 (S.I. No. 130 of 2008);
- the Safety, Health and Welfare at Work (Construction) (Amendment) (No. 2) Regulations 2008 (S.I. No. 423 of 2008);
- the Fishing Vessels Regulations (S.I. No. 325 of 1999); and
- the Chemical Agents Regulations (S.I. No. 619 of 2001).

Employees' Duties

The duties of employees while at work are set out in section 13 of the 2005 Act. These include the following:

(a) to take reasonable care to protect the health and safety of themselves and of other people in the workplace;
(b) not to engage in improper behaviour that will endanger themselves or others;
(c) not to be under the influence of any intoxicant in the workplace; and
(d) to undergo any reasonable medical or other assessment if requested to do so by the employer in discharging the employer's duties.

Employers' Duties

The general duties of employers are set out in section 8 of the 2005 Act, which provides that every employer will ensure as far as is practicable the safety, health and welfare at work of employees. This extends, in particular, to:

- performing risk assessments, which should identify any hazards in the workplace, assess the risks arising from such hazards and identify steps to be taken to deal with the risks;
- preparing written safety statements based on the risk assessments;
- providing and maintaining a safe workplace, which uses safe plant and equipment;
- preventing risks from use of any article or substance and from exposure to physical agents, noise and vibration;
- preventing any improper conduct or behaviour likely to put the safety, health and welfare of employees at risk;
- providing instruction and training to employees on health and safety;
- providing protective clothing and equipment to employees; and
- appointing a competent person as the organisation's safety officer.

Offences and Penalties

Section 77 of the 2005 Act splits offences under the Act into two categories:

- less serious offences are punishable upon summary conviction by a fine not exceeding €3,000 or imprisonment for up to six months or both; and
- serious offences are punishable on indictment by a fine of up to €3 million or imprisonment for up to two years or both. Section 79 of the Act also provides for on-the-spot fines of €1,000.

Section 80 also provides for the liability of directors and officers of undertakings. This provision says that, if any offence has been committed by a company and that offence has been authorised by a director, manager or other similar person, then that person as well as the company is guilty of the offence and can be prosecuted.

Enforcement: The Health and Safety Authority

The Health and Safety Authority (HSA) has overall responsibility for the administration and enforcement of health and safety at work in Ireland. The HSA monitors compliance in the workplace and can impose on-the-spot fines or bring prosecutions against offenders. The HSA is the national centre for information and advice to employers, employees and the self-employed on all aspects of workplace health and safety.

The HSA carries out pro-active and reactive inspections of the workplace to ensure compliance with the legislation. Reactive inspections may arise following an accident, incident or complaint. Pro-active inspections may be routine or targeted.

DATA PROTECTION

The main Irish law dealing with data protection is the Data Protection Act 1988 (DPA) as amended by the Data Protection (Amendment) Act 2003. The DPA gives individuals certain rights regarding information held about them, and imposes certain obligations on data controllers. The Act regulates the collection processing, keeping, using and disclosure of certain information relating to individuals that is processed automatically. With some exceptions, it covers all computerised data relating to individuals.

Personal information is any information about a living identifiable individual held on a computer, on paper or in other manual form, such as part of a filing system. Personal information includes photos or video recordings of a person's image, recordings of a person's voice, fingerprints or e-mail or text messages.

Data Controllers

A data controller is an entity that controls the contents and use of personal information. A data controller can be a person, a company, a firm, etc.

Data Processors

A data processor is an individual who processes personal information on behalf of the data controller. This does not include employees who process data in the course of their work.

Personal Information

Under the Data Protection Acts, "*personal data* means data relating to a living individual who is, or can be, identified either from the data or from the data in conjunction with other information that is in, or is likely to come into, the possession of the data controller". The definition of 'personal data' is quite broad as it encompasses any information that relates to a living and identifiable individual. Additionally, there is no distinction between technologies or how the data is stored, e.g. on paper, on a computer, on a CCTV system and so on.

Disclosure by Data Controllers

Data controllers must disclose certain matters to the person whose information is being gathered:

- the identity of the data controller;
- the reasons for which the data is being gathered; and
- any other relevant information the data subject may require, e.g. whether the data controller plans to use this information with others.

Consent to Processing

As a general rule, personal information cannot be processed without the consent of the person to whom it relates. Consent is not necessary for certain purposes, including:

- pre-contractual activities;
- to carry out a contract;
- to comply with a legal obligation;
- to avoid injury or damage; and

- to satisfy the legitimate business needs of the data processor, but only where there is no prejudice to the individual, or 'data subject' (e.g. transferring the files to another format).

Sensitive Data

Sensitive data is afforded special protection and is governed by stricter rules. It includes information relating to:

- physical or mental health;
- racial or ethnic origin (but not nationality);
- criminal convictions and details relating to an alleged offence;
- sexual life; and
- religious beliefs and political opinions.

The explicit consent of the individual concerned must be sought before sensitive information can be gathered or processed, except where the information is being gathered or used:

- in connection with rights or obligations imposed by law on employers;
- for tax collection purposes;
- by non-profit organisations for political, religious or trade union purposes;
- for statistical purposes;
- by a health professional or for medical purposes;
- for purposes of obtaining legal advice or in connection with legal proceedings;
- to prevent injury or damage to the health of the person concerned or others or to protect their vital interest, where consent cannot be reasonably obtained (e.g. if the person is suffering from a mental illness);
- in circumstances where the person has already made the information public; or
- by a political party or election candidate.

Processing Information

Processing is defined widely by the Act as performing any operation on data, automatic or not, and includes obtaining, recording, storing, keeping, retrieving, altering, disclosing, disseminating, etc. (Case studies that illustrate the number of rules governing the processing of information are available at www.dataprotection.ie.)

The Rules of Data Processing

There are eight rules of data processing.

1. Information should be obtained and processed in a fair manner.

2. The information may only be kept for one or more specified, explicit and lawful purposes.
3. It may only be processed in a way that is compatible with the reason for which it was gathered.
4. The information must be kept safe and secure.
5. It should be kept accurate, complete and up-to-date.
6. The information obtained should only be relevant to the purpose of the data controller and should not go beyond that.
7. It should be retained no longer than is necessary.
8. A copy of personal information kept should be given to the individual if requested.

Data Protection Commissioner

The role of the Data Protection Commissioner is to ensure that data controllers processing personal information comply with the provisions of the Data Protection Acts. The Commissioner investigates complaints made by the public and also carries out pro-active investigations to ensure compliance with the Acts. If found guilty of an offence under the Acts, a data controller could be ordered to purge all or part of the database where the information is stored, and may be fined up to €100,000.

Registration

Certain categories of data controller (those who control the contents and use of personal data) and certain categories of data processor (those whose business consists wholly or partly in processing such data for others) must register their details with the Data Protection Commissioner. These include:

- government bodies/public authorities;
- banks and financial/credit institutions;
- insurance undertakings (not including brokers);
- persons whose business consists wholly or mainly of direct marketing;
- persons whose business consists wholly or mainly of providing credit references;
- persons whose business consists wholly or mainly of collecting debts;
- internet service providers (ISPs);
- telecommunications network or service providers;
- anyone processing personal data related to mental or physical health (e.g. health care professionals);
- anyone processing genetic data; and
- anyone whose business consists of processing personal data for supply to others, other than for journalistic, literary or artistic purposes.

THE CONTRACT OF EMPLOYMENT

Employment law developed under common law principles has been supplemented by legislation to give the employee protection in such areas as working conditions, adequate notice, provision of holidays and unfair dismissal.

Contract of Service vs Contract for Services

The determination of whether an individual is an employee or a contractor is far from straightforward and the courts have developed a number of tests in establishing whether it is a contract **of** service or a contract **for** services. A contract of service refers to an employee relationship where one of the essential elements is the employer's control over the individual's working terms and conditions. A contract for services refers to an independent contractor/sole trader/consultant relationship where individuals control their own working terms and conditions. The courts have made it clear that no one test is conclusive and the importance of each factor will depend on the circumstances of each situation.

A number of determining tests or factors will not be clear cut when looking at the facts of a situation and may be argued either way. All the factors must be looked at and the tests/factors weighed up to determine towards which status they are leaning and also to explain the factors that indicate a contrary status.

The tests and determining factors are as follows.

The Control Test

Did the person alleged to be the employer control the alleged employee, both in respect of the work that was done and the manner of performance of the work?

In *Lynch v. Palgrave Murphy Ltd* (1964), Palgrave Murphy Ltd were stevedores who hired a forklift operator from Crosbie Forklift for £1 an hour. The forklift operator injured the plaintiff, a casual labourer employed by Palgrave Murphy. The plaintiff sued Palgrave Murphy Ltd, claiming that it was vicariously liable for the injury caused. **Held**: the Supreme Court looked at the extent of control the defendants were entitled to exercise in relation to the negligently performed act. The forklift driver was employed, paid and subject to dismissal by Crosbie Ltd, but was assigned tasks, e.g. what load to take, by Palgrave Murphy Ltd. The mere fact that it could assign him tasks was not sufficient to make Palgrave Murphy liable.

In *Mersey Docks & Harbour Board v. Coggins & Griffiths* (1947) Coggins and Griffiths hired a crane and driver from Mersey Docks & Harbour Board. The contract between the Board and Coggins & Griffiths stated that the driver was to become the firm's employee for the duration of the hire. The crane driver performed his duties negligently, injuring a third party in the process. The question was whether the Board was liable to the injured man as the driver's principal employers, or whether the hirers now bore responsibility. The House of Lords **held** that the hirers could only be treated as employers of the driver if they could control in detail how he did his work. Although it could instruct him what to do, it could not control him in how he operated the crane. The Harbour Board was, therefore, still the driver's employer.

The Business Integration Test

The control test is not always of assistance in deciding whether a contract of service exists, i.e. where employees are so skilled that they cannot be controlled in the performance of their duties. An example would be a surgeon in a hospital. A test of control is not of benefit here. Instead, the courts will ask whether the worker was integrated into the employer's business. The business integration test was first stated by Lord Denning in *Stevenson, Jordan and Harrison Ltd v. MacDonald & Evans* (1952):

> "[o]ne feature which seems to run through the instances is that, under a contract of service, a man is employed as part of the business; whereas, under a contract for services, his work, although done for the business, is not integrated into it but is only accessory to it."

In the *Stevenson* case, an accountant was **held** to be an accessory to a business, and not part of it, and therefore self-employed.

In *Cassidy v. Ministry for Health* (1951), a resident surgeon in a hospital was **held** to be an employee, with the result that the hospital was liable for his negligence.

The Economic Reality Test/'Mixed Test'

This approach incorporates both the control and the integration tests. It allows for everything to be taken into account, and such things as control and integration are merely factors that contribute to a decision.

The 'mixed' text was developed in *Ready Mixed Concrete (South East) Ltd v. Minister of Pensions and National Insurance* (1968) in which a contract between Ready Mixed Concrete (RMC) and a lorry driver stated that the driver was self-employed. He owned, insured and maintained his own lorry; however, RMC had helped finance its purchase, and the driver wore a company uniform and painted the truck in the company colours. An issue relating to National Insurance contributions arose which brought into question whether he was an employee. A major factor in finding the lorry driver was an independent contractor was that he could appoint a substitute lorry driver. Mr Justice McKenna identified conditions to be satisfied to find a contract of service:

- that there is an agreement from the worker that he or she will provide work for their employer in exchange for remuneration;
- that the worker agrees, either expressly or implicitly, that the employer can exercise control over his or her performance;
- that there are other factors in the contract which make it consistent with a contract of service.

The case of *Ó Coindealbháin (Inspector of Taxes) v. Mooney* (1990) concerned the question of whether Mr Mooney should be assessed for income tax under Schedule E as an employee or under Schedule D as an independent contractor. Mr Mooney was allegedly employed by the Department of Social Welfare as the branch manager of an employment exchange office in Tullamore, County Offaly. Mr Justice Blayney reviewed the authorities on the issue and looked at the relationship that existed between Mr Mooney and the Department of Social Welfare. In the judge's opinion, the following were critical facts in determining the relationship that existed.

- Mr Mooney did not have to perform the work personally.
- He had to provide a furnished office, a deputy and clerical staff.
- He was entirely responsible for the employing of the deputy and all other clerical staff.
- His pay was not salaried, but he was given allowances and other payments relative to the amount of work done by him.
- His remuneration could be changed without his agreement.
- He was obliged to provide certain services as per guidelines issued to him by the department.
- He was given a gross annual budget and with this money he was to run the office following the department's guidelines.

On the facts, it was **held** that the relationship between the Department and Mr Mooney was inconsistent with that of a contract of service.

The Enterprise/Entrepreneurial Test

The 'enterprise test' examines whether or not persons are in business on their own account and is illustrated by the case of *Henry Denny & Sons (Ireland) Ltd t/a Kerry Foods v. Minister for Social Welfare* (1998) in which the court considered whether a supermarket food demonstrator was an employee or not. Her contract with Denny's stated that she was not an employee but an independent contractor responsible for her own tax affairs. The court found that, in reality, she was an employee as she did not provide an independent input into her role or invest money in equipment. The terms of her contract required her to work specified hours, wear a particular uniform and carry out her tasks in a particular way using Denny's equipment. Keane J stated that:

> "in general a person will be regarded as providing his or her services under a contract of service and not as an independent contractor where he or she is performing those services for another person and not for himself or herself."

Although the various tests are useful in deciding whether a contract of service or a contract for services exists, no one test is fundamental or exhaustive and each case should be decided on its own facts. This point was reiterated in the case of *Minister for Agriculture and Food v. Barry and Others* (2008). In this case, the court found that five temporary veterinary inspectors (TVIs) engaged by the Department of Agriculture were contractors and not employees. The TVIs had brought a claim under the Redundancy Act against the Department following the closure of the Galtee Meats plant in Cork. The court concluded that the *Henry Denny* test was not a "one size fits all" test and emphasised the need to consider each case on its own individual facts.

In considering the enterprise test the court found the following factors relevant:
- whether he or she provides the necessary premises, or equipment or some other form of investment;
- whether he or she employs others to assist in the business; and
- whether the profit which he or she derives from the business is dependent on the efficiency with which it is conducted.

The Department had argued that the TVIs were private veterinary practitioners who were also in business on their own and continued in private practice along with undertaking temporary work for the Department. The TVIs' remuneration was also paid on an hourly-fee basis at rates fixed between the Department and their union, Veterinary Ireland. The court **held** that the 'control' found in the employer–employee relationship was absent between the TVIs and the Department, as the level of work available to them was dictated by Galtee and not the Department.

Formation of the Contract of Employment

The normal rules with regard to contract law apply. The contract may be oral or in writing. However, if it is not to be performed within one year, it must be evidenced in writing, otherwise it is unenforceable.

The Terms of Employment (Information) Act 1994, as amended by the Terms of Employment (Information) Act 2012, states that new employees must be given a written statement of the principal terms and conditions of their employment within two months of commencing work. If existing employees request a statement of the principal terms and conditions of their employment, the Act states that it must be given to them in writing within two months. The details listed in the Act are:

- full name of the employer and employee;
- address of the employer and the principal place of business;
- the place of work or, if there is no fixed place, a statement that the employee is required to work at various places;
- a job description and title;
- the commencement date;
- details about holidays and paid leave;
- notice requirements;
- reference to any collective agreements that may be applicable;
- provisions relating to pay; and
- hours of work.

Implied Terms and the Main Duties of an Employer

There are certain duties employers owe an employee that are so central to the contract of employment that they are implied by common law or legislation into the contract, such as minimum levels of remuneration and holiday leave.

Remuneration

If there is no express term in the contract of employment as to pay, the employee will be entitled to **reasonable remuneration**. However, the National Minimum Wage (Low Pay Commission) Act 2015 empowers the Minister for Trade, Enterprise and Employment to prescribe a national minimum hourly rate of pay. Any term in an employment contract that attempts to exclude or reduce this rate is automatically void.

Method of Remuneration

The Payment of Wages Act 1991 enshrines the right of every employee:

- to a readily negotiable mode of wage payment;
- to protection against unlawful deductions; and
- to a written statement of wages, plus any deductions required by statute (income tax and social welfare) or agreed between the employer and employee (pension, health insurance, trade union subscription, etc.)

The Act also provides that all wages should be paid by cheque, bank draft, credit transfer, cash or, more commonly, electronic fund transfer (EFT).

To Provide Work

There is a duty on the part of the employer to provide work, although there is no obligation on an employer to provide work for an employee, provided he continues to pay the agreed wages. This was seen in the case of *Collier v. Sunday Referee Publishing Co Ltd* (1940) where Asquith J. stated:

> "[p]rovided I pay my cook her wages regularly she cannot complain if I choose to take any or all of my meals out."

There are exceptions to the employer's duty to provide work:
- when the employment is on a piecemeal or commission basis, i.e. work must be provided as the basis for pay; and
- with skilled employees where there is a need to work on a regular basis in order to maintain their skills.

To Provide for the Safety of Employees

The employer has a duty to provide:
- a safe place of work;
- proper plant and equipment; and
- a safe system of work.

This area of employer's duties is generally governed by the Health, Safety and Welfare at Work Act 2005. In addition, the employer also has a common law duty to take reasonable care for the safety of employees by providing a safe place of work; safe system of work; safe access to and from work; competent co-workers; properly maintained equipment, etc. Failure to comply will render the employer liable for an action in negligence.

Duty with regard to Employee References

Employers have a duty to **take reasonable care** in preparing references. In *Spring v. Guardian Assurance plc* (1994), the plaintiff, Mr Spring, sold life assurance policies. The company he worked for, C Ltd, was taken over by Guardian Assurance plc and, shortly thereafter, he was dismissed from his post. He attempted to obtain employment elsewhere. Under the rules of the industry's self-regulatory body, members were to provide references in respect of their former employees that made "full and frank disclosure of all relevant matters which are believed to be true" to other members. Guardian Assurance provided references in relation to the plaintiff to various other members of the self-regulatory body. Each such reference was in similar terms and contained a number of false and damaging assertions to the effect that the plaintiff had acted dishonestly on a number of occasions. The trial judge found that the statements were not made maliciously, but were made without exercising reasonable care in investigating their correctness. **Held**: the House of Lords found the defendants liable in failing to take reasonable care in preparing the reference.

To Provide Holidays/Annual Leave

Statute prescribes minimum holiday periods for certain employees. The Organisation of Working Time Act 1997 provides that an employee is entitled to:

(a) four working weeks in a leave year in which he or she works at least 1,365 hours;
(b) one-third of a work week for each month in the leave year in which he or she works at least 117 hours; or
(c) 8% of the hours that he or she works in a leave year, subject to a maximum of four working weeks.

The annual leave of an employee who works eight or more months in a leave year generally includes an unbroken period of two weeks. The dates or times that annual leave may be taken by an employee are determined by agreement with the employer, taking into consideration work requirements, family responsibilities and the opportunities for rest and recreation available to the employee. The dates should be agreed at least one month before the annual leave is due to commence. Remuneration for annual leave must be paid in advance. Where the employee becomes ill while on annual leave, and furnishes medical evidence to this effect, the period covered cannot be counted as annual leave.

Employee's Right to an Indemnity

The employer receiving the benefit of the employee's service must indemnify the employee against all liabilities and expenses incurred in the proper performance of the employment.

To be Mutually Respectful

The employment relationship is assumed to be based on mutuality of respect, trust and confidence.

The following terms are implied on the part of the employee, and therefore are duties of the employee:

Implied Terms/the Main Duties of an Employee

There are certain duties employees owe that are so central to the contract of employment that they are implied by law into the contract, such as the duty to exercise reasonable care and skill, and to act in good faith.

To be Available for Work

Employees are expected to be available for work during their agreed work shift.

To Obey the Reasonable Orders of the Employer

In the case of *Pepper v. Webb* (1969), a couple consulted their gardener before going away for a holiday. Mrs Webb instructed the gardener, Mr Pepper, to put in some plants while they were gone; however, Mr Pepper replied that he was leaving at noon and "you can do what you like about them. If you don't like it, you can give me notice." Later that day he told Mr Webb: "I couldn't care less about your bloody greenhouse or your sodding garden." The court **held** that his dismissal was justified in that: (i) he had refused to obey the lawful and reasonable order to put in the plants; (ii) he had said that he did not care about the grounds and the greenhouse; and (iii) he was insolent to the employer.

To Exercise Reasonable Care and Skill

In *Lister v. Romford Ice and Cold Storage Co Ltd* (1957) a father and son were employed by the same company. The father was directing the son to park a lorry and owing to the son's negligence the father was injured. The father sued the company as being vicariously liable for the son's negligence. The company in a later action succeeded in obtaining similar damages from the son for failure to exercise reasonable care and skill.

To Act in Good Faith

In *Faccenda Chicken Ltd v. Fowler* (1986) the plaintiff company operated a mobile service selling frozen chickens to retail shops and catering companies. Fowler, an ex-employee, set up in competition with Faccenda Chicken and it attempted to prevent him from continuing to do so. It alleged that Fowler had wrongfully made use of confidential 'sales information', such as names and addresses of customers, best routes to take, etc., acquired during his employment. Mr Justice Goulding **held** that information acquired by an employee during the course of employment could be divided into three categories.

1. Information either trivial in nature or available from public sources that could not be regarded as confidential. For example, details of van routes that could be ascertained by following the plaintiff's delivery vehicles would fall within this category.
2. Information that an employee must treat as confidential either because this is expressly communicated to him or because the information is obviously confidential in nature. This information may become part of the employee's own skill and knowledge and, if so, can be protected during the continuance of employment, but can be used for the employee's benefit once he leaves.

If an employer wishes to protect such information, he must do so by express contractual provision, usually in the form of a confidentiality clause or restrictive covenant. Price lists and sales information fall into this category.

3. Specific trade secrets so confidential that they cannot be lawfully used for anyone's benefit except the original employer, notwithstanding that the employee may have learned this information by heart.

The court found that the information that Fowler used fell into the first two categories, and so he was not liable to his previous employer for a breach of confidence.

To Disclose Breaches of Duty by Fellow Employees

In general, the higher the position the employee holds, the greater the burden placed upon him or her to disclose such breaches.

Termination of the Contract of Employment

Under the general rules of contract law, a contract of employment can be terminated, either by agreement between the parties, or as a result of breach of contract by performance or by frustration.

By Agreement

A contract of employment can be terminated by agreement between the parties:

(a) if the contract is for a fixed term and this expires without renewal;
(b) if the contract provides for termination by notice and the relevant notice is given. Here either party may give the required notice according to the terms of the contract; and
(c) it may be discharged by mutual agreement or by frustration.

Termination without Notice

The only situation at common law in which a contract can be terminated without notice by an employer is where an employee is guilty of serious misconduct.

Serious misconduct includes:

(a) wilful and serious defiance of authority;
(b) misconduct such as disclosing confidential information;
(c) negligence or incompetence of an employee in the course of his or her employment; and
(d) drunkenness or immorality, particularly if it affects the performance of the employee's duties or the reputation of the business in which he or she is employed.

Dismissal of Office Holders

At common law an **office holder** is a person who generally holds a fairly high position and so the principles of natural justice must be observed in the dismissal of office holders. They should be given the reason for the dismissal and an opportunity to defend themselves.

In *Carvill v. Irish Industrial Bank Ltd* (1968), Mr Justice Kenny stated that the grounds relied on to justify a dismissal without notice of an employee must be actions or omissions by the employee that are inconsistent with the performance of the express or implied terms of his contract of service. In *Gunn v. NCAD* (1988), the Supreme Court **held** that the distinction between an office holder and an employee was becoming increasingly blurred.

Constructive Dismissal

Where the employer is in serious breach of an express or implied term of the contract, the employee is entitled to terminate the contract. This amounts to constructive dismissal by the employer and entitles the employee to leave the job with or without giving notice, and to sue.

Section 1 of the Unfair Dismissals Act 1977 defines constructive dismissal as:

> "the termination by the employee of his contract of employment with his employer, whether prior notice of the termination was or was not given to the employer, in circumstances in which, because of the conduct of the employer, the employee was or would have been entitled, or it was or would have been reasonable for the employee, to terminate the contract of employment without giving prior notice of the termination to the employer".

The mutual bond of trust and confidence between the employer and the employee is a vital component of the employment relationship. Where this bond of mutual trust and confidence has been broken as a result of the employer's actions, the employee may be entitled to resign and claim constructive dismissal.

The employee bears the burden of proof to show that the circumstances amounted to constructive dismissal. An employee will be expected to exhaust all internal grievance procedures prior to embarking on this cause of action.

Two tests are applied when considering an action for constructive dismissal.

1. *The Contract Test*

This was set out in the English case of *Western Excavating Ltd v. Sharp* (1978):

> "If the employer is guilty of conduct which is a significant breach going **to the root of the contract of employment** [emphasis added], or which shows that the employer no longer intends to be bound by one or more of the essential terms of the contract then the employee is entitled to treat himself as discharged from any further performance."

2. *The Reasonableness Test*

This test focuses on the conduct of the employer. Has the employer conducted itself so unreasonably that the employee cannot be expected to continue in its employment?

One year of continuous service is required to take an action; however, this is waived where employees can show the constructive dismissal came about as a result of:
- (a) trade union membership;
- (b) pregnancy; or
- (c) exercising a statutory right to maternity or other protected leave.

In *Keogh v. Green Isle Foods* (2007), the claimant believed that his employer was questioning his ability to do his job, as he was put on lighter duties after a period of sick leave. As a result, he tendered his resignation and subsequently brought an action for constructive dismissal. However, as he had not initiated the company's grievance procedures prior to resigning, his action was dismissed on the grounds that he had not exhausted the procedures of the company. The Tribunal stated that as there were options other than resignation available to him, he could not claim that it was impossible to continue his employment due to unreasonableness.

In *Liz Allen v. Independent Newspapers* (2001), Ms Allen was a former crime correspondent for the *Sunday Independent* newspaper. The hearing at the Employment Appeals Tribunal (EAT) was informed that two colleagues in particular has been hostile towards Ms Allen and she had been told that other crime correspondents were being recruited for the paper. Despite Ms Allen's attempts to resolve matters internally, she felt that she had no option but to resign due to being isolated at work. The EAT accepted that her confidence and health had been undermined as a result of her employer's conduct. Ms Allen won her constructive dismissal case, and was awarded 78 week's pay plus compensation for future losses.

Termination by Notice

The Minimum Notice and Terms of Employment Act 1973–2001 deals with the entitlement of employees to certain minimum notice. It only applies to employees who have been continuously employed for 13 weeks by the same employer. The amount of notice depends on the length of the employment:

- 13 weeks to two years: the minimum notice is one week;
- two years to five years: the minimum notice is two weeks;
- five years to 10 years: the minimum notice is four weeks;
- 10 years to 15 years: the minimum notice is six weeks; and
- 15 years and over: the minimum notice is eight weeks.

Excluded from the provisions of the Act are members of An Garda Síochána, the Defence Forces and the immediate family of the employer who live with the employer and are employed in the same private house or farm.

If an employee is dismissed on the spot or without notice, this is known as **summary dismissal**. Section 8 of the 1973 Act states that an employee may be dismissed without notice for misconduct.

Wrongful Dismissal

A wrongful dismissal is a dismissal in breach of contract by the employer and/or where proper procedures were not followed. Generally, the only effective remedy available to an employee who has been wrongfully dismissed is to claim for damages based on loss of earnings. The measure of damages is usually the sum which would have been paid if proper notice had been given.

Employees who qualify for both wrongful dismissal and unfair dismissal must choose their course of action: they are not entitled to both remedies.

Dismissals

The area of dismissals is governed by the Unfair Dismissals Acts 1977–2007. The law is designed to question the fairness of a dismissal after it has occurred. Legislation lays down criteria whereby the fairness of a dismissal can be judged and provides redress in cases where an unfair dismissal has occurred.

The legislation is based on two fundamental principles:

- there must be substantial grounds to justify the termination of an employment contract; and
- fair procedures must be followed in effecting the termination of an employment contract.

Requirements to Bring a Claim under Unfair Dismissals Legislation

In order to bring a claim for unfair dismissal, the employee must have:

- a contract of service;
- one year (52 weeks) continuous service with the employer;
- bring the action for unfair dismissal within six months of the dismissal (this can be extended to 12 months in exceptional circumstances); and
- show that he or she has been actually dismissed.

One year of continuous service, referred to above, is not required where employees can show they were:

(a) dismissed by reason of trade union membership;
(b) pregnancy; or
(c) exercising a statutory right to maternity or other protected leave.

Certain categories of persons are excluded from the protections of the Unfair Dismissals Acts:

- officers of Vocational Education Committees (VECs);
- employees working and ordinarily resident outside the State; and
- employees with less than one year of continuous service.

The legislation divides dismissals into two categories:

1. dismissals that are *prime facie* unfair; and
2. dismissals that are *prime facie* fair.

Dismissals that are Prima Facie *Unfair*

A dismissal will be deemed to be unfair if it occurs for any of the following reasons:

- **Trade union membership of the employee** – dismissal for trade union activity or membership is automatically unfair under the Unfair Dismissals Acts 1977–2007. In *McCormack v. Ross* (1979), the employer claimed that McCormack was dismissed because he had caused disruption by calling meetings during working hours, he was generally a trouble-maker, he refused to accept a new lunch break system that the other staff had accepted, and because of his bad manners. The dismissal was **held** to be unfair. It was **held** that he was dismissed due to his trade union activities: the employer had not expressed dissatisfaction with him until he tried to introduce the union to other colleagues; only then did the employer decide to dismiss him.
- **Trade union activities carried on by the employee.**
- **Ethnicity of the employee.**
- **Engagement of the employee in civil or criminal proceedings against the employer** – if an employee is dismissed due to his embarking on legal proceedings against his employer, this is an unfair reason for dismissal.

- **Religious or political beliefs of the employee** – in *Merriman v. St James's Hospital* (1986) the plaintiff was dismissed after she refused on religious grounds to bring a crucifix and candle to the bed of a dying patient. This was **held** to be an unfair dismissal.
- Taking part in a lawful industrial action or strike against the employer.
- Exercising the right to be paid the minimum wage.
- **Unfair selection for redundancy** – in *Hurley v. Royal Yacht Club* (1997) Hurley was told that the company was under severe financial pressure and that he had been selected for redundancy accordingly. The AGM accounts of the Royal Yacht Club showed that, in fact, the company was performing well. Hurley was found to have been unfairly selected for dismissal.
- **Pregnancy of the employee** – in *Flynn v. Sisters of the Holy Faith* (1985) a secondary school teacher was dismissed in New Ross, County Wexford. She claimed that she was dismissed due to her pregnancy. **The dismissal of an employee who takes maternity leave in accordance with the Maternity (Protection of Employees) Act 1981 is automatically unfair**. However, the Sisters of Holy Faith claimed that she had been dismissed for misconduct. The plaintiff was cohabiting with a separated father of three. It was alleged that there had been several complaints from parents and that the teacher had been warned to desist from the relationship. The High Court found that the conduct of the employee was not in keeping with the ethos of the Catholic school and that she also had a high absence record. Her dismissal was therefore lawful.

The Unfair Dismissals (Amendment) Act 1993 was the first major change in the law regarding unfair dismissals since the Unfair Dismissals Act of 1977 and came into force on 1 October 1993. The Unfair Dismissals (Amendment) Act 1993 added to the categories of dismissal that would be deemed to be automatically unfair. The new categories are:

- dismissal by reason of the employee's **age**;
- dismissal by reason of the **sexual orientation** of the employee; and
- dismissal by reason of the employee's **membership of the Traveller Community**.

Dismissals that are Prima Facie *Fair*

Section 6(1) of the Unfair Dismissals Act 1977 provides that "the dismissal of an employee shall be deemed, for the purposes of this Act, to be an unfair dismissal unless, having regard to all the circumstances, there were substantial grounds justifying the dismissal." Section 6(6) further states that the onus is on the employer to demonstrate that the dismissal was fair, either wholly or mostly, from the conditions set out in section 6(4), or from any "other substantial grounds" that would legitimately justify the dismissal.

Section 6(4) of the Act specifies a number of circumstances that render a dismissal fair:

(a) The employee lacks the capability, competence or qualification to perform work of the kind that he or she was employed to do. In *Reardon v. St Vincent's Hospital* (1979), it was **held** that dismissal arising from absences due to illness over a long period (amounting to three-quarters of the of total employment period) was fair, providing adequate warning was given and fair procedures followed.

(b) The conduct of the employee, e.g. being drunk on duty, or being violent. In *Murray v. Meath County Council* (1978), a dismissal was deemed to be fair where the employee assaulted his superior.

(c) Redundancy of the employee: an employer is entitled to dismiss an employee on the grounds of redundancy. Redundancy is defined by the Redundancy Payments Acts 1967–2012. However, it will not be a fair ground where a selective redundancy is made.

(d) Where continuation of employment would result in contravention of the law.

(e) The dismissal of a civilian from the Defence Forces for the purpose of safeguarding national security.

Code of Practice on Disciplinary Procedures

The Code of Practice on Grievance and Disciplinary Procedures (S.I. No. 146 of 2000) contains general guidelines for employers and employees on the application of grievance and disciplinary procedures. The Code outlines the acceptable fair procedures that should be maintained in order to promote good industrial relations. These procedures includes requirements that:

- "employee grievances are examined and processed fairly;
- details of any allegations or complaints are put to the employee involved;
- the employee concerned is given the opportunity to respond fully to allegations or complaints;
- the employee concerned is given the opportunity to avail of the right to be represented during the procedure; and
- the employee concerned has the right to a fair and impartial determination of the issues concerned, taking into account any representations made by, or on behalf of, the employee and any other relevant or appropriate evidence, factors or circumstances."

'Disciplinary action' includes:

- an oral warning;
- a written warning;
- a final written warning;

- suspension without pay;
- transfer to another task or section of the organisation;
- demotion;
- some other appropriate disciplinary action short of dismissal; and
- dismissal.

The steps in the procedure are normally progressive and happen in stages. However, there may be circumstances where serious action such as dismissal is warranted at earlier stage.

(**Note:** warnings given as part of a disciplinary process should be removed from an employee's record after a specified period.)

Procedures under the Code of Practice

An employee has six months from the date of dismissal to take action, or 12 months in exceptional cases. Cases are either referred to a Rights Commissioner (who is appointed by the Minister to investigate disputes or grievances that workers may have) for a non-binding recommendation, or are taken to the Employment Appeals Tribunal (EAT). Cases can be appealed to the EAT from a Rights Commissioner, and from the EAT to the Circuit Court and High Court. Appeals must generally be made within six weeks.

Remedies for Unfair Dismissal

Where an employee has been deemed to be unfairly dismissed in accordance with the terms of the Unfair Dismissals Acts 1977–2007, a Rights Commissioner, the EAT or the Labour Court have equal power to award any of the following:

Reinstatement

The employer has to reinstate the employee to his or her former position with the effect that there has been no break in the employment contract. Under the 1993 Act, an employee, upon reinstatement, will benefit from any improvements in the terms and conditions of employment that occurred after his or her dismissal.

Re-engagement

The employer must re-employ the employee, although not necessarily in the same position as he or she had held before his or her dismissal, provided the terms of such alternative employment are reasonable.

Damages

This is the most common remedy, particularly where the employer and employee consider that a reinstatement or re-engagement would be unworkable.

The maximum amount of compensation allowed by the Unfair Dismissal Acts is the equivalent of 104 weeks' pay, although deductions will be made for any money received by the employee and for any fault or contributory negligence on the part of the employee in bringing about the dismissal.

An employee is entitled to request from the employer a written statement of the reasons for dismissal, which must be supplied within 14 days.

A claim under the terms of the Acts must be brought within six months of the dismissal, or possibly within 12 months where exceptional circumstances prevented the making of the claim. There are three possible stages of adjudication on claims for unfair dismissal. These include a Rights Commissioner, the Employment Appeals Tribunal (EAT) and an appeal to the Circuit Court, with a possible appeal to the High Court.

REDUNDANCY

Redundancy law is governed by the Redundancy Payments Acts 1967–2012. Redundancy is a dismissal resulting 'wholly or mainly' from:

- cessation of business, e.g. the winding up of a company;
- cessation of the business in the place where it is currently carried out, e.g. moving operations to a different jurisdiction;
- the employer's requirements for particular work have ceased or diminished; or
- a change in the requirements of the job with which the employee cannot comply.

In short, it is a redundancy if the job has become redundant, and not the person.

In *Byrne v. Trackline Crane Hire Ltd* (2003) Byrne was made redundant as the crane he operated on was no longer profitable and it would have taken an excessive period of time to retrain the plaintiff on the new cranes. The EAT found that his position "no longer existed" as the greater part of his employment had been spent driving a specific crane which was no longer in use and had been sold on by the company.

In *Vaux & Associated Breweries v. Ward* (1968), a 57-year-old female bar tender was dismissed because the hotel she worked for wanted to re-brand its bar with 'bunny girls' and she did not fit the new requirements. It was found that this was not a legitimate case of redundancy as her job still existed.

Redundancy vs Unfair Dismissal

A real redundancy is fairly implemented and cannot be considered an unfair dismissal. The employer will be able to show that selection was based on objective criteria and that a valid redundancy situation had arisen, such as cessation of the business.

An invalid, unfair or 'sham' redundancy is considered an unfair dismissal, with a potential liability under the unfair dismissals legislation of up to two years' wages.

Qualification for Redundancy

The conditions that must be met to qualify under the redundancy payment legislation are as follows:

- the person made redundant must be aged 16 or over;
- a contract of service must exist (employee);
- the dismissal must be as a result of redundancy; and
- continuous service of at least 104 weeks (two years).

Statutory Entitlements under the Redundancy Legislation

If eligible, the statutory entitlements under the legislation are as follows:

- two weeks' statutory redundancy payment for each year of service; and
- a 'bonus' week's pay.

There is a maximum earnings limit of €600 per week (€31,200 per annum) for this statutory redundancy payment, and it is automatically tax-free – although an employer may choose to pay more.

'Short-time' Workers

Employees may be able to claim redundancy without being dismissed where they are earning half their weekly amount or doing half their weekly hours due to lack of work. If a lay-off or a short-time situation exists and has continued for four weeks or more, or for six weeks in the last 13 weeks, employees may then provide their employer with a notice in writing of their intention to claim redundancy. Unless their employer serves them with a counter-notice restoring their normal conditions within seven days, redundancy can be claimed, provided the other qualification requirements are met.

Collective Redundancy

Collective redundancy is a redundancy on a large scale. The minimum requirement for a redundancy to be known as a collective redundancy is that five employees out of a workforce of at least 20 are made redundant.

The legislation applicable to collective redundancies is the Protection of Employment Act 1977, which is separate to the Redundancy Payment Acts 1967–2007.

The 1977 Act provides that:

- representatives of the employees should be consulted at least 30 days in advance of people being made redundant; and
- the Minister for Jobs, Enterprise and Innovation should be notified 30 days in advance of redundancies.

The aim of this is to investigate through consultation with the employees' representatives if redundancies can be avoided and, if not, to work out the terms of redundancy. However, there is no obligation to reach an agreement.

Transfer of Business

The EC (Protection of Employees on Transfer of Undertakings) Regulations 2003 apply where ownership of a business is transferred from one employer to another as a result of a legal transfer or merger. In this situation, the statutory rights of the employee to notice, redundancy and unfair dismissal, as well as their contractual rights, are preserved on the transfer.

Fair Dismissal and Grounds for Fair Dismissal

Once a dismissal is proven, the burden of proof lies with the employer to prove that the dismissal was fair. The employer also has to prove that proper procedures existed and were followed throughout the process of dismissal. Fair grounds for dismissal are listed in Section 6 (4) in the Unfair Dismissals Act 1977 and are as follows.

1. **Capability** – employees have to be either physically or mentally capable to do their job. This would cover a situation where employees become incapable of performing their job due to an illness or loss of memory.
2. **Competence** – where an employee's work performance is sub-standard, the employer has to be extremely cautious before a dismissal can be effected. The employer has to follow the proper procedures of warnings and goals for improvement. Only if these targets are not met should the employer dismiss the employee.
3. **Qualification** – there are some roles for which a qualification is essential, e.g. a full driving licence. Should the employee not meet these requirements or, for example, in the case of an accounting qualification, where he or she have been expelled from membership of a professional body, it would be considered a fair dismissal of the employee.
4. **Conduct** – an employee must show serious misconduct to be fairly dismissed. This is usually confined to misconduct in the work place.

5. **Redundancy** – redundancy is permitted as a fair ground for dismissal if it is within the remit of the Redundancy Payments Acts 1967–2012. The employer must show that the circumstances surrounding the application of redundancy was equitable and not due to an unfair selection or a contravention of agreed procedures.
6. **Contravention of Statute** – if the employer dismisses an employee due to the fact that the employment contravenes or will contravene a statute, this will be considered a fair dismissal. This can be seen in the case of *Ponnampalam v. Mid Western Health Board* (1979) where an Indian doctor's qualification was not recognised by the Health Board and thus he could not be retained in employment.
7. **Other Substantial Grounds** – this category is rarely used and is designed to include any situations not covered in the categories above.

Fair Procedures

The employer is considered to have acted fairly if there are disciplinary procedures that were followed by the employer. Disciplinary procedures set out the stages and process the employer has to follow in relation to any alleged shortcomings of an employee. Generally, the procedure allows for informal warnings leading to written warnings and ultimately to dismissal as described in the Code of Practice on Grievance and Disciplinary Procedures (S.I. No. 146 of 2000).

The employer must follow fair procedures and is required to give appropriate warnings, make the employee fully aware of the allegations and give the employee an opportunity to present his or her side. The employee must also be allowed the right to be represented in any disciplinary procedures by, for example, a trade union official.

EMPLOYMENT EQUALITY

The Employment Equality Acts 1998 and 2004 deal with discrimination in employment. The Acts apply to all employees whether full-time, part-time or temporary. They extend to the self-employed, partnerships and to people employed in another person's home. They also govern access to employment and therefore advertisements and interviews for jobs.

The grounds for discrimination are as follows:

- gender;
- civil status;
- family status;

- age;
- race, colour, nationality, ethnic or national origins;
- religion;
- disability;
- sexual orientation; and
- membership of the Traveller Community.

Making a Claim under the Employment Equality Acts

All claims (except for gender discrimination claims, which have the option of going to the Circuit Court) must be referred in the first instance to the Equality Tribunal. The Equality Tribunal is the quasi-judicial body established to investigate, hear and decide on claims of discrimination. The tribunal is headed up by the Director of the Equality Tribunal. A complaint of discrimination or harassment must be made within six months from the last act of discrimination. The six-month time limit can be extended up to 12 months by the director "for reasonable cause".

The Equality Tribunal

Mediation

The director of the Equality Tribunal can at any stage with the consent of both parties, appoint an Equality Mediation Officer. If a settlement is reached, it is legally enforceable. If either party objects to the appointment of a mediator or if the process of mediation is unsuccessful, the case will be referred to an Equality Officer for investigation.

Investigations are held in private (people can represent themselves or be represented). The Equality Officer will issue a determination, which is enforceable through the Circuit Court.

Remedies Available

The remedies available under the Employment Equality Acts for people who are found to have been discriminated against include:

"1. In equal pay claims an order for equal pay and arrears in respect of a period not exceeding three years.
2. In other cases an order for equal treatment and compensation for the effects of discrimination of up to a maximum of 2 years' pay or €12,700 where the person was not an employee (the maximum compensation applies notwithstanding that there was discrimination on more than one ground).

3. An order for reinstatement or re-engagement with or without an order for compensation.
4. An order that a named person(s) take a course of action which is set out, e.g. to follow proper procedures on promotion panels.
5. In gender discrimination claims that are initiated in the Circuit Court, the Circuit Court in equal pay claims may order arrears of pay in respect of six years before the date of referral.
6. There is no limit to the amount of compensation that may be ordered by the Circuit Court."

(Source: www.iboa.ie)

REVIEW QUESTIONS

(See Solutions to Review Questions at the end of this text.)

Question 7.1

In relation to employment law explain:
(a) the grounds upon which dismissal may be fair; and
(b) the meaning and effect of constructive dismissal.

Question 7.2

James Holmes Snr died in October 2013. Under the terms of his will, he bequeathed his printing business, Printshop, equally to his two sons, Robert and Matthew Holmes. At the date of his death, James Holmes Snr employed 12 staff in Printshop. No member of staff has ever been given a contract of employment. You advise the brothers that they are obliged to issue each member of staff with a written statement of employment in accordance with the provisions of the Minimum Notice and Terms of Employment Acts 1973–2001, as amended.

Requirement List any **five** terms required to be included in a statement of employment under the provisions of this legislation.

(Based on Chartered Accountants Ireland, CAP 1 Law for Accountants, Autumn 2014, Question 3(b))

Question 7.3

Porter was an executive director and *de facto* managing director of Cupcake and Coffee Ltd ('Cupcake'), a nationwide coffeehouse chain, since the company's incorporation in 2001. Last month, at an extraordinary general meeting of the company, a resolution was passed removing Porter as a company director.

The rationale for this decision is that the company discovered that Porter had lodged a number of cheques payable to Cupcake into his personal bank account. It was also noted that Porter had entered into a number of profitable leases with Cupcake, using a company that, on paper, was owned by his brother to disguise his true identity. Since his removal Porter has contacted Cupcake seeking redundancy for the termination of his appointment, based on his 13 years of service. To date Cupcake has refused to pay any redundancy to Porter, claiming that he is not entitled to this payment.

Requirement:

(a) Define the meaning of the term 'redundancy'.

(b) Outline any **two** eligibility requirements to obtain a redundancy payment.

(c) Assess whether Porter is entitled to a redundancy payment in these circumstances.

(Based on Chartered Accountants Ireland, CAP 1 Law for Accountants, Summer 2014, Question 3(a))

Question 7.4

Dylan has recently been contacted by one of its part-time lecturers, Mary. Mary is querying why she has not received any leave entitlements since she commenced employment with Dylan nine months ago. Dylan's human resource manager, Sheila Murray, met Mary to discuss her query. Sheila explained to Mary that she was hired as an independent contractor (under a contract for services) and, as such, had no entitlement to annual leave. Mary commented that she considers herself an employee (and not a contractor) as she is required to attend all staff meetings, is always invited to all social activities connected with Dylan (such as Christmas parties and student graduations), and has her own office on Dylan's campus. Sheila explained that as she is paid an hourly rate to attend staff meetings and student graduations she is unquestionably a contractor. According to Sheila, the fact that Mary is also paid a fee without any statutory deductions is conclusive evidence of her contractor status. Mary is confused and seeks your advice.

Requirement Explain any **two** tests used by the courts to determine whether a worker is employed under a 'contract of service' as an employee or a 'contract for services' as a contractor. In light of this explanation, assess how Mary is likely to be classified.

(Based on Chartered Accountants Ireland, CAP 1 Law for Accountants, Autumn 2013, Question 1(b))

Question 7.5

Last month one of the employees of Regal was injured when he was hit by a bus that was shuttling passengers out to a plane. Regal discovered that the employee had only commenced employment the week before the incident and had not been wearing high-visibility clothing, as it had none in stock in his size and was awaiting a delivery.

Regal's human resource manager has advised the directors that this incident must be reported to the Health and Safety Authority and that it is likely that Regal will be prosecuted for breach of its duties as an employer.

Requirement Advise the board of directors of Regal of any **three** duties an employer owes to an employee pursuant to the Health, Safety and Welfare at Work Act 2005, as amended. Comment also on whether Regal breached its duty to the injured employee.

(Based on Chartered Accountants Ireland, CAP 1 Law for Accountants, Autumn 2013, Question 4(b))

Question 7.6

List any **two** sanctions that can be imposed by the Health and Safety Authority where a breach arises.

(Based on Chartered Accountants Ireland, CAP 1 Law for Accountants, Summer 2013, Question 1(b)(ii))

Question 7.7

Following Lola's resignation as director of Cherry, she incorporated a rival company, Indigo Holidays Limited ('Indigo'). Lola and Edward, Cherry's current sales manager, are the sole directors/shareholders of Indigo. Cherry intends to dismiss Edward for breach of his employment contract, which states that he cannot work for any direct competitor of Cherry's while still in its employment.

Requirement List any **two** grounds that may constitute a **fair** dismissal under the terms of the Unfair Dismissal Acts 1977–2007, as amended. Advise Cherry on the procedure it should follow to effect a **fair** dismissal of Edward.

(Based on Chartered Accountants Ireland, CAP 1 Law for Accountants, Summer 2013, Question 3(c))

Question 7.8

Fiona has worked for Cruise Publications Limited since 2000 as an accounts assistant. Twelve months ago, Cruise Publications Limited was taken over by another company, Parkway Publications Ltd. Since this takeover Fiona has been experiencing problems with her new manager who wants her to change certain aspects of her employment contract. To date Fiona has refused to make any alterations to her contract.

Last week Fiona was called to a meeting with her manager and told that she was being given a final written warning arising from her missing a deadline to return completed accounts to the company's head office last month. Fiona believes that the real reason for the warning is that the company wants to get rid of her, based on the fact that she has refused to change the terms of her employment contract. Based on these events, Fiona is now considering resigning from her position and claiming constructive dismissal.

Requirement:

(a) Outline any **four** procedures that employers should follow when subjecting employees to grievance and disciplinary actions (as outlined in the Code of Practice on Grievance and Disciplinary Procedures (S.I. No. 146 of 2000)).

(b) Determine whether you consider the actions of Fiona's employer in giving her a final written warning for a missed deadline to be fair or unfair, providing reasons for your answer.

(c) Assess whether the actions of Fiona's employer are likely to be classified as a constructive dismissal.

(Based on Chartered Accountants Ireland, CAP 1 Law for Accountants, Autumn 2012 Question 3(a))

Question 7.9

Define the term 'constructive dismissal'.

(Based on Chartered Accountants Ireland, CAP 1 Law for Accountants, Autumn 2012, Question 3(a))

Question 7.10

List any **two** prerequisites to bring a claim for constructive dismissal.

(Based on Chartered Accountants Ireland, CAP 1 Law for Accountants, Autumn 2012, Question 3(a))

Question 7.11

Sarah has worked at a university since 2000 as a clinical demonstrator in the biology department. On commencement of her employment, Sarah's contract stated that she was being employed under a "contract for services". Since her appointment Sarah has worked for 12 weeks in the first semester, eight weeks in the second semester and four weeks in the third semester.

Before each semester commenced, she was always told the start and end time for classes. She was also given a teaching syllabus, told what was required in each class and had set hours each week. Sarah was also required to write an exam paper, and after correction of exam papers, she was required to be present at an exam board, where results were being reviewed and validated.

In September 2011, Sarah was told that the university would no longer be requiring her services and not to return for the next semester. Sarah is now considering suing the university for unfair dismissal, but has been told by a colleague that she does not have a contract of employment but instead works under a contract for services and so cannot bring such a claim.

Requirement:

(a) Outline any **two** prerequisite to bring a claim for unfair dismissal.

(b) List any **four** tests and explain any **two** tests used by both the tribunals and the courts to determine whether or not someone is classified as an employee or as a contractor for the purpose of employment law.

(c) State whether you consider that Sarah is likely to be classified as an employee or as a contractor, providing reasons for your answer.

(d) Sarah thinks that her claim for unfair dismissal is going to be heard in the Circuit Court, but you have explained to her that employment matters can be dealt with in the Employment Appeals Tribunal (EAT), which is a quasi-judicial tribunal. Explain briefly the nature of a quasi-judicial tribunal, outlining any **three** advantages and any **one** disadvantage of these tribunals.

(Based on Chartered Accountants Ireland, CAP 1 Law for Accountants, Summer 2012, Question 3(a))

Question 7.12

List any **four** duties owed by an employer to an employee.

(Based on Chartered Accountants Ireland, CAP 1 Law for Accountants, Summer 2011, Question 2(a)(i))

Question 7.13

List any **two** main sources of implied terms in employment contracts.

(Based on Chartered Accountants Ireland, CAP 1 Law for Accountants, Summer 2011, Question 2(a)(ii))

Question 7.14

XYZ Ltd ('XYZ') is a recently-formed business and wishes to be advised of the rights that it should provide to its employees.

Requirement:

(a) Advise XYZ of the information that is required to be included in a statement of employment, under the terms of the Minimum Notice and Terms of Employment Act 1973–2001, as amended by the Terms of Employment (Information) Act 1994.

(b) Outline **five** implied duties of an employer in an employment contract.

(c) Outline **five** implied duties of an employee in an employment contract.

(Based on Chartered Accountants Ireland, CAP 1 Law for Accountants, Autumn 2010, Question 4)

Question 7.15

Shoreland Enterprises Ltd ('Shoreland'), a furniture manufacturing company, has recently been experiencing cash flow problems as a consequence of the failure by its customers to pay invoices on time. To overcome this crisis Shoreland has decided to make 20% of its workforce redundant.

Requirement Shoreland does not have a human resource department and therefore would value your advice in relation to the following matters.

(a) The legal definition of redundancy.

(b) Any **three** requirements to qualify for redundancy under the terms of the legislation.

(c) The amount of compensation payable.

(Based on Chartered Accountants Ireland, CAP 1 Law for Accountants, Summer 2010, Question 1(a))

Chapter 8

THE LAW OF AGENCY

The law of agency is concerned with a delegation of power, by which one party (**the principal**) authorises another (**the agent**) to enter into legal relations on his or her behalf.

Categories of Agent

Agents are divided into three main categories:
1. general agents;
2. special agents; and
3. universal agents.

General Agents

A general agent is someone who has general authority to enter into a specific area of business.

Special Agents

A special agent is someone whose authority is limited to a special authority given by the principal for a specific purpose. An example would be the sale of a house.

Universal Agents

A universal agent is someone authorised to transact every kind of business for the principal.

Types of Agents

Factor

A factor is a person who transacts business for another. An example is a motor dealer.

Broker

A broker is a middle man who contracts on behalf of another.

Del Credere *Agent*

A *del credere* agent is responsible for a contract with third parties, but also takes an extra commission from the principal for ensuring that the parties the agent is dealing with are solvent.

Auctioneer

An auctioneer is an agent who sells property at an auction.

Commercial Agent

A commercial agent is an agent who solicits and procures business from potential customers on behalf of one or more principals, usually against payment of a percentage. Each country has specific laws to regulate and protect a commercial agent.

Creation of an Agency

The relationship of agency is usually created by mutual consent. This consent is generally not formal, except for the creation of a power of attorney. Agency may be created:

1. by express appointment; or
2. by operation of law:
   - agency by estoppel;
   - agency of necessity; and
   - agency by ratification.

By Express Appointment

This is usually by mutual consent, which need not be formal or evidenced in writing.

By Operation of Law

This arises when the law may infer an agency from the relationship between the parties, the conduct of the parties or the circumstances of the case.

Agency by estoppel An agency by estoppel may arise in one of two situations:

1. where someone was previously an agent and continues to act as such after the agency agreement has been terminated, but the person they are dealing with is unaware of this; or

2. where someone to your knowledge enters into contracts on your behalf with another person and you fail to inform that person that the former is your agent.

In *Freeman & Lockyer v. Buckhurst Park Properties (Mangal) Ltd* (1964), the director of a company, who managed the company's property portfolio, hired the plaintiff, an architect, to draw up plans. The architect later sued for non-payment. The company claimed that the director did not have the authority to bind the company. **Held**: although the director had never been appointed as managing director and therefore had no actual authority, express or implied, his actions were within his ostensible authority and the board had either been aware of his actions or had acquiesced. Lord Justice Diplock identified **four factors** that must be present before a company can be bound by an agent that had no authority to enter into an agreement:

1. that a representation that the agent had authority to enter on behalf of the company into a contract of the kind sought to be enforced was made to the contractor;
2. that such a representation was made by a person or persons who had 'actual' authority to manage the business of the company, either generally or in respect of those matters to which the contract related;
3. that the contractor had in fact relied upon it; and
4. that the Memorandum of Association meant the company was not deprived of the capacity either to enter into a contract of the kind sought to be enforced or to delegate authority to enter into a contract of that kind to an agent.

In *Panorama Developments (Guildford) Ltd v. Fidelis Furnishing Fabrics Ltd* (1971), the defendant's company secretary, Mr Bayne, hired cars from Panorama Development's business. He represented that he wished to hire a number of Rolls Royces and Jaguars on behalf of the managing director who was away. He used them himself. **Held**: a company secretary has ostensible/apparent authority to act as an agent of a company and therefore Fidelis was bound by the contract with Panorama.

Agency of necessity An agency of necessity occurs when a person is entrusted with another's property and it becomes necessary to do something with that property. The contract of agency of necessity arises from the circumstances of the case. The law may confer authority where:

- the property is at risk; and
- the instructions of the owner cannot be obtained.

In *Sachs v. Miklos* (1948), the defendant ran a boarding house and agreed to store the plaintiff's furniture free of charge. After three years and several attempts to contact the plaintiff by phone and letter, the defendant sold the furniture. The plaintiff then returned to claim his furniture and discovered that it had been sold. The defendant argued that he was an 'agent of necessity', but the court rejected this argument. **Held**: the defendant sold the furniture as he wanted to rent out the room where it was stored. Lord Goddard warned that:

> "the court should be slow to increase the classes of those who can be looked upon as agents of necessity in selling or disposing of other people's goods without the authority of the owners."

Therefore the defendant was **held** liable for the cost of the plaintiff's furniture.

In *Springer v. Great Western Railway Company* (1921), a consignment of tomatoes was shipped from Jersey to London. The ship was delayed and arrived three days late. A railway strike resulted in a further delay of two days, so the railway company sold them at the port. **Held**: the railway company should have contacted the plaintiff for instructions; failure to do so was a breach of duty on its part.

In summary, for agency of necessity to arise, the following conditions must be satisfied:
1. there must be an emergency;
2. it must be impossible to contact the owner to get instructions; and
3. the agent must have acted in good faith and in the interests of all parties.

Agency by Ratification

An agency by ratification occurs if an agent makes a contract on behalf of the principal, but at that time the agent had no authority from the principal. This contract may later be ratified by the principal.

The principle of retrospective effect imposes the following conditions on agency by ratification.
1. The principal must be disclosed at the time of the contract. In *Keighley, Maxsted & Co v. Durant* (1901), an agent bought corn without disclosing that he was buying for the principal at a price higher than he had been authorised to do. The principal later purported to ratify the contract but failed to pay the agreed price. The defendant sued. **Held**: there is no contract as the agent had no authority as an undisclosed principal lacks authority to ratify the contract.
2. The principal must have capacity and must be in existence at the time of the contract. In *Kelner v. Baxter* (1866), Baxter conveyed that he was an agent of the company that had yet to be formed and ordered stock from

the plaintiff. The company was formed and accepted and traded the stock, but failed to pay for it. **Held**: the defendant was personally liable as the company could not ratify a pre-incorporation contract with retrospective effect to a date before the company existed.

3. The principal must, before ratification, have full knowledge of all material facts pertaining to the contract.
4. The principal must ratify the whole contract. The reason for this is that to ratify only part of the contract would impose a new contract on the third party.
5. The contract must be valid. Consequently, if it is a void contract or a forgery it cannot be ratified.
6. The principal must ratify the contract within the time period fixed under the purported contract or, if no time period has been fixed, within a reasonable period.

The Authority of an Agent

The most important aspect of the agency relationship is the power of the agent to affect the principal's relationship with third parties. A contract entered into by an agent will only bind the principal if the agent was acting within the limits of his or her authority. The actual authority of an agent may be express or implied.

Express Authority

Express authority is authority specifically given to make a particular contract.

Implied Authority

In addition, the agent must also have implied authority. This is authority to do everything necessary for, or incidental to, the execution of his or her express authority.

Implied authority enables the agent to complete his or her express function. If the principal wishes to restrict the agent's usual authority in any way, then he or she must inform third parties.

In *Watteau v. Fenwick* (1893), H owned a hotel. He sold it to the defendants, who gave him the job of manager and told him that under no circumstances was he to buy cigars. The plaintiff supplied cigars to H, believing him to be the owner. The plaintiff later sued for non-payment. **Held**: the court ruled in the plaintiff's favour. It was within the implied authority of a manager of a hotel.

Apparent Authority

The apparent authority (also known as 'ostensible authority') of an agent is that which his or her principal represents to other persons (with whom the agent deals) that he or she has given to the agent. Apparent authority (unlike implied authority) is not restricted to what is normal in the circumstances.

Relationship between the Principal and Agent

Although the relationship between the parties is based on contract, there is also an important fiduciary element to the relationship that creates rights and obligations between the parties.

The Duties of an Agent

When an agent agrees to perform services for his or her principal and there is consideration, then there is a contract. Out of this contract stem rights and obligations. The duties that exist between an agent and principal are as follows:

- duty of care and skill;
- delegation;
- accountability;
- conflict of interest;
- secret profit; and
- confidentiality.

Rights of the Agent

As discussed above, when a contract exists between an agent and a principal, then there are rights and obligations. The rights are as follows:

- the agent has a right to remuneration;
- the agent is entitled to be repaid his or her expenses and to be indemnified against any losses or liabilities;
- where remuneration or expenses to which the agent is properly entitled are not paid by the principal, the agent has a right to exercise a possessory lien over the goods of the principal.

Remedies Available to a Principal

If the agent is in breach of any of the above fiduciary duties, the principal may:

- seek an account and payment of secret profits;
- refuse to pay commissions;
- dismiss the agent; and
- if a bribe has been paid, he or she may recover the amount.

Effects of Contracts made by Agents

The effects of a contract entered into by an agent depend on whether:

- the agent discloses the identity of the principal;
- the agent discloses the existence but not the identity of the principal;
- the existence of the principal is not disclosed; or
- the principal does not exist.

The Identity of the Principal is Disclosed

Usually, an agent will disclose the identity of the principal to the third party and the agent is not liable under contract to the third party. However, there are some exceptional circumstances where the agent may be liable to the third party.

If an agent fails to declare to a third party that he or she in fact an agent acting on behalf of a principal, the third party has the choice of treating either the principal or the agent as bound by the contract.

The Existence but not the Identity of the Principal is Disclosed

When an agent discloses to the third party that he or she is the agent for the principal but does not disclose the principal's identity, the agent will not be liable under the contract.

The Existence of the Principal is not Disclosed

When an agent enters into a contract apparently on his or her own behalf, the doctrine of undisclosed principal comes into existence. On discovering the true situation, the third party may:

- personally hold the agent bound; and
- elect to sue the principal.

The Principal Does Not Exist

When an agent enters into a contact with a third party and the principal is non-existent, then the contract is enforceable against the agent only by the third party.

Termination of the Agency

Agency may be terminated either by the acts of the parties, or by the operation of law.

- **By the acts of the parties:**
    - where the authority is given for a single transaction, the authority expires once the transaction is complete;

  - by notice of revocation given by the principal to the agent;
  - by the expiration of the period stipulated in the contract of agency; and
  - by mutual agreement between the parties.
- **By the operation of law:**
  - by death of either party;
  - by insanity of either party;
  - by bankruptcy of either party; and
  - by destruction of the subject matter of the agency (frustration).

REVIEW QUESTIONS

(See Solutions to Review Questions at the end of this text.)

Question 8.1

Alan delivers his goods to his agent, Brian, with the instructions that they are not to be sold for less than €2,000. Consider the legal situation of the parties for each of the following:

(a) Brian sells the goods to Paula for €500.

(b) Brian buys the goods himself for €2,000 sends on the money to Alan and soon afterwards sells the goods to Paula for €4,000.

Question 8.2

Porter was an executive director and *de facto* managing director of Cupcake and Coffee Ltd ('Cupcake'), a nationwide coffeehouse chain, since the company's incorporation in 2001. Last month, at an extraordinary general meeting of the company, a resolution was passed removing Porter as a company director. The rationale for this decision is that the company discovered that Porter had lodged a number of cheques payable to Cupcake into his personal bank account. It was also noted that Porter had entered into a number of profitable leases with Cupcake, using a company, which on paper was owned by his brother, to disguise his true identity. Since his removal Porter has contacted Cupcake seeking redundancy for the termination of his appointment, based on his 13 years of service. To date Cupcake has refused to pay any redundancy to Porter, claiming that he is not entitled to this payment.

Prior to his removal, Porter entered into a contract with the Aromatic Coffee Company ('Aromatic') to purchase a large consignment of Italian coffee beans on behalf of Cupcake for €3,000. These coffee beans were delivered to an address specified by Porter, but Cupcake has since discovered that this was the address of a restaurant owned by Porter's wife. Cupcake is refusing to pay Aromatic for the coffee beans supplied on foot of this contract, arguing that Porter had no authority to create this contract.

Requirement Examine whether Cupcake and Coffee Ltd is legally obliged to pay the €3,000 due to the Aromatic Coffee Company by reviewing the law in relation to agency by estoppel (also known as ostensible or apparent authority).

(Based on Chartered Accountants Ireland, CAP 1 Law for Accountants, Summer 2014, Question 3(b))

Question 8.3

Rose, Hyacinth and Petunia are the sole shareholders and directors of Daffodils and Dandelions Ltd, a company that specialises in providing floral displays for corporate clients. Rose has been appointed managing director of the company by the board.

Daffodils and Dandelions Ltd has been trading successfully for the past eight years, and recently the directors have been considering moving the business to larger premises. Last week they looked at a vacant store in Dublin's dockland. They all agreed that the store was an ideal location, but both Hyacinth and Petunia considered the cost of the lease excessive and decided to keep looking for a more cost-effective solution.

Rose was very disappointed with Hyacinth and Petunia's decision and, after two weeks of viewing other premises and having found nothing suitable, she signed a lease with the proprietors of the Dockland store on behalf of the company, without consulting her co-directors.

Hyacinth and Petunia have discovered that Rose has ignored their wishes and signed the lease, and are extremely annoyed. They are considering removing Rose as a company director and replacing her with Lilly. They also inform the Dockland store proprietor that they are challenging the validity of the lease on the basis that Rose did not have the authority to create this contract.

Requirement Applying the law of agency, assess whether Rose had the capacity to sign the lease agreement, and its validity.

(Based on Chartered Accountants Ireland, CAP 1 Law for Accountants, Summer 2011, Question 4(b))

Question 8.4

Edward is an executive director of Giselle Ltd ('Giselle'), an accessories manufacturing company, and is employed under a contract of service. Fairways Fabric has been a supplier to Giselle for the past five years. Two months ago Edward ordered a large quantity of fabric from Fairways Fabric and billed it to the company's account. However, there is no record of this order arriving at the company. Upon examination the company discovers that this order was sent to a different delivery address, which is in fact Edward's home address. The company undertakes an investigation of this incident and discovers that Edward has been using the company account to order goods to establish a rival accessories manufacturing business from his home. Upon making this discovery, Giselle removes Edward as a director and is refusing to pay for the fabric supplied by Fairways Fabrics.

Requirement Through an examination of the law of agency, assess whether Giselle is legally obliged to pay Fairways Fabrics for the supply of the fabric.

(Based on Chartered Accountants Ireland, CAP 1 Law for Accountants, Summer 2010, Question 3(a))

CHAPTER 9

SOLE TRADER

A sole trader is a self-employed individual. It is the simplest of businesses to set up as there are very few formalities. No permission is required to operate as a sole trader. This was the most traditional method used in doing business in Ireland.

The main characteristics of a sole trader are:

1. there is no formal permission required to commence a business as a sole trader;
2. generally, sole traders operate as small businesses;
3. the sole trader has to make all decisions for the business;
4. the sole trader is only accountable to themselves;
5. there is a greater degree of flexibity in the setting up of the business.

Legal requirements must be complied with, which include:

- registering as a sole trader with the Revenue Commissioners for the purposes of being assessed as a self-employed person and for VAT; and
- registering his or her business name when using a name that is different to his or her own surname. This is a requirement of the Registration of Business Names Act 1963.

The main disadvantages of being a sole trader are:

- he or she has unlimited personal liability for the debts of the business; and
- individuals may lack specific skills and expertise (which might otherwise be available in a partnership or a company).

REVIEW QUESTION

(See Solutions to Review Questions at the end of this text.)

Question 9.1

Bertie has been a client of your accounting firm for over 20 years. He has always operated his business as a sole trader. Bertie attends your offices with his son and daughter to discuss a future business plan for the business. One option that they are considering is to convert the business into a partnership.

Requirement Advise Bertie on the main advantages and disadvantages of continuing to trade as a sole trader.

(Based on Chartered Accountants Ireland, CAP 1 Law for Accountants, Autumn 2011, Question 2(a))

Chapter 10

PARTNERSHIPS

Formation of Partnerships

The Partnership Act of 1890 defines the nature of a partnership in section 1 as follows:

> "Partnership is the relation subsisting between *persons* [emphasis added] carrying on a *business* [emphasis added] in common with a view to profits."

The Act also clarifies that:

- 'persons' may include a company; and
- 'business' includes every trade or occupation.

The sharing of net profits is *prima facie* evidence of the existence of a partnership. It is not conclusive evidence, but gives rise to a presumption which places the burden of proof on the shoulders of the person who denies the existence of a partnership.

No formalities are required for the formation of a partnership, unlike a company which cannot exist without a formal constitution and due registration (see **Chapter 11**). This is because the intention of company legislation is to maintain control of larger organsations, and it is not necessary to be as restrictive with smaller organisations. However, there are still some restrictions placed on a partnership, which are outlined below.

Choice of Name

The following restrictions arise in relation to the matter of the name of a firm.

Registration

Under the Registration of Business Names Act 1963, registration is required where the firm name contains anything other than true surnames of each partner. Failure to comply with this provision gives rise to the following sanctions:

1. a fine of €5 per day so long as the firm remains unregistered; and
2. the firm cannot enforce its contracts unless the court feels that the other party to the contract has not been prejudiced by the failure to register; for example, where he or she has not dealt previously with any of the partners and would not, therefore, have been put off by the fact that one of them might be uncreditworthy.

With regard to the registration of partnerships, section 381 of the Companies Act 1963 provides that the use of the description "Company" or "and Company" is permitted in a partnership even though this suggests corporate status.

Capacity of a Person to Form a Partnership

Every person is entitled to form a partnership with the following exceptions:

Minors

A minor is entitled to form a partnership, but as regards his or her relationship with other partners, a minor who has not reached 18 years of age is entitled to repudiate the contract of the partnership:

(a) at any time during his or her minority; or
(b) within a reasonable time thereafter.

A minor is not personally liable for debts of the firm incurred during his or her minority. He or she is liable for debts incurred after majority unless he or she has repudiated the partnership contract before the debt was incurred.

Persons of Unsound Mind

At common law, a person of unsound mind may avoid a contract of partnership if he or she can prove:

1. that they did not understand the nature of the contract; and
2. that the other partners were aware of this at the time.

As long as a person of unsound mind remains a partner, he or she is fully liable for the debts and liabilities of the partnership except to those who knew that he or she did not understand the nature of the transaction involved.

The Partnership Agreement

Written agreements of partnerships are known as partnership agreements. Partnership agreements are not compulsory but are recommended, as otherwise the default position is that set out in the Partnership Act, which may have unintended consequences. Section 19 of the Partnership Act provides that the mutual rights and duties of partners, whether ascertained by agreement or defined by the Act, may be varied by the consent of all the partners, and such consent may be either expressed or inferred from a course of dealings. Thus, an agreement to vary the partnership articles may be implied from the conduct of the partners.

Usual Clauses in an Partnership Agreement

The following are the usual clauses found in a partnership agreement, also known as a 'deed of partnership'. They are the basis of a contract between the partners. They are as follows.

- Nature, objective, place and name of business.
- Commencement and duration of the partnership.
- The property of the partnership: land; appointments; trade secrets; and goodwill.
- Contributions of capital by each partner.
- Accounts to be kept and taken.
- Division of profits and losses. Generally, these are this is divided equally among the partners;
- Powers and duties of partners
- The amount of attention to be given to the affairs of the firm should be stipulated; as should agreements as to the carrying out of other business and the restraint of business.
- Retirement from the firm. The Articles should include under this heading matters relating to the sale of the partner's share on retirement, death, mental disorder or bankruptcy.
- Dissolution of the firm. The Articles should stipulate when a firm may be dissolved in the absence of an agreement between the partners. For example, if one partner does certain specific forbidden acts, the partnership may be dissolved by the other partner.
- Powers of expulsion.
- Resolution of disputes, for example, an arbitration clause.

Section 25 of the Partnership Act expressly states that no majority of partners can expel any partner unless the power to do so has been conferred by express agreement between the partners. Such clauses are construed strictly.

Relationship of Partners to Each Other

The rights and duties of partners to each other depend primarily on the articles of partnership. Only in the absence of a partnership agreement are these rights and duties governed by section 24 of the Partnership Act:

- section 24(1) states that all the partners are entitled to share equally in profits and must contribute equally to the losses; and
- section 24(2) states that the firm must indemnify every partner in respect of payments made and liabilities incurred by them:
  - in the ordinary and proper conduct of the business of the firm; and
  - for or about anything necessarily done for the preservation of the business or property of the firm.

Section 29 of the Act provides that: "every partner must account to the firm for any benefit derived by him without the consent of the other partners from any transaction concerning the partnership or from any use by him of the partnership property, name or business connection."

Section 30 of the Partnership Act provides that: "if a partner, without the consent of the other partners, carries on any business of the same nature as and competing with that of the firm, he must account for and pay over to the firm all the profits made by him in that business."

Section 31 of the Partnership Act provides that: "an assignment by any partner of his share in the partnership ... does not ... entitle the assignee ... to interfere in the management or administration of the partnership business or affairs, or to require any accounts of the partnership transactions, or to inspect the partnership books, but entitles the assignee only to receive the share of profits to which the assigning partner would otherwise be entitled".

Remedies for the Breach of the Partnership

Damages may be awarded if loss has been caused to the firm, e.g. where a partner has failed to turn up for work.

An injunction may be granted to prevent a partner from carrying out other business activities; for example, a partnership deed providing that partners 'will not work for anyone else'. On the other hand, if the partnership deed provides, for example, that the partners will 'give all their time to the business' then there is no negative stipulation and an injunction will not be granted. Injunctions of this nature will only be granted where there is a negative stipulation in the partnership agreement.

Specific performance will not be granted in general terms because the contract is one of personal service. However, the court will enforce the signing of the partnership deed so as to give partners their rights under that deed where previously they had been operating in business on an informal basis.

Relationship of Partners to Third Parties

Partnership law is an extension of the law of agency. Section 5 of the Partnership Act provides that every partner is an agent of the firm and is jointly and severally liable for the purpose of the business of the partnership:

- "the acts of every partner who does any act for carrying on in the usual way business of the kind carried on by the firm of which he is a member bind the firm and his partners, unless the partner so acting has in fact no authority to act in the particular matter, and the person with whom he is dealing either knows that he has no authority or does not know or believe him to be a partner."

- A firm will be bound by "any act for carrying on in the usual way business of the kind carried on by the firm".

In *Mercantile Credit Company Ltd v. Garrod* (1962) a partnership agreement clearly stated that the partners could only repair cars, not buy and sell them. One of the partners sold a car. The credit company brought an action against the partnership. The question at issue in the case was whether the partnership was bound to pay the credit company. **Held**: the partner who sold the car had apparent authority to bind the firm and, thus, the firm was bound to pay the amount owing to the credit company.

A partner's authority to bind the firm in respect of transactions with third parties may be either:

- **actual** authority; or
- **apparent** authority.

Powers not Held by any Partner

No partner, whether in a trading partnership or not, has apparent authority in the following cases:

(a) they cannot bind the firm by deed (i.e. a contract that does not need consideration) unless they have been given express authority under seal to do so by the other partners;

(b) they cannot give a guarantee in the firm's name even in relation to the firm's business; and

(c) they cannot compromise debt by taking something else instead of the money owed, for example shares in a company.

Liability of Incoming and Outgoing Partners

As a general rule, liability for contract and torts may only be incurred by persons who were partners at the time when the liability was incurred. The topic of liability of incoming and outgoing partners is governed by section 17 of the Partnership Act which states:

"1. A person who is admitted as a partner into an existing firm does not thereby become liable to the creditors of the firm for anything done before he became a partner.

2. A partner who retires from a firm does not thereby cease to be liable for partnership debts or obligations incurred before his retirement.

3. A retiring partner may be discharged from any existing liabilities, by an agreement to that effect between himself and the members of the firm as

newly constituted and the creditors, and this agreement may be either express or inferred as a fact from the course of dealing between the creditors and the firm as newly constituted."

In *Tower Cabinet Co Ltd v. Ingram* (1949) the plaintiff sued a firm for furniture sold and delivered to it. He tried to enforce the judgment against a retired partner, Ingram. Upon retiring, Ingram informed persons with whom the firm had previous dealings that he had retired. He did not advertise in the *London Gazette* that he had done so. The remaining partner later ordered the furniture on notepaper that listed Ingram as a partner, but Ingram did not know of this. The court **held** that Ingram was not liable, as he had not represented himself as a partner or knowingly allowed himself to be represented as a partner.

Duties of Partners

The duties of partners are set out in sections 28, 29 and 30 of the Partnership Act 1890.

Section 28 – Duty of Disclosure

All partners have to disclose all aspects of their dealings with the business and/or partnership to each of their partners.

This was seen in the case of *Law v. Law* (1905) where one partner accepted an offer from the other to buy his share of the firm. At a later date he discovered that certain partnership assets had not been disclosed to him and he sought to have the contract set aside. **Held**: as the purchasing partner had breached the duty of disclosure, the agreement could have been set aside. This order was not necessary on the facts as the parties had come to an arrangement.

Section 29 – Duty to Account

All partners have a duty to account for all monies used from the business. This only applies to monies that the other partners are not aware of.

This principle of law was best illustrated in the case of *Bentley v. Craven* (1853) where Craven was a partner in a sugar refinery business. He bought sugar on his own and sold it to the partnership at a profit without declaring his involvement to the other partners. **Held**: the partnership was entitled to recover the profit from Craven.

Section 30 – Duty not to Compete

All partners are not to carry on a business in competition with the partnership without the other partners knowing.

In *Pathirana v. Pathirana* (1966) the plaintiff and defendant were partners in the selling of Caltex petrol and kerosene oil from a service station belonging to Caltex Ltd. After the termination of the partnership by due notice given by the defendant to the plaintiff, the defendant continued to carry on business on the premises in his own name and did not account to the plaintiff for his share of capital or any profits. The court **held** that section 42(1) of the Partnership Act entitles a partner to claim such share of the profits made since the dissolution of the partnership as the court may find to be attributable to the use of his share of the partnership assets:

1. that under section 29 of the Partnership Act a partner must account to the firm for any benefit he may derive which is obtained by him (without the assent of the others) through a partnership transaction;
2. that goodwill of a business may exist "notwithstanding that it is incapable of being ascertainable in pounds, shillings and pence";
3. that where a partner who manages the business fails to produce books of account, the court may assess the profits of the business in a practical way upon the evidence.

Retirement of Partners

It is usual to provide for retirement in the partnership articles on terms that the partnership shall continue. Unless this is agreed, retirement automatically dissolves a partnership, in accordance with the provisions of section 26(1) of the Partnership Act.

Liability of Retiring Partners

As partnership depends on mutual agency, any outsider who does not know of the retirement of the partner may bring an action against the retiring partner. As stated above, under section 36(2) a person is entitled to treat all apparent members of the old firm as still being members of the firm until he or she receives notice.

Retiring Partner Binding the Firm

Where a retiring partner holds himself out to an outsider as a partner of the firm, or is known to the outsider as having been a partner of the firm and does not give notice that he or she has retired, the retiring partner *does* bind the firm.

Section 26(2) provides that, before a partner can retire, he or she must give notice in writing, if the partnership was constituted by deed, to the other partners of the intention to retire. In order to avoid continuing liability, notice should also be given to all present customers of the firm.

Grounds for Dissolution of Partnership

A partnership is dissolved by an expressed or implied agreement, by court decree or by retirement on the following grounds:

1. by expiration of the term or giving of notice (section 32 of the Partnership Act);
2. by bankruptcy, death or change of any partner's share of the partnership property (section 33);
3. by illegality (section 34);
4. by fraud or misrepresentation (section 41); or
5. by court decree. Under section 35, a partnership may be dissolved on the application to the court by a partner:
   (a) when any partner is of unsound mind;
   (b) when any partner becomes permanently incapable of performing their part of the contract;
   (c) when any partner has become guilty of conduct prejudicial to the business;
   (d) when any partner wilfully or persistently commits a breach of agreement;
   (e) whenever circumstances arise that would render it just and equitable to dissolve the partnership; or
   (f) where the business can only be carried on at a loss.

Retirement of a Partner

As indicated above, retirement dissolves the partnership unless there is provision for retirement without dissolution or unless all partners consent. In such a case, partners may surrender their share and interest in the firm to their co-partners on terms to which they agree. This will not apply where the firm is insolvent.

Expulsion of a Partner

Section 25 of the Act provides that, unless agreed, there is no right to expel a partner, to forfeit his or her shares or to compel them to resign. Where a power to expel is included in the partnership agreement, it will be construed strictly.

Partnership Dissolution

The partnership articles may determine the effects of dissolution. If not so determined, then the whole of the partnership property must be converted into money and dealt with in accordance with the Partnership Act.

Section 44(a) of the Act provides for the *final distribution* of the assets (profit and capital) of a partnership as follows:

- losses are paid first out of profits;
- next out of capital; and
- lastly, by partners individually in the proportion in which they are entitled to share the profits.

If there are surplus assets on dissolution, these will be divided among the partners according to the proportion in which they share profits.

On dissolution, the order of priority that the debts (money owed by the firm) should be paid are set out in section 44(b) of the Act, as follows:

- to persons who are not partners;
- to partners for advances, as distinguished from capital; and
- to partners in respect of capital.

As previously stated, if partnership funds are insufficient to pay external debts then the partners are personally liable.

Where a partner is required to contribute to the assets owing to the lack of funds, and if they are unable to pay their quota, the deficiency is borne by the other partners in the proportion of their last agreed capitals and not in the proportion in which they share ordinary losses. This is known as the 'Rule in *Garner v. Murray*' (1904).

Goodwill of a Business

Goodwill was defined in the case of *Trego v. Hunt* (1896) as

> "the whole advantage, whatever it may be, or the reputation [or] connection of the firm, which may have been built up by years of honest work or gained by a lavish expenditure of money."

If the goodwill of a business is sold, in the absence of an agreement to the contrary, the following rules will apply.

1. The purchaser will acquire the right to represent himself or herself as carrying on the business, which he or she purchased, as well as the right to the sole use of the old firm name.
2. The vendor may carry on a similar business in competition with the purchaser under a new name as long as he or she does not represent himself or herself as continuing or succeeding to the same business.
3. The vendor may publicly advertise his or her business but he or she cannot solicit customers of the old firm.

4. The sale carries the exclusive right to use the name of the former firm, subject to the qualification that the vendor is not thereby exposed to liability, i.e. where the name of the business is still used, it must be clearly stated that it is under new management and, thus, the new owners will be liable for any loss.
5. The assets may, of course, be divided physically among the partners. In this situation there is no goodwill and any partner may use the firm's name, though he or she must not involve his or her former partners in liability. The physical division of the assets is by agreement.
6. If there is no agreement, a court will order a sale, whereupon goodwill becomes an asset.

Limited Partnership

A limited partnership is a partnership in which some members have limited liability for the debts of the firm. Their liability is limited to the extent of the amount of capital that they contribute to the partnership. A limited partnership is not a separate legal entity.

Such a partnership is created under the Partnership Act 1907. The following are the characteristics of a limited partnership:

- under this creation, at least one partner has to be a general partner, i.e. with unlimited liability, while the other partners may have limited liability;
- a limited partner cannot take part in the management of the firm, as unlimited partners can;
- death, bankruptcy, or insanity does not dissolve the partnership; and
- a limited partnership must be registered with the Registrar of Companies.

Types of Partner

In an ordinary partnership, there are two types of partner: silent and active.

Silent Partner

A silent partner is not an active participant in a partnership business and does not have an input into the day-to-day management. He or she is a partner who invests cash or other assets, such as business premises or machinery, but has no say in the application of that property to partnership business. A silent partner is silent by agreement, i.e. in the partnership agreement. Such arrangements usually cater for investors in partnerships.

Active Partner

An active partner has the right to be involved in the management of the partnership and has the right to be involved in key decisions relating to the business. In some partnerships, roles are defined, with a particular partner assigned a particular role. For example one partner may be responsible for sales and marketing, another for financial management, etc. This is common where all partners are actively engaged in the business of the partnership.

Table 10.1 Partnerships compared with Companies

Companies	*Partnerships*
Every company is legally distinct from its members.	A partnership cannot exist apart from its members.
The creation of a company involves legal formalities as specified in the Companies Act.	The creation of a partnership can be very informal; it is simply an agreement between partners and need not be written.
A company has perpetual succession.	A partnership ceases on the death of a partner as far as that partner is concerned.
A company's members can have limited liability for its debts.	A partner's liability is unlimited. (Though a form of limited liability is admitted, one partner must always have unlimited liability.)
Creditors have no right of action against the members of a company.	Where the firm defaults, the creditors have rights against the individual partners.
There is no limit to the number of members in a public company. A private company limited by shares ('Ltd') must have at least one member and cannot have more than 149.	A partnership must have a minimum of two partners.
The constitution of a limited company is laid down in its constitution. These powers are alterable only in certain ways.	No constitution is necessary for a partnership, if it exists at all it is freely alterable on agreement of the partners.
The constitution is a public document.	The constitution documents (if any) are private.

Table 10.1 *(Continued)*

Companies	*Partnerships*
Shares are freely transferable between members and those who are not current members. (This is restricted in the case of a private company.)	A partner cannot transfer his shares or assign his interest in a partnership without the consent of the other partners.
Companies are subject to the strict regulations of the Companies Act and are obliged to hold certain meetings, file certain documents and observe administrative formalities.	A partnership is not subject to such formalities and does not have to file returns, although the name of the partnership must be registered in certain circumstances.
Management is delegated to directors.	Each partner can take part in the management of the business.

REVIEW QUESTIONS

(See Solutions to Review Questions at the end of this text.)

Question 10.1

List and explain the duties that the members of a partnership owe to one another.

Question 10.2

James Holmes Snr died in October 2013. Under the terms of his will, he bequeathed his printing business, Printshop, to be shared equally between his two sons, Robert and Matthew Holmes. James Holmes Snr set up Printshop in 1960 and, up until the date of his death, he had always operated the business as a sole trader. Robert and Matthew have now taken legal advice and have decided to continue running Printshop but they wish to establish it as a partnership. They have been advised to draft a deed of partnership.

Requirement Outline the purpose of a deed of partnership and list **four** items normally contained in a partnership agreement.

(Based on Chartered Accountants Ireland, CAP 1 Law for Accountants, Autumn 2014, Question 3(a))

Question 10.3

Bertie has been a client of your accounting firm for over 20 years. He has always operated his business as a sole trader. Bertie attends your offices with his son and daughter to discuss a future business plan. One option they are considering is to convert the business into a partnership.

Bertie is concerned about the potential liability that he and his family are exposed to if the partnership fails. He has heard that he may be able to establish a limited liability partnership (LLP) but he is not sure what this is.

Requirement Explain the meaning of the term 'limited liability partnership' and assess the suitability of this business form in these circumstances.

(Based on Chartered Accountants Ireland, CAP 1 Law for Accountants, Autumn 2011, Question 2)

Question 10.4

List the three main provisions in the Partnership Act 1890 governing the termination of a partnership.

(Based on Chartered Accountants Ireland, CAP 1 Law for Accountants, Autumn 2011, Question 2(c))

Question 10.5

State the main advantage and the main disadvantage of operating as a partnership as opposed to a company.

(Based on Chartered Accountants Ireland, CAP 1 Law for Accountants, Autumn 2010, Question 1(a))

Question 10.6

Briefly describe a deed of partnership and advise of the essential terms that should be included in an agreement.

(Based on Chartered Accountants Ireland, CAP 1 Law for Accountants, Autumn 2010, Question 3(a))

Question 10.7

Discuss the statutory duties owed between the partners as stipulated in the Partnership Act 1890.

(Based on Chartered Accountants Ireland, CAP 1 Law for Accountants, Autumn 2010, Question 3(b))

Question 10.8

Explain the various methods of termination of a partnership under the terms of the Partnership Act 1890.

(Based on Chartered Accountants Ireland, CAP 1 Law for Accountants, Autumn 2010, Question 3(c))

Chapter 11

COMPANY FORMATION

Introduction

A company has a separate legal identity (also known as a *corporate* personality) once it is incorporated and registered with the Companies Registration Office (CRO).

There are a number of advantages to carrying out business as a company. These include:

- limited liability for members, i.e. the liability of its members are limited to the amount, if any, on the shares taken by them;
- the company can sue and be sued, i.e. it has the power to conduct business in its own name;
- tax advantages;
- ability to raise finance on foot of additional security, i.e. the company has assets that it could borrow against;
- ability to have a large number of members;
- perpetual succession, i.e. the company does not dissolve when the directors of the company leave or when the shareholders of the company die;
- clear definition and delineation of management and company;
- the assets of the company are vested in and owned by the company, rather than its members.

The Companies Act 2014 (CA 2014 or 'the Act') was passed by both houses of the Oireachtas on 10 December 2014 and signed by the President on 23 December 2014. The Act was commenced (i.e. became operative) on 1 June 2015. The purpose of this Act is to simplify and modify company law, especially the laws relating to private companies limited by shares. Its main aim is to make the law as clear and accessible as possible.

The Act is set out in 25 Parts; the first 15 Parts set out comprehensively the law applying to private companies limited by shares ('LTDs'). The remaining 10 Parts deal with the other types of companies under the Act, e.g. designated activity companies (DACs), public limited companies ('PLCs'), etc. (see below).

In the Companies Act 2014, the different company types are as follows:

- private company limited by shares **(LTD)**;
- designated activity company limited by shares/limited by guarantee with share capital **(DAC)**;
- public limited company **(PLC)**;
- company limited by guarantee **(CLG)**; and
- unlimited companies: private unlimited company having a share capital **(ULC)**; public unlimited company having a share capital **(PUC)**; and public unlimited company not having a share capital **(PULC)**.

Limited Liability – Company Limited by Shares

If a company has limited liability it means that, in the event that the company fails, the debts of the company are not the debts of the members, i.e. the members' liability is to the company and is limited to the amounts unpaid in respect of shares issued to them. Members are not liable to creditors of the company for debts of the company.

The issuing of shares is where a company raises capital in exchange for ownership of the company (see **Chapter 13**). The only liability of such shareholders for the debts of the company is the amounts unpaid in respect of shares issued to them. For example, if a share's issue price is, say, €1.00 but each shareholder has only been required by the company to pay €0.80 per share, the shareholders' liability for the debts of the company is limited to a maximum of €0.20 per share.

Limited Liability – Company Limited by Guarantee

A company limited by guarantee is a company that does not issue shares and, therefore, does not have shareholders – it only has members. Membership in such a company is by subscription and members give a guarantee to the company that they will be liable to the company to the extent of the specific figure that they have agreed in the event of insolvency. Common examples of companies limited by guarantee include clubs and social societies.

Unlimited Companies

In the case of an unlimited company, the liability of the members is unlimited and, in the event that the company is wound up, the members shall be liable to contribute to the assets of the company an amount sufficient for the payment of the company's debts (i.e. the members have unlimited liability for the debts of the company).

Types of Company

Private Company Limited by Shares (LTD)

The LTD is the model company and has been given centre stage in the Act. The first 15 Parts of the Act are dedicated to the company limited by shares.

The LTD is the most common type of company in Ireland and the primary focus of the Act is to simplify the law relating to LTDs, making it clear and accessible to all. It is thought that this new LTD will be the 'workhorse' of the Irish small and medium-sized business (SME) sector.

Key features of this type of company are:

- it may have one or more directors (though it must have a separate company secretary if it has only one director);
- it must have a company secretary;
- it can have between one and 149 members (in reckoning this limit of 149 members the following shall be disregarded: a person employed by the company who is also a member of it and a person who was formerly employed by the company and has continued after termination of the employment to be a member of it (section 17 CA 2014));
- liability is limited to the amount unpaid on the shares registered in the member's name;
- it does not need to hold an annual general meeting (AGM), but can instead adopt written procedures for passing resolutions – see **Chapter 12**;
- it has a single-document constitution that does not have an objects clause because a LTD has full unlimited capacity to carry on any legal business;
- it can claim eligibility for audit exemptions and dormant company audit exemptions – subject to compliance with statutory prerequisites (audit exemptions are discussed further in **Chapter 12**);
- it can pass majority written resolutions – special and ordinary (resolutions are discussed under 'Meetings' in **Chapter 12**);
- the board (including a sole director) and a registered person (a person authorised by the board with the CRO) has the authority legally to bind the company in contracts; and
- the company name must end in 'Limited' ('Ltd') or 'Teoranta' ('Teo').

The advantages of a LTD include:

- the incorporation process is simplified to having only one document for its constitution;
- the contractual capacity of the LTD is simplified in that there is no *ultra vires* rule (discussed further on in this chapter) and a registered person can bind the company;

- the management of a LTD is simplified in that the company requires only one director and there is no requirement for a physical Annual General Meeting.

Designated Activity Company (DAC)

The designated activity company (DAC) is the main alternative to the LTD. Typically, this type of private company is chosen when a company is being set up, or converted, for a specific purpose, i.e. when the members want to define or limit its activities, or a more complex company management structure is required.

A DAC is defined under Part 16 of the Act as a private company limited by shares or guarantee with the capacity to do only things set out in both its Memorandum of Association and Articles of Association, collectively referred to as its 'constitution'. (The Memorandum and Articles are explained later in this chapter under separate headings.)

Key features of a DAC are:

- it must have at least two directors, one of whom may be the company secretary;
- it must have a company secretary;
- it can have between one and 149 members (in reckoning this limit of 149 members, the following shall be disregarded: a person employed by the company who is also a member of it and a person who was formerly employed by the company and has continued after termination of the employment to be a member of it);
- it is required to hold an AGM when it has two or more members;
- it has a two-document constitution which includes a Memorandum of Association and Articles of Association;
- it has stated objects (an objects clause) for which the company was and is incorporated (although the Act seeks to reduce the effect of the operation of the doctrine of *ultra vires* – discussed later in this chapter – by providing that the validity of an act done by the company shall not be questioned on the ground of lack of capacity);
- it can claim eligibility for audit exemptions and dormant company audit exemptions (audit exemptions are discussed in **Chapter 12**);
- it can be a company either limited by a share capital or limited by guarantee;
- it can pass majority written resolutions (unless its constitution states otherwise);
- it will not be prevented from having its debentures admitted to trading or listed on a stock exchange (debentures are discussed in **Chapter 14** under 'Loan Capital'); and

- the company name must end in 'Designated Activity Company' ('DAC') or 'Cuideachta Ghníomhaíochta Ainmnithe' ('CGA') unless it qualifies for an exemption in this regard, i.e. the company shall enjoy all the privileges and obligations of a DAC but will be exempt from using the words 'designated activity company', etc., as part of its name if it is a company whose objects are the promotion of commerce, art, science, education, religion, charity or any other prescribed object and its profits are to be only so applied.

The advantages of a designated activity company (DAC) include:

- the company has an objects clause, which it can tailor to the aims and objectives of the company and to which it can be confined;
- it must hold a physical AGM, which is beneficial for members and directors, so that they can meet and discuss the strategic performance of the company; and
- it can list debt securities on a stock exchange.

Table 11.1 Comparison of LTDs and DACs

LTD	DAC
May have just one director (but it must have a separate company secretary if it has only one director).	Must have at least two directors (one of whom must be the company secretary).
Can have between one and 149 members.	Can have between one and 149 members.
Does not need to hold an AGM.	It is required to hold an AGM if the company has two or more members.
Single-document constitution.	Constitution includes a Memorandum and Articles of Association.
Its constitution does not have an objects clause as the company has the capacity to carry on any legal business.	It has stated objects (an objects clause in its Memorandum and Articles of Association) for which the company is incorporated.
Can claim eligibility for audit exemption and dormant company audit exemption.	Can claim eligibility for audit exemption and dormant company audit exemption.
It has limited liability and has a share capital.	It has limited liability and has a share capital or is a private company limited by guarantee with a share capital.

Table 11.1 ***(Continued)***

LTD	DAC
It can pass majority written resolutions (both special and ordinary).	It can pass written resolutions (unless its constitution states otherwise).
Company name must end in 'Limited' ('LTD') or 'Teoranta' ('Teo').	Company name must end in 'Designated Activity Company' ('DAC') or 'Cuideachta Ghníomhaíochta Ainmnithe' ('CGA').

Public Limited Company (PLC)

A PLC is a company that may list its shares on a stock exchange and offer its shares to the public. This is the key distinguishing feature of a PLC compared to a LTD or a DAC.

The key features of a PLC are:

- it must have two directors;
- it can be incorporated with one member, though the Acts do not set a maximum number of members;
- it must have a Memorandum of Association and Articles of Association as its constitution (see '**The Constitution of a Company**', below);
- it must have a minimum share capital of €25,000, or a greater sum as may be specified by an order made by the Minister for Jobs, Enterprise and Innovation;
- it must obtain a trading certificate before the commencement of business (a trading certificate is a certificate that is applied for after a company receives its certificate of incorporation to verify that the minimum amount of share capital requirement is adhered to);
- it can list its shares and debentures and offer them for sale to the public;
- directors are required to retire by rotation, i.e. at every AGM, with the exception of the first AGM; one-third of them must offer themselves for retirement by rotation (see **Chapter 12**) and may be eligible for re-election; and
- its name must end with 'Public Limited Company' ('PLC') or 'cuideachta phoiblí theoranta' ('CPT').

The advantages of a PLC are:

- the shares of the company can be advertised for sale to the public;
- shares can be sold through the stock exchange to raise capital;
- a larger PLC may find it easier to borrow from the banks; and
- shareholders have limited liability.

The main difference between a public and a private company is that a public company can invite the public to subscribe for shares and debentures, while a private company is prohibited from doing so. A public company must have a minimum share capital of €25,000 and does not have a maximum number of members. There are other differences between public and private companies, as presented in the table below, which summarises the differences between and a PLC and a LTD.

Table 11.2 Comparison of PLCs and LTDs

PLC (Public)		LTD (Private)
Must end in 'public limited company' ('Plc') or cuideachta phoiblí theoranta ('Cpt')	**Name**	Must end in 'Limited' ('Ltd') or 'Teoranta' ('Teo').
A two-document constitution, i.e. a Memorandum and Articles of Association, has to be lodged with the CRO.	**Constitution**	A single-document constitution to be lodged with the CRO.
Objectives of the company have to be stated.	**Objectives**	Company has full and unlimited capacity to carry on any activity.
Requirement of minimum authorised share capital of €25,000.	**Share capital**	No minimum share capital required.
Required to have an authorised share capital.	**Authorised capital**	Can choose not to have an authorised share capital.
Minimum one member. No maximum.	**Members**	Minimum one member. Maximum 149 members.
At least two directors with special rules regarding remuneration and retirement by rotation.	**Directors**	At least one director with no special rules.
Needs a certificate of incorporation and a certificate of trading to commence trading.	**Certificate of trading**	Can commence trading with a certificate of incorporation only.
No restrictions on transfer of shares.	**Transfer of shares**	Transfer usually restricted by directors.
Can list shares on a stock exchange.	**Public listing**	Cannot list shares on a stock exchange.

Company Limited by Guarantee (CLG)

A CLG is a private company limited by guarantee without a share capital. With this type of company, the members guarantee to contribute a certain amount of money, if necessary, in the event of the company being liquidated. The members' liability is limited to the amount that they have guaranteed in the constitution of the company. Organisations such as charities, sports and social clubs, whose main aim is to come together for charitable or social purposes, tend to use this type of company, which offers the benefits of incorporation (i.e. limited liability) but does not require that funds be raised from its members. Furthermore, any profit the CLG makes must be re-invested in the company.

The key features of a company limited by guarantee (CLG) are:

- it must have at least two directors;
- it does not have share capital; it has members who are not shareholders;
- it must have at least one member but there is no restriction as to the maximum number of members;
- it must have a Memorandum of Association and Articles of Association in its constitution;
- its Memorandum has an objects clause although the Act seeks to oust the operation of the doctrine of *ultra vires* (discussed later in this chapter) by providing that the validity of an act done by the company shall not be questioned on the ground of lack of capacity;
- it can list its debentures and offer them for sale to the public.
- directors are required to retire by rotation, i.e. at every AGM, with the exception of the first AGM; one-third of them must offer themselves for retirement by rotation (see **Chapter 12**) and may be eligible for re-election;
- it is required to have an AGM if there is more than one member; and
- its name must end with "company limited by guarantee" ('Clg') or "cuideachta faoi theorainn ráthaíochta" ('Cfr') unless it qualifies for an exemption in this regard, i.e. the company shall enjoy all the privileges and obligations of a CLG but will be exempt from using the words 'company limited by guarantee', etc., as part of its name if it is a company whose objects are the promotion of commerce, art, science, education, religion, charity or any other prescribed object and its profits are to be only so applied.

The advantages of a CLG include:

- the members are protected by limited liability to the extent of their guarantee;
- it has a specific objects clause to state the main objective for incorporation; and
- the company is a separate legal entity.

Unlimited Liability Companies

Members of an unlimited company pay an unlimited amount towards the company's debts in the event of it being liquidated. The Companies Act 2014 recognises three types of unlimited companies:

- private unlimited company having a share capital (ULC);
- public unlimited company having a share capital (PUC);
- public unlimited company not having a share capital (PULC).

The key features for all unlimited liability companies are:

- they can have one member; there is no maximum number of members;
- they must have both a Memorandum and Articles of Association;
- they will have an objects clause although the Companies Act seeks to oust the operation of the doctrine of *ultra vires* (discussed later in this chapter) by providing that the validity of an act done by the company shall not be questioned on the ground of lack of capacity;
- they do not have to prepare a Director's Compliance Statement (see **Chapter 12**);
- they do not have to file accounts with the CRO;
- if the company is public it can list its debt securities on a stock exchange, while private unlimited companies cannot;
- they may not dispense with having an AGM if there is more than one member;
- they must have at least two directors; and
- their name must end with 'unlimited company' ('Uc') or 'cuideachta neamhtheoranta' ('Cn').

The advantages of an unlimited company (UC) include:

- it does not need to file accounts with the CRO;
- it can have a single member;
- it does not have to prepare a directors' compliance statement (see **Chapter 12**).

Promoters

We will now discuss the formation and the registration of companies. The people who form a company are called 'promoters' and sometimes to start the business, even before the company is incorporated, these promoters have to enter into pre-incorporation contracts.

A promoter is a person who undertakes the formation of a company. While promoters are referred to in the Companies Act 2014, there is no general definition of a 'promoter'. Whether or not a person is a promoter of a company is a question of fact based on each case and therefore encompassed in common law.

In *Twycross v. Grant* (1877), Cockburn J. stated:

> "[A] promoter is one who undertakes to form a company with reference to a given project and to set it going, and who takes the necessary steps to accomplish that purpose."

The Duties of a Promoter

A promoter owes certain fiduciary duties both to the company and its shareholders. A promoter is considered a trustee on behalf of the assets of the company. He or she is therefore obliged:

- not to make any secret profit out of promotion and to account for any profits made;
- to disclose to the company any interest he or she has in any transaction entered into by the company, and to get its consent to keep any profit or gain; such profits must be disclosed to:
  1. an independent board of directors; and
  2. the shareholders of the company at a general meeting or in the prospectus of a PLC.

In addition, these disclosures must be accepted. Thus, if disclosure cannot be made to an independent board, it must be made to existing and future shareholders.

In *Gluckstein v. Barnes* (1900), Gluckstein and three others bought the Olympia exhibition building for £140,000 and promoted the company Olympia Ltd, to which they sold the property at a substantial profit. They did not fully disclose this profit. The company became insolvent and investors sought repayment of the hidden profit. **Held:** the action succeeded – the promoter, as a fiduciary, may not make a secret profit while acting in that capacity and he will have to account to the company for any profit he has made.

In *Hopkins v. Shannon Transport Systems Limited* (1972), the plaintiff, in partnership with another person, acquired ferries and options on terminal sites. The two partners were also the promotors of a company set up to operate a Shannon ferry service. Money was raised from the sale of shares to the public and grant aid received from the Department of Finance, and the defendant company was formed. The promoters sold the ferries and options on terminal sites to the defendant company at a profit, but did not disclose the profit to the company. When this fact was discovered, the Department of Finance decided not to proceed with the grant and shareholders left the company. At this point, the plaintiff left the partnership and sued the partnership for his share of the profits. **Held:** the contract for the sale of the ferries and options on terminal sites to the company was voidable as the promotors had breached their fiduciary duties to the company.

Remedies for a Breach of Promoters' Duties

The remedies that are available to a company for a breach of promoters' duties are contractual, tortious and equitable, and are as follows:

- a company may rescind the contract but only where *restitutio in integrum* is possible, i.e. the parties involved can be restored to their original position;
- as the promoter is a trustee of the company, a company may claim restitution of any profit on the basis of a constructive trust;
- the promoter may be obliged by the court to disgorge the profit due to his fiduciary duty to account to the company for any secret profit that he may have made (see the *Gluckstein v. Barnes* case discussed above);
- a company can sue the promoter for damages for breach of his or her fiduciary duty/breach of trust;
- the promoter can be sued in tort for deceit where a fraudulent misrepresentation was made;
- a company can sue the promoter for damages for breach of contract; and
- the law of evidence may provide the remedy of estoppel (**see Chapter 3**); here the promoter can be *estopped* from denying that he bought the property on his own behalf.

In addition, an action may be brought to the High Court for the imposition of a discretionary disqualification order against a promoter based on a breach of duties.

Pre-incorporation Contracts

In business, it is sometimes necessary for negotiations and contracts to be signed before a company is formed. However, when a company is not yet formed, and therefore has no legal existence, it has no capacity to contract. This situation can cause practical difficulties.

These difficulties can be illustrated by the case of *Kelner v. Baxter* (1866) in which Baxter conveyed that he was an agent of a company that had yet to be formed and ordered stock from the plaintiff. The company was formed, accepted and traded the stock but failed to pay for it. **Held:** the defendant promoter was personally liable as the company could not ratify a pre-incorporation contract with retrospective effect to a date before the company existed.

However, section 45 CA 2014 legislates for this in that it empowers the company to ratify pre-incorporation transactions and contracts entered into by it or by persons acting on its behalf. Section 45(1) provides:

> "Any contract or other transaction (including any application to any lawful authority) purporting to be entered into by a company prior to its formation,

or by any person on behalf of the company prior to its formation, may be ratified by the company after its formation."

The Act also states that the company shall not only be bound by the contracts ratified by it, but may also benefit from such contracts.

If, however, ratification does not occur (i.e. the contract is not confirmed at a later date), any person who acted on behalf of the company shall, in the absence of an express provision, be personally bound by the contract (section 45(3)). This legal principle was applied in the case of *Phonogram Ltd v. Lane* (1982) where a company known as Fragile Management Ltd was being formed for the purposes of managing a band, which Phonogram Ltd agreed to finance. As Fragile Management had not yet been incorporated, the cheque was made payable to Jelly Music Management, of which the defendant was a director, "for and on behalf of Fragile Management Ltd". Fragile Management was never incorporated and the plaintiff sued the defendant, who argued that as the company had never been incorporated, he could not have acted as its agent. **Held:** the defendant had purported to act for the company, or as an agent of the company, and was personally liable to account for the sum to Phonogram Ltd.

Registration

A company needs to go through a process of registration so that it can be incorporated as a company. Once a company is incorporated, it is subject to all the obligations pertaining to a company and it may commence trading.

Before a company can be incorporated, certain documents must be lodged with the Companies Registration Office (CRO). This section discusses the documents required for LTDs, DACs and PLCs as these are the most common types of company incorporated in Ireland.

Registering a Private Company Limited by Shares (LTD)

The Companies Act 2014 requires the following documents to be submitted to the Registrar CRO for the valid incorporation of a LTD:
1. the constitution of the company;
2. the "statement to be delivered with the constitution" (section 22); and
3. the declaration.

Each of these will be discussed separately.

1. **Constitution of a LTD** This document must contain the following information (section 19(1) CA 2014):
   (a) the company's name;
   (b) that it is a private company limited by shares registered under Part 2 of the Act;
   (c) that the liability of its members is limited;
   (d) with regards to its share capital, either:
      "(i) the amount of share capital with which it proposes to be registered ('its authorised share capital'), and the division of that capital into shares of a fixed amount specified in the constitution, or
      (ii) without stating [an authorised share capital], that the share capital of the company shall, at the time of its registration, stand divided into shares of a fixed amount specified in the constitution". (This means that a LTD is no longer required to have an authorised share capital and therefore has the option to leave an unstated share capital in its constitution. It must always state the issued share capital.)
   (e) the number of shares taken by each subscriber (see **Chapter 13**); and
   (f) any supplemental regulations that the company is adopting.
2. **Statement to be delivered with the constitution** This statement must contain the following information:
   - the name of each of the persons who are to be the first directors of the company;
   - the name of the person who is to be the first secretary of the company (as well as the names of the deputy secretary or first assistant, where appropriate);
   - the address of the company's registered office; and
   - the location where the central administration of the company will normally be carried on.

The statement must be signed by, or on behalf of, each subscriber to the constitution of the company or authenticated in accordance with section 888 CA 2014.

3. **Declaration** A declaration to the Registrar must accompany the above statement stating that: all requirements and obligations for registration have been complied with, the aim of forming the company is within the law of the State; and, finally, the particulars contained in the statement are correct.

This statement must be made by a company director, secretary or the company solicitor.

Registering a Designated Activity Company (DAC)

As explained above, there are two types of DACs: a company limited by guarantee or limited by shares. The Companies Act 2014 requires the following documents be submitted to the Registrar at the CRO for the valid incorporation of both types of DAC:

1. **Constitution of a DAC** The constitution of a DAC shall be in the form of a Memorandum of Association and Articles of Association which together are referred to as its 'constitution'.
   (a) *The Memorandum of Association* This is a document stating the aims and objectives of the company and regulating its external activities. (The Memorandum of Association in general and specific provisions relating to those of DACs are discussed further below.)
   (b) *The Articles of Association* This is a document that regulates the internal activities of the company (see discussion of Articles of Association below).
2. **Statement** A statement must be delivered to the Registrar at the CRO with the Memorandum and Articles containing the following particulars:
   - the name and registered office of the company;
   - particulars of the directors, including their signatures; and
   - a statement of the company's issued capital.
3. **Declaration** A statutory declaration must also be lodged to the effect that all the terms of the Companies Act 2014 have been complied with.

Registering a Public Limited Company (PLC)

1. **Constitution of a PLC** The constitution of a PLC shall be in the form of a Memorandum of Association and Articles of Association, which together are referred to as its 'constitution'.
   (a) *The Memorandum of Association* The Memorandum of a PLC shall state:
      - the company's name;
      - that it is a public limited company;
      - its objects;
      - that the liability of its members is limited;
      - its authorised share capital; and
      - the number of shares (which shall not be less than one) taken by each subscriber to the constitution (see '**The Constitution of a Company**' below).
   (b) *The Articles of Association* The Articles of a PLC may contain any type of regulations that the company cares to apply to the management of the company, i.e. it can regulate its own internal management rules as long as it complies with the Companies Act 2014 and does not contradict its Memorandum.

2. **Statement** A statement must be delivered to the Registrar at the CRO with the Memorandum and Articles containing the following particulars:
   - the name and registered office of the company;
   - particulars of the directors, including their signatures;
   - a statement that the company's minimum issued capital is not less than the authorised minimum of €25,000.
3. **Declaration** A declaration shall be included in the prescribed form and signed by a director or secretary of the PLC and shall state:
   - the amount paid up on the PLC's allotted share capital;
   - the amount, or estimated amount, of the preliminary expenses of the PLC and the persons by whom any of those expenses have been paid or are payable; and
   - any amount or benefit paid or given or intended to be paid or given to any promoter of the PLC, and the consideration for that payment or benefit.

Certificate of Incorporation

Once all the above documents have been delivered to the Registrar at the CRO who is satisfied with the proposed name for the company and that all the documents are in order according to the Act, the company will be issued with a certificate of incorporation.

The issue of the certificate of incorporation is conclusive evidence that the requirements for registration have been met and that the company is duly registered. Within 10 days of its delivery or issue, the CRO must publish a notice of its incorporation in the *CRO Gazette* informing the public of the company's valid incorporation.

The certificate of incorporation contains the following information:
1. the name and registered number of the company;
2. the date of incorporation of the company;
3. whether the company is limited by shares or guarantee;
4. whether the company is private, designated activity or public; and
5. the signature of the Registrar and official seal of the company.

Company Names

The Companies Act 2014 provides that the company must use the corporate identifier in its name (with minor exceptions). The name clause in a company's constitution states the name of the company and includes the appropriate term identifying the business form (such as LTD, DAC or PLC). Where a company intends carrying on business under a name other than its corporate name, it is required to register that name in accordance with the obligations imposed by the Registration of Business Names Act 1963). The legislation prohibits the use of the following names:

- a name identical to one already on the register;
- a name that is deemed to be offensive, blasphemous or immoral;
- a name that would suggest state sponsorship;
- a name that includes 'bank', etc.;
- a name that includes 'insurance';
- a name that includes 'society' or 'co-op' or 'co-operative'; or
- a misleading name.

Section 27 CA 2014 prohibits individuals or bodies other than companies, trading under a misleading corporate name, e.g. only a company limited by shares can use the abbreviation 'LTD'. Contravention of this is a category 3 offence under the Act (see **Chapter 15**).

A company may not use a name that is the same or similar to that of another company to make a profit or to rely on the reputation of the other company. This is called the tort of 'passing-off', the law that is used to protect the goodwill associated with the name of a business. A classic example of where the court **held** that there was a tort of passing off was in the case of *Ewing v. Buttercup Margarine Co Ltd* (1917). In this case, the plaintiff, whose business was named The Buttercup Dairy Company, was successful in his attempt to prevent the defendant company from continuing to use its name because it would be likely to cause consumer confusion and lead the public to think that the two businesses were connected.

In *Guinness Ltd, Smithwick & Sons of Kilkenny v. Kilkenny Brewing Company Ltd* (1999) the court ordered the defendant to change its name as there was uncertainty with 'Kilkenny Irish Beer', which was brewed by the plaintiffs. The court found that goodwill had been established by the plaintiffs when used in conjunction with beer.

Company Seals

A company seal is an official seal used by a company to imprint the company's legal name as additional evidence that a document was executed by its directors. Official documentation, e.g. share certificates, must be embossed with a company seal beside the officers' signatures.

Section 41 CA 2014 requires every company to have a company seal(s) stating the company's name engraved in legible characters. The company seal is to be used only with the authority of the directors of the company or a committee of directors, or by a registered person, provided its use is countersigned by the directors or secretary or their authorised representatives.

The Constitution of a Company

With the exception of LTDs (see below), the Memorandum of Association and Articles of Association together form the constitution of a company. The Memorandum regulates the external activities of the company and the Articles regulate its internal management. Together they determine the legal boundaries within which the company and its officers must operate.

The Memorandum of Association

The Memorandum of a company states its aims and objectives and sets out the purpose for which it was formed. It is included in the two-document constitutions of all companies, except LTDs, which have a single document constitution.

A company is bound by the contents of its Memorandum, which are:

- the company name;
- that it is a DAC, PLC, CLG or UC;
- the objects clause;
- the liability clause (which states the nature of the liability of the members of the company, e.g. limited or unlimited);
- the amount of share capital clause/guarantee clause (which is discussed in **Chapter 13**); and
- the association clause.

Name clause See under 'Company Names' above.

Objects clause Every company (except a LTD) is required to state the objects of the company in its Memorandum of Association. The objects clause determines the capacity of the company to act. Any act outside the terms of the objects clause is deemed to be *ultra vires*, i.e. outside the powers of the company and is, therefore, void. (See below for a discussion of the doctrine of *ultra vires*.)

The objects clause can be amended by a special resolution. Such alteration must be *bona fide* and in the interests of the company as a whole.

Liability clause The Memorandum of Association must state that the liability of the members is limited where a company is to be limited by shares or by guarantee, or that the liability of the members is unlimited.

Share capital clause The capital clause must set out the total amount of the company's authorised share capital and the division of it into shares of a fixed amount.

Association clause The Memorandum ends with a statement that the members wish to form a company and that each member agrees to take out the number of shares that is set out against his or her name. The minimum number of shares that a shareholder can subscribe for is one.

DACs (special requirements of the Memorandum of a DAC) The constitution of a DAC shall be in accordance with Schedule 7 CA 2014 for a DAC limited by shares and Schedule 8 CA 2014 for a DAC limited by guarantee.

The Memorandum of a DAC must state that it is a designated activity company "having the status, as the case may be, of—

(i) a private company limited by shares, or
(ii) a private company limited by guarantee, and having a share capital" (section 969 CA 2014).

A DAC can only carry on business in the State (section 966 CA 2014) providing that it is "an activity that is mentioned in its Memorandum".

PLCs (special requirements of the constitution of a PLC) The Memorandum of Association of a PLC shall state:

- its name;
- that it is a public limited company;
- its objects;
- that the liability of its members is limited;
- its authorised share capital, being the amount of share capital with which the PLC proposes to be registered (which shall not be less than the authorised minimum of €25,000) and the division of it into shares of a fixed amount;
- the number of shares (which shall not be less than one) taken by each subscriber to the constitution.

The objects clause must also state that an act done by a PLC shall not be called into question on the ground of lack of capacity by reason of anything contained in it.

Articles of Association

A company's Articles of Association govern its internal dealings, including matters such as company meetings, transfer of shares, voting rights, the appointment and removal of company officers, transfer of shares and payment.

Where there is a conflict between the Articles and the Memorandum the latter prevails. All registered companies, except LTDs, have a separate Articles of Association.

The Companies Act 2014 states that the Articles of Association may be drafted by the company or may consist solely of a statement to the effect that Schedule 9 of the Companies Act 2014 is adopted as the regulations of the company. If the Articles of Association are adopted in this format, the management of the company is carried out with no restriction, provided it is compliant with the Companies Act.

The Articles must be printed, divided into paragraphs, numbered consecutively, stamped and signed by each subscriber to the Memorandum. This serves to create a contract between the members and the company, and the members *inter se*, as stated in section 31 CA 2014:

> "subject to the provisions of this Act, the constitution shall, when registered, bind the company and the members of it to the same extent as if it had been signed and sealed by each member, and contained covenants by the company and each member to observe all the provisions of the constitution and any provision of this Act as to the governance of the company."

The Companies Act 2014 provides for the fundamental right of a company to alter its Articles by special resolution. A special resolution is passed by a 75% majority of members present in person or by proxy at a general meeting of the company, as well as compliance with notice requirements. There are restrictions on the right to alter the Articles:

- alterations contrary to the law are not permitted; and
- alterations must be *bona fide* and in the interest of the company as a whole.

Alterations of the Articles of Association must be made on equitable principles. An interpretation of the meaning of equitable principles and the concept of *bona fide* alterations arose in the case of *Clemens v. Clemens Bros Ltd* (1976). In this case, the plaintiff held a 45% share and her aunt a 55% share in the family company. The plaintiff's aunt used her voting rights to alter the Articles to issue new shares. The effect of this issue reduced the plaintiff's shareholding from 45% to 25% of the company. This allowed her aunt to pass special resolutions. **Held:** the aunt had not acted in the best interests of the company as a whole. The court concluded that her primary motivation was the removal of the plaintiff's influence over the company. The resolutions to alter the Articles were put aside as the aunt had acted for her own personal reasons and not for the benefit of the company.

The Single-document Constitution (LTDs)

LTDs have only a single-document constitution, which does not have an objects clause because a LTD has full unlimited capacity to carry on any legal business. The contents of the constitution of a LTD are as set out in section 19(1) CA 2014 (see above under 'Registration') and must be in the form of Schedule 1 CA 2014 ('Form of Constitution of Private Company Limited by Shares') or as near to it as possible. They must also be divided into paragraphs, numbered consecutively, signed and witnessed. These signatures by the subscribers must be in the presence of at least one attesting witness or authenticated in accordance with section 888 CA 2014.

The Contractual Nature of a Company's Constitution

By virtue of section 31 CA 2014, every shareholder of a company must have his or her name registered in the Register of Members and is a party to a contract from which flow various rights and duties. It is the same as if each member has signed and sealed a legally binding contract with each other and the company.

The constitutional document binds the company and its members and is enforceable by the members against the company, and vice versa, in respect of shareholder rights only. In *Hickman v. Kent & Romney Marsh Sheep Breeders* (1915) the Articles of Association stated that any dispute in the company was to be resolved through arbitration. A member initiated court proceedings and the company successfully secured a stay on the proceedings pending the outcome of arbitration.

The constitution also binds members *inter se* (between themselves). In *Rayfield v. Hands* (1960), the Articles of Association contained a pre-emption clause stating that directors had to buy shares that were offered to them at a fair price. **Held:** the member was successful in the proceedings.

As noted above, this contract only applies to rights and obligations *qua* members (i.e. in their capacity as members). In *Eley v. Positive Government SLA Co Ltd* (1876), Eley was a shareholder in PGSLA and was named in the Articles of Association as its solicitor 'for life'. PGSLA used another solicitor and Eley sought to enforce the Article in question. **Held:** the Article in question did not confer rights on him in his capacity as a member. Therefore, he could not use it to ground his action.

Corporate Personality

Once incorporated, a company acquires a corporate personality, i.e. rights and duties that are separate from its members, and it is considered a legal person in the eyes of the law. This means the company can buy and sell assets, own property in its own name and has perpetual existence. The implications of a corporate legal personality, which is sometimes referred to as the 'veil of incorporation' or 'Salomon's veil', can be seen in the case of *Salomon v. Salomon & Company Ltd* (1897).

The 'Salomon Veil'

The seminal case that established the concept of the registered company having a corporate personality is *Salomon v. Salomon & Company Ltd* (1897). Salomon was a leather merchant who for many years operated as a sole trader. He decided to incorporate his business as a limited company and complied with the requirements for incorporation. Salomon owned 20,001 of the 20,007 shares issued by the company and the other six were held by the other shareholders, who were members of his family. He then sold his business to the company for £39,000 of which £10,000 was in the form of debentures in his favour (debentures are a written acknowledgement of a debt, similar to a mortgage). The company later entered insolvent liquidation. On liquidation, the validity of the debenture was challenged on the basis that Salomon and Salomon & Company Ltd were in fact the same legal entity. **Held:** a company has a separate legal personality to its shareholders. *Salomon & Company Ltd* was separate in law to Mr Salomon. Mr Salomon was a secured debenture holder and was entitled to be repaid first as a secured creditor above the other creditors of the company.

The *Salomon* judgment was reiterated in *Macaura v. Northern Assurance Company* (1925). Mr Macaura, the owner of a quantity of timber, sold it to a company, of which he was the main shareholder. The insurance of the timber was taken out in his own name and not that of the company. Two weeks later the timber was destroyed by fire and the insurance company refused to pay out. **Held:** the company's asset was uninsured as the company had a separate corporate personality to that of its main shareholder.

Separate personality was affirmed again in *Lee v. Lee's Air Farming Company Ltd* (1961). Mr Lee incorporated Lee's Air Farming Company Ltd in which he held all the shares. In the course of his work as a chief pilot he was killed. The issue for the court was whether he was a "worker" of the company, thereby entitling his family to compensation for his death. **Held:** the company and Mr Lee were distinct legal entities and thereby capable of entering into legal relations with each other. He was employed by the company as its chief pilot and his family were entitled to compensation for his death.

Lifting the Veil by the Courts

There are situations in which the court will disregard separate personality and hold a controller or another company in a group of companies responsible for a company's debts.

Lifting the veil can occur in one of the following contexts:

- lifting the veil between the directors and the shareholders;
- lifting the veil between a group of companies, e.g. between subsidiaries or between a holding company and its subsidiaries; and
- disregarding the company altogether where the company was incorporated to defraud others.

The situations in which the courts will look behind the veil in certain circumstances are discussed below:

- human characteristics;
- fraud;
- avoidance of legal duty;
- agency; and
- single economic entity.

Human characteristics De Beers Consolidated Mines v. Howe (1906) concerned whether a South African company was resident in England for tax purposes. The head office was in South Africa, as were all the general meetings. All the directors lived in England and the board meetings were held there. **Held:** the company resided in England as that is where the head and brains of the company operated.

Fraud If a company is an instrument of fraud, the courts will lift the corporate veil. In *Creasey v. Breachwood Motors Limited* (1993), the manager of a garage owned by Breachwood was dismissed from his post and he sued for wrongful dismissal. The proprietors formed another company and transferred the entire business of the old company to it. **Held:** Creasey obtained judgment against Breachwood. The court would not allow a "phoenix company" to be used to defraud an employee of his legal rights.

Avoidance of legal duty In *Gilford Motor Company v. Horne* (1933), the defendant's contract of employment with the plaintiff incorporated a restraint of trade clause stating that he would not poach customers belonging to the plaintiff. On leaving, the defendant set up a company with his son, in direct competition with the plaintiff, but was neither a director nor a shareholder. **Held:** the court set aside the separate legal personality of the company, as the reality of the situation was that the defendant had used the guise of a company in order to avoid the non-compete clause.

In *Jones v. Lipman* (1962), the defendant conveyed a house to a company which he owned and controlled, in an effort to evade the plaintiff's enforceable contract for sale. The court **held** that the company was a sham, but ordered specific performance of the contract, as opposed to setting aside the company and ordering the defendant to comply directly.

The agency or alter ego principle The presumption is that a company is not the agent of its members, but such a relationship may be created between the two. Subsidiaries are frequently found to be the agent of the parent company. This is demonstrated by the case of *Smith, Stone and Knight v. Birmingham Corporation* (1939), where SSK was the parent company of Birmingham Waste Co Ltd, which carried on business on behalf of SSK. SSK owned all of the capital and took all of the profits. SSK claimed that BWC was an alter ego and that SSK was entitled to be compensated for the compulsory purchase by the corporation of the company's property. The courts had to consider the issue of agency in deciding whether or not to lift the veil and allow the plaintiff to be compensated. **Held:** the court undertook a *de facto* (factual) analysis of the economic circumstances of BWC. It was decided that the subsidiary was an agent of the parent and compensation was payable. The court was influenced by six factors, all of which should be answered in the affirmative in deciding to lift the veil:

1. The profits of the subsidiary were treated as profits of the parent.
2. The parent was the so called "head and brains" of the business.
3. The persons conducting BWC were appointed by the parent.
4. The parent effectively governed the running of the business.
5. The profits made were a result of skill and direction of the parent.
6. The parent was in effective and constant control of BWC.

Single economic entity This ground arises where, although the companies are registered as separate entities, they are in fact all part of the same single economic entity. Mr Justice Costello adopted this rationale in *Power Supermarket Limited v. Crumlin Investments Ltd & Dunnes Stores Ltd* (1981). Here the plaintiff was a tenant that operated a large supermarket in a shopping centre in which the first named defendant was the landlord. The lease agreement contained a covenant that the landlord would not permit the sale of grocery or food produce by any party from a unit exceeding 3,000 square feet within the shopping centre for the duration of the lease. Cornelscourt Shopping Centre Ltd, a member of the Dunnes Stores group, acquired the shopping centre and wanted to establish its own outlet in the centre. A separate company was set up, Dunnes Stores (Crumlin) Limited, and Cornelscourt Shopping Centre Limited as controlling shareholder caused the first named defendant to convey the freehold of a large unit in the centre to this new company, which then set up in competition with the plaintiff. **Held:** the plaintiff was successful in obtaining an injunction restraining the second named defendant from trading in the centre. Dunnes Stores (Crumlin) Ltd was bound by the terms of the lease, even though it had not formally been a party to it on the basis that it was part of the same single economic entity as Cornelscourt Shopping Centre Ltd.

In deciding to pierce the veil, Mr Justice Costello described Dunnes Stores Crumlin Ltd as a mere "technical device" with a £2 share capital and no real independent life of its own. He stated:

> "It seems to me that a court may, where the justice of the case so requires, treat two or more related companies as a single economic entity so that the business notionally carried on by one will be regarded as the business of the other group or another member of the group if this conforms to the economic and commercial realities of the situation."

In *Allied Irish Coal Supplies v. Powell Duffryn International Fuels* (1998) the defendant company was one of 25 subsidiary companies of Powell Duffryn PLC. The plaintiff sought to have the parent and subsidiary treated as a single economic entity. The High Court and Supreme Court **held** there were no grounds on which to pierce the corporate veil. They rejected arguments that separate legal personality should be disregarded in a group of companies merely because there is a close relationship between the companies. Consequently, the significance of *Salomon v. Salomon* was re-affirmed.

Lifting the Veil under Statute

The corporate veil can also be lifted by statute law and the members or officers of the company held personally liable. The following are some situations in which the veil of incorporation can be lifted under statute.

Fraudulent trading Section 722 CA 2014 provides that, if any person is knowingly a party to the carrying on of the business of a company with intent to defraud its creditors or the creditors of any other person, or for any fraudulent purpose, he or she shall be guilty of a category 1 offence (see **Chapter 15**). Therefore, the company is not liable, the veil of incorporation is lifted and the person committing the fraudulent act becomes personally liable.

Reckless trading Section 610 CA 2014 states that, where a company officer is a party to carrying out business in a reckless manner, the court may, if it considers it proper to do so, upon application by a liquidator/creditor, hold such person personally responsible for all or any of the debts that the court directs. Again, the veil of incorporation is pierced and the officer is made personally liable.

Restriction Section 819 CA 2014 provides that, on the application of either a liquidator or a receiver, the courts shall declare that a person who was a director or shadow director of an insolvent company at the date of, or within 12 months before, the commencement of its winding up shall not for a period of five years be appointed or act in any way, directly or indirectly as a director or secretary of a company, or take part in the formation or promotion of a company. Therefore, the veil of incorporation is lifted and either the director or shadow director is held to be personally responsible for the company winding up.

Disqualification Section 838 CA 2014 provides that a person may be disqualified from being appointed or acting as a director or other officer, statutory auditor, receiver, liquidator or examiner, or being in any way, whether directly or indirectly, concerned or taking part in the promotion, formation or management of a company for a period of five years or more and may be guilty of a criminal offence or may be personally liable for the debts of the company should it become insolvent within 12 months of the disqualification order being made. Thus, the veil of incorporation is pierced and a person is made personally responsible for the debts of the company.

Name irregularities If an officer of a company or any person on its behalf uses a name other than the official company name, he or she shall be personally liable, on summary conviction, to a fine of €5,000 or imprisonment for a term not exceeding six months or both (section 27 CA 2014).

Other miscellaneous examples of where the veil can be lifted by legislation and company officers deemed criminally liable for their actions include:

- failing to provide a member with a copy of the company's constitution upon request (section 37(3) CA 2014);
- where a LTD offers its shares or debentures to the public or invites them to purchase them, or where it applies to have its securities (or interests in them) admitted to trading or to be listed on a public market (section 68(9));
- failing to deliver to the CRO within 30 days after the date of its being passed a copy of a resolution to vary the capital of a company (section 83(7));
- where a person acts in the capacity of a director while an undischarged bankrupt (Section 132(1));
- failing to comply with the obligations regarding directors' compliance statements (section 225(1)).

The Doctrine of *Ultra Vires*

A company is not permitted to go beyond its objects and this is known as the doctrine of '*ultra vires*', i.e. beyond the [company's] powers. Other than a LTD, all other types of company must have an objects clause in the Memorandum of Association. The objects of a company are its aims and objectives, i.e. what it was set up to do. The doctrine of *ultra vires* arises when a company contracts outside the scope of its objects clause. Such a contract is void in common law. To avoid the *ultra vires* rule, companies have tended to register very long lists of all their aims and objectives.

The Companies Act 2014 tries to reduce the effect of the doctrine of *ultra vires* to some degree by stating that the validity of an act done by the company shall not be called into question on the grounds of lack of capacity by reason of anything that should be contained in objects clause. This means that, in practice, companies may still need a specific objects clause and thus the *ultra vires* rule is still relevant, though a third party dealing in good faith will not be prejudiced if the company acts outside its corporate capacity.

Constructive Notice

The application of the doctrine of 'constructive notice' heightened the harshness of the *ultra vires* rule for those dealing with a company. The constructive notice doctrine, supported by the 'Ashbury Rule', provides that a person who deals with a company is deemed to be aware of the contents of a company's public documents, i.e. its Memorandum and Articles of Association. Therefore, a third party who is contracting with the company should check to see if the company has the capacity to enter into this contract.

The Old Position – the Ashbury *Rule*

The old position states that contracts entered into by a company for purposes other than set out in the objects clause of the Memorandum are void and unenforceable. This was set out in the case of *Ashbury Railway Carriage and Iron Company v. Riche* (1875) (known as the *Ashbury* Rule). In this case the objects of the company were to make and sell railway carriages. The directors started to construct a railway using a loan given by the company. The directors later refused to repay the loan claiming it was *ultra vires*. The House of Lords **held** that the contract was unenforceable as it went beyond the stated objects of the company.

In *Re German Date Coffee Co* (1882), a company, using a Swedish patent, manufactured coffee from dates, although the Memorandum of Association specifically provided that the business of the company could only be carried out once the German patent had been obtained. **Held:** the company must be wound up as it had not obtained the German patent and the main objects of the company could only be conducted when the German patent had been obtained. Thus, the full rigour of the *Ashbury* Rule was applied.

Circumventing the Ashbury *Rule*

The *Ashbury* Rule led to hardship both for controllers of the company and outsiders dealing with it. There are a number of ways in which companies tried to circumvent the harshness of the rule in the *Ashbury* case. These are:

- the endless objects 'shopping list';
- the main objects rule;
- the independent objects rule; and
- the *Bell Houses* clause.

The endless objects 'shopping list' This method involves inserting an 'endless' and lengthy objects clause. In *Cotman v. Brougham* (1918), the court referred to a multiplicity of objects as "pernicious", but due to the fact that a certificate of incorporation had been granted, it could not do anything to curtail it as "the certificate is conclusive evidence that all requirements of the company's acts in respect of registration and matters precedent and incidental thereto have been complied with". Lord Finlay LC stated that all the courts could do was to construe the Memorandum as it stood.

The objects clause at issue contained no fewer than 30 sub-clauses that permitted the company (involved in the rubber business) to carry on almost any business. The Memorandum stated that every sub-clause should be regarded as a substantive clause in its own right. The company purchased shares in an oil company. The oil company subsequently went into liquidation. **Held:** the rubber company was held liable.

The independent objects clause In the *Cotman* case, a clause had been inserted in the Memorandum stating that each of the clauses listed in the Memorandum was independent and could stand on its own.

In *Introductions Ltd v. National Provincial Bank* (1970), a company formed for tourist purposes eventually went into pig rearing and ended up insolvent. The company had an outstanding overdraft with the bank. The bank had a copy of the company's constitution. The objects clause stated that the purpose of the company was the business of "tourism". It also contained a clause empowering the company to borrow money with a statement to the effect that each clause should be read independently. The bank argued that the power to borrow money was an object of the company. **Held:** borrowing was a power and not an object. The company had the power to borrow money as a means to achieve the object of the company, which in this case was "tourism" and not "pig breeding". The borrowing of money for another purpose other than its object was *ultra vires* as it was a purpose beyond the capacity stated in the Memorandum of Association.

The Bell Houses *clause* The practice developed of inserting a clause enabling the directors absolute discretion to enter into a contract if it was advantageous to the company. In *Bell Houses Limited v. City Wall Properties Limited* (1966), the main business was property development. A sub-clause stated that the company could:

> "carry on any other trade or business whatsoever, which can, in the honest opinion of the board of directors, be advantageously carried on by the Company in connection with or ancillary to … the general business of the Company".

Bell Houses entered into contract with another company under which Bell Houses would introduce Swiss financiers to them for a fee. The other company then refused to pay the fee, claiming arranging of finance was *ultra vires* and, therefore, it was not liable to pay the fee. **Held:** Bell Houses was allowed to rely on its "other business clause", which was held to cover the company taking advantage of the directors' specialist knowledge or connections. The act of introduction was therefore within the objects clause and was not *ultra vires*.

Powers and Objects

In interpreting whether the company has the capacity to act, the courts will have to discern between objects, express and implied powers, and express and implied ancillary powers.

Therefore, some clauses can be termed the objects of the company. This is quite straightforward and, if exercised correctly, will be *intra vires* (within the powers) of the company's Memorandum and thus valid.

However, the company's objects clauses will often have sub-clauses and not all of these sub-clauses are actually objects of the company. These are 'ancillary powers'. These powers can be either express or implied.

The following acts are examples of a power of the company that may be included in the objects clause:

- to borrow money,
- to give guarantees;
- to take shares in another company;
- to acquire similar businesses; or
- to sell or dispose of any of the property belonging to the company.

Exercising a Power

The law concerning the exercising of an express power is divided into traditional and newer views.

An express power The traditional view on the exercise of an express power not in furtherance of an object was that it was *ultra vires* the company. This can be seen in the case of *Introductions Ltd v. National Provincial Bank* (1970) (as discussed previously).

The more contemporary view on the exercise of an express power is that it is an abuse of directorial powers and not a question of being *ultra vires* the company. The Irish case of *Parkes & Sons Ltd v. Hong Kong and Shanghai Bank* (1990) accepted the distinction between *ultra vires* and abuse of directors' powers. In this case, Mr Collier owned a company that acquired control of the plaintiff's company. A fire destroyed the stock and premises of the plaintiff, and they moved to the premises owned by Mr Collier's company, which owed the defendant bank £20,000, which Collier had guaranteed. Shortly afterwards Mr Collier's company ceased trading and transferred all its stock to the plaintiff which gave a guarantee for the money and a charge over its property, even though it too was insolvent. The plaintiff was then wound up and the question was whether the new guarantee and charge were *ultra vires*. The court stated that:

> "While a disposition in such circumstances may constitute a breach of duty on the part of the directors, it does not follow that it would be *ultra vires* the company."

This distinction was also recognised by the Supreme Court in *Re Frederick Inns Ltd* (1994).

An implied power The law in this regard is settled in that the implied power must be reasonably incidental to the furtherance of the company's objects. This can be seen in the case of *Parke v. Daily News Ltd* (1962) where it was **held** that there was no implied power in the objects to make ex-gratia gifts.

Ultra Vires *Gifts*

An *ultra vires* gift is also relevant in relation to gifts made by companies. If a company decides to donate money to charity or to give gifts to its employees, it could be argued that the gift is *ultra vires*. The general rule is that the power to bestow gifts must be expressed in the Memorandum of Association. Where there is no express provision, such power may be implied as long as it is for the benefit of the company as a whole. Again, this can be illustrated by the case of *Parke v. Daily News Ltd* as the ex-gratia gift was not beneficial to the company as a whole.

In contrast, the court **held** that a gift made by the company in *Evans v. Brunner Mond Limited* (1921) for research was *intra vires* as it benefited the company as a whole.

Effects of Ultra Vires *Contracts*

As stated previously, the Companies Act 2014 has diminished the strength of the *ultra vires* rule. It has achieved this by stating that the validity of an act shall not be brought into question on the grounds of lack of capacity by reason of anything contained in the objects of the company (sections 973, 1012, 1183 and 1240).

However, it remains the duty of the directors to observe any limitations on their powers flowing from the company's objects, and any action by the directors that would be beyond a company's capacity may only be ratified by the company by special resolution. A resolution ratifying such actions shall not affect any liability incurred by the directors or any other person; if, however, relief from any such liability is to be conferred by the company, it must be agreed **separately** by a special resolution.

A party to a transaction with a company is not bound to enquire as to whether the transaction is permitted by the company's objects clause or not. This removes the need for actual or constructive notice, which had previously been required.

Conclusion

This chapter has discussed the different types of companies, their formation and registration. In the next chapter we will examine the law relating to the manner in which these companies are managed, and the duties and responsibilities of the people who manage them.

REVIEW QUESTIONS

(See Solutions to Review Questions at the end of this text.)

Question 11.1

(a) Jane Matthews has just won €10 million in the weekly lottery and wants to invest the money and set up a business baking and selling cakes. She is taking legal advice from your firm about setting up the business as a company but is unsure of the different types of company that can be set up.

Requirement Explain to Jane any **four** different types of company that can be set up.

(b) Jane is planning on operating the business under the name "Jane's Little Cupcake Café Limited". However, further down the street from where Jane proposes to set up her business is another business called "John's Little Cupcake Cafe". John has threatened to seek an injunction against Jane if she calls her business "Jane's Little Cupcake Café Limited".

Requirement:

(i) Discuss the various classifications of names likely to be denied registration as a business name under the provisions of the Registration of Business Names Act 1963.

(ii) Comment whether John will be successful in obtaining this injunction to prevent Jane's use of this name, providing a reason for your answer.

(c) You explain to Jane that certain types of business must have a Memorandum of Association, with an objects clause defining the powers and objectives of the company. Jane tells you that she wants the business only to bake and sell cakes and asks you to draft an objects clause accordingly. However, Jane's 10-year business plan states that she would like the company to expand into selling clothing, household items and other handmade craft items. You explain to Jane that if she wants to expand the business in this way she will have to amend the objects clause, otherwise her actions will be *ultra vires.*

Requirement:

(i) Explain the concept of *ultra vires.*

(ii) Discuss the validity, or otherwise, of *ultra vires* actions carried out by the company.

Question 11.2

The Joe Glass Partnership operates a successful recycling business based in Munster and has recently become a client of your firm. You have been brought along by the firm's senior partner to a meeting with Joe Glass. Joe explains to you that every year he prepares a business plan for the partnership. One of his goals for the next financial year is to expand the business into a public limited company, but he is unsure of the advantages and disadvantages in changing his corporate form.

Requirement Outline any **three** advantages and any **three** disadvantages of operating as a public limited company, as opposed to a partnership.

Question 11.3

MS Printing Services, an expanding client of your firm, has decided to change its status from that of partnership to that of a private limited company.

The client asked your partner to permit you to go on secondment to the business for a year as the company accountant. Prior to starting your secondment, you are tasked with ensuring that the company has a proper constitution.

Requirement:

(a) Advise MS Printing Services as to the nature of a company's constitution, commenting (briefly) on its content.

(b) Explain how the constitution can be altered.

Question 11.4

Purity plc ("Purity"), a public limited company, is a pharmaceutical company. The directors of the company are of the opinion that it should be re-registered as a private limited company and are seeking to put a proposal before the shareholders at an extraordinary general meeting to effect this alteration.

Requirement Identify any **three** differences between the characteristics of a public limited company and a private limited company.

Chapter 12

COMPANY MANAGEMENT

Introduction

This chapter discusses the people that are needed to manage a company, namely the company directors, company secretary and the auditor. This chapter also discusses company meetings, with which the directors manage the company, and the documentation that is required to comply with the Companies Act, i.e. company accounts, returns, registers and reports.

COMPANY DIRECTORS

A director is an officer of the company and is involved in its management. Directors receive the power delegated to them by the members of the company under the constitution of the company and the Companies Act 2014.

A company is required to have at least one director (section 128 CA 2014) who must be a person resident in an EEA state (European Economic Area) which includes the EU Member States plus Iceland, Liechtenstein and Norway (section 137), though a company may opt to place a bond to the value of €25,000 as an alternative to this residency requirement with a "nominated person" who may be appointed by the Registrar or the Revenue Commissioners.

Appointment of Directors

The first directors of a company are those who consent to being listed as such and shall be those persons determined in writing by the subscribers to the company's constitution or a majority of them.

Subsequent directors of a company may be appointed by the members in general meeting, unless a retiring director has been recommended and is eligible for re-election.

Ineligibility

Persons ineligible to become a director are:

- a company;
- an undischarged bankrupt (someone who has not paid off the debt that resulted in them becoming bankrupt) – if he or she acts as a director, they will be guilty of a category 2 offence (section 871(1) – see **Chapter 15**);
- an auditor of the company or its holding company;
- a minor (under the age of 18);
- a restricted person (subject to exceptions);
- a disqualified director (discussed later in this chapter).

In addition to the above, the maximum number of company directorships that a person can hold is 25. There are some exceptions to this rule, for example groups of companies are treated as one company and companies that have a real continuous link with an economic activity being carried out in the State are excluded.

Categories of Directors

There are different categories of directors:

- formally-appointed directors (known as *de jure* directors);
- shadow directors
- alternate directors
- *de facto* directors
- managing director (agent of the company)
- executive directors
- non-executive directors
- directors for life.

Shadow Directors

A shadow director is "a person in accordance with whose directions or instructions the directors of a company are accustomed to act" (section 221 CA 2014). While a shadow director may not want to be known as a director, as he or she works behind the directors who are properly appointed and frequently instructs the whole board of directors on how to act, he or she will be classified as such. As a shadow director will be classed as a director, he or she will have the same liabilities as a director.

Alternate Directors

Alternate directors are persons who are nominated by a director to act in his or her absence. An alternate director can only be appointed with the agreement of the majority of the directors. Only one person may stand appointed as an alternate director at any one time in respect of the particular director (section 165 CA 2014).

De Facto *Directors*

De facto directors are persons who, although not formally appointed as directors, hold themselves out to be directors and are treated as such (section 165 CA 2014).

In *Re Hydrodam (Corby) Ltd* (1994), a distinction was drawn between those who claim or purport to act as directors even though they have not been appointed (*de facto*) and those who claim not to be directors (shadow) even though they direct those who are the formally appointed 'real' directors.

Managing Directors

The managing director is responsible for the day-to-day running of the company and is accountable to the board of directors and shareholders of the company. The managing director is appointed from the board of directors (section 159 CA 2014).

Executive Directors

Executive directors are involved in the operational management of the company.

Non-executive Directors

Non-executive directors are directors who are not involved in the operational management of the company. The key role for every non-executive director is to bring an independent, objective and external perspective to the board of the company – therefore, this role is more strategic than operational. (The role of a non-executive director will be discussed in more depth in **Chapter 18**.)

Directors' Duties

It is the duty of each director of a company to ensure that the Companies Act 2014 is complied with by the company (section 223 CA 2014). The consent of each director must accompany a statement by that director (immediately above his or her signature on the consent) in the following terms:

> *"I acknowledge that, as a director, I have legal duties and obligations imposed by the Companies Act, other statutes and at common law."*

A director of a company shall owe the duties set out in section 228 CA 2014 (the "relevant duties") to the company (and the company alone).

Part 5 of the Act sets out or enumerates in statute for the first time the fiduciary duties (duties based on trust and honesty) of company directors, most of which were previously recognised only in common law. Section 228 sets out the following eight director's duties:

1. to act in good faith in what the director considers to be the interests of the company;
2. to act honestly and responsibly in relation to the conduct of the affairs of the company;
3. to act in accordance with the company's constitution and exercise his or her powers only for the purposes allowed by law;
4. not use the company's property, information or opportunities for his or her own or anyone else's benefit (unless in specific allowed circumstances – see below);
5. not to agree to a restriction of his or her exercise of independent judgement (unless in specific allowed circumstances);
6. to avoid any conflict of interest between the director's duties to the company and his or her own interests (unless in specified allowed circumstances);
7. to exercise the care, skill and diligence that would be exercised in the same circumstances by a reasonable person;
8. to have regard to the interests of the members of the company, in addition to the duty (under section 224) to have regard to the interests of the company's employees in general.

Each of these duties is discussed separately below.

1. To act in good faith and in the interests of the company

The powers that directors use must be exercised *bona fide* and for the benefit of the company as a whole. In *Parke v. Daily News Ltd* (1962), it was **held** by the court that an ex-gratia gift (not compelled by legal right) of £1.5 million to employees was not in the best interests of the company as a whole.

In the case of *Re Smith v. Fawcett* (1942), the court stated that the directors must exercise their powers in the best interest of the company and not what the courts believed to be the best interest. In other words, this is a subjective test and the burden of proof lies on those alleging that the powers have been exercised improperly.

2. To act honestly and responsibly in relation to the conduct of the affairs of the company

Directors have a duty to act honestly and responsibly in managing the affairs of the company. If a director does not act in this manner, then it would be just and equitable to subject him or her either to a restriction or a disqualification order. (Restriction and disqualification is discussed later in this chapter.)

In *La Moselle Clothing Ltd v. Soualhi* (1998), the court set out factors to consider in determining whether a director was acting honestly and responsibly:

- the extent of the compliance with the Companies Acts;
- whether the director's conduct was so incompetent as to be irresponsible;
- the extent of the director's responsibility for any insolvency;
- the extent of the director's responsibility for the net deficiency in assets at winding up;
- the extent to which the director displayed a lack of commercial probity or want of proper standards.

Soualhi was a director and 99% shareholder of La Moselle, and was restricted as director after the company became insolvent. **Held**: in making Soualhi a restricted director, the court was heavily influenced by his failure to wind up the company, even when it was clear that the company was insolvent; and also that he had been very unforthcoming with books of account and the existence of unaccounted-for expenses and withdrawals.

The above test was approved by the Supreme Court in *Re Squash (Ireland) Ltd* (2001). The Supreme Court also agreed that, when evaluating whether a director acted responsibly, regard should be had to his entire tenure as director and not just the few months leading up to the liquidation.

In *Re Mitek Holdings Limited* (2010) a restriction order was made by the liquidator against the two directors of Mitek Pharmaceuticals Limited. The Supreme Court upheld a High Court decision to grant restriction orders and noted the difference between the duties of executive and non-executive directors, stating that "even non-executive directors of companies must be increasingly conscious in the time we live that they cannot be mere ciphers or purveyors of votes at the whim of management".

The Supreme Court reiterated that the court would take into consideration the following factors when assessing whether directors had acted honestly and responsibly:

- their compliance with statutory obligations;
- their commercial management of the company, particularly when it was facing insolvency;
- their compliance with the obligation to ensure that the assets of a company facing insolvency were dealt with in the law.

3. To act in accordance with the company's constitution and exercise powers only for the purposes allowed by law

Directors can act only in accordance with the powers that are conferred upon them. First, the existence of the lawful power has to be determined; if it is, then a determination as to whether it was lawfully used must be made. The powers of directors are determined in the company's constitution and by statute. These powers must only be exercised for a proper purpose.

In *Smith Howard Ltd v. Ampol Petroleum Ltd* (1974), two companies held a substantial percentage of the shares in a third company. The third company was in need of capital, and the other two companies sought to acquire the remaining shares by way of a takeover. However, another company, the appellant in the case, was willing to make a higher bid for the shares. The directors of the third company allotted sufficient shares to the appellant company so as to enable it to complete the takeover of the third company. One of the original two companies, Ampol, then brought proceedings to challenge the validity of the allotment. **Held**: the allotment had an improper purpose and was accordingly held to be invalid. The primary purpose of the allotment had been to reduce the shareholding of the two companies in question, in order that the appellant might complete the takeover (i.e. the allotment was not for a legal purpose).

In *Nash v. Lancegaye (Ireland) Ltd* (1958), the respondent held 49% of the votes, the remainder was held by Nash and others. Following a dispute, the respondent decided to allot more shares and increased his vote to 51%. The court **held** that the main reasoning behind this allotting of more shares was to relegate the plaintiff to a minority. This was not in the best interests of the company as a whole and, therefore, the allotment was ineffective.

In *Re Looe Fish Ltd* (1993), a director who allotted shares to himself and who used his position to block the appointment of directors of whom he did not approve was disqualified for two and a half years.

4. Not use the company's property, information or opportunities for own or anyone else's benefit

A director may not benefit from his or her position as a director or must account to the company for any benefit he or she has accrued unless specified circumstances are involved, which are:

- the company's constitution expressly permits such a benefit;
- there has been a full disclosure and approval by the company in general meeting.

5. Not to agree to a restriction of his or her exercise of independent judgement (unless in specific allowed circumstances)

This duty is derived from the duty of directors to act in the best interest of the company. Directors should not unlawfully fetter their own judgement or discretion, or the judgement of other directors, in their future decision-making powers unless it is expressly permitted in the company's constitution or approved by resolution in general meeting.

An example of this duty can be seen in the case of *Fulham Football Club Ltd and others v. Cabra Estates plc* (1992) in which the court **held** that the directors were in breach of their duties when they received substantial sums in return for undertakings to object to or support, or provide evidence in support of, an application by the council for the compulsory acquisition of the defendant's property.

On appeal it was found that the agreement with the landlords was part of a contract that conferred significant benefits on the company and therefore the directors, in giving their undertaking to Cabra, had **not** improperly fettered the future exercise of their discretion. The court drew a distinction between directors fettering their discretion, which is a clear breach of duty, as opposed to directors exercising their discretion in a manner which restricts their future conduct for the benefit of the company, which is not a breach of duty.

6. To avoid conflicts of interest between themselves and the company

A company director has a duty to avoid any conflict between his or her director's duties to the company and his or her other (including personal) interests, unless it is specifically stated in the company's constitution and agreed in a general meeting (section 228(1)(f) CA 2014).

Conflicts of interest may take one of two forms:

- **(a) Taking a business opportunity for his or her own benefit** Directors may not usurp business opportunities that arise for the company in order to make their own personal profit. In *Cook v. Deeks* (1916) three directors negotiated a contract on behalf of the company and then took it for themselves. **Held**: they had to pay the company the profit they made as a result of the deal (see also *Industrial Development Consultants Ltd v. Cooley* (1972)).
- **(b) A secret interest in another's business** If the director has an interest in another business, he or she must disclose this to the company prior to dealings with the business. In *Aberdeen Railway Co v. Blaikie Bros* (1854), Blaikie Bros had a contract with Aberdeen Railway to make iron rail sockets at £8.50 a ton. Aberdeen Railway argued that they

were not bound by the contract because at that time the chairman of Aberdeen Railway was the managing director of Blaikie Bros and that, therefore, there was a conflict of interest. **Held**: the basic rule is that if a director has an interest in a corporate transaction, the transaction is voidable at the company's will, and it is the duty of the directors to avoid a conflict of interest situation.

7. To exercise reasonable care, skill and diligence

Directors owe a duty to exercise reasonable care, skill and diligence according to their level of knowledge and experience in the discharge of their duties. This duty is owed to the company and aims to protect the company from abuse of power by the directors.

The seminal case in this area is *Re City Equitable Fire Insurance Company Ltd* (1925) in which the liquidators of a company sought to sue the directors for negligence in the manner in which they had made certain investments. The company lost £1.2 million in assets as a result. It turned out that this was mainly due to the deliberate fraud of the managing director of the company. The liquidator sought to make the honest directors personally liable for the loss when the company went into liquidation. The directors escaped liability as the Articles limited their liability for breach of duty. In discharging the duties of his or her position thus ascertained, a director must, of course, act honestly; but he or she must also exercise some degree of both skill and diligence.

Re City Equitable Fire Insurance Company Ltd established three principles:

- the duty to exercise proper skill, care and diligence is subjective in nature and is based on the knowledge and experience of the particular director (objective duty subjectively applied);
- directors can delegate or leave the normal running of the business to the management of the company; and
- a director's duty of care is owed at board meetings only. A director need only attend board meetings regularly.

In *Re Barings plc (No 5)* (2000), Nick Leeson was a futures trader in Singapore for Barings Bank. He fraudulently doctored the bank's accounts, reporting that the bank was making large profits while, in truth, the bank was incurring losses. After an earthquake in Japan, the stock market went into a downward spiral and the truth of the losses was discovered. An action was brought against three of the bank's directors for their failure to supervise Nick Leeson's activities. **Held**: the three directors should be disqualified.

In *Dorchester Finance Co v. Stebbing* (1977), all three directors of a money-lending company were **held** liable in damages for negligence. It was also **held** that the three directors had failed to exhibit the necessary skill, care and diligence in the performance of their duties as directors of the company.

Mr Stebbing was the only director involved full-time in the company's affairs; no board meetings were held; directors signed blank cheques drawn on the company; and the company made a number of loans, on the advice of Mr Stebbing, which, because they were not adequately secured, could not be recovered. The company brought an action against all three directors.

8. To have regard to the interests of the members of the company as well as those of the company's employees

Directors must have regard to the interests of the members of the company as well as the interests of its employees (section 224) in the performance of their duties. This duty does not displace the fact that the directors' duty is to the company alone; it merely imposes an obligation to have regard to the interests of members and employees in exercising this duty to the company. If there are two routes to an end that benefits the company, one route which benefits the members and/or employees and one route which does not, then, in fulfilling this duty, the route which benefits the members and/or employees should be chosen. Directors do not owe duties directly to the shareholders. If duties were owed to the company and the shareholders, this could lead to a conflict of interest for the directors.

Some Other Statutory Duties of Directors

Duty to Provide a Directors' Compliance Statement with the Directors' Report

Directors have a duty to provide a financial report every year to the company (discussed later in this chapter). For all PLCs and all limited companies with turnovers exceeding €25 million and where the balance sheet totals exceeding €12.5 million, a directors' compliance statement must be included (section 225 CA 2014). This is a statement by the directors acknowledging that they are responsible for securing the company's compliance with its legal obligations.

The company's relevant obligations are its obligations under the Companies Act 2014 and the Taxes Consolidation Act 1997. In the compliance statement, the directors must also confirm that a statement setting out the company's policies (which, in the opinion of the directors, are appropriate to the company) respecting relevant obligations has been drawn up, and if this has not been done, specify why not. The directors' compliance statement must also confirm that there are appropriate arrangements and structures designed to secure material compliance with the company's relevant obligations and that a review is conducted every financial year to which the directors' report relates and, if this has not been done, why not. Appropriate structures and procedures includes obtaining professional advice.

Failure to comply with these statutory obligations is classed as a category 3 offence (see **Chapter 15**).

Duty to Disclose any Interest in Contracts made by the Company

In accordance with section 231 CA 2014 directors have a duty to disclose to the board the existence and nature of any personal interest in a contract to be made by the company before a decision is made on it. This disclosure must be made at the first meeting of the directors at which the contract is considered, or the first meeting at which the director is aware of the conflict. A director who fails to disclose his or her interest has committed a category 2 offence.

Duty Regarding Employment Contracts

In accordance with section 249 CA 2014 a director cannot be granted an employment contract with a company for a period exceeding five years and during which his or her employment cannot be terminated by the company by giving notice, or can only be terminated in specified circumstances, unless first approved by a resolution of the company in general meeting.

Other miscellaneous statutory duties include:

- a director is not entitled to a payment for loss of office unless it is disclosed to the members and approved by a resolution of the company at a general meeting (section 250 CA 2014);
- a director has a duty to disclose to the company any payments to be made to him or her in connection with a transfer of shares in the company (section 253 CA 2014). Breach of this duty is classed as a category 3 offence (see **Chapter 15**);
- a director has a duty to disclose his or her interests in company shares and debentures. Such disclosures must be entered into a Register maintained by the company for this purpose (sections 256–266 CA 2014). Breach of this duty is classed as a category 3 offence; and
- a director has a duty to ensure that all reasonable steps are taken by the company to secure compliance with its obligations to maintain accounting records (section 286 CA 2014). Breach of this duty is classed as a category 1 or 2 offence.

Breach of Duties

In accordance with section 232 CA 2014, where a director breaches any of the above duties, he or she may be liable to account to the company for any gain made, directly or indirectly, from the breach of duty, and indemnify the company for any loss or damage resulting from that breach. Any provision exempting officers of the company from liability in respect of a breach of these duties is void (subject to limited statutory exceptions) (section 235 CA 2014).

Transactions with Directors

Part 5 of the Act provides for substantive prohibitions or restrictions on loans to directors and other transactions between a company and its directors.

Substantial Transactions in Respect of Non-cash Assets

The Companies Act 2014 requires a resolution at a general meeting before any substantial property transaction involving the sale of non-cash assets between directors and the company can take place. For these purposes a 'non-cash asset' is of the "requisite value if at the time the arrangement in question is entered into its value is not less than €5,000 but, subject to that, exceeds €65,000 or 10 per cent of the amount of the relevant company's relevant assets", whichever is lower (section 238 CA 2014).

Prohibition of Loans to Directors

Section 239 of the Companies Act 2014 prohibits loans, quasi-loans, credit transactions and guarantees to a director or to connected persons of the company. The **exceptions** to this prohibition on directors' loans include:

- where the value of the arrangement or loan is less than 10% of the value of the net assets of the company;
- where funds are advanced to a director to cover reasonable expenses which are properly incurred and provided within a reasonable time-frame;
- intra-group transactions;
- where the transaction is in the normal course of the company's business (e.g. if the company is an authorised lending institution).

In addition, section 242 does not prohibit a company from making a loan or quasi-loan, entering into a credit transaction, or entering into a guarantee or providing any security, where the summary approval procedure has been followed.

Note: If the terms of loan to a director are not in writing, then it shall be presumed, until the contrary is proved, that the loan is repayable on demand and will be interest-bearing until the time that it is repaid (section 236 CA 2014). On the other hand, if a director or a person connected to that director has made a loan to the company and the loan is unwritten, then there is a presumption that this is not a loan at all, has no interest bearing on the amount and is not repayable by the company (section 237 CA 2014).

Any transaction in contravention of section 239 is voidable by the company, unless restitution is not possible, or where it affects innocent third-party rights. A breach may also result in personal liability without limit where the transaction results in an insolvent liquidation or contributes to the company being unable to pay its debts. Furthermore, the breach is also actionable as a category 2 offence in criminal law.

Removal of Directors

Directors may be removed at a general meeting by ordinary resolution (section 146 CA 2014). An extended notice of 28 days is required in respect of any such resolution to remove a director. The company shall send a copy of this intent to the director and the director has the right to be heard at the meeting, and have a statement by him circulated to the shareholders in advance of the meeting.

A director may have the right to damages for breach of contract for wrongful dismissal or for unfair dismissal if he or she was an employee of the company.

Vacation of Office

A director will have to vacate (step down from) his office as a director should he or she not meet the company's share qualification as set by the constitution of the company. In addition to this requirement, a director must also vacate his or her office as a director if he or she is adjudicated bankrupt or:

- (a) is subject to a disqualification order (see below);
- (b) resigns by notice in writing to the company (see below);
- (c) does not have the capacity to make decisions due to ill health;
- (d) is restricted (see below);
- (e) is sentenced to a term of imprisonment (whether suspended or otherwise) following conviction for an indictable offence; or
- (f) is absent for six months or more from directors' meetings held during this period, without the permission of the other directors.

Remuneration of Directors

Director's salaries must be clearly stated in the company's constitution and will be approved by the board of directors. As mentioned above, directors are also allowed to claim for expenses that are reasonably incurred in connection with the business of the company.

Resignation of Directors

Directors may resign in writing by giving notice as required in their employment contracts.

Restriction and Disqualification of Directors

Restriction

Restriction orders against directors were brought into law by the now obsolete Companies Act 1990. These provisions have been re-stated in sections 818–836 of the Companies Act 2014. Such an order may be brought against directors, as defined under the Act, of a company that is insolvent or going through a process of liquidation to prevent irresponsible directors from writing off the debts of one company to start up another company (this is known colloquially as 'phoenix trading').

A director of an insolvent company is restricted from acting directly or indirectly as a director or a shadow director, or from taking part in the formation or management of a company, for a period of five years. An application for a restriction order can be brought by a director, a liquidator, a receiver or made by the courts. The courts will take into consideration the following requirements of those likely to be restricted:

1. whether the director acted honestly and responsibly in relation to the company;
2. whether the director co-operated with the liquidator in relation to the conduct of the winding up of the company;
3. even where the director has complied with the aforementioned obligations, whether there is any other reason why it would be just and equitable to restrict him or her.

Under certain circumstances, it is possible to continue to act while restricted. A restricted officer of a company may still act as a company director or company secretary where a public limited or unlimited company has an issued share capital of €500,000 and for any other company that has an issued share capital of €100,000. This share capital must be fully paid up in cash.

In discussing the case of *La Moselle Clothing Ltd v. Soualhi* (1998) in the context of a director's duty to act honestly and responsibly in relation to the conduct of the affairs of the company, we have already seen the factors the court will consider in determining whether a director was acting responsibly:

- the extent of the compliance with the Companies Act;
- whether the director's conduct was so incompetent as to be irresponsible;
- the extent of the director's responsibility for any insolvency;
- the extent of the director's responsibility for the net deficiency in assets at winding up;
- the extent to which the director displayed a lack of commercial probity or want of proper standards.

In *Re Tralee Beef and Lamb Ltd: Kavanagh v. Delaney, Dunne & Coyle & Ors* (2008) the applicant, Mr Coyle, was a non-executive director in Tralee Beef and Lamb Ltd, which became insolvent. He was nominated as a director by investors in the company and was a Chartered Accountant by profession. A restriction order was made and he appealed this to the Supreme Court. The terms of his appointment as a non-executive director were that he should receive and review financial information from the executives of the company and attend certain directors' meetings as a non-executive director. He was not, however, to play any active part in the management of the company. The liquidator made a request that he be relieved of his duty to bring a restriction order against Mr Coyle because he himself had formed the view that Mr Coyle had acted honestly and responsibly. The Supreme Court stated that the same duties cannot be expected from executive and non-executive directors. Applying such criteria would not be in line with the realities of what was a small rural company run by the sole executive director, Mr Delaney. Accordingly, the Supreme Court set aside the restriction order placed on Mr Coyle.

A restricted director who continues to act as director of a company may be made personally liable without limit for the debts of the company in a civil action and be guilty of a category 2 offence (see **Chapter 15**).

Disqualification

A disqualification order prohibits a director from any involvement in any company. This is a severe sanction and can be brought against directors, promoters, auditors, officers, liquidators and examiners who may be disqualified for a period of five years or more, according to the discretion of the courts (section 838 CA 2014). In effect, the disqualification order prohibits a person from becoming involved in the formation, promotion or management of any company for the prescribed period.

A person who contravenes a disqualification order may have the period of disqualification extended for a further period of 10 years, may be guilty of a category 2 offence or may be personally liable for the debts of the company should it become insolvent within 12 months of the disqualification order being made.

The following may apply for a disqualification order against a director:

- the Director of Corporate Enforcement;
- the Director of Public Prosecutions;
- the Registrar of Companies;
- any member, contributory, officer, employee, receiver, liquidator, examiner or creditor of the company.

Automatic disqualification orders The common circumstances where the imposition of a disqualification order is automatic include:

- upon conviction for an indictable offence relating to the management of the company;
- upon conviction for an offence involving fraud or dishonesty;
- failing to notify the Registrar of Companies about disqualification in another state;
- being convicted of acting while already restricted;
- conviction for acting while already disqualified.

Discretionary disqualification orders Disqualification orders can be made at the discretion of the courts under the following circumstances:

- when a person has been found guilty of any fraud in relation to the company, its members or creditors;
- when a person has been found guilty of any breach of duty as an officer of the company;
- when a person has been found guilty of fraudulent or reckless trading;
- when the conduct of any officer of a company makes them unfit to manage the company;
- when a report by a court-appointed inspector finds his or her conduct unfit to manage the company;
- when a person has been persistently in default of relevant filing requirements (where three or more instances of default can be shown);
- when a person has been disqualified under the law of another state from being appointed or acting as a director or secretary of a company, and it would be deemed appropriate to make a disqualification order against the person based on his or her conduct or the circumstances which gave rise to the foreign disqualification if it had occurred or arisen in the State.

Burden of proof required for a disqualification order A disqualification order will place significant restrictions on the ability of a person to earn a livelihood and the courts therefore impose a high burden of proof. In *Re Kentford Securities* (2007), the court stated that "given the penal consequences. … A court must feel a high degree of confidence before making such a disqualification order".

In *Chercrest Limited and Riverstown Industrial Estate Management Company Limited v. Slattery and Slattery* (2014) the High Court found that the burden of proof had not been met and declined to impose either a disqualification or restriction order against the directors of the company, which was a family-run business. The rationale for this refusal was that the Slatterys had engaged the services of a professional accountant who advised that they seek an additional investor to put more cash into the business, as opposed to liquidating it. Ultimately, the company's fortunes did not improve and eventually the company was struck off the register by the CRO for failure to file books of account. A strong element of this decision was based on the fact that:

- when financial difficulties arose in the company, the directors engaged *appropriate advice from an accountant* as how best to restructure the business and had acted in good faith based on the advice given; and
- that the parties had acted honestly and reasonably in their dealings in the circumstances.

Relief from a disqualification order A person who is disqualified may apply to the courts for relief and, if the court deems it to be just and equitable, it may grant partial or full relief as it sees fit.

Fraudulent Trading

Fraudulent trading is where any person connected with a company trades with the intention to defraud its creditors.

Section 722 of the Companies Act 2014 provides that, if any person is knowingly a party to the carrying on of the business of a company with intent to defraud creditors of the company or creditors of any other person or for any fraudulent purpose, the person shall be guilty of a category 1 offence.

In *Re Hunting Lodges Ltd* (1985), the company's only asset was a public house called "Durty Nelly's", which was valued at €950,000. The company was insolvent and owed money to the Revenue Commissioners. The pub was sold for €610,000 with an additional €254,000 paid "under the table". **Held**: the sole purpose of the under-the-table payment was to defraud the Revenue Commissioners. The court also held that this single act would constitute fraudulent trading.

In *Re Kelly's Carpetdrome Ltd* (1983), Kelly's Carpetdrome was wound up by the High Court in 1981 at the petition of the Revenue Commissioners. The liquidator brought proceedings against the two directors, Matthew and Eamon Kelly, after discovering falsification and destruction of records at the company. **Held**: the High Court declared that the business of the company was carried on from October 1976 to February 1980 with intent to defraud creditors of the company and for other fraudulent purposes and that the two directors were aware of this. They had acted deliberately to defraud the Revenue Commissioners and were made personally liable for the debts of the company.

Liability for Fraudulent Trading

This offence attracts both civil and criminal liability:

- *civil liability* – the court has the power to declare any person personally liable without limitation for the debts of the company.
- *criminal liability* – as a category 1 offence, the court may impose imprisonment and/or a fine if any person is found guilty of fraudulent trading.

Reckless Trading

Reckless trading is where an officer (i.e. director or company secretary) carries on the business of the company in a reckless manner if, having regard to the general knowledge, skill and experience that may reasonably be expected of a person in that position, the person ought to have known that his or her actions. or those of the company, would cause loss to the company's creditors or if they did not believe on reasonable grounds that the company could pay its debts as they fell due (section 610 CA 2014).

Defence of Acting "Honestly and Reasonably"

In relation to reckless trading, where a court is satisfied that the officer of the company acted "honestly and responsibly" in relation to the conduct of the affairs of the company, this may relieve him or her, either wholly or in part, from personal liability on such terms as the court may think fit.

In the case of *Re Heffernan Kearns (No 2)* (1993), the defendants were directors of a building company that never showed a profit. Both directors took out personal loans and invested them in the company. The company finally went into creditors' liquidation and a liquidator was appointed (see **Chapter 14**). The liquidator sought to hold the directors personally liable. It was **held** that the directors did not act in a reckless manner because they had acted honestly and responsibly in a bid to save their company. The court laid down a number of points regarding the rules on reckless trading, as follows:

- directors do not need to have acted fraudulently to have acted recklessly;
- reckless trading cannot be imposed on the board of directors collectively; the court will need to be satisfied that a director, as an individual, acted in a manner likely to cause loss to creditors;
- the court will engage in objective analysis to ascertain if a director was 'knowingly' trading in a manner likely to cause the creditors loss; this is akin to the 'reasonable man' test, in that the director must have known that he was carrying out business in a manner that would cause loss to his creditors;
- to prove reckless trading, the directors must "know of an obvious and serious risk of loss or damage to others and ignore this risk or be careless or indifferent to the consequences".

STATUTORY AUDITORS

A 'statutory auditor' is an external auditor whose appointment is required by law to review the financial statements of certain companies. The function of an auditor is to provide the shareholders with an independent report as to whether, in the auditor's opinion, the financial statements presented by the directors give a true and fair view of the state of affairs of the company, its profits (or losses) for the relevant period and its financial position.

It is important to distinguish the function of the accountant from the auditor. Accounting is concerned with the process of identifying, measuring and communicating financial and related information. The function of the auditor is to:

- form and express an opinion on the financial statements;
- ensure that the financial statements have been properly prepared in accordance with the accounting provisions of the Companies Act;
- make certain disclosures in the public interest.

The Auditor's Report

Auditors must report to the members of the company on the statutory financial statements (discussed further in this chapter) and present the report at the general meeting (section 391 CA 2014). They must report their opinion as to whether the directors' report is consistent with the statutory financial statements and whether, in the auditors' opinion, these statements are properly prepared in accordance with the relevant financial reporting framework and the legal requirements, and they provide a true and fair view of the financial affairs of the company.

In accordance with section 336(4) CA 2014, this report should also include:

1. whether the auditor has obtained all the information and explanations which, to the best of his or her knowledge and belief, are necessary for the purposes of the audit;
2. whether, in his or her opinion, the accounting records of the company were sufficient to permit the financial statements to be readily and properly audited;
3. whether, in their opinion, information and returns adequate for the audit have been received from branches of the company not visited by him or her; and,
4. in the case of entity financial statements, whether they are in agreement with the accounting records and returns.

Appointment and Re-appointment of Auditors

The first statutory auditors of a company may be appointed by the directors at any time before the first annual general meeting and shall hold office until the conclusion of the annual general meeting (section 382 CA 2014). The tenure of the auditors is from one AGM to the conclusion of the next. At the next AGM, a retiring statutory auditor will be reappointed without any resolution being passed unless:

- he or she is not qualified for re-appointment (e.g. due to bankruptcy or disqualification);
- a resolution has been passed at that meeting appointing another person as auditor;
- a resolution has been passed by the company providing expressly that he or she shall not be re-appointed; or
- the auditor has given express notice in writing of his or her unwillingness of to be re-appointed.

Sometimes a vacancy for the position of statutory auditor may arise between AGMs (due to death, retirement, incapacity or removal of an auditor). This vacancy is known as a 'casual vacancy'. In this situation, the directors of the company have a duty to fill this vacancy as soon as it arises and any person appointed to fill this vacancy as statutory auditor will hold office until the next annual general meeting.

Where a company fails to appoint an auditor, the Office of the Director of Corporate Enforcement (ODCE) must be notified within one week and the director has the power to appoint an auditor. If a company fails to inform the ODCE, then the company and any officer in default may be guilty of a category 3 offence (see **Chapter 15**).

Qualifications of Statutory Auditors

Section 1441 CA 2014 requires that a public auditor must hold a relevant qualification from one of the six professional accounting bodies recognised by the Irish Auditing and Accounting Supervisory Authority (IAASA) and hold a valid practising certificate. These bodies (known as 'recognised accountancy bodies' (RABs)) are:

(a) the Association of Chartered Certified Accountants;
(b) the Institute of Chartered Accountants in Ireland;
(c) the Institute of Chartered Accountants in England and Wales;
(d) the Institute of Chartered Accountants of Scotland;
(e) the Institute of Certified Public Accountants in Ireland; and
(f) the Institute of Incorporated Public Accountants.

Ineligibility of Statutory Auditors

The following persons are ineligible to act as the statutory auditor of a company:

1. an officer or employee of the company;
2. an ex-officer or ex-employee of the company within a period in respect of which accounts would be audited by him or her if appointed auditor;
3. a parent, spouse, brother, sister or child of an officer of the company;
4. a partner or employee of an officer of the company;
5. a person disqualified from being an auditor of the company's holding company or subsidiary;
6. a body corporate;
7. a person in whose name a share in the company is registered, whether or not that person is the beneficial owner of the share.

Resignation of Statutory Auditors

A statutory auditor may resign on giving written notice to the company (section 400 CA 2014). A statutory auditor who has resigned may attend the next annual general meeting, as well as any meeting where a vacancy has arisen due to his or her resignation, and must be given a copy of all communication regarding that meeting. The statutory auditor also has the right to be heard at this meeting, on any matter concerning the audit. If default is made in complying with the above requirements, the company and any officer of it who is default shall be guilty of a category 3 offence (see **Chapter 15**).

Removal of the Statutory Auditor

An auditor may be removed from office by an ordinary resolution passed by the shareholders of a company (section 394 CA 2014). This resolution requires an extended notice of 28 days. The statutory auditor who is removed must be sent a copy of the intended resolution and in return should be given the opportunity to make written representations to the company in general meeting. The removal of a statutory auditor must only be due to his or her lack of performance or conduct, and that it is in the best interest of the company.

Rights, Obligations and Duties of Statutory Auditors

The rights, obligations and duties of statutory auditors are outlined in sections 368 to 393 CA 2014. The statutory auditor has certain rights to enable him or her to gather the information required to prepare the report to be presented to the company at general meeting. He or she has the right to:

- access at all reasonable times to the accounting records of the company;
- question the relevant persons in the company and receive explanations and information;
- information and explanations concerning subsidiary companies;
- attend any general meetings of the company and to receive all notices and communications regarding the general meetings;
- be heard at the general meetings on matters concerning the auditors.

If a company officer knowingly or recklessly makes a statement in a written or oral form to the auditor that is misleading or false in a material manner, then that officer is guilty of a category 2 offence.

The main duties of an auditor are:

- **Duty to report to members** – the auditor must report to the members via the auditor's report, confirming "as to whether, in the auditor's opinion, the financial statements presented by the directors give a true and fair view of the financial affairs of the company". (The auditor's report is discussed later in this chapter.)
- **Duty to report any failure by the directors to keep proper books of account** – the auditor is under an obligation to report to the Registrar of Companies within seven days if the directors do not keep proper accounting records.
- **Duty to act with professional integrity** – a statutory auditor has a duty under the codes of practice of the professional accountancy bodies to which he or she belongs to act with professional integrity.
- **Duty to ensure compliance with taxation law** – where an auditor becomes aware that the company is committing an offence in relation to taxation, the auditor must communicate the offence to the company and request that it take remedial action to rectify the situation or the auditor must notify an officer of the Revenue Commissioners.

- **Duty to notify the Director of Corporate Enforcement** and provide details where an auditor is of the opinion that a company, its officers or agents have committed a category 1 or 2 offence under the Companies Act.

Common Law Duty of Skill and Care

In addition to their statutory duties, auditors owe a duty to act with due skill and care in the performance of their role as company auditors.

This duty was seen in the case of *Hedley Byrne & Co. Ltd v. Heller and Partners Ltd* (1964). The plaintiffs, Hedley Byrne & Co, were advertising agents who intended to engage in an advertising programme for Easipower Ltd, which would cost about £100,000. They asked their own bankers, National Provincial Bank Ltd, to obtain a reference for Easipower; National Provincial wrote to the defendants, Heller and Partners, Easipower's bankers, who replied in a letter stating that it was:

> "For your private use and without responsibility on the part of the bank or its officials".

The letter went on to say that Easipower was a

> "respectably constituted company, considered good for its ordinary business engagements. Your figures are larger than we are accustomed to see".

Easipower went into liquidation and the plaintiffs lost £17,000. The House of Lords **held** that, on the facts, there was no liability due to a valid disclaimer. However, the House of Lords accepted the principle that a duty could arise if an auditor fails to perform his or her duty with reasonable skill and care.

There was a contrary decision in the English case of *Caparo Industries plc v. Dickman* (1990) where a shareholder in Fidelity Plc bought shares in a company after receiving the audited accounts and later made a takeover bid. Following the takeover, the plaintiff sued the auditors alleging that the audited accounts were misleading in that they showed a profit where in fact there had been a loss. It was **held** by the court that auditors of a public company owe no duty of care to the public at large who rely on accounts when purchasing shares in a company; nor was any duty owed to individual shareholders who purchased additional shares. The precedent of *Caparo* has not yet been followed in this jurisdiction. In Ireland, an auditor is only liable in negligence to a third party where he or she knew or ought to have known that the third party would act in reliance on his or her report.

Liability of Statutory Auditors

An auditor is liable to the company for a loss caused by negligent performance of his duty. In *Re Kingston Cotton Mill* (1896) the duty to investigate and report was described by the court as a duty to be "a watch-dog, but not a bloodhound".

In *Re Thomas Gerrard & Sons Ltd* (1967), a managing director falsified accounts by including non-existent stock. As a result of these overstated profits, additional taxes were paid by the company and dividends declared which otherwise would not have been. The auditors became suspicious when they noticed altered invoices, but accepted the MD's explanation. **Held**: the auditors were found to be negligent. The discovery of altered invoices put the auditors on enquiry and, by not investigating the irregularities further, they failed in their duty to exercise reasonable care and skill. Their breach of duty was a direct cause of loss to the company in tax revenues and dividends otherwise payable so that the firm of auditors and the MD were both liable to the company for this loss. The court noted that standards of reasonable care and skill were more exacting than in 1896. However, they affirmed the view expressed in *Kingston* that:

> "If there is nothing which ought to excite suspicion, less care may properly be considered reasonable than can be so considered if suspicion ought to have been aroused".

In *Kelly v. Haughey Boland & Co* (1989), Cavan Crystal expressed an interest in taking over Royal Tara Ltd, and asked to have a look at its accounts for the years 1972–1976. The years 1972–1974 were already prepared by the auditors and handed over to Cavan Crystal. They subsequently prepared the years 1975–1976 with knowledge of the plaintiff's interest. The defendant had not attended physically at stocktakes over a 20-year period. **Held**: physically attending stocktakes, although not compulsory, was considered "good practice" in the industry. While not attending all of the stocktakes would not amount to a breach of duty, failure to attend any over a 20-year period amounted to negligence. They should have foreseen at the time the second set of accounts were audited that the third party would rely upon them.

As discussed above in *Caparo Industries plc v. Dickman* (1990), the English Court of Appeal adopted a narrow approach to the duty owed by auditors to third parties in tort.

Audit Exemption

Private Company Limited by Shares (LTD)

A small private company is exempt from an audit provided it meets two of the following criteria:

- turnover of the company does not exceed €8.8 million;
- the balance sheet total of the company does not exceed €4.4 million;
- the average number of employees of the company does not exceed 50.

The company also cannot be classified as a subsidiary, a bank, an insurance company or a stockbroking or investment company to qualify for exemption.

A medium-sized private company is exempt from an audit if it meets the following criteria:

- the turnover of the company does not exceed €20 million; and
- the balance sheet total does not exceed €10 million.

Only private companies can avail of an exemption from audit on the basis of size – PLCs, PUCs and PULCs will not be able to avail of such an exemption.

Company Limited by Guarantee (CLG)

The availability of the audit exemption has been extended to CLGs, providing that, if any one member does **not** wish the audit exemption to be available to the company in that financial year, the CLG will **not** be entitled to avail of the audit exemption in that financial year.

Dormant Company

A "dormant" company (a company which has no significant accounting transactions during the year and has only intragroup assets and liabilities) may avail of a "special" audit exemption.

THE COMPANY SECRETARY

The role of the company secretary is to advise the board on its responsibilities under company law and to ensure that these are complied with. Every company must have a company secretary, who can also be a company director (section 129 CA 2014), though if a company has only one director (i.e. a LTD), that person may not also be the company secretary.

Under the Companies Act 2014, the obligation to ensure compliance with company law now rests entirely on the company's director or directors and is no longer a requirement of the company secretary (although in reality the tasks he or she performs revolve around regulatory compliance). The company secretary is an officer of the company.

Appointment of the Company Secretary

On a company's initial formation, the name of the first company secretary must be provided to the CRO along with the constitution of the company.

Qualifications of a Company Secretary

PLCs, under CA 2014, may now have only one director; however, if the company has only one director it must have a company secretary, although this secretary is not required to have any formal qualifications.

Directors have a duty to ensure that the company secretary has the necessary skills and resources to fulfil his or her statutory duties (section 129(4) CA 2014).

In the case of a PLC, section 1112 CA 2014 states that the qualification/experience requirements for the company secretary are as follows:

- the person appointed must have held the office of secretary of a company for a minimum of three of the five years immediately preceding the appointment as secretary to that company; or
- the person must be a member of a body recognised as appropriate by the minister; or
- he or she, by virtue of holding or having held another position or being a member of another body, appears to the directors to be capable of discharging company secretarial duties.

Persons Prohibited from being a Company Secretary

A person who is a minor (under 18 years of age), an undischarged bankrupt or a restricted or disqualified person are prohibited from acting as a company secretary.

Duties of a Company Secretary

Section 226 of the Companies Act 2014 explains that the duties of the secretary of a company shall, without derogating from the secretary's statutory and other legal duties, be such duties as are delegated to him or her from time to time by the board of directors of the company.

The secretary, although an officer of the company, fulfils an administrative rather than managerial role. Though his or her duties are determined by the company's directors upon appointment, rather than set out explicitly in the Companies Act, some common tasks of the company secretary are as follows.

The company secretary maintains registers required under company law, such as the:

- register of members;
- register of directors and secretaries;
- register of directors' and secretaries' interests in shares and debentures;
- register of the instruments which create charges.

With regard to company meetings, the company secretary:

- convenes meetings of members,
- maintains minutes of meetings,
- supplies financial statements to members in advance of meetings within specified timeframes; and
- ensures financial statements are available for viewing by those who are entitled to do so.

The secretary also safeguards the company seal, files the necessary forms within applicable deadlines with the CRO, as well as delivering resolutions, and ensures that the requisite details are supplied on company correspondence.

The secretary is obliged to provide sufficient details to the company to enable it maintain an accurate register and is required to:

- disclose any interests he or she may have in any shares and or debentures held in the company or any holding in subsidiary companies; and
- notify the company where he or she enters into a contract to sell or exercise a right to subscribe or assigns a right to subscribe for shares or debentures in that company, its parent or subsidiaries.

Powers of a Company Secretary

A company secretary has authority to enter into contracts within his or her sphere of competence, i.e. the day-to-day administration of the company. The company secretary has the authority to bind the company, as the constitution puts no limits to the officer's authority, although this has historically been interpreted to include only actions that fall within the normal remit of the secretary's duties.

In *Panorama Developments (Guildford) Ltd v. Fidelis Furnishing Fabrics Ltd* (1971), the English Court of Appeal **held** that a company secretary was entitled to sign contracts connected with the administrative side of a company's affairs, such as employing staff, ordering cars, etc. All such matters now come within the ostensible authority of a company's secretary.

MEETINGS

All directors manage the company through meetings. This is also the forum where the board members and directors act collectively. The rules on meetings reflect the division of power between the members who exercise their powers through the general meetings, and the board of directors who exercise their powers through board meetings. There are five main types of company meeting:

- annual general meetings;
- extraordinary general meetings
- meetings of the board of directors;
- class meetings; and
- court-ordered meetings.

Annual General Meetings

A single-member company (i.e. a company with only one member) may dispense with holding an annual general meeting (AGM).

With the exception of single-member companies, all companies are required by section 175 CA 2014 to hold annual general meetings (AGMs) every calendar year, not more than 15 months after the previous one. Newly incorporated companies are allowed an 18-month period from incorporation within which to have their first meeting.

In the case of a private company limited by shares, section 175(3) allows it to dispense with this requirement provided the members entitled to attend and vote at this meeting sign a written resolution: (a) acknowledging receipt of the financial statements that would have been laid before the meeting; (b) resolving all such matters as would have been resolved at that meeting; and (c) confirming no change is proposed in the appointment of the person (if any) who stands appointed as statutory auditor of the company.

The AGM can be held within or outside the State. Should it be held outside the State, the company, at its expense, must ensure that people can attend it using technological means, without having to leave the State.

Section 186 CA 2014 requires the annual general meeting to consider the following:

- the company's statutory financial statements (balance sheet, profit and loss account, etc.);
- the auditor's report;
- the directors' report.

These must be placed before the members for their approval. In addition, the meeting must facilitate a review by the members of the company's affairs.

The constitution of the company will then outline any other ordinary business that needs to be carried out by the AGM, including:

- declaration of dividends;
- the election of directors and auditors in place of those retiring, or the reappointment of retiring directors or auditors;
- fixing the remuneration of auditors or directors.

Under section 175 CA 2014, a copy of the financial statements and the reports must be sent to the members, any debenture holders and any other entitled persons, at least 21 days before the AGM.

Extraordinary General Meetings

A company requires an extraordinary general meeting (EGM) if it is proposed to do something new. All business at an EGM constitutes special business (i.e. business other than ordinary business of the company). An EGM can be convened by:

- a member or members, unless the constitution of the company provides otherwise; or
- members of a company with 50% or more of paid-up share capital or voting rights; or
- the directors, following a request by members of a company with a shareholding of not less than10% of the paid-up capital; or
- by a court in accordance with section 179 CA 2014. (This right will be discussed in greater detail in the latter part of this chapter.)

Members of the company must deposit at the registered office of the company a signed requisition stating the resolutions that they propose. The directors are obliged, within 21 days of the requisition deposit, to convene an EGM to be held within two months of the deposit of the requisition. If they fail to so do, half of the members requisitioning the meeting can convene a meeting within three months of the requisition date.

Meetings of the Board of Directors

Meetings are held so that the board of directors can make decisions regarding the direction of the company. The directors vote on decisions that need to be made and the chairperson has the casting vote. The basic rules of a meeting apply, in that it must have the requisite forum (see below), the appropriate notice and the proceedings must be conducted properly.

The best practice procedures for a meeting of a board or directors are as follows:

- the directors elect a chairperson of the meeting among themselves;
- the chairperson has a casting vote; and
- the managing director has the second casting vote.

The minimum quorum for a directors' meeting is two directors. Minutes must be kept of all board meetings.

Indoor Management Rule

The 'indoor management rule' (also known as the Rule in *Turquand*'s case) provides that outsiders to the company are entitled to presume that the internal regulations of the company are adhered to correctly according to the company's constitution.

This presumption was first set out in the case of the *Royal British Bank v. Turquand* (1856). In this case, the directors borrowed in excess of an authorised amount without the approval of the shareholders, and then argued that the loan from the Royal British Bank was invalid (due to its *ultra vires* nature). The company directors were only entitled to borrow above a certain sum if they were authorised by an ordinary resolution of a company meeting. The directors borrowed the money from the bank without ensuring the proper procedures were adhered to. It was **held** that the bank could presume that the internal regulations of the company were correctly adhered to. Therefore, the borrowing was within the company's powers. The court held that the loan was valid and accordingly it had to be repaid.

It is important to note, however, that the indoor management rule does not apply if the facts of the case cause suspicion, and the third party should make further enquiries. In *AL Underwood Limited v. Bank of Liverpool & Martins* (1924), Mr Underwood, who was the director of his company, AL Underwood Ltd, had a personal account with the defendant's bank. He paid company cheques into his personal bank account. When the company got into financial difficulty the receiver sued the bank for the money lodged into Underwood's personal account. The court **held** that the lodging of company cheques into a personal account was so unusual that the bank should have been on notice of a suspicious transaction and should have made further enquiries. Thus the bank was not successful and had to return the monies to the company.

Class Meetings

The company generally convenes a meeting with holders of different classes of shares when it is necessary to obtain approval from that class. This is usually when there is a proposed variation of class rights (e.g. if the company wants to change the rate of dividend payable to preference shareholders). Generally, class meetings are likely to be held at the same time as general meetings.

Court-ordered Meetings

Under section 179 CA 2014, the High Court may order a meeting to be convened, held and conducted on the application of the following persons:

- a director of the company;
- a member of the company who would be entitled to vote at a general meeting;
- the personal representative of a deceased member of the company;
- the assignee in bankruptcy of a bankrupt member of the company.

This only arises where the court is satisfied that it is impracticable or undesirable for any person to call a general meeting of the company or to conduct a general meeting in any manner provided by the Companies Act 2014 or the company's constitution. For example, in *Re El Sombrero Ltd* (1958) the company comprised three shareholders; one shareholder held 90% of the shares and the other two held 5% each. However, the majority shareholder was not a director of the company – but both minorities were. When the majority shareholder wanted to remove the minority shareholders from their position as directors as a consequence of mismanagement, he requisitioned an EGM to pass an ordinary resolution. However, the minority shareholders failed to attend this meeting and subsequent meetings requisitioned for this same purpose and as the quorum for the meetings was set at two, he could not conduct the meeting or pass the resolution in their absence. After numerous failed attempts to conduct this meeting, he made an application to the court. The court subsequently requisitioned the meeting allowing a quorum of one to facilitate the majority shareholder in passing the resolution to effect the removal of the company's directors.

Validity of Meetings

To constitute a valid meeting, there must be a chairperson and a quorum.

Quorums

A quorum is the minimum number of persons that, according to the company's constitution, is necessary in order that the meeting commences business. The quorum constitutes those members present in person, as well as those present by proxy.

Section 182 CA 2014 states that "[n]o business shall be transacted at any general meeting of a company unless a quorum of members is present at the time when the meeting proceeds to business".

Unless its constitution provides otherwise, two members of a company present in person or by proxy at a general meeting shall be a quorum. In the case of a single-member company, one member of the company present in person or by proxy at a general meeting shall be a quorum. The quorum must be present within 15 minutes of the commencement of the meeting, otherwise the chairperson must adjourn the meeting. It is not necessary that the quorum is present when voting on resolutions takes place.

If a meeting is not properly constituted, the outcome of the meeting is voidable, but not void. The courts have discretion as to whether they will set aside particular resolutions or not.

Chairperson

A chairperson must preside over the meetings. The chairperson of the general meeting is generally the chairperson of the board of directors or may be appointed by the company's constitution. The chairperson's duties include:

- ensuring that the meeting is conducted properly;
- preserving the order of the meeting and adjourning it where necessary;
- deciding on matters relating to motions and amendments;
- demanding a poll, if appropriate; and
- declaring the result of a poll.

The chairperson has the authority to adjourn a meeting with the consent of the members or where it becomes disorderly. In *Kinsella v. Alliance & Dublin Gas Consumer Company* (1982), the court **held** that the chairman had no power to adjourn a meeting without the consent of the majority, as it was not a disorderly meeting.

Procedural Requirements

There are a number of requirements to ensure that the proceedings of a meeting are valid. These are as follows:

Notice for Meetings Except where the constitution of a company provides for the giving of greater notice, the required notice for general meetings is as set out in section 181 CA 2014:

- the minimum notice period for an AGM is 21 days;
- the notice requirement for an EGM is seven days if an ordinary resolution is required but the company must give a notice of 21 days if it is a special resolution.

However, this requirement of a formal notice can be waived if 90% of members entitled to vote agree and also the statutory auditor agrees in writing.

Form of notice required Notice must be in writing and must specify:

- the place, date and time of the meeting;
- the general nature of the business to be transacted at the meeting;
- in the case of a proposed special resolution, the text or substance of that proposed special resolution; and
- with reasonable prominence a statement that:
    - a member entitled to attend and vote is entitled to appoint a proxy using the form set out (see section 184 CA 2014) or, where that is allowed, one or more proxies, to attend, speak and vote instead of him or her;
    - a proxy need not be a member; and

- the time by which the name of the proxy must be received at the company's registered office or some other place within the State as is specified in the statement for that purpose.

Resolutions A resolution is a decision requiring approval by the voting members of the company. There are two types of resolutions: ordinary and special:

- **Ordinary resolutions** are resolutions that require a simple majority of the votes cast, in person or by proxy, by members of the company entitled to vote at a general meeting (section 191(1) CA 2014).
- **Special resolutions** are required for alteration to the authorised capital, most of the provisions of the company's constitution, change of company name, reduction in share capital, certain types of company liquidations, or variation of class rights. They require a majority of not less than 75% of the votes cast, in person or by proxy, by members of the company entitled to vote at a general meeting (section 191(2)). The 21-day notice period required for a general meeting at which a special resolution is proposed can be reduced if 90% of the members agree.

In addition to ordinary and special resolutions, other resolutions of the company include:

- **Unanimous written resolutions** This is a resolution in writing signed by all members of a company entitled to attend and vote on such resolutions at a general meeting. It is deemed valid and effective as if the resolution had been passed at a general meeting (section 193 CA 2014). If a company or a signatory fails to comply with the above requirements, the company and any officer of it who is in default shall be guilty of a category 4 offence (see **Chapter 15**).
- **Majority written resolutions** An ordinary or special resolution can also be passed by a majority written resolution. This resolution is deemed to be passed at a meeting held seven or 21 days after the last member to sign (depending upon whether it is ordinary or special). All such resolutions must be delivered to the CRO. This does not apply to:
  - a resolution to remove a director; or
  - a resolution to effect the removal of a statutory auditor from office.

Voting

In order to vote on a resolution, a member must be registered in the Register of Members. There are two methods for voting, namely on a show of hands or on a poll:

1. on a show of hands, every member, or proxy, present has one vote only;
2. on a poll, every member, whether present in person or by proxy, has one vote for every share held.

Where a contentious issue is being decided, or where the outcome of a show of hands is unclear, members may wish to call for a poll vote. This poll vote takes place by means of a secret ballot. Under section 188 CA 2014, a poll can only be validly demanded by:

(a) the chairperson;
(b) at least three members present in person or their proxies;
(c) members or proxies representing not less than 10% of the total voting rights or 10% of the paid-up capital.

Proxies

A 'proxy' is a person appointed by shareholders to attend, speak and vote on their behalf at a general meeting (section 186 CA 2014). A proxy need not be a member of the company.

Unless the company's constitution provides otherwise, a member of the company may not appoint more than one proxy to attend at the same occasion.

The right to appoint must be contained in every notice of a meeting to members. Under section 183(6) CA 2014, members cannot be compelled to submit proxy forms to the company more than 48 hours before the meeting.

An instrument appointing a proxy, must state the name of the company, the name and address of the member, the name and address of the proxy and which way the proxy is to vote on behalf of the member.

There are several types of proxy, including:

- A **general proxy** which can give the power to represent the member at more than one general meeting.
- With a **special proxy**, the authority only covers one meeting. The proxy form will indicate who is appointed as proxy. It can be the chairman or another individual, often a solicitor or an accountant. If the member is a company, the proxy must be signed by two directors and sealed.
- The **two-way proxy** entitles the proxy to vote for or against a particular motion in accordance with the member's wishes. Results may then enable the proxy to act as he or she wishes on other matters, which may arise at the meeting.

Minutes of Meetings

Minutes are an official account of a meeting. They must be taken by one individual and then approved at the next meeting, once all board members have had the opportunity to review and make any corrections (section 199 CA 2014). They are signed by the chairperson of the meeting at which the minutes were taken. Therefore, they are *prima facie* evidence of what took place at the meeting.

A company shall, if required by the Director of Corporate Enforcement, produce to the Director for inspection its minute book and provide the Director with facilities for inspecting and taking copies of its contents.

The minutes of meetings must be properly maintained. These minutes must be maintained at the company's registered office and must be open to inspection by company members without charge for at least two hours per day.

If a company fails to comply with its obligations regarding the proper maintenance of minutes, the company, and any officer of it who is in default, shall be guilty of a category 4 offence.

COMPANY ACCOUNTING RECORDS, RETURNS, REGISTERS AND REPORTS

Company accounting records must record and explain the day-to-day transactions of a company. These records should enable users to determine the overall state of the company's financial status accurately at any time. Records should be accurate and correct to enable the directors to comply with the Companies Act and to allow proper auditing of the company.

A company must keep adequate accounting records that enable statutory financial statements to be prepared, and must file annual returns with the CRO.

Accounting Records

A company's accounting records represent the financial memory of the company; they are important for the analysis of company performance and for ensuring regulatory compliance.

According to section 282 of the Companies Act 2014, these accounting records must be kept to:

(a) record and correctly explain the transactions of the company;
(b) enable, at any time, the assets, liabilities, financial position and profit or loss of the company to be determined with reasonable accuracy;
(c) enable the directors to ensure that the statutory financial statements of the company and the directors' report comply with company law; and
(d) enable the financial statements of the company to be audited.

The accounting records must be kept on a continuous and consistent basis, i.e. the entries in them shall be made in a timely manner and be consistent from one period to the next.

Accounting records must be kept at the registered office of the company or at such other place as the directors think fit. If these books are kept outside the State, the company must send to and keep at a place in the State such information and returns relating to the business dealt with in the accounting records as discloses with reasonable accuracy the assets, liabilities, financial position and profit or loss of that business at intervals not exceeding six months, and enables the preparation of the company's statutory financial statements required by section 290 or 293 and the directors' report required by section 325 CA 2014.

An accounting record is required to be kept by the company concerned for at least six years after the end of the financial year containing the latest date to which the record, information or return relates.

If a company officer fails to maintain accounting records, he or she may be guilty of a category 1 or 2 offence (see **Chapter 15**).

Financial Statements

The financial statements are presented to members of the company at the AGM. They should include a record of all the assets and liabilities of the company. Section 338 CA 2014 requires the directors of the company to lay before the AGM financial statements, annexed to a copy of the directors' report and the auditor's report. The financial statements must also be filed with the CRO. Small and medium-sized companies may avail of exemptions when returning financial statements with the annual return.

Annual Returns

All companies with a share capital are obliged to file an annual return on an annual basis with the CRO (with the exception of those in the course of winding up or strike off – see **Chapter 14**) within 28 days of the annual return date. The annual return is a document containing general information about a company's directors and registered office, shareholders and share capital. It is a separate document to the company's annual accounts and must contain certain prescribed information, including:

- the name and registered number of the company;
- the address of the registered office of the company;
- the financial period covered by the return;

- details of all shares issued for cash or other consideration, any calls made on shares that have been received or remain unpaid, any commission paid or discounts given on shares or debentures;
- particulars of the total amount of indebtedness of the company that is secured by mortgages or charges, which are required to be registered;
- a list of all persons, including names and addresses, who are members of the company, and of persons who have ceased to be members since the date of the last return;
- details of shares held by each of the existing members, specifying the shares transferred since the date of the last return;
- particulars of the directors and secretaries to be entered in the company's register of directors and secretaries.

The annual return should have attached to it the annual financial statements as defined above. Every company must deliver to the CRO successive annual returns in compliance with the company's annual return date. These annual returns can be filed electronically or in a paper format. The company and any officer of it in default of these requirements will be guilty of a category 3 offence (see **Chapter 15**).

Except for the first annual return made by the company after it is incorporated, the following documents that have been, or are to be, laid before the relevant general meeting, must be annexed to the annual return:

- the statutory financial statements of the company (balance sheet and profit and loss account);
- the directors' report, including the directors' compliance statement (see **Chapter 13**); and
- the statutory auditors' report.

Annual Return Date

On the commencement of the Companies Act 2014, on 1 June 2015, all existing companies retain their existing annual return date (ARD). Companies incorporated after this Act came into existence are allocated an annual return date six months after its date of incorporation, and, in each subsequent year, the ARD will be the anniversary of its first annual return date (section 345 CA 2014).

Directors' Report

Section 325 of the Companies Act 2014 requires that a report by the directors on the state of the company's financial affairs must be appended to the accounts laid before the general meeting.

This report must include a review of general matters in relation to the company and the directors, a business review of the financial year, information on the acquisition or disposal of own shares by company officers, information on interests in shares or debentures held by company officers and a statement on any relevant audit information. Where appropriate, it should also contain statements regarding audit committees and compliance statements.

The directors' report must contain the following information:

- the names of the persons who, at any time during the financial year, were directors of the company;
- the principal activities of the company during the year;
- a statement of the measures taken by the directors to secure compliance with the requirements regarding the maintenance of accounting records, and the exact location of those records;
- the amount of any interim dividends paid by the directors during the year and the amount, if any, that the directors recommend should be paid by way of final dividend.

Where relevant in a particular financial year, the directors' report should also state:

- particulars of any important events affecting the company which have occurred since the end of that year;
- an indication of the activities, if any, of the company in the field of research and development;
- an indication of the existence of branches of the company outside the State and the country in which each such branch is located;
- details of political donations made during the year that are required to be disclosed by the Electoral Act 1997;
- the directors' compliance statement, where relevant.

Registers that must be Maintained by a Company

There are a number of different books and records that must be maintained under the provisions of the Companies Acts, in order to make them available to members of the public, including the company's shareholders. These are among others:

- register of members
- register of directors and secretaries
- register of interests;
- register of debenture holders
- the minute books.

Register of Members The register of members is required to be kept under section 169 CA 2014. It must contain:

- the names and addresses of the members;
- a statement of the shares held by each member, including the amount paid on these shares;
- the date at which each person was entered in the register as a member; and
- the date at which any person ceased to be a member.

The register is a public document that must be available to members of the public. The company must return details of any allotment of shares to the Registrar of Companies within one month. A company cannot refuse to register a person who has lawfully acquired shares as a member, unless the company's rules allow it.

Register of Directors and Secretaries Section 149 CA 2014 requires a company to keep, at its registered office and available for inspection, a register of directors and secretaries. This must contain the following in relation to every director:

- his or her present forename and surname and any former forename and surname;
- his or her date of birth;
- his or her usual residential address;
- his or her nationality;
- his or her business occupation, if any; and
- details of any other directorships held by him or her or that have been held by him or her.

In relation to the company secretary, the register must contain the following information:

1. in the case of an individual:
   (a) his or her present forename and surname and any former forename and surname;
   (b) his or her usual residential address; and
   (c) his or her date of birth; and
2. in the case of a company, the company name and, if the company is registered:
   (a) its registered office;
   (b) the register in which it is registered; and
   (c) the number under which it is registered in that register.

Where any information in these registers is amended, notification must be made to the Registrar with 14 days.

Register of Interests Section 267 CA 2014 places minimum disclosure requirements on every company in relation to the disclosure of the interests of directors or the secretary of the company every time it grants a right to subscribe for shares in, or debentures of, the company. The company is required to enter in the register of interests against the relevant director or secretary's name the date on which shares or debentures were granted, the period during which they are exercisable, the amount paid and the description of shares and debentures.

If default is made by a company in complying with the above, the company and any officer of it who is in default shall be guilty of a category 3 offence (see **Chapter 15**).

Minute Books

As discussed above, a minute book of company board meeting and members' meetings must be kept. The minutes of the company's general meetings must be made available to members of the public for inspection.

Conclusion

This chapter discussed: the roles of directors, the company secretary and the auditor; the scope and procedures of the different types of company meeting; and the requirements for the maintenance of the records of the company. In short, the entire management of the company was discussed.

The next chapter discusses the financing of a company, including how the company may raise finance, the different types of shares and the roles and responsibilities of the shareholders.

REVIEW QUESTIONS

(See Solutions to Review Questions at the end of this text.)

Question 12.1

(a) Explain the distinction between executive and non-executive directors.
(b) Explain the procedure for the appointment of company directors, after their initial appointment.
(c) Explain the difference between an ordinary resolution and a special resolution under any **three** headings.

Question 12.2

Porter has received a letter from the Director of Corporate Enforcement notifying him that an application has been brought to the High Court seeking his disqualification as a company director. Porter has contacted you for advice in this regard.

Requirement Write a **memo** to Porter that:

(a) Explains the effect of a disqualification order.
(b) States any **six** grounds upon which such an order can be imposed, either automatically or at the absolute discretion of the court.
(c) Advises Porter on the effect of acting in breach of a disqualification order.

Question 12.3

Regal Airways Limited ('Regal') was dissatisfied with the quality of passenger meals being provided by its catering contractor and the directors decided to look for alternate caterers. After much debate and following some lobbying from one of Regal's directors, Sam, they decided to offer the contract to Dragon Catering Services ('Dragon').

Two months after this decision was taken, it came to the attention of Regal's board of directors that Sam's sister is the managing director of Dragon and has a 50% ownership interest in it. Following further investigation, Regal's directors also discovered that Sam has a 25% ownership interest in Dragon and the remaining 25% is held by Sam's brother-in-law.

Following this discovery, Regal is considering taking legal action against Sam for breach of his statutory duties and are also considering removing him as a company director of Regal.

Requirement:

(a) Explain the statutory duty in relation to directors' disclosure obligations regarding contracts. Determine whether Sam's actions amount to a breach of his statutory duties to Regal.
(b) Give the procedure that Regal must comply with in order to effect a lawful removal of Sam as company director.

Question 12.4

Allen Enterprises Limited ('Allen') is an on-line gambling company. In the first three years of operation, Allen's turnover was less than €7.3 million and therefore the company was eligible for an audit exemption. This year, Allen's turnover is in excess of €10 million and Allen's accountant has informed the directors that the accounts will need to be audited before presentation to the shareholders at the annual general meeting (AGM).

Requirement Last month, the directors of Allen appointed Paddison Chartered Accountants ('Paddison') as Allen's auditor. Paddison has been asked to prepare an explanatory note for Allen's shareholders which:

(a) Outlines the role of an auditor and his or her respective requisite qualifications.
(b) Lists any **three** powers available to an auditor when conducting an audit.
(c) States the procedure necessary to effect the removal of an auditor.

Question 12.5

Fiona has worked for Cruise Publications Limited since 2000 as an accounts assistant. Twelve months ago, Cruise Publications Limited was taken over by another company, Parkway Publications Ltd. Since this takeover Fiona has been experiencing problems with her new manager who wants her to change certain aspects of her employment contract. One of the new tasks that Fiona's manager wishes to add to her job description is the preparation of the company's annual return. Fiona has never completed an annual return and is unsure what it involves.

Requirement:

(a) Give any **four** pieces of information included in an annual return, and list the documents that must be annexed to the annual return.
(b) Outline the date on which the annual return must be filed and assess any **two** consequences of failure to file an annual return.

Question 12.6

Brendan and Barbara are a husband and wife team who have been running a successful hairdressing business, in the form of a partnership, for the last 10 years. They now want to expand the business and to open branches across the Republic of Ireland. To support this, they are considering converting their partnership to a limited company. They now seek advice in relation to the following matters:

Requirement:

(a) They wish to know the people who are ineligible to act as a director of a company. List any **four** people who are ineligible to act as a company director and state the minimum number of directors that an Irish private limited company must have.
(b) In relation to directors' duties:
    (i) Define a substantial transaction in respect of non-cash assets involving directors (known as substantial property transactions), and explain the statutory duty imposed upon a director when a substantial property transaction occurs.

(ii) Explain the fiduciary duty imposed upon directors to act with proper care, skill and diligence in the performance of their duties.

(iii) Aside from the duty referred to in (b)(ii) above, list any **three** other fiduciary duties that directors owe a company in accordance with sections 227 and 228 of the Companies Act 2014.

Question12.7

Arlington Enterprises Ltd is a Cork-based manufacturing company. In 2010, the company experienced quite significant financial problems and, as a consequence, it has accumulated considerable unpaid debt. In April 2011, an application was made to the High Court by one of the creditors of the company to have it placed in compulsory liquidation on the grounds of insolvency. This application was granted and Ryan was appointed as the compulsory liquidator. Since his appointment, Ryan has discovered the following irregularity. In January 2011, Ethan, one of the directors of Arlington, purchased new haulage vehicles on behalf of the company at a cost of €100,000. However, the constitution of Arlington states that the directors are prohibited from creating credit contracts on behalf of the company in excess of €50,000 without first calling a meeting of the board of directors and obtaining its authorisation. According to Arlington's company secretary, no such meeting has taken place.

Requirement Ryan seeks your advice in relation to the following matter.

Evaluate whether the credit contract created by Ethan on behalf of Arlington Enterprises Ltd is valid and binding upon the company, or whether it can be invalidated based on Ethan's lack of authority to create this contract.

Question 12.8

Ralph is a director of a company, Ardmore Consulting Plc. He is considering borrowing money from this company to repay some of the debts of another company that he is involved in.

Requirement Outline the rules regarding directors' loans and assess whether this loan is permissible under the Companies Act 2014.

Chapter 13

SHARES, SHAREHOLDERS AND SHARE CAPITAL

Introduction

This chapter discusses the long-term funding contributed by the members of a company in the form of share capital. Share capital is needed to finance a company's day-to-day operations and to expand the business of the company. If it does not expand or grow, the company will stagnate and will ultimately be in financial difficulties. This chapter also discusses the various classes of shares that confer different rights and liabilities to their owners, i.e. a company's various classes of shareholders. Furthermore, this chapter includes a discussion of the different classifications of capital, the rules on capital maintenance and the necessity for these rules. The remedies available to shareholders whose rights have been oppressed or disregarded are also addressed.

In terms of capital different rules apply to different business entities. For example, there is no restriction on the transfer of shares in a public limited company, whereas this restriction applies in private companies limited by shares and in designated activity companies. For the purpose of this chapter the rules stated specifically relate to private companies limited by shares (LTDs – see **Chapter 11**), unless otherwise specified.

SHARES

When a company is incorporated, those persons named as subscribers to its constitution are automatically deemed to be members of that company. These are the *original members* of the company. This applies even if the names of these individuals are not entered on the register of members (discussed later in this chapter).

All other subsequent members must agree to become members by purchasing shares in the company and consenting to have their names registered in the register of members.

Shares were defined in *Borlands Trustee Company v. Steel* (1901) as the interests of a shareholder in a company measured by a sum of money. They are intangible property, as you cannot see or touch them; a share is an intangible accumulation of rights, interests and obligations.

The ownership of shares does not confer upon shareholders ownership of the assets of the company. For example, a shareholder with a 20% capital holding is **not** entitled to ownership of 20% of the company's assets. In *Kerry Co-op Creamery Ltd v. An Bord Bainne Co-op Ltd* (1990), the court **held** that "no shareholder has any right to any specific portion of the company's property". This distinction arises due to the fact that the company and its shareholders are classed as separate and distinct legal entities.

Sections 66 and 67 of the Companies Act 2014 (CA 2014) further define shares, stating that:

- shares in a company must have a nominal value (see below);
- a company may allot (issue) shares of different values and currencies;
- the company may issue redeemable shares (i.e. where the company may buy back its shares);
- the shares or other interest of any member in a company shall be classed as personal estate and not be of the nature of real estate – this is a legal distinction in that real estate is defined as land and anything attaching to that land and personal estate is defined as all other property; and
- each share in a company shall be distinguished by its appropriate number.

Nominal Value

Every share must have a nominal or 'par' value. This is the base value of the share as set by the company upon its formation. The nominal value is calculated by way of the authorised share capital divided into a fixed number of shares as stated in its constitution, e.g. when there is €200,000 in 200,000 shares, each share has a nominal or par value of €1. Alternatively, upon formation, the company's constitution may state the fixed (nominal or par) amount of each share as per section 19(1)(d). This nominal value is the measure of the shareholder's liability to the company (where the shares are only partly-paid upon subscription) as well as the company's liability to the shareholder (upon liquidation). All shares rank *pari passu*, i.e. equally in every respect, within a class, for all purposes (see also below).

Allotment of Shares

As mentioned above, a company may allot new shares to increase the amount of capital that can be obtained by the company. The process of allotment is subject to certain restrictions. The company has to be authorised to allot shares by its constitution or by an ordinary resolution of the members in general meeting. Shares can only be allotted at their nominal (par) value or at a premium (above par), but not a discount (below par), which is discussed further below under 'Maintenance/Protection of Share Capital'.

At the company's discretion, shares need not be paid for in full at the time of allotment. When the full amount has not been paid, the holder of the share remains liable for the unpaid amount. When this happens, these shares are known as partly-paid shares and the holder has a liability in relation to the unpaid portion until the company 'calls' for the unpaid amount and that payment is made by the shareholder.

Calls on shares A 'call' is where the company calls on its members to pay the unpaid amounts on their shares (see also below in the section on 'Shareholders'). The call date may be specified at the time that these shares are issued. However, a call may be revoked or postponed, as the directors of the company may decide.

The company has a lien on its shareholders for unpaid amounts on allotted shares. The liability of the shareholders is limited to the amount unpaid on shares that have been allotted to them.

Lien This can be defined as the right to retain possession of something until a claim is satisfied. In the context of company law, a lien arises when shareholders are in debt to the company for the unpaid portion of their shares and the company has the right to retain possession of the shares until the outstanding payment is made. The right of first claim only arises where the company's constitution permits this. In effect, a company shall have a first and paramount lien on every share (not being a fully paid share) for all monies (whether immediately payable or not) called, or payable at a fixed time, in respect of that share. This lien is for the full amount outstanding on the share, even if a call has not been made and prior to the fixed date for payment. In general, the effect of this lien is that the owner of these shares cannot transfer them until the debt due to the company in respect of them is paid.

A company's lien on a share shall extend to all dividends payable on it. This right empowers a company to off set any monies due to it by a shareholder against the dividend debt due by the company to that shareholder. A director of the company may sell the shares that the company has a lien over if the sum unpaid on the shares is immediately payable, and a notice in writing has been given to the registered holder of the shares demanding payment 14 days prior to the transfer.

Surrender of Shares

A shareholder who has bought allotted shares but has unpaid amounts on the shares may decide to surrender them to the company rather than pay the outstanding amounts. In this circumstance, the surrender results in a reduction of the company's issued capital.

To surrender property is to give it voluntarily – but where the company compels the giving up of shares, it is deemed a forfeiture and not a surrender. Both surrender and forfeiture mean the transfer of both possession and title of the goods.

Forfeiture of Shares

Where a person buys partly-paid shares and subsequently fails to meet a call for payment in respect of the unpaid portion of these shares, then the constitution of a company may provide that the shares will be forfeited to the company. The forfeiture also results in a reduction of the company's issued capital.

A forfeited share may be sold or otherwise disposed of on such terms and in such manner as the directors of the company think fit, and at any time before a sale or disposition the forfeiture may be cancelled on such terms as the directors think fit.

The main distinction between the surrender and the forfeiture of shares is that surrender involves a voluntary act of the shareholder, whereas forfeiture arises at the behest of the company.

Classes of Shares

Prima facie, all shares are equal, i.e. they rank *pari passu*. This means that each share conveys entitlement to the same rights, interests and obligations as every other share. However, a company can create whatever category of shares it wishes – and each category may have different rights, interests and obligations. The following are the most common categories:

- equity shares – referred to colloquially as 'ordinary shares'; and
- preference shares.

In addition, these equity (ordinary) and preference shares may be issued as:

- redeemable shares,
- bonus shares, or
- employee shares.

Ordinary Shares

Ordinary shares are the basic and most common type of shares. They usually carry the following rights and duties:

1. the right to a variable dividend, when declared by the company – this dividend varies according to the amount of profit that a company has available for distribution;

2. the right to repayment of capital upon liquidation once all other debts of the company have been settled. In addition, where there is a surplus of funds available on liquidation, ordinary shareholders have the right to share in this surplus; and
3. the right to attend all company meetings and exercise their shareholder rights at these meetings (such as the right to appoint a proxy and vote on resolutions – see **Chapter 12**).

Not all ordinary shares carry these rights and entitlements. The company may create ordinary shares that encompass some or all of these rights or any other rights that the company determines.

Furthermore, because these shareholders rank lowest in terms of repayment of debt upon liquidation, they represent the greatest speculative risk. This disadvantage can be balanced against the advantage that these shares often have strong representation on the board of directors, and greater influence in relation to the running of the company arising from their voting rights.

Preference Shares

Preference shares are shares that carry certain preferential rights over other categories of share. The most common types of preferential treatment are as to their:
- dividend; and
- capital repayment.

The main disadvantage in relation to these shares is that they generally do not confer the right to influence how the company is being run.

When the company creates preference shares, it must clearly outline the type of preference shares that are being allotted – this requires it specifically to express the nature of the preference being attached to these shares.

Dividend Where the share is preferred as to dividend, it is usual for that shareholder to be paid his dividend prior to the ordinary shareholder. It is normal practice for the terms of the share to express the dividend as a percentage of the nominal value of the share per annum (e.g. 6% preference shares). Therefore, the preference dividend is usually at a fixed rate, and this is expressly stated by the company when these shares are being allotted. This preference dividend is only payable when declared by the company. The company has no obligation to pay the preference dividend, even if there are profits available for distribution. This payment is at the absolute discretion of the directors of the company, who may elect to retain the company profits for asset acquisition, expansion or any other relevant purpose. However, if the company's constitution mandates the payment of this dividend upon certain conditions being satisfied, then this would become a contractual right of the shareholders, who can demand that the company make the payment.

In *Re Lafayette Ltd* (1950), it was **held** that, where the company's constitution provides that a preference shareholder would receive a dividend every year, it should be paid, irrespective of whether it was declared or not.

In *Re Imperial Hotel (Cork) Ltd* (1950), the company's constitution gave preference shareholders the right to an annual 6% dividend, including all arrears "independent of any recommendation by the board of directors, and independent of any declaration of dividend by the company in a general meeting …". This was **held** to be a debt of the company and that it should have priority of payment.

Once declared, the dividend is payable to preference shareholders. However, if the dividend on a preference share is not declared in any particular year, that share becomes a cumulative preference share. In this event, any unpaid dividend is added to the amount payable the following year and no dividends can be paid by the company on ordinary shares until the entire amount of unpaid dividends on cumulative preference shares is cleared. As the right to a dividend is a contractual right, the right to the repayment of the arrears of cumulative preference dividends lasts for a period of six years.

Capital repayment Another type of preference share is one that is preferred as to capital. This means that a preferred shareholder will have his or her capital paid back before any ordinary shareholder at the winding up of the company. This preferential right must be expressly stated by the company upon the allotment of these shares. With regard to capital, unless otherwise stated in the company's constitution, these shares are entitled to participate in any surplus funds available following the liquidation of the company.

Note: Although preference shareholders are entitled to attend the general meetings of the company, they do not normally have voting rights. These rights are only acquired if the dividends payable are in arrears.

Redeemable Shares

Redeemable shares are shares that the company issues with the intention of redeeming them (or buying them back) at a later date. For example, a company may issue shares in 2015 in order to finance the expansion of the business and state that they plan on buying back those shares in 2025, in order to reduce their capital liabilities. In effect, redeemable shares allow a company to increase its capital for a prescribed period of time in order to meet the financial requirements of the company, and then to extinguish this liability when this capital is no longer necessary to run the company.

Furthermore, save to the extent that its constitution otherwise provides, section 83 CA 2014 states that a company may, by special resolution, and subject to the provisions governing the variation of rights attached to classes of shares and the amendment of a company's constitution, convert any of its shares into redeemable shares. This provision empowers a company to convert any of its existing shares into redeemable shares, which can be bought back to reduce the company's capital. This power is often used when the directors of the company consider that it is over-capitalised.

After redeeming the shares the company has the following options:

1. **Cancel the shares** A company may redeem the shares and upon redemption cancel these shares. In this situation, the shares no longer exist and the company's issued share capital is reduced by the redeemed amount. The authorised share capital (the maximum amount of capital that a company can issue) would not be affected by this redemption.
2. **Treasury shares** Instead of cancelling the shares upon redemption, a company may retain the shares as 'treasury shares'. This right is subject to the requirement that the nominal value of treasury shares held by a company may not, at any one time, exceed 10 per cent of its company's capital. Treasury shares do not carry any tangible benefits to the holder, i.e. the company, as they carry no voting rights and no dividend is payable on them as per section 109(4) CA 2014. Although a company may cancel these treasury shares at a later date, the real benefit to the company of having treasury shares is that they may also be re-issued by the company at a later date.

The general rule is that the issue of redeemable shares has to be contingent on certain events taking place. They are most often used in business expansion schemes where a company, as a way of obtaining funding, will issue redeemable shares. The shares may give the provider of the finance (usually a fund) a say in the running of the company (and usually a seat on the board). After a certain period of time (commonly five years), the shares may be redeemed, often at a premium. The company will have benefited from the use of the finance provided. The providers of the finance benefit because they will receive dividends on the shares as well as any premium on redemption; additionally, there are tax breaks for the money invested.

Funding the Redemption

Redeemable shares may be redeemed out of profits, but only out of profits that are available for distribution to shareholders. Section 107(2) CA 2014 defines 'profits available for distribution' as the company's accumulated, realised profits, which have not previously been utilised by a distribution or capitalisation, less its accumulated, realised losses, which have not been previously written off in a reduction or reorganisation of capital.

A company may redeem shares out of a fresh issue of shares and cancel the old issue of shares.

- When redeemable shares that are being redeemed out of the proceeds of a fresh issue of shares were originally issued at a premium (above their par value), any premium payable on redemption can be paid out of the share premium account, providing it is equal to or less than the premium received on the issue of the shares, as per section 105 CA 2014.
- When redeemable shares that are being redeemed out of the proceeds of a fresh issue of shares were **not** originally issued at a premium, the premium must be paid out of distributable profits.

If the shares are cancelled on redemption, the company's issued share capital can be reduced by the nominal value of the redeemed shares. In accordance with section 106(4) CA 2014, where the redemption is from profits available for distribution, then a sum equal to the nominal value of the redeemed shares must be transferred to the undenominated capital account (discussed below in the section 'Company Capital'), which is treated as capital. Where the redemption is from a fresh issue of shares but the funds raised are less than the aggregate of the nominal value of the shares redeemed, then an amount equivalent to the aggregable difference must be transferred to the undenominated capital account. Both of these transfers reflect the fact that, if these shares are cancelled, they are no longer available to issue in the future. For example, if a company had an authorised capital divided into one million €1 shares, and an issued capital of 500,000 €1 shares (and unissued capital of 500,000 €1 shares), if €100,000 of these issued shares were redeemed, then the issued capital would be reduced to 400,000 €1 shares. Even though the authorised capital is one million, this does not mean that the company now has 600,000 €1 unissued shares – as 100,000 of these shares have been cancelled. Accordingly the accounts should reflect this fact by stating that the authorised capital is one million €1 shares, the issued capital is 400,000 €1 shares, the undenominated capital is 100,000 €1 shares and the unissued capital is 500,000 €1 shares.

As previously stated, if redeemable shares are not cancelled, they must be retained as 'treasury shares' to maintain the current level of issued capital, i.e. the company's capital is not altered.

Bonus Shares

Bonus shares are shares issued by a 'healthy' company to existing shareholders in recognition of their loyalty and without any payment being made by the existing shareholders to the company. They are issued in proportion to the existing holding of a shareholder. For example, a company may decide to allot one bonus share to every ordinary shareholder for every 10 shares held – so a shareholder who owns 20,000 ordinary shares may receive 2,000 bonus shares as a gift. The rules regarding bonus shares are contained in sections 123–126 CA 2014. Bonus shares can only be issued out of profits, and issued as wholly-paid or partly-paid bonus shares on the recommendation of directors in general meeting (section 126(4) CA 2014).

Unless the company's constitution provides otherwise, the directors of that company may recommend the capitalisation of monies (1) credited to the undenominated capital account, (2) representing profits available for distribution, or (3) representing unrealised asset revaluation reserves, to the members of the company as bonus shares. In effect, the company may use these funds to finance the purchase of its own unissued shares, which are then distributed as a bonus or gift to its shareholders.

Employee Shares

Employee shares arise where employees are gifted shares in the company by which they are employed. Their purpose is to incentivise employees to be more loyal to the company and to be more productive, which means that if the company makes more profit, the employees benefit by earning a greater dividend. It is a 'win-win' situation for all concerned. These shares may be ordinary or preference shares and the rights of these must be expressed by the company at the time of their allotment.

Transfer of Shares

A transfer of shares is where a shareholder decides to transfer shares to another person either by a sale or by gift. A transfer of shares is done by a voluntary act (i.e. an *inter vivos* act) of a member of the company. This is to be compared with 'transmission', which is usually involuntary and occurs upon either the death or bankruptcy of the shareholder (see below). Section 94 CA 2014 states that a transfer of shares must be done:

- in writing;
- in a proper instrument of transfer delivered to the company (this is usually a form approved by the directors to effect the transfer of the shares).

The shares shall be deemed to be in the name of the transferor until the name of the transferee is entered into the register of members. When this occurs, the transferee becomes the legal owner of the shares.

Restrictions on Transfer of Shares

Certain formalities need to be adhered to pursuant to section 95(2) CA 2014 in relation to any proposed transfer of shares. This provision empowers the company's directors (unless the company's constitution states otherwise) to decline to register any instrument of share transfer unless:

- a fee of €10.00, or such lesser sum as stipulated by the company, is paid to the company in respect of the transfer;
- the instrument of transfer is accompanied by the certificate of the shares; and
- the instrument of transfer is in respect of one class of share only.

Furthermore, the directors of a company may also decline to register the transfer of any share (though this power expires two months after the date of delivery to the company of the instrument of transfer of the share). This right reflects the fact that companies, and in particular private companies, want some control over the transfer of their shares.

According to common law when directors are exercising this right they are required to be acting in good faith and in the best interest of the company as a whole. In *Re Hafner: Olhausen v. Powderley* (1943), Mr Justice Black stated that "[directors] must not exercise [this right] arbitrarily, capriciously, or corruptly". Where they are found to be acting in breach of these obligations, the court can make an order for rectification.

Transmission of Shares

A transmission arises without the consent of the owner of the shares. It is an involuntary process involving the registration of the name of the transferee after the death of a shareholder or the registration of the name of a personal representative after the death of a shareholder. It can also arise in a bankruptcy situation (section 96(4) CA 2014) where the shares of a declared bankrupt are transmitted to the transferee in accordance with an order of the court.

The instances of the operation of the transmission of shares that are provided by section 96 CA 2014 are as follows:

- the shares automatically vest in the personal representative of the deceased shareholder on death;
- the surviving owner of joint shares becomes the sole owner of the shares upon death of the other owner.

The directors of the company shall have the same right to decline or suspend registration as they would have had in the case of a transfer of shares, as discussed above.

Transmission of Shares in Special Circumstances

Section 97 of the Companies Act 2014 confers a power on the Minister for Jobs, Enterprise and Innovation to prescribe procedures whereby the registration of shares in a company may be validly effected in the following cases:

- the death of the sole member of a single-member company where that member had been the only director of the company;
- other cases of difficulty in effecting such registration. There are no examples given in the Act, but in all likelihood this would include any situation where it would be otherwise impossible to effect the registration, e.g. due to the death or permanent incapacity of all a company's directors, as well as its secretary. Likewise, upon the merger of two companies, the minister may authorise the use of alternative procedures than those previously discussed to effect the transfer of shares from one company to another.

Certification of Shares

A share certificate is a document issued by a company certifying that, on its date of issue, a person is the *prima facie* registered owner of shares in the company.

> "A certificate under the common seal of the company specifying any shares held by any member shall be *prima facie* evidence of the title of the member to the shares." (Section 99 CA 2014.)

A company must, within two months after the date of allotment of any of its shares, have these certificates ready. If a company contravenes this requirement it, any of its officers who are in default shall be guilty of a category 4 offence (see **Chapter 15**).

SHAREHOLDERS

The shareholders of a company are the persons who acquire shares in that company; they become members of the company when their names are entered into the company's register of members. When a company is incorporated, those who subscribe to its constitution are automatically members. As discussed previously, these are the *original members.* This applies even if the name of the individual is not entered on the register of members (see below).

The Register of Members

The register of members is an important document and regulated by section 169 CA 2014. A register of members must be kept by every company, stating:

1. the names and addresses of the members;
2. a statement of the shares held by each member;

3. the share numbers, where they exist (i.e. the distinguishing numbers on the share certificates used to identify the shares);
4. the amount paid up on the shares;
5. the date each person's details were entered into the register of members; and
6. the date at which any person ceased to be a member (through the transfer, transmission or forfeiture of his or her shareholding).

With the exception of the first shareholders of the company, all relevant details must be entered in the register of members within 28 days of conclusion of the agreement with the company to become a member. Regarding the first shareholders of the company, their details must be registered in the register of members within 28 days of the registration of the company. Default in complying with these requirements is a category 3 offence.

This register must be kept at the registered office of the company or where the company's work is carried out within the State.

The register is the *prima facie* (and, therefore, not conclusive) evidence of membership of a company. It must be open for inspection to members and non-members. The general rule is that it should be made available for not less than two hours per day during normal business hours and days. This rule is subject to the exception that a company may, provided it gives notice through an advertisement in a newspaper local to the registered office of the company, close the register for a period of time not exceeding 30 whole days per year. Inspection of the register is free for members but may be subject to the payment of a small fee by non-members.

Shareholders' Rights

Shareholders' rights, duties and obligations depend on the terms of the issue of the shares. Shares confer many rights on shareholders. These may include the following:

- the right to a dividend, if a dividend is properly declared;
- the right to attend and vote at general meetings of the company;
- on winding up, the right to participate in any surplus of assets; and
- statutory rights to notices, information that is allowed under the Companies Act, unless the constitution of the company provides otherwise.

Other rights include access to the constitutional documents of the company, copies of the financial reports and the statutory registers. Shareholders also possess the right to take an action against the company where their rights as shareholders have been breached.

Fiduciary Duties

The fiduciary duties that directors owe the company were conceived in common law but are now encompassed in section 228 CA 2014. These duties originate from the fact that directors have a fiduciary relationship with the company in that they hold a position of trust. They hold the assets of the company in trust for the company's stakeholders. Any actions deemed to be in breach of this trust are actionable.

Some of the rights of shareholders are derived from directors' fiduciary duties. These duties require the directors to act in the best interests of the company as a whole – this encompasses the duty to act in the best interests of the shareholders as a collective entity. Therefore, the general rule of law is that directors owe their duty to the company, but that in exercising their powers they also owe duties to the collective shareholders of that company.

The case of *Percival v. Wright* (1902) related to the duty of directors to shareholders concerning the value of shareholders' shares when the directors are secretly negotiating the sale of the business. The directors cannot make a profit from the shareholders on the basis of their secret knowledge, as they have a fiduciary relationship with the shareholder.

Personal Rights

A shareholder retains some rights that are personal to the individual and, if infringed, the wrong is done to him or her personally and actionable by him or her personally. Section 31 CA 2014 is one source of these personal rights in that any actions by company directors in breach of the company's constitution may be actionable by the shareholders directly affected by that breach. For example, a failure by a director to permit a shareholder to appoint a proxy (to attend and vote at a general meeting of the company on his or her behalf) would be personally actionable by that shareholder. Similarly, refusing to allow a shareholder to exercise his or her voting rights would be in breach of the shareholder's personal rights.

Another personal right of shareholders is the right of pre-emption – a company that is allotting shares must first offer them to the existing shareholders in the same proportion as their existing shareholdings before offering them to non-members. This means that existing shareholders have the right of first refusal on issues of shares. Pre-emption clauses are usually found in a company's constitution or in a shareholders' agreement. Unless a company's constitution states otherwise, the shares of a company may only be allotted by its directors. Any director of a company who knowingly contravenes its constitution or the shareholders' agreement, or knowingly permits or authorises such a contravention, shall be guilty of a category 3 offence (see **Chapter 15**).

Shareholders' Duties

A shareholder's principal duty is to pay what remains unpaid on a share, when a 'call' is made (see also above in the section 'Shares'). Each member shall pay the company (subject to receiving at least 30 days' notice specifying the time(s) and place of payment), the amount called on the shares. The directors may revoke or postpone the call on shares. A call will be deemed to have been made at the time when the resolution of the directors authorising the call was passed and may be required to be paid by instalments.

Shareholder Protection and Remedies

The Companies Act 2014 has not removed the derivative actions that have been in place since even before the Companies Act 1963. These actions are derived from the general rule that the majority voice of the members prevails. Consequently, if the shareholders approve a course of action to be undertaken by a company, a minority shareholder generally cannot challenge that action on the grounds that he or she disagrees with it. However, the exceptions to the legal principles established in *Foss v. Harbottle* (1843) have managed to give minority shareholders some protection through the courts.

In the *Foss* case, a company was formed by an Act of the British Parliament for the purposes of acquiring land. The land was purchased from one of the 15 defendants. After the project was advertised, the two plaintiffs subscribed for two and 12 shares respectively. Subsequently, the company was incorporated. The plaintiffs alleged that the defendants, who had become directors of the company, had charged the company an exorbitant price for the land. The plaintiffs accused the defendants of having raised money through mortgaging the land, which was not allowed by the objects clause of the company. **Held**: the company was the proper vehicle for the bringing of an action where the company suffers the wrong. In essence the power of the company is vested by the members in the board and, if the members do not like what the board does, it is up to them to appoint a different board.

The *Foss* case is a precedent for two important propositions:

1. If some wrong has allegedly been committed in the course of a company's affairs, it is the company, in its corporate capacity, that should seek redress, i.e. the proper plaintiff is the company.
2. Shareholders of a company may not bring proceedings to overturn a decision of the company where that is a decision that a majority could confirm, i.e. the wishes of the majority prevail in a company.

The Supreme Court reaffirmed this in the case of *O'Neill v. Ryan, Ryanair Ltd and Others* (1990). The plaintiff was the CEO and minority shareholder in Ryanair. He sued the principal shareholder and the company itself based on the reduction in the value of his shareholding. **Held**: shareholders cannot sue for reduction in share value. If the company suffers a loss, the company can sue the wrongdoer in respect of that loss, but an individual shareholder has no right of action.

There are, however, several grounds on which the courts will intervene in a company's affairs on the side of the minority and a shareholder can bring:

1. a personal action;
2. a derivative action; or
3. an action for oppression and/or disregarding members' interests.

Each of these will be discussed separately.

Personal Actions

The rule in *Foss* does not interfere with a member's personal rights. This is best illustrated by the case of *Pender v. Lushington* (1877) where the chairman of a general meeting refused to take the votes of certain shareholders into account. The members were able to bring a personal action to have their votes counted. It was **held** that members have a personal right, which derives from the company's constitution, to have their votes counted. As mentioned earlier in this chapter, this personal right is derived from section 31 CA 2014.

Derivative Actions and Exceptions to Foss

A derivative action is one taken by a shareholder, representing all the shareholders, on behalf of the company to redress a wrong committed against that company by a third party. This action derives from the injury to the company rather than the injury to individual shareholders. The right to bring this type of action arises where the wrong is done by those who control the company.

The following are derivative actions that can be brought by the minority. These actions are based on the exceptions to the Rule in *Foss v. Harbottle.*

1. The minority may bring an action if an act perpetrated by the company is *ultra vires* or an illegal act. In *Parke v. Daily News Ltd* (1962), the plaintiff disapproved of an *ultra vires* gift of £1.5 million to redundant employees. **Held**: it was *ultra vires* (beyond the powers of the company's constitution) and the company could not pay it out.
2. The minority may bring an action if there is a failure to observe proper procedure. In *Edwards v. Halliwell* (1950), a secret ballot was supposed to be taken at a general meeting. However, an open vote was taken and the court held that the minority could set aside the vote.

3. Where the members' personal rights are infringed. In *Pender v. Lushington* (1877), certain votes were rejected and not counted. This was held by the courts to be an infringement of personal rights. (Members' personal rights are discussed in the previous sub-section.)
4. The minority may bring an action against the majority if a fraud has been committed against the minority. (See *Cook v. Deeks* (1916), which is discussed under 'Directors' Duties' in **Chapter 12**.)
5. The minority may issue proceedings against the majority if the justice of the case demands it (*per* Hamilton J. in *Moylan v. Irish Whiting Manufacturers* (1980). To invoke this ground, a very strong case (which does not fall under any of the other exceptions) has to be made.

Oppression and Disregard of Members' Interests

Section 212 CA 2014 provides minority shareholders with a powerful tool to protect themselves against the company if the affairs of the company or the powers of the directors are being exercised oppressively or in disregard of the interests of the minority.

Section 212(1) states that:

> "Any member of a company who complains that the affairs of the company are being conducted or that the powers of the directors of the company are being exercised—
> (a) in a manner oppressive to him or her or any of the members (including himself or herself), or
> (b) in disregard of his or her or their interests as members, may apply to the court for an order under this section."

In *Scottish Co-operative Wholesale Society Ltd v. Meyer* (1959) 'oppression' was defined as arising where the conduct of the company is "burdensome, harsh and wrongful" to a member or members of the company. The Scottish Co-operative Wholesale Society Ltd set up a new company called Scottish Textile & Manufacturing Co Ltd with Dr Meyer and Mr Lucas. They manufactured rayon cloth. At that time one required state licensing and, to get a licence, experienced managers were needed. Dr Meyer and Mr Lucas were the managing directors, with some shares, while the Scottish Co-operative held the majority of the company's shares and appointed the other three directors to the board. These three were also directors of the Scottish Co-operative itself. In 1952, the licensing system was ended by the British government. So Scottish Co-operative used its majority of votes to transfer all the business to a branch of the Co-op. It also cut off the supplies of raw materials. The company could not continue, no profits were made and the share value crashed. Dr Meyer and Mr Lucas felt oppressed and petitioned for relief. The House of Lords held that the conduct of the majority was indeed oppressive, and ordered that Dr Meyer's and Mr Lucas's shares be bought at a price that was fair.

Oppressive behaviour is considered by objective standards and on a case-by-case basis.

The oppression in question need not be suffered by a member as a member (*qua* member). This was seen in the case of *Re Murph's Restaurant* (1979). The company had three shareholder directors involved in the restaurant business. Two were brothers and the other was their friend. The friend left his well-paid job to run one of their restaurants. The finances of the company were run in an unusual way. The three met every Monday over dinner where they each took a wage from the company. Great effort went into maintaining equality between the three. The two brothers decided to remove their friend as a director after personal relationships soured. The friend sought to have the company wound up. Mr Justice Gannon observed that evidence clearly showed that the members were "[e]qual partners in a joint venture and that the company was no more than a vehicle to secure limited liability for possible losses and to provide a means of earning and distributing profits to their best advantage and minimum disclosure". The court went on to hold that the actions of the two directors in removing the third constituted a "deliberate and calculated repudiation … of that relationship of equality, trust and confidence between the three which constituted the very essence of the company". **Held**: it was just and equitable to wind up the company in the circumstances.

Exclusion from management is also oppression The case of *Re Murph's* (as cited above) is also the relevant authority for exclusion from management.

Disregard of members' interests: a single act can be regarded as oppression When members are of the opinion that their interests have been disregarded, they can petition the court on the grounds that the interests of the members have not been taken into consideration. The leading case in this area is *Re Williams Group Tullamore Ltd* (1985) in which ordinary shareholders sought relief for oppression. The company attempted to create a new category of preference shareholders, who would then receive €169,000 in dividends, which otherwise would have gone to the ordinary shareholders. **Held**: a single act is sufficient to give rise to actionable oppression.

The remedies to "end the matters complained of" If the court is satisfied that the claim of a shareholder is well founded, it may invoke the remedies set out in section 212 CA 2014 to "end the matters complained of".

The following are the remedies available, pursuant to section 212(3) CA 2014:

1. an order directing or prohibiting any act or cancelling or varying any transaction (as in *Re Williams Group Tullamore Ltd* (1985) where the resolutions passed by the members were cancelled);
2. an order regulating the conduct of the company's affairs in future;
3. an order for the purchase of the shares of any members of the company by other members of the company or by the company and, in the case of a purchase by the company, for the reduction accordingly of the company's capital (this order can relate to the purchase of the petitioner's shares, properly valued as in *Re Greenore Trading* and in *Re Clubman Shirts* (1983), or the purchase of the respondent's shares, properly valued as in *Irish Press plc v. Ingersoll Irish Publications Ltd* (1995)); and
4. an order for the payment of compensation.

Note: if, in the opinion of the court, the hearing of proceedings under section 212 would involve the disclosure of information the publication of which would be seriously prejudicial to the legitimate interests of the company, the court may order that the hearing of the proceedings or any part of them shall be *in camera* (i.e. private).

COMPANY CAPITAL

A company needs to raise capital from its members (as discussed earlier in the section on 'Shareholders') or from creditors in the form of loan capital (which will be discussed in **Chapter 14**).

According to section 64 CA 2014, 'company capital' is defined as the aggregate value, received by the company in respect of the allotment of shares of the company and that part of the company's undenominated capital constituted by the transfer of sums. Section 64(1) CA 2014 defines 'undenominated capital' as the excess of company capital over the nominal value of issued shares.

There are different types of share capital. They are:

- **Nominal/authorised share capital** This is the total amount of shares that a company has the authority to issue, either at formation or at a subsequent date. This figure is expressly stated in a company's constitution. However, a company is entitled to choose not to have an authorised share capital, but instead state that the share capital of the company at formation is divided into shares of a fixed amount specified in its constitution.
- **Issued/allotted share capital** This is the nominal value of shares that the company has already issued/allotted. A company is not required to issue/allot all of its share capital, and most companies reserve the right

to issue/allot shares at a later date to raise capital as required. The unissued/unallotted portion of a company's nominal share capital is known as 'unissued/unallotted capital'.

- **Called-up share capital** When a company issues shares it may ask for payment in full, or it may ask for payment of a specified amount with the obligation to pay the outstanding balance at a later date. As mentioned when discussing the allotment of shares, such shares are referred to as partly-paid shares. In the context of these shares, the value of the shares that members have paid to date is known as called-up capital (also referred to as paid-up capital). This term also includes shares upon which a call for payment has been made, irrespective of whether the payment has been received by the company, as well as any share capital to be paid on a specified future date as stated in the company's constitution, or the terms of the issue or any other arrangements made by the company. The remaining amount per share that each shareholder owes to the company is known as the 'uncalled share capital'.
- **Reserve capital** This is uncalled capital that is reserved for a special purpose. Under section 1295 CA 2014, where an unlimited company re-registers as a limited company it may pass a special resolution stating that some or all of the uncalled capital may only be called up when the company is being wound up.

Variation of Class Rights

If the constitution attaches different rights to different classes of shares, those rights can be altered by a written resolution of holders of 75% in nominal value of the issued shares of that class, or a special resolution passed at a separate extraordinary general meeting sanctions this variation (section 88 CA 2014).

A decision that adversely affects a particular class does not necessarily amount to a variation of rights. In *Greenhalgh v. Arderne Cinemas Ltd (1951)*, the company had two classes of ordinary shares: 50p shares and 10p shares. Every share carried one vote. A resolution was passed to subdivide each of the 50p shares into five 10p shares, thus multiplying the votes of that class by five. The courts **held** that the rights of the 10p shareholders had not been varied since they still had one vote per share as before, even though their voting power had been diluted.

Accounting for Company Capital within the Legal Framework

As discussed earlier in this chapter, capital is defined as the company's share capital, share premium, capital conversion reserve fund and capital redemption reserve fund. Undenominated capital comprises the excess of company capital over the nominal value of issued shares. Thus to maintain proper books of account and to maintain the capital of the company (discussed below), separate capital accounts have to be kept by the company. These accounts are the share capital accounts, share premium account and capital redemption reserve fund, which are discussed separately below.

Share Capital Account

For accounting purposes, when the company issues shares for their nominal value, the amount of money paid up for these shares is transferred into an account called a share capital account. This money is not considered profit and therefore cannot be distributed to the shareholders – see 'Maintenance/Protection of Share Capital' below.

Share Premium Account

When a company issues shares at a premium (above their nominal value), the premium is part of the undenominated capital of the company, and should be transferred to a share premium account (section 71 CA 2014). The monies in this account represent the profit made from the sale of shares (capital gains) – they are not part of the trading profits of the company. As this account is part of the company's capital there are restrictions on the use of the funds accumulated in this account, to which the rules on capital maintenance (explained later in this chapter) apply.

Capital Redemption Reserve Fund

A company that redeems or purchases its own shares out of funds that have not been generated by a new issue of shares must transfer money from its distributable profits into an undenominated capital account called the 'capital redemption reserve fund' account. This fund appears as a reserve on the company's balance sheet.

Maintenance/Protection of Share Capital

A private company limited by shares has three basic options through which it may generate the necessary funds it requires to operate:

1. Borrowing – a company may borrow the funds it requires.
2. Investment – a company may raise funds through an allotment of shares.
3. Profits – a profitable business may use funds it has generated by making profits a source of finance.

It is a fundamental principle of company law that, throughout the lifetime of the company, its share capital and undenominated capital must be protected. The rationale behind this rule is that a company's capital has always been seen as a secure fund (or a buffer fund) maintained for the purpose of paying creditors in the event of the liquidation of the company. Consequently, it cannot be distributed as profit to the shareholders of the company while it is still trading. Any activity that may diminish the share capital or undenominated capital of the company must be closely examined and is subject to a number of rules known as capital maintenance rules.

1. Prohibition on Issuing Shares at a Discount

The general rule is that a company may not allot shares at a discount, i.e. below the par value of the shares. The purpose of this prohibition is to protect the company's capital for its creditors, and to ensure that the shares are not devalued. Section 73(3) CA 2014 provides that, where a company issues shares in contravention of this rule, then the person receiving these shares will be liable to repay the company an amount equal to the amount of the discount and interest thereon at the appropriate rate.

Company officers who issue shares in breach of this rule may also be sanctioned.

2. Reduction in Company Capital

The common law principle that a company may **not** reduce its capital was decided in the case of *Ooregum Gold Mining Co v. Roper* (1892). However, under the Act, a company **may** reduce its capital if it thinks that it is **expedient** to do so (section 84 CA 2014).

There are numerous ways in which a company can reduce its capital, as follows:

1. by extinguishing or reducing the liability on any of its shares in respect of share capital not paid up – this may arise where the company decides to write off obligations in relation to monies outstanding on foot of partly-paid shares or by reducing the authorised share capital of the company;
2. by cancelling any paid-up company capital that is lost or unrepresented by available assets – this amounts to a reduction/revaluation in capital in order to write off a trading loss; or
3. by paying off any paid-up company capital that is in excess of the wants of the company – this would arise where a company proposes to buy back

its own shares from existing shareholders in order to reduce its capital, for example, by asking shareholders to sell one share back to the company for every ten shares that they hold.

In order to effect any of these types of reduction, strict requirements must be followed in that the company must either:

- employ the summary approval procedure (as discussed in **Chapter 14**); or
- pass a special resolution that is confirmed by the **court**.

If a company contravenes this section, the company and any of its officers who are in default shall be guilty of a category 3 offence (see **Chapter 15**).

Where a company has passed a special resolution for reducing its company capital, before it seeks confirmation from the court, it must:

- advertise its intention at least once in a daily newspaper; and
- notify all its creditors that it proposes to apply to the court for an order to reduce its capital.

Otherwise, where the reduction arises from cancelling any paid-up company capital that is lost or unrepresented by available assets, the creditors of the company may object to the proposed reduction, and the court will consider this objection when deciding whether or not to confirm the reduction. If the court does confirm a reduction of capital, it can require the company to publish the reasons for this reduction, the causes that led to the reduction or any other such information that it considers expedient in order to ensure that proper information is provided to the public.

Upon confirmation of the reduction, the Registrar of Companies must be notified.

3. *Financial Assistance by a Company in the Purchase of its Own Shares*

The general prohibition for a company to give financial assistance to a third party to purchase its shares, either directly or indirectly or by means of a loan or guarantee, is given by section 82 CA 2014. Aside from the fact that a company obtains no financial benefit if it engages in such a transaction, the main purpose behind the rule is to prevent capital manipulation.

The prohibition does not prevent a company from providing this assistance if the purpose of it is not just to give the assistance but for a much larger purpose that is in good faith and in the best interests of the company. Accordingly, there are exceptions to this general rule prohibiting the provision of financial assistance.

The provision of financial assistance by the company to a party for the purchase of the company's own shares is permitted if such financial assistance is:

- in accordance with the summary approval procedure (discussed in **Chapter 14**);
- in accordance with employee share schemes;
- in its ordinary course of business;
- in accordance with lending money to non-director employees; or
- in accordance with a refinancing or re-arrangement of the company.

In addition, this rule does not prevent the company from: (1) paying dividends or distributing company profits that are available for distribution; (2) discharging a liability lawfully incurred by the company; (3) the purchase or redemption of redeemable shares; or (4) the payment of fees or expenses to advisors of purchasers in relation to the subscription or purchase of shares.

If a company does not abide by these strict requirements, the company and any of its officers who are in default shall be guilty of a category 2 offence (see **Chapter 15**).

Therefore, it is left to the company giving the financial assistance to void the contract against any person, whether he is a party to the transaction or not, who had notice of the facts that constitute the breach. In effect, where a person obtains financial assistance from the company to purchase shares in contravention of the stated exceptions, then the company, upon becoming aware that its own directors may have authorised this prohibited transaction, has the authority to void the contract.

Notice Notice in this situation must be "actual notice". Therefore, the party must have *actually* known of the breach. In *Bank of Ireland v. Rockfield* (1979) the plaintiff advanced money to a company. It was offered as security a mortgage over the company's property. The money was being used by a third party to acquire shares in the company. The plaintiff was not aware what the money was being used for. Had it made inquiries it would have discovered this. The plaintiff bank sought repayment of the loan. The company resisted claiming that this transaction was void. **Held**: the plaintiff had taken the security without actual notice that the prohibition was being breached. The transaction stood.

In *Lombard & Ulster Bank Ltd v. Bank of Ireland* (1987), a number of people wished to purchase a school by purchasing shares in the company that owned it. As they did not have the necessary funds to buy the company, they sought a bank loan. The company that owned the school agreed to create a charge over the school property in favour of the bank in return for the bank giving a loan to the proposed buyers. No statutory declaration or special resolution was made, only an informal agreement of all shareholders to permit the transaction. The validity of the transaction was challenged. **Held**: Mr Justice Costello stated that, as the transaction was in breach of the legislation, it was voidable by the company providing the assistance, where: (1) the recipient of the assistance (the bank) knew of the facts that resulted in non-compliance, (2) the bank had notice of the non-compliance, and (3) the notice was actual notice. In this instance, in order to void the transaction, the bank would have to have known that there had been no formal adherence to the procedures necessary to ensure compliance with the obligations regarding the exceptions to the provision of financial assistance. As the bank had been assured that proper procedures had been followed in accordance with company law, and was unaware that only an informal agreement had been effected, which did not comply with statutory obligations, the transaction was upheld and was not voidable against the bank as it had no actual notice of the breach.

4. Purchase by a Company of its own Shares

The general rule that a company cannot purchase its own shares originated in the case of *Trevor v. Whitworth* (1887).

In this case, the executors of Whitworth's estate sold the shares that Whitworth had held in a company back to the company. This transaction was permitted by the company's constitution. The company went into liquidation and the executors sued for the amount owing by the company on the shares transferred. **Held**: the purchase of its own shares by the company was prohibited as it would cause a reduction in the company's capital.

However, there are numerous statutory exceptions to this rule given in section 102 CA 2014. This section states that a company **may** acquire its own fully paid shares in the following circumstances:

1. by transfer or surrender to the company other than for valuable consideration;
2. by cancellation pursuant to a reduction of company capital;
3. pursuant to an order of the court in relation to minority rights;
4. where those shares are redeemable shares;
5. by the purchase of shares that have been re-classed as redeemable, where they were not originally issued as such;
6. pursuant to the redemption of preference shares; or
7. pursuant to a merger or division.

If a company purports to act in contravention of the above requirements, the company and any of its officers who are in default shall be guilty of a category 2 offence (see **Chapter 15**).

In order to invoke any of these exceptions, the acquisition by a company of its own shares must also be authorised by:
(a) the constitution of the company;
(b) the rights attaching to the shares in question; or
(c) the passing of a special resolution.

5. Dividends and Distribution of Profits

A shareholder normally invests in a company in the hope of receiving a return on his or her investment either in the form of a profit (by selling the shares for more than they were purchased for) or by earning a dividend on the shares. A dividend is a periodic payment from the company's profits that are available for distribution. Unless a company's constitution states otherwise, section 124 CA 2014 regulates the payment of the dividend. The rules regarding dividends are as follows:

- a dividend must be declared in general meeting by ordinary resolution;
- the declaration cannot exceed the amount recommended by directors;
- the directors may declare an interim dividend if they see fit;
- the directors may, before paying dividends, set aside profits to be used for other purposes;
- a shareholder is not entitled to a dividend unless it is declared according to the constitution and the date of payment has arrived;
- dividends are declared as payable on paid-up amounts of shares only; and
- no dividend shall bear an interest against a company.

REVIEW QUESTIONS

(See Solutions to Review Questions at the end of this text.)

Question 13.1

Following the death of his great uncle Nelson, Cranston inherited 75,000 €1 ordinary shares in Finest Cuisine Catering Ltd ('Finest'). This is the first time that Cranston has owned company shares and he knows nothing about company law or how companies operate.

Last week he received a notification from the company secretary of Finest informing him that an extraordinary general meeting of the company was being requisitioned and that this meeting would consider the sale of 100,000 €1 ordinary shares in the company to a new private investor, Hamilton. Hamilton has offered to pay a share premium of €0.30 on every €1 share purchased. In addition, this notice also stated that a special resolution was being proposed to avoid pre-emption so that these shares could be offered directly to Hamilton and an ordinary resolution was being proposed to appoint Hamilton as a non-executive director in the company (if he was successful in acquiring these shares).

Cranston does not understand the meaning of any of these terms and seeks your advice.

Requirement:

(a) Explain the meaning of the term 'share premium', commenting also on how share premium is accounted for in a company's accounts, and any **two** purposes for which this premium can be utilised.

(b) Define the meaning of the term 'pre-emption' in the context of an issue of shares.

Question 13.2

Bextor Manufacturing Plc ('Bextor') was incorporated in 2005 with an authorised share capital of 5,000,000 €1 ordinary shares. At incorporation, 1,000,000 of these shares were issued and since then Bextor has not issued any further capital.

Upon incorporation, Mark purchased 300,000 Class A ordinary shares. At the point of subscription, Mark was only required to pay €0.50 for every €1 share purchased. Since incorporation, Mark has made no other payment on foot of these shares.

Unfortunately, in recent years Bextor has experienced a significant decline in sales and Bextor's most recent financial statements highlighted that the company had incurred a trading loss of €200,000. In addition, Bextor is also carrying a retained loss of €500,000 from previous trading periods. As a consequence of these losses, Bextor is now insolvent and the board of directors has decided to put Bextor into liquidation.

Bextor has contacted you for advice in relation to this situation.

Requirement Write a memo to Bextor that:

(a) Lists **three** of the main characteristics of an ordinary share.

(b) Outlines the nature of a partly-paid share and states how these shares are accounted for in the Bextor's share capital account.

(c) Outlines the potential liability of Mark on the liquidation of Bextor.

Chapter 14

COMPANY INSOLVENCY AND BUSINESS RECOVERY

LOAN CAPITAL

All companies need to raise capital with which to operate. This capital can be raised either by issuing share capital or by borrowing capital. Where capital relates to borrowing it is called loan capital. 'Loan capital' comprises debentures and other long-term loans to a business. Companies often use their assets to secure these loans, and this is known as placing a charge on an asset. In this section we will examine the different types of charges that can be placed against a loan and the significance of these charges in the event of a company being wound up.

Debentures

A 'debenture' is a type of loan and is defined by Courtney, *The Law of Companies* (Bloomsbury Professional, 3rd Edition, 2012) as a written document acknowledging the debt owed by a company. Most debentures contain a security or a charge that improves the lender's prospect of being repaid if the company becomes insolvent.

There are three forms of debenture:

- **Single debenture** An individual loan to a company and the most common type of debenture in Ireland.
- **Series of debentures** A group of separate loans, which rank equally, used to raise a total amount.
- **Debenture stock** Used by PLCs to raise money from the public at large. A large number of lenders subscribe for debentures and the loan is treated as part of an overall stock figure.

Debenture Trust Deed

Where companies issue a series of debentures or debenture stocks, the number of subscribers may be numerous. To facilitate the administration of these large numbers of subscribers, a 'trust deed' is executed by the company.

A debenture trust deed appoints a trustee to act on behalf of all debenture holders to regulate administrative matters in relation to the debenture, where necessary to enforce the security and, in default, to appoint a receiver.

Secured and Unsecured Debentures

Debentures may be secured or unsecured, but are normally secured to improve the debenture holders' prospects of being repaid if the company becomes insolvent. The most common means of granting security are charges, legal and equitable mortgages, and pledges.

Charges

The most common type of security used by a company is a charge on its assets, which are pledged as collateral for borrowings. A charge is an acknowledgement, either in a written or oral form, that is created over any interest in any property of the company. However, section 408 CA 2014 specifically excludes the following from the definition of a charge:

- a mortgage or charge created over cash;
- money credited to an account of a financial institution, or any other deposits;
- shares, bonds or debt instruments;
- units in collective investment undertakings or money market instruments; or
- claims and rights, such as dividends or interest, in respect of any of the foregoing, except for cash.

Charges can be secured either by a **fixed** or a **floating** charge. A fixed charge attaches to a specific asset and restricts the borrower's ability to deal with the charged asset. This does not mean that the company cannot use the asset that is the subject of a fixed charge, but that the company cannot sell this asset or use it as collateral for future borrowing, without the permission of the charge holder.

A floating charge does not attach to specific assets – the borrower is free to deal with them (sell them, replenish them, etc.) as the charge hovers/floats over them until the moment of crystallisation (e.g. winding up of the company). Upon crystallisation, the charge attaches to the assets over which it previously floated. (Crystallisation is discussed further below.)

Fixed Charges

Fixed charges are beneficial to the lender in that they rank above all other existing creditors on liquidation in relation to those assets that the charge affects.

There is no statutory prohibition on the creation of fixed charges within 12 months of the liquidation of the company.

A fixed charge may also take the form of a legal mortgage or be by way of an equitable mortgage (see 'Mortgages' below).

Floating Charges

A floating charge is a general security over things such as 'stock in trade'. The benefit to the company of this type of charge is that it does not impede its ability to deal with these assets day-to-day as it does not attach to the asset until a crystallising event occurs.

Lord Justice MacNaughton in *Illingworth v. Houldsworth* (1904) defined fixed and floating charges as follows:

> "A specific [fixed] charge, I think, is one that fastens more on ascertained and definite property or property capable of being ascertained and defined; a floating charge, on the other hand, is ambulatory and shifting in it's nature, hovering over and so to speak floating with the property which it is intended to affect until some event occurs or some act is done which causes it to settle and fasten on the subject of the charge within its reach and grasp."

In *Re Yorkshire Woolcombers Association Ltd* (1903), three characteristics of a floating charge were listed as follows:

1. it is a charge on a class of assets of a company present and future;
2. that class is one which, in the ordinary course of the business of the company, would change from time to time; and
3. that until some future step is taken by or on behalf of those interested in the charge, the company may carry on its business in the ordinary way so far as concerns the particular class of assets being dealt with.

Crystallisation of Floating Charges

Crystallisation is the occurrence of a special event that causes the floating charge to cease floating and become attached to the class of assets that it affects. The rights of the charge holder are dormant until the moment of crystallisation, which confers tangible equitable rights on the assets within the ambit of the charge.

Floating charges crystallise when:

1. a receiver is appointed;
2. the company is being wound up;
3. there is cessation of business;

4. there is automatic crystallisation (a clause may state that the charge will crystallise automatically upon the occurrence of some specified event); or
5. the giving of notice by the debenture holder can cause crystallisation where the debenture provides for this.

In *Re Brightlife Ltd* (1987), the debenture provided that there was a fixed charge over the book debts and a floating charge over all the undertakings of the company, present and future. There was also a provision that the floating charge could be converted into a fixed charge at any time before the liquidation of the company if the debenture holder gave notice of crystallisation to the company. **Held**: on the facts that there was no reason the debenture holder should not be capable of crystallising the charge by giving notice.

Negative Pledge Clause

A 'negative pledge clause' is a clause to protect the holder of a floating charge against any subsequent charges that may have priority of payment over the floating charge. This clause now appears in most standard charges and it binds both parties, as well as any subsequent secured creditors, provided they have actual notice of the clause. For example, if a floating charge containing a negative pledge clause was created by X Ltd in December 20X4 and a fixed charge was subsequently created by X Ltd in June 20X5, the fixed charge would be in breach of the negative pledge due to its priority of payment, and all parties who were aware of the negative pledge and those who acted in contravention of it would be liable. The key issue regarding liability is knowledge of the existence of the clause.

In *Welch v. Bowmaker and Bank of Ireland* (1980), a company issued a debenture in favour of Bowmaker that created a fixed charge over three of the four parcels of land owned by the company and a floating charge over its remaining assets, which included the fourth parcel known as 'Ivy Lawn'. The floating charge over the remaining assets contained a negative pledge clause. A month later the company deposited the title deeds of 'Ivy Lawn' as security with Bank of Ireland, which was aware of the earlier floating charge but unaware of the terms of the debenture. The company subsequently went into liquidation and Bowmaker argued that the Bank of Ireland should have had constructive notice of the negative pledge clause. **Held**: the court found that although unusual, it is possible to create a floating charge over land. The bank did not have actual knowledge of the negative pledge clause, so the court ruled that the fixed charge created by the depositing of the deeds with the bank took priority over the earlier floating charge.

Mortgages

A fixed charge is often created by means of a mortgage over the securitised property. With a mortgage, the borrower pledges a property as security to the lender in case it fails to repay their mortgage loan. Mortgages involve the transfer of ownership and a mortgage can be legal or equitable:

- **Legal mortgage** The mortgagee has the legal title of the property in return for lending, subject to an equitable right of the mortgagor to recover the legal title by fulfilling the terms of redemption (by repaying the mortgage). If the mortgagor defaults in repayment, the mortgagee may be entitled to sell the property to recoup any unpaid loan amount.
- **Equitable mortgage** The mortgagor transfers the equitable interest in the property to the mortgagee (e.g. by depositing the title deeds of the property with the lender). If the mortgagor defaults in repayment, the mortgagee may be entitled to sell the property to recoup any outstanding debt.

Registration of Charges Created by Companies

All charges that are not registered with the Companies Registration Office (CRO) become void against any liquidator or creditor of the company. When the charge becomes void, the money secured becomes payable immediately, and may be ranked as an unsecured debt.

The company, as the borrower, has the legal obligation to register the charge (section 419 CA 2014). In reality, this function usually falls within the remit of the company secretary. The Act also allows any interested person to invoke the procedure for registration, though this rarely happens.

Section 409(1) CA 2014 provides for two methods by which a charge can be registered, i.e. the 'one-stage' procedure or the 'two-stage' procedure:

- The one-stage procedure involves the CRO receiving an application for registration of the charge, not later than 21 days after the date of the creation of the charge, in its prescribed form.
- The two stage-procedure involves the CRO receiving a notice stating the company's intention to create the charge in two separate forms:
  - the first form is a notice of intention by the company to create a charge, which must be submitted to the CRO in advance of the charge being created;
  - the second form, which includes details of the charge to be registered, must be delivered to the CRO within 21 days of the submission of the notice of intention.

The application for registration of the charge must contain the following details: (1) the name of the company; (2) the description of the charge; (3) the date of creation; (4) short particulars of the property charged; (5) the presenter's details; and (6) details of the persons entitled to the charge.

Register of Charges

Section 414 CA 2014 requires the CRO to maintain, in relation to each company, a register of all registered charges. A copy of the instrument creating these charges must also be maintained at the registered office of the company (section 418). In addition, where a company breaches its obligations pursuant to section 418, it may be guilty of a category 3 offence (see **Chapter 15**).

Certificate of Registration

The Registrar (CRO) shall give a certificate of the registration of any charge registered and this certificate shall be conclusive evidence that the requirements of the registration of the charge have been complied with (section 415 CA 2014).

Time Extension for Registration of Charges and Rectification of Register

As discussed above, if a charge is not registered within the 21-day timeframe with the CRO it becomes void against a liquidator or relevant company creditors. When this arises, the charge holder may demand repayment and, if the company is unable to do so at that time, the charge holder may demand that the company be wound up. The Companies Act provides for a procedure to apply to the High Court for an extension of time for registration or rectification of the charge. This will only be granted where the court is satisfied that:

- the omission was accidental or due to inadvertence or is not of a nature to prejudice the position of creditors or shareholders of the company; or
- that on other grounds it is just and equitable to grant that relief in respect of such an omission or misstatement.

Priority of Charges

According to section 412 CA 2014, charges have to be paid in order of priority. The basic order of priority for the payment of debts owed by a company is:

1. fixed charges (ranked in order of date of registration);
2. preferential debts (ranked *pari passu*, i.e. paid equally) under section 621 CA 2014 (see later);
3. floating charges (ranked in order of date of registration).

This means that the first fixed charge registered with the CRO is the first charge to be repaid. If, however, there are two charges on the asset, a fixed charge and a floating charge, the fixed charge is always paid first in order of date of registration and then the floating charge according to date of registration.

RECEIVERSHIP

Introduction

A receiver is someone who is appointed when a debenture holder needs to realise his or her security. This usually arises where the company defaults in its obligation regarding the repayment of the debenture loan. The receiver takes control of the charged asset, sells the asset, applies the proceeds of the sale and discharges the debt.

The classic common law definition of a receiver was given in *Re Manchester and Milford Railway Company* (1880) where it was stated that:

> "'Receiver' is a term which was well known in the court of chancery as meaning a person who receives rents and other income-paying ascertained outgoings, but who does not, if I may say so, manage the property in the sense of buying or selling or anything of that kind … if it was desired to continue to trade at all it was necessary to appoint a manager, or a receiver and manager as it was generally called. He could buy and sell and carry on trade."

Appointment of Receivers

A Receiver Appointed by a Debenture Holder

Most debenture documents empower the lender to appoint a receiver where the borrower defaults on the repayment of the debt. When a receiver is appointed by a debenture holder, he is a creature of contract and not an officer of the court. The debenture will usually state that he is an agent of the company, and therefore, the company is responsible for his acts, defaults and remuneration.

A Receiver Appointed by the Court

Another situation in which a receiver may be appointed is by order of a court, following an application by a creditor. In this situation, he is a court officer, and therefore is subject to its directions and not the directions of the applicant creditor. However, he must still have regard to the creditors' interests.

An application for the appointment of a receiver by the court is usually made where the debenture document is vague as to the appointment of a receiver. Therefore, the court will only appoint a receiver on one of the following grounds:

- if the security that is pledged is in jeopardy;
- if the company has begun proceedings to be wound up;
- if the principal sum or interest due on the debenture is in arrears.

Notification that A Receiver has been Appointed

Section 429 of the Companies Act 2014 states that where a receiver of the asset charged has been appointed, all documentation pertaining to the company, all electronic correspondence and the company's website must state that the company is in receivership and that a receiver has been appointed.

If this requirement is not complied with, any person acting on behalf of the company who knowingly and intentionally authorises or permits the default, the company itself and any of its officers who are in default shall be guilty of a category 4 offence (see **Chapter 15**).

Persons Ineligible for Appointment as a Receiver

Under section 433 CA 2014, the following persons are disqualified/ineligible from acting as a receiver:

- an undischarged bankrupt;
- a person who was an employee or officer of the company within 12 months of the commencement of the receivership;
- a parent, spouse, civil partner, brother, sister or child of an officer of the company;
- a partner or employee of an officer or employee of the company;
- any person likely to classed as a connected person to the company's parent or subsidiary;
- a body corporate (company).

Resignation of a Receiver

A receiver appointed under a deed may resign from office if he gives one month's written notice to the charge-holders, the company or its liquidator.

A receiver appointed by the court may resign only with the consent of the court.

A person in default of the above criteria will be guilty of a category 4 offence (see **Chapter 14**).

Removal of a Receiver

The court has the power to remove a receiver if:

- the company in receivership has gone into liquidation; or
- a cause has been shown, such as where the court believes it to be in the best interest of the creditors or where there has been an act of misconduct by the receiver.

Powers and Duties of Receivers

Powers of a Receiver

The statutory powers of the receiver of a company are set out in section 437 CA 2014. A receiver's powers are subject to the terms of the relevant debenture document, or order of the court.

Subject to the terms of the debenture document, or the court order, the receiver has the power to take possession of and control the company's property and can:

- lease it, hire it out or dispose of it;
- grant options over the propery on such conditions as he thinks fit;
- borrow money, using it as security;
- insure it;
- repair, renew or enlarge it; and/or
- convert it into money.

A receiver (subject to the terms of the debenture document, or the court order), has the power to carry on any business of the company, including to:

- take on lease or on hire, or otherwise acquire, property;
- execute any document, bring or defend any proceedings or do any other act or thing in the name of and on behalf of the company;
- draw, accept, make and endorse a bill of exchange or promissory note;
- use a seal of the company;
- engage or discharge employees on behalf of the company;
- appoint:
  - a solicitor, accountant or other professionally qualified person to assist him; or
  - an agent to do any business that he is unable to do, or that it is unreasonable to expect him to do in person;
- enforce payment of any call on the company's shares that is due and unpaid;
- make or defend an application for the winding up of the company;
- refer to arbitration or mediation, any question affecting the company.

Where a debt or liability is owed to the company, the receiver has the power to prove it in a bankruptcy, insolvency or winding up and, in connection with such a debt or liability, to receive dividends and to assent to a proposal for a composition or a scheme of arrangement.

If the receiver was appointed under an instrument that created a charge on uncalled share capital of the company, he has the power:

- to make a call in the name of the company for the payment of money unpaid on the company's shares; or
- on giving a proper indemnity to a liquidator of the company, to make a call in the liquidator's name for the payment of money unpaid on the company's shares.

Duties of a Receiver

A receiver's main duty is to receive and realise the assets of the company that are the subject of a charge. The receiver then discharges this debt and vacates his office. The receiver's responsibility is to the debenture holder and not the company. However, in discharging these duties, the receiver's actions may affect on the company, as the sale of a company asset may result in the company having to be brought to an end, or the downsizing or restructuring of the business. The main duties owed by a receiver are further discussed below.

Duty of receiver to sell property at the best price reasonably obtainable, etc.
In the case of *Ruby Property Company Ltd v. Kilty* (1999), the receiver sold company property on the advice of an estate agent, but without advertising it publicly. **Held**: the receiver may have a duty to consider representations from the company as to how to conduct a sale to comply with section 316(A) of the Companies Act 1963 (now section 439 CA 2014). However, the court held that the receiver was not liable, as he did not have the benefit of hindsight.

In *Bula Ltd v. Crowley* (2003), the receiver was appointed to a mining company and he wrote to other major mining companies seeking expressions of interest. It was argued that the receiver had gone to the market at a bad time. **Held**: the court rejected the argument and stated that the receiver is not obliged to postpone the sale until the market rises; his primary duty is to the debenture holder.

Furthermore, under section 439(3) CA 2014, a receiver shall not sell any assets of the company by private contract to a person who was an officer of the company within a three-year period prior to the date of his appointment, unless the creditors have been notified within 14 days of this fact.

Duty of Receiver to apply to the Court for direction The receiver and any officers and members of the company may apply to the court for direction in relation to any potential liability of the receiver in relation to contracts created by him in the performance of his duties.

Duty of Receivers to notify and account to the Registrar The receiver also has a duty to notify the Registrar of his appointment and the cessation of this appointment (section 436 CA 2014). Within a prescribed timeframe during his appointment and following cessation of his appointment, the receiver has a duty to notify the Registrar which of the assets of the company he or she has taken into his or her possession, the value and the proceeds of sale of any such asset and his or her expenses (section 430 CA 2014).

A receiver in default of this requirement shall be guilty of a category 4 offence (see **Chapter 15**).

Duty of receivers to report to the company Within 14 days of his appointment the receiver is entitled to receive a statement of affairs in relation to the company, which must state the following:

- particulars of all of the company's assets, debts and liabilities at the date of appointment of the receiver;
- the names and residences of the company's creditors;
- the securities held by those creditors;
- the dates when the securities were respectively given;
- any further or other information that may be required.

Within two months of his appointment, the receiver must send a copy of this statement of affairs to: (1) the CRO; (2) the court; (3) the company; and (4) the debenture holders and/or their trustees, including any comments regarding this statement that the receiver sees fit to make.

When a person ceases to act as a receiver, he or she is also required to report on his or her opinion as to whether or not the company is solvent to the CRO which, upon receiving this statement, will forward a copy of it to the Director of Corporate Enforcement.

Duty of receiver to comply with requests of the Director of Corporate Enforcement A receiver has a duty to furnish the Director of Corporate Enforcement with his or her books for examination, either in regard to a particular receivership or to all receiverships undertaken by the receiver up to six years from the date of the receivership. If a receiver fails to comply with this request, he or she shall be guilty of a category 3 offence (see **Chapter 15**).

Duty of receiver to report to the Director of Public Prosecutions In the course of a receivership, a receiver has a duty to report to the DPP any past or present officer, or any member, of the company who may be guilty of any offence in relation to the company.

Duty of receiver to pay the company's debts in a manner fixed by law If a receiver is appointed by a debenture holder and realises assets on a fixed charge or a legal mortgage, he has an obligation to pay the debenture holder first. Any surplus over the realisation of the asset should be returned to the company.

However, if a receiver is appointed by a debenture holder and realises assets secured by a floating charge, the Companies Act provides that the receiver can apply the proceeds realised to discharge the debt owed to the debenture holder, provided the receiver uses these proceeds to pay the debts due to the preferential creditors first. Any surplus can then be used to repay the debt outstanding on foot of the floating charge. This obligation arises as a consequence of the following prescribed priority for the repayment of company debts on receivership:

- the costs of receivership;
- the fixed charges in the order that they were registered;
- the preferential debts;
- the floating charges in the order they were registered;
- the unsecured creditors.

EXAMINERSHIP

Introduction

Examinership is a process that offers protection to failing companies and affords them the opportunity to implement plans to facilitate any required changes in order to achieve their long-term survival.

In effect, with examinership a company is awarded temporary protection by the court. The purpose of this protection is to prevent actions taken by creditors that may result in the demise of the company, as well as allowing the company the time to investigate its own business affairs and make a proposal for changes within the company to enable its survival.

The examiner is an officer of the court who investigates the company's affairs and reports to the court on its prospects of survival.

In *Re Atlantic Magnetics Ltd* (1993), Mr Justice McCarthy stated that the purpose of examinership:

> "... is protection, protection of the company and consequently of its shareholders, workforce and creditors. It is clear that Parliament intended that

> the fate of the company and those who depend on it should not lie solely in the hands of one or more large creditors, who can by appointing a receiver effectively terminate its operation to the inevitable disadvantage of those less protected."

In *Re Holidair Ltd* (1994), Chief Justice Mr Finlay stated that the construction of any provision of the Companies Act (1990) should be mindful of the twin objectives of:

- provision of a period of protection; and
- if possible, that a company be enabled to continue as a going concern.

Examinership enables a company to avoid being wound up during a period of court protection and facilitates the rescue and return to health of ailing but potentially viable companies.

The period of court protection is 70 days.

Power of Court to Appoint an Examiner

The examiner is appointed by the High Court if the company (other than companies deemed to be a 'small company' under section 350 CA 2014, wherein the process is overseen by the Circuit Court) can satisfy the court that it has a reasonable chance of survival as a going concern. During the period of examinership, the appointed examiner will prepare a report on the possible future of the company and possible schemes of arrangement for the company's survival.

As stated by section 509 CA 2014, the grounds for the appointment of an examiner are that a company has a reasonable prospect of survival as a going concern and that:

1. the company is, or is likely to be, unable to pay its debts; and
2. no resolution subsists for the winding up of the company; and
3. no order has been made for the winding up of the company.

In determining whether a company is unable to pay its debts, one of the key factors is whether the value of its assets is less than the amount of its liabilities, taking into account its contingent and prospective liabilities.

Petition to Appoint an Examiner

The process of appointing an examiner commences with the lodging of a petition to the High Court. A petition may be presented to the court by one or more of the following:

- the company;
- the directors of the company;

- a creditor, or a contingent or prospective creditor (including an employee) of the company; or
- a member or members of the company holding at least 10% of the fully paid-up voting capital.

The Application to the Court

An application to the court to appoint an examiner is an *ex parte* application, i.e. the company does not have to be in court on that day. The *ex parte* application to have an examiner appointed has been described as an *uberrimae fidei* procedure, i.e. it is an application that must be made in the utmost good faith. This requires that all information relevant to the examinership must be brought to the attention of the court at the application stage, and the application must be for the primary purpose of rescuing the company – not for any other ulterior purpose.

In *Re Wogan's (Drogheda) Ltd* (1992), the court rejected the application because the company's real motive of bringing such an application was that it did not want to pay the Revenue Commissioners. Furthermore, the directors deliberately misstated the value of Revenue debts in the balance sheet presented on foot of the petition.

On hearing the application, the High Court may appoint an examiner, refuse to appoint an examiner, adjourn the petition to enable the applicant to present further evidence, make an interim order or make such order as it thinks fit.

The appointment lasts for 70 days and must be advertised in *Iris Oifigúil* and two daily newspapers. The company must amend all its documentation to include the word "in examination".

The Petition

Section 511 CA 2014 requires that the petition to the High Court be accompanied by a report of an independent expert. This is usually the statutory auditor of the company or a person who is qualified to be appointed as an examiner of the company. The report must contain the following:

(a) the names and addresses of the officers of the company;

(b) the names of other companies of which the directors of the company are also directors;

(c) a statement as to the affairs of the company, showing particulars of the company's assets and liabilities (whether any deficiency between the assets and liabilities of the company has been satisfactorily accounted for);

(d) whether the company, and the whole or any part of its undertaking, would have a reasonable prospect of survival as a going concern;
(e) whether the formulation, acceptance and confirmation of proposals for a compromise or scheme of arrangement would offer a reasonable prospect of the survival of the company, and the whole or any part of its undertaking, as a going concern;
(f) whether an attempt to continue the whole company would be more advantageous than a winding up of the company;
(g) recommendations as to the course that should be taken in relation to the company;
(h) whether the facts disclosed would warrant further inquiries with a view to proceedings;
(i) details of the extent of the funding required to enable the company to continue trading during the period of protection and the sources of that funding;
(j) recommendations as to which liabilities incurred before the presentation of the petition should be paid;
(k) an opinion as to whether the work of the examiner would be assisted by a direction of the court in relation to the role or membership of any creditor's committee;
(l) such other matters as he or she thinks relevant.

Before the court will appoint an examiner, it must appear to the court that:

- the examiner is suitably qualified (see below);
- no winding up of the company has commenced;
- the company has not been in receivership for more than three continuous days before the petition was presented;
- it appears to the court that the company is likely to be unable to pay its debts;
- the person designated to act as examiner by the petitioners consents to the appointment in writing;
- the examiner was not within the previous 12 months an officer or servant of the company or a partner of that person.

The court will take the report of an independent expert into consideration, but retains the discretion not to grant an application for examinership. For example, in *Re Missford Limited t/a Residents Club* (2010), Missford Ltd traded as a private members' club on St Stephen's Green, Dublin, managed by two brothers. The club never showed a profit. The company petitioned the court to have an examiner appointed. The application for examinership was supported by the company's creditors. **Held**: in exercising its discretion not to grant examinership the court was critical of both the independent accountant's report and the management of the company. The court was highly sceptical of the independent accountant's opinion that the company had a reasonable prospect of survival. The independent accountant had based this view in part on the business plan which was in the court's view overly optimistic, projecting profits for 2010 and 2011 for a company with liabilities of €4 million in a time of economic downturn. The court strongly criticised the management of the club, in particular the use by the club of PAYE and VAT monies owed to the Revenue Commissioners.

The court will also allow the creditors to be heard at the petition stage.

Qualifications of an Examiner

A person shall not be qualified to be appointed or act as an examiner of a company unless he or she would be qualified to act as its liquidator, i.e. with the same qualifications and experience as a liquidator, with the exception that the examiner does not have to comply with the requirements regarding professional indemnity cover (see later in this chapter). A person who acts as examiner of a company when he or she is not qualified to do so shall be guilty of a category 2 offence (see **Chapter 15**).

Powers of an Examiner

An examiner has the following powers under section 524 CA 2014:

- the powers of the company's directors can be transferred to him or her;
- he or she may obtain information in the same way as the company's auditor;
- he or she may convene, preside over and is entitled to receive notice and be heard at all directors and general meetings;
- he or she may seek direction from the court to assist him;
- he or she may sell property that has a charge with the approval of the court;
- he or she may certify expenses and ascertain and agree claims against the company;
- he or she may halt, prevent or rectify the effects of any act, omission, course of conduct, decision or contracts made in relation to the income, assets or liabilities of the company – where such is likely to be detrimental to the company or any interested party.

The examiner's ability to repudiate contracts is now confined to contracts entered into during the period of examinership only.

Duty of an Examiner

The examiner has the duty to examine the affairs of the company and report within 21 days to the court. Also, the examiner must report if the company has a reasonable prospect of survival and what procedures should be taken to ensure this.

The Effect of the Examiner's Protection

Once the company is awarded protection, creditors will be prevented from taking the following actions against it for the next 70 days from the date of petition:

- no winding up or receivership may commence against the company;
- where a receiver has been appointed within three days before the examiner's appointment, the receivership is to cease;
- no legal action can be taken against the company except with the consent of the examiner;
- no attachment, sequestration, distress or execution shall be put into force against the property or effects of the company, except with the consent of the examiner;
- where any claim against the company is secured by a mortgage, charge, lien or other encumbrance or a pledge of, on or affecting the whole or any part of the property, effects or income of the company, no action may be taken to realise the whole or any part of that security, except with the consent of the examiner;
- no steps may be taken to repossess goods in the company's possession under any hire-purchase agreement, except with the consent of the examiner;
- no application for relief by a minority shareholder may be made during the period of examinership;
- no other proceedings in relation to the company may be commenced except by leave of the court and subject to such terms as the court may impose, and the court may, on the application of the examiner, make such order as it thinks fit.

A person who fails to comply with the above requirements shall be guilty of a category 4 offence.

Reports to the Court made by the Examiner

The most important duty of the examiner is to report to the court. Section 534 CA 2014 states that the examiner shall:

- formulate proposals for a compromise or scheme of arrangement (see below);
- report on those proposals to the court, within 35 days after the date of his or her appointment (the court may, of its own motion or on the application of the examiner, extend the period concerned by a further 30 days);
- perform such functions as the court may direct the examiner to perform;
- convene and preside at such meetings of members and creditors as he or she thinks proper for the purpose of formulating proposals and obtaining agreement for the compromise or scheme of arrangement;

- supply a copy of his or her report under this section to:
    - the company concerned on the same day as he or she causes the report to be delivered to the office of the court; and
    - any interested party on written application being made to him in that behalf.

Content of the Examiner's Report

An examiner's report under section 534 shall include:

- the proposals for a compromise or scheme of arrangement;
- any adopted modifications to these proposals;
- the outcome of each of the meetings held regarding these proposals;
- the recommendation of the committee of creditors, if any (see below);
- a statement of the company's assets and liabilities (including contingent and prospective liabilities);
- a list of the company's creditors and the amount owed to them;
- a list of the officers of the company;
- the examiner's recommendations;
- such other matters as the examiner deems appropriate or the court directs.

Appointment of Committee of Creditors

An examiner may, and if so directed by the court shall, appoint a committee of creditors to assist him in the performance of his functions. This committee shall consist of not more than five members and shall include the holders of the three largest unsecured claims who are willing to serve on such a committee.

Proposals for Compromises or Schemes of Arrangement

Where a company enters examinership in order for the company to continue to survive, it is likely that changes will need to be made, the majority of which are likely to affect the financial structure of the company, although other changes, such as in the management structure, may also be necessary. These proposed changes are known as 'proposals for a compromise' or 'schemes of arrangement'.

For example, the examiner might propose a reduction in unsecured debt, the waiving of interest or the freezing of certain debts, the elimination of the cumulative preference dividend or a reduction in the rate of preference dividends.

Proposals for a compromise or schemes of arrangement shall:

- specify each class of members and creditors of the company;
- specify any class of members and creditors whose interests or claims will not be impaired by the proposals;

- specify any class of members and creditors whose interests or claims will be impaired by the proposals;
- provide equal treatment for each claim or interest of a particular class provide for the implementation of the proposals;
- specify what changes should be made in relation to the management or direction of the company;
- specify any changes the examiner considers should be made in the constitution of the company, including such other matters as the examiner deems appropriate.

A statement of the assets and liabilities should be submitted to the members and creditors at the meeting at which these proposals are to be considered.

Confirmation of Proposals

Once formulated the proposals for a compromise or scheme of arrangement must be put before the creditors and members for approval. In order to be valid they must be accepted by the majority of the different classes of creditors that will be affected by them. Once approved, these proposals will be binding on everyone.

Following his appointment, if the examiner feels that the company is not viable or if he cannot obtain agreement from the creditors regarding the proposals for a compromise or scheme of arrangement, the examiner must notify the court of this fact, which will generally grant an order for the liquidation of the company. If the company is viable and the proposals are approved, then the examiner must notify the court of this fact.

Termination of Court Protection

The protection granted to a company in examination shall cease either on the coming into effect of a compromise or a scheme of arrangement, or on such earlier date as the court may direct (section 552 CA 2014).

LIQUIDATION

The liquidation of a company is a process involving its winding up. Dealt with in Part 11 of the Companies Act 2014, it is where a company's corporate life is brought to an end and its property realised and distributed for the benefit of its creditors and members.

Section 561 CA 2014 states that there are two modes of winding up:

"(a) by the court; or
(b) voluntary."

Court-ordered Winding Up

Court-ordered winding ups are also knowns as compulsory or official liquidations. This type of winding up begins with a petition to the High Court on any of the grounds stated in section 569(1) CA 2014. A company may be wound up by the court if:

- the company has passed a special resolution to be wound up;
- the company does not commence trading within 12 months of its incorporation;
- the members of the company are all deceased or no longer exist;
- the company is unable to pay its debts;
- the court is of the opinion that it is just and equitable that the company should be wound up;
- the court is satisfied that the company's affairs are being conducted in a manner oppressive to any member; or
- the court is satisfied that it is the public interest that the company be wound up.

In addition, the company may also be placed in compulsory liquidation where it has failed at examinership (section 535 CA 2014).

Only those with an interest may bring a petition to wind up a company. These persons are called persons who have *locus standi*. The persons with *locus standi* are:

- the company itself;
- creditors;
- contributories and members;
- the Registrar of Companies;
- the Director of Corporate Enforcement.

The most common grounds to bring a petition for compulsory liquidation are:

1. if the company is unable to pay its debts;
2. if the court is satisfied that the company's affairs are being conducted in a manner oppressive to any member; and
3. if the court is of the opinion that it is just and equitable that the company should be wound up.

These grounds are discussed in more detail below.

1. If the Company is Unable to Pay its Debts

A company is deemed to be unable to pay its debts in three different circumstances: when:

- when a creditor has served a demand in writing to the company for a sum owed that exceeds €10,000 and this demand has not been satisfied within 21 days;

- when two or more creditors have served on the company a demand for a sum owed exceeding €20,000 and this demand has not been satisfied within 21 days;
- when a creditor has attempted to execute a judgment, decree or order of the court and this has been returned unsatisfied by the County Sheriff. This may arise where a claim is made to the court regarding the non-payment of a debt and the court makes an order in favour of the applicant requiring the respondent to pay the debt.

2. 'Oppression'

Section 569(1)(f) CA 2014 provides a ground to bring a winding up order where "the court is satisfied that the company's affairs are being conducted, or the powers of the directors are being exercised, in a manner that is oppressive to any member or in disregard of his interests as a member ..." and where the court is satisfied that winding up is justified in the circumstances.

(***Note:*** The court will dismiss any application if it is of the opinion that proceedings under section 212 CA 2014 – which provides alternative remedies for oppression – are, in the circumstances, a more appropriate remedy.)

In *Scottish Co-operative Wholesale Society Ltd v. Meyer* (1959) 'oppression' in this context was defined as behaviour that is "burdensome, harsh and wrongful to the other members of the company, or some of them, and lacks the degree of probity which they are entitled to expect in the conduct of the company's affairs".

Oppressive behaviour is considered by objective standards and on a case-by-case basis. See, for example, the discussion of the case of *Re Murph's Restaurant* (1979) in **Chapter 13** in the context of oppression and members' interests.

3. Where it is Just and Equitable that a Company be Wound Up

As stated above, and as per section 569(1)(e) CA 2014, a company may be wound up by the court if the court is of the opinion that it is just and equitable to do so.

As 'just and equitable' grounds are discretionary, the courts have concluded that they must be assessed on a case-by-case basis. The following are examples of cases where the courts have justified the liquidation of a company on just and equitable grounds.

Quasi-partnership Cases In *Re Murph's Restaurant* (1979) (which is also an example under this category), the compulsory liquidation of the company on just and equitable grounds was granted, based on the fact that the company was being run more like a partnership and the actions of the directors had breached the requirements of trust and confidence that are required in the context of partnerships. In this case, Mr Justice Gannon relied heavily on the House of Lords decision in *Ebrahimi v. Westbourne Galleries Ltd* (1973) and cited the judgment of Lord Wilberforce with approval:

> "[P]eople do not become partners unless they have confidence in one another and it is of the essence of the relationship that mutual confidence is maintained. If neither has any longer confidence in the other so that they cannot work together in the way originally contemplated then the relationship should end—unless, indeed the party who wishes to end it has been solely responsible for the situation which has arisen."

Deadlock in Corporate Management In *Re Yenidje Tobacco Co Ltd* (1916), a company was formed by two tobacco manufacturers who were equal shareholders and the only directors of the company. They had a disagreement and refused to talk to each other. Their only communication was through a secretary. **Held**: despite the profitability of the company, it had to be wound up on the "just and equitable" ground that they refused to talk to each other directly, as this created a deadlock in corporate management.

Similarly, in *Re Vehicle Buildings and Insulations Ltd* (1986), a company was involved in the repair of and dealing in motor vehicles. The petitioner of the winding up was an equal shareholder in the company and alleged that a state of deadlock existed in the management of the company. **Held**: the court ordered that the company be wound up. The court pointed to the complete unwillingness of either party to co-operate with each other and the objective fact that shareholders/directors could not legally or practically administer a company in such circumstances.

Where the Substratum of the Company has Failed/Disappeared This is when the substratum and/or the objects of the company have failed. Since the enactment of the Companies Act 2014, this ground can only be cited by companies that have an objects clause in their constitutions, such as designated activity companies or public limited companies. The use of this ground was seen in the case of *Re German Date Coffee Company* (1882). The company was formed with the object of making coffee from dried dates. It could not get a permit to do so (as a patent had already been granted to another company) and instead began making coffee from coffee beans. A shareholder objected to this change in the business and sought to have the company wound up. **Held**: in the circumstances it was just and equitable to liquidate the company because it had exceeded its powers as the whole substratum of the company had failed.

Illegal Objects The court will order that the company be wound up where its objectives are illegal, i.e. where the company was set up to achieve an illegal purpose. This was seen in the case of *Re Shrinkpak Ltd* (1989) where the liquidator succeeded in having the company compulsorily wound up on the grounds that it was used to divert money from another insolvent company.

Fraud Where the purpose of a company is to perpetrate a fraud, an application for compulsory liquidation may be granted. In the case of *Cook v. Deeks* (1916), three directors negotiated a contract on behalf of the company and then took it for themselves. **Held**: they were accountable to the company for profits made and thus one of the contributors could look to wind up the company, as the company was an instrument of fraud.

(***Note:*** Although fraud is a just and equitable ground for compulsory liquidation, the fact that company officers are engaged in fraudulent, reckless or insider trading is **not** automatically a ground for compulsory liquidation. The officers may be sanctioned without affecting the company.)

In addition to the above, the court will not make an order for compulsory liquidation unless it is satisfied that the company has no obligations in relation to a bank asset that has been transferred to the National Assets Management Agency (Nama) or a Nama group entity, or where they has been notification of the application.

Voluntary Winding Up

A voluntary liquidation is when a company initiates its own winding up and has control over the process. A company can be liquidated voluntarily in one of the following three circumstances:

1. the company resolves by special resolution to wind itself up voluntarily (known as member's voluntary winding up or liquidation);
2. the company resolves by resolution that it cannot by reason of its liabilities continue in business and a resolution is passed to liquidate the company voluntarily (known as creditors' voluntary winding up or liquidation);
3. a period fixed for the duration of the company expires or on the occurrence of an event that the company's constitution provides.

A copy of the resolution must be sent to the Registrar within 14 days of its passing at the general meeting.

Members' Voluntary Winding Up

A members' voluntary winding up is when the members declare in general meeting that the company is solvent and should be liquidated. This liquidation must commence with a Summary Approval Procedure (unless the liquidation arises where the company has a fixed duration or on the occurrence of a liquidating event) which requires:

- a declaration of solvency by the directors of the company;
- the passing of a special resolution or a written resolution to liquidate the company within 30 days of the declaration of solvency;
- a report by a person qualified to act as a statutory auditor confirming that the declaration is not unreasonable.

A copy of the declaration must be delivered to the Registrar within 21 days of the commencement date of the members' voluntary winding up. A copy of the special resolution must be delivered to the Registrar within 15 days of the date on which it is passed.

Companies of Fixed Duration, etc.

For a company that was established for a fixed duration that has expired, or for a fixed purpose that has been achieved, the Companies Act provides for an alternative procedure to be followed:

- a special resolution must be passed by the members, in general meeting, to voluntarily liquidate the company;
- the directors of the company must swear a declaration of solvency no more than 30 days prior to the passing of the resolution;
- the declaration must state that the directors have made a full inquiry into the affairs of the company and that, in their opinion, the company will be able to pay its debts in full with interest, within a period not exceeding 12 months from the commencement of the winding up;
- the declaration must have attached to it a statement of the company's assets and liabilities;
- an independent report by a person qualified to act as the statutory auditor of the company must be attached to the declaration and must state whether or not the declaration of solvency and the statement of affairs are reasonable.

The voluntary liquidation is deemed to have commenced at the time of passing the resolution at the general meeting and the general meeting must also have appointed one or more liquidators for the purpose of winding up the company's affairs.

The declaration must be delivered to the Registrar (CRO) within 14 days of the passing of the resolution to wind up the company.

Where a company has effected a members' voluntary liquidation by either method, notice of this fact must be made by placing an advertisement in *Iris Oifigiúil.* Default is classed as a category 3 offence.

Creditors' Voluntary Winding Up

A creditors' voluntary winding up occurs when the company is insolvent and the members in general meeting pass an ordinary resolution to state that the company cannot by reason of its liabilities carry on with its business. In this scenario, what generally happens is that the directors realise that the company is insolvent and, not wanting to trade recklessly, request that the members agree to pass a resolution to effect a creditors' voluntary liquidation. In some cases this may begin as a members' voluntary winding up and be converted to a creditors' voluntary winding up where the members or a liquidator believe that the company is unable to pay its debts within 12 months, despite having sworn a declaration of solvency to this effect.

Following the members' resolution, a meeting of creditors must be called on either the same day or the next day after the members' meeting. Creditors must be given at least 10 days' written notice of this meeting. This notice must also be advertised in two daily newspapers in the locality of the company and must state who the proposed liquidator is, and be accompanied by a list of creditors or notification of where this list is available for their review.

At this creditors' meeting, the directors must present a full statement of the affairs of the company together with a list of creditors of the company and the estimated amounts that are owed to them.

The creditors at this meeting may pass a resolution allowing the liquidation to proceed as a creditors' voluntary liquidation. The creditors may also appoint a committee of inspection to assist the liquidator with his powers and duties in winding up the company. The committee may be made up of a maximum of eight creditors.

LIQUIDATORS

A liquidator is a person who administers the property of the company. This means that the liquidator has responsibility for collecting and gathering the company's property, realising its value and distributing the proceeds of sale to repay the company's debts. Regardless of the type of winding up or liquidation involved, the liquidator's duties are the same. The main powers and duties of a liquidator, in accordance with section 627 CA 2014, are to:

- bring or defend any action or legal proceeding in the name of and on behalf of the company;
- carry on the business as far as is necessary for the beneficial winding up of the company;

- ascertain the debts and liabilities of the company;
- sell any part of the company's property, including the goodwill and book debts of the business, whether by public auction or private contract. To fulfil this duty the liquidator is empowered to apply to the court to vest any property belonging to the company in his or her official name (section 614 CA 2014);
- execute deeds, receipts and other documents that require the company seal in the name of the company;
- raise security on the assets of the company (e.g. subject an asset to a mortgage or charge in exchange for credit);
- pay any class of creditors in full;
- make any compromises or arrangements with creditors;
- appoint a legal practitioner to assist him;
- appoint an agent;
- participate in the bankruptcy of any contributor or debtor;
- do all such other things necessary for winding up the company's affairs and distributing the assets.

In relation to the administration of a company's assets the liquidator must comply with the following rules:

1. Paying Debts in Order of Priority

Liquidators must follow the rules set out in section 617 CA 2014 as to how the costs incurred in the winding up of a company are payable out of the property of the company assets and according to the following order of priority:

- in the case of winding up by the court, the cost of the petition;
- the cost and expenses necessary for the liquidation including the remuneration of the liquidator;
- fixed charges in the order they are registered;
- preferential debts as defined in section 621 CA 2014 (see below);
- floating charges in the order they are registered;
- unsecured creditors;
- dividends to members that have been declared payable but have not yet been paid; and
- the return to shareholders of any remaining monies.

Preferential Payments in a Winding Up

Preferential debts are unsecured debts as outlined in the legislation that are paid in priority to both floating charges and all other unsecured debts.

Section 621 CA 2014 defines the priority of payment of preferential debts in a winding up as follows:

- all taxes and local rates due at the time of the appointment of the liquidator and having become due and payable within the period of 12 months before that date;
- all wages or salaries of any employee for services to the company during the period of four months before the date of appointment of the liquidator;
- all accrued holiday remuneration payable 12 months before the date of liquidation;
- all sums due to any employee pursuant to any scheme for provision of payments to the employee while he or she is absent from employment due to ill health or in respect of superannuation benefits
- all amounts due from the company in respect of damages and costs or liability for damages and costs, payable to an employee.

In relation to payments to employees in respect of salaries, benefits or leave, the amount payable as a preferential debt cannot exceed €10,000 in respect of any one employee.

2. Avoiding Fraudulent Preferences

A liquidator also has a duty to ensure that the company does not enter a transaction that favours a creditor while the company was insolvent but before the commencement of the winding up order. This type of transaction is a called a 'fraudulent preference' and can be set aside by the liquidator.

A fraudulent preference is where a creditor is "fraudulently preferred" over another and is paid off first. A charge that has been paid due to fraudulent preference will be considered invalid.

In accordance with section 604 CA 2014, a charge may be invalid due to fraudulent preference if:

- it was created within six months of the company being wound up. This section prohibits "any conveyance, mortgage, delivery of goods, payment, execution or other act relating to property";
- where it is done with a view to preferring one creditor over another; and
- the company at the commencement of winding up is unable to pay its debts.

If a preference is in favour of a director or connected person, however, the six-month period is extended to two years. A connected person is defined as either a shadow director or a spouse, parent, child or sibling of a director or a related company.

In *Re M Kushler Ltd* (1943), it was **held** that liquidators must prove their intention to prefer at the time the transaction was made. An inference may be drawn from the facts where there is no other possible explanation.

In *Station Motors Ltd v. Allied Irish Banks Ltd* (1985), the overdraft of a company was guaranteed personally by two of its directors. Three months later the company went into creditors' voluntary liquidation. Prior to the liquidation, about half of the overdraft had been repaid and the liquidator argued that these payments were a fraudulent preference. **Held**: pre-liquidation payment was done to prefer AIB directly and the two directors indirectly. The transaction was set aside and AIB had to repay the money.

3. Avoidance of Certain Floating Charges

Section 597 CA 2014 states that a liquidator may avoid a floating charge (as explained earlier in this chapter) if it was registered within 12 months of liquidation and the company was not solvent at the time of its creation.

This 12-month period is extended to two years if the charge was created in favour of a director or connected person. This does not mean that the debt is invalid; rather that the debt is no longer secured and will now be ranked as unsecured debt.

In *Re Creation Printing Company Ltd* (1981), the test for deciding the solvency of a company for the purpose of ascertaining the validity of a floating charge is whether the company was able to pay its debts as they fell due.

4. Obtaining a Court Order for Return of Assets Improperly Transferred

A liquidator is empowered to apply to the court to return any asset of the company to him or her if the effect of the disposal of the asset was to perpetrate fraud on the company, its creditors or members (section 608 CA 2014).

5. Accepting Shares as Consideration for Sale of Property of Company

In the context of a members' voluntary liquidation, section 601 CA 2014 empowers the liquidator to accept payment-in-kind (payment other than in cash) in return for the sale of the whole or part of the business of the company. This payment may be in the form of shares, policies or other like interests in the transferee company, which are then distributed among the members of the transferor company. Alternatively, the members of the transferor company may agree to participate in the profits of, or receive any other benefit from, the transferee company.

To effect such a transaction, the members of the company in liquidation must give their consent to the liquidator to proceed in this manner through the passing of a special resolution.

6. Disclaiming Unprofitable Contracts

With the permission of the court, the liquidator may disclaim unprofitable company contracts and disclaim property that has onerous obligations attached to it (section 615 CA 2014). For example, if the liquidator is selling the entire business of the company to another company, but the company being liquidated has a lease on a property for a value that exceeds current market value, the liquidator may apply to the court to cancel the lease in order to make the business more attractive for sales purposes.

Personal Liabilities on Liquidation

The liquidator is empowered in certain situations to seek the imposition of personal liability upon company officers in respect of actions committed by them prior to the liquidation of the company. These include the following:

1. Failure to Maintain Adequate Accounting Records

Where adequate accounting records were not kept, and this contributed to the company being unable to pay its debts, resulted in substantial uncertainty as to the assets and liabilities of the company or substantially impeded the orderly winding up of the company, then the liquidator may apply to the court to declare that the officers of the company are made personally liable without any limitation of liability, for all, or such part as may be specified by the court, of the debts and other liabilities of the company (section 609 CA 2014).

2. Fraudulent and Reckless Trading

If in the course of the winding up of a company it appears that any person:

- was, while an officer of the company, knowingly a party to the carrying on of any business of the company in a reckless manner; or
- was knowingly a party to the carrying on of any business of the company with intent to defraud creditors of the company, or creditors of any other person or for any fraudulent purpose;

the court has the power, on the application of a liquidator (examiner or receiver), to make that person personally liable (section 610 CA 2014).

3. Damages against Certain Persons

Where a company officer is guilty of misfeasance, breach of duties or trust, both the liquidator and the Director of Corporate Enforcement are empowered to apply to the court to compel any such officer to compensate the company, or repay or restore the money or property to the company which has been lost as a consequence of these actions (section 612 CA 2014). This provision may also be used against the liquidator himself or herself where he or she commits a misfeasance, breach of duty or trust. In this latter situation the action is brought by the Director of Corporate Enforcement.

Qualifications of a Liquidator

Section 633 CA 2014 specifically provides that a liquidator must have one of the following qualifications:

- be a member of a prescribed accountancy body, i.e. any accountancy body that comes within the supervisory remit of IAASA (see **Chapter 17**), such as Chartered Accountants Ireland.
- be a practising solicitor, who is a member of the Law Society of Ireland under the Solicitors Act 1954–2002;
- be a member of other professional bodies recognised by IAASA;
- be qualified under the laws of another EEA Member State; or
- have practical experience of winding up and knowledge of the relevant law, as recognised by IAASA.

The following persons are disqualified from acting as a liquidator:

- a person who is, or within 24 months of the commencement of the winding up has been, an officer or servant of the company;
- except with the leave of the court, a parent, spouse, civil partner, sibling or child of an officer of the company;
- a person who is a partner or in the employment of an officer or servant of the company;
- a person who is an undischarged bankrupt;
- a person who is not qualified for appointment as a liquidator due to his or her connection to the liquidating company's subsidiary or holding company.

Resignation of a Liquidator

In both compulsory and voluntary winding up, a liquidator may resign from office by giving notice in writing within two days after the date of resigning to the Registrar (CRO) and the Director of Corporate Enforcement and, within 14 days after the date of resigning:

- in the case of a winding up by the court, to the court, and:
    - if a committee of inspection has been appointed — to the members of that committee, or

  - if no committee of inspection has been appointed — to the creditors of the company;
- in the case of a creditors' voluntary winding up:
  - if a committee of inspection has been appointed — to the members of that committee, or
  - if no committee of inspection has been appointed — to the creditors of the company, or
- in the case of a members' voluntary winding up — to the members of the company.

If a liquidator fails, without reasonable excuse, to provide such notice, he or she shall be guilty of a category 3 offence.

The Liability of a Liquidator

The duties of a liquidator are fiduciary in nature. As an agent of the company the liquidator will not be personally strictly liable, as **held** in *Knowles v. Scott* (1891) where it was stated that, in the absence of fraud, bad faith or personal misconduct, an action for damages will not lie against a liquidator. However, the liquidator will be liable for injury caused to creditors through breach of his statutory duties. Furthermore, as mentioned earlier in this chapter, the liquidator may also be liable for acts of misfeasance and breach of trust.

The Liquidator and the Director of Corporate Enforcement

The liquidator has certain obligations vis-à-vis the Office of the Director of Corporate Enforcement (ODCE). These can be summarised as follows:

1. Section 682 of the Companies Act 2014 provides that a liquidator of an insolvent company must within six months after the date of his appointment, and at intervals as required by the ODCE, report to the Director of Corporate Enforcement on the affairs of the company and the conduct of the company's officers for the purpose of determining whether restriction/disqualification (Part IV CA 2014) proceedings are justified. Where they are justified, the liquidator is obliged to bring proceedings unless excused by the ODCE (section 683).
2. The liquidator also has a duty to report any suspicion of criminal offences committed by a company, or its past or present officers, to the ODCE and the DPP, and may be required to provide information to the DPP and assist him by giving him access to facilities for inspecting and taking any copies of any company documents as he or she may require (section 723).
3. The liquidator has a duty to produce books and records for examination to the ODCE, and to answer any questions of the ODCE concerning the conduct of the particular liquidation (section 653).

REVIEW QUESTIONS

(See Solutions to Review Questions at the end of this text.)

Question 14.1

Robert and Matthew own a property business called RM Ltd ('RM'). RM is struggling to pay its debts and has sought your assistance. RM is considering appointing a compulsory liquidator, although no petition has yet been brought in the High Court for a compulsory liquidation of RM.

Requirement:

(a) Explain any **two** grounds (excluding insolvency) under which the court may accept a petition for the compulsory liquidation of a company.

(b) Outline and briefly describe any **two** alternatives that RM could consider other than putting the company into compulsory liquidation.

Question 14.2

Aunty Em's Catering School Ltd ('Aunty Em') has been trading successfully since 1963. Since its incorporation, its founder and primary shareholder, Emilia, has acted as the company's managing director. Emilia celebrated her 75th birthday last year and at this stage she decided to sell the business. She received an offer from the Dingle Catering School Ltd ('Dingle') proposing to purchase all of the assets of Aunty Em for €2.5 million. Emilia accepted this offer and has been advised by her solicitor to effect a members' voluntary liquidation of Aunty Em in order to distribute the €2.5 million to the company's shareholders. Emilia does not understand the meaning of the term 'members' voluntary liquidation' and seeks your advice.

Requirement:

(a) Outline any **two** reasons to effect a members' voluntary liquidation.

(b) State the main prerequisite to effect such a liquidation.

(c) Explain the Summary Approval Procedure that may be followed to effect a members' voluntary liquidation.

Question 14.3

Outline the procedure necessary to effect a creditors' voluntary liquidation.

Question 14.4

Peacock Books Ltd ('Peacock') is a private limited company, owned and managed by James and John, the sole directors and shareholders of the company. Peacock has been experiencing a downturn in its business in recent years.

In April 2013, the Revenue Commissioners applied to the High Court for the compulsory liquidation of Peacock on the grounds that it could not pay its debts. The court granted this application and Robert Barry was appointed as the official liquidator. On liquidation, the assets of Peacock were valued at €300,000 but the liabilities were valued at €485,000. These liabilities comprise, among other things:

1. Unpaid salaries in the last six months of €30,000;
2. Revenue debts of €20,000;
3. A loan of €40,000 in favour of Provincial Bank secured on the stock by a floating charge, created on 21 September 2004 and registered on 4 October 2004;
4. A loan for €100,000 in favour of Bank of Galway secured on the stock by a second floating charge, created on 24 September 2004 and registered on 26 September 2004;
5. A loan of €30,000 from James' father;
6. €165,000 of a mortgage, secured on Peacock's business premises in favour of Trinity Bank Plc, created and registered in March 2000; and
7. Unpaid trade creditors in the amount of €40,000.

Requirement As a trainee accountant in the firm acting as liquidator to Peacock, you have been asked to draft a memo to James and John that:

(a) Outlines the characteristics of a floating charge.
(b) Lists the priority of payment of a company's debts upon liquidation.
(c) Lists the priority of the debts due to the creditors in 1–7 above.

Question 14.5

Outline the duties imposed upon a company liquidator to the Director of Corporate Enforcement, pursuant to the provisions of the Company Law Enforcement Act 2001.

Question 14.6

Liston and Partners, a firm of chartered accountants, has recently been appointed receiver to a Cork-based hotel, the Boston Isle Hotel Ltd. The appointment is as a consequence of a fixed charge on the hotel's business premises, and a floating charge on the goodwill of the business in favour of the People's Bank of Dublin. The majority shareholder in the Boston Isle Hotel Ltd knows little about company law and comes to you for advice.

Requirement Write a memo to this shareholder explaining the following matters:

(a) The nature of a fixed charge.

(b) The definition of a receiver and any **three** effects of the appointment of a receiver.

(c) The distinction between receivership and liquidation.

Chapter 15

COMPLIANCE AND ENFORCEMENT

Part 14 of the Companies Act 2014 addresses compliance with and enforcement of the Act and of company law generally. The most important innovation of the Companies Act 2014 is its simplification and streamlining of **all** offences under company law. It codifies and categorises company law offences into four categories according to their gravity. This categorisation of offences introduces a more structured and consistent process, with clearly defined lines that enhance enforcement. This makes it very easy for the public at large to understand that, should there be a breach of company law, the person offending could be in breach of a category 1, 2, 3 or 4 offence, with a category 1 offence at the most serious end of the scale and the least serious a category 4 offence. Part 14 covers:

1. the power of courts to make orders to remedy any actions in breach of the legislation committed by company officers;
2. the categorisation of offences under the Act;
3. the restriction of directors; and
4. disqualification orders.

The restriction of directors and disqualification orders have already been discussed in **Chapter 12**. Therefore, the areas that are left to be discussed are court orders and, most importantly, the categorisation of offences.

Court Orders

In the course of the performance of their duties, company officers may act in breach of their obligations as established by the Companies Act 2014. The company itself may also act in a manner prohibited by the legislation. Where either situation arises, the court may make an order to remedy these breaches.

In accordance with section 797 CA 2014, where a company, or an officer of a company, has failed to comply with a provision of the Act, and failed to remedy the default within 14 days after the date of service on the company or officer of a notice requiring remedy of the default, the court, on the application of the following persons:

- any member of the company;
- any creditor of the company;

- the Director of Corporate Enforcement (the 'Director'); or
- the Registrar of Companies (the 'Registrar')

may order the company or officer in default to remedy the default within such time as the court specifies.

In this context, 'officer' means director, shadow director, promoter, receiver, liquidator, statutory auditor or secretary.

Where such an order is granted, the court is empowered to compel the defaulting party to pay all costs and expenses incidental to the application. Furthermore, such an application does not preclude the imposition of a restriction or disqualification order in respect of the same defaulting behaviour.

Orders Restraining Directors from Removing Assets

Under section 798 CA 2014, the court may restrain directors and other officers from the following acts:

- removing their or the company's assets from the State; or
- reducing their or the company's assets within or outside the State below an amount specified in the order. For example, if a claim is made against a director for fraudulent trading in the amount of €100,000, then the court may order that the assets of the director are not transferred to another party within Ireland or moved outside of Ireland, unless a minimum value of €100,000 is maintained in the director's name within the State to meet the claim against the director if it is successful.

Historically, these orders were known as 'freezing orders'.

The court will only make the order where it is satisfied that the applicant (see below) has a qualifying (see also below) claim, and where there are grounds for believing that the director or officer, or the company, may remove or dispose of their assets or the assets of the company, with a view to evading their obligations or those of the company, thereby frustrating an order of the court. In effect, the objective of this order is to prevent company officers from reducing/removing their assets in order to negate any civil claim against them.

The court may make the order only on the application of:

- the company;
- a director, member, liquidator, receiver or creditor of the company; or
- the Director.

A 'qualifying claim' is a claim that is a substantive civil cause of action, or right to seek a declaration of personal liability or to claim damages against a director, an officer or the company, and that arises under the Companies Act, the company's constitution or from the position of an officer of the company.

Such claims may include claims arising from corporate offences, such as fraudulent/reckless trading or insider dealing, or they may arise where a breach of duty by a company officer has resulted in a loss to the company, such as illegal loans, diverting business from the company, making a secret profit, etc.

Disclosure Orders

A disclosure order is an order of the court compelling the disclosure of documents and information and is often granted to assist an applicant in bringing legal proceedings in respect of an alleged wrongdoing. It can be used in order to ascertain the proper defendant in a legal action or to obtain information in order to support a claim. They are colloquially referred to as '*Norwich Pharmacal* orders', as they were first granted by the House of Lords in *Norwich Pharmacal Co v Customs and Excise Commissioners* (1974). Such an order is generally an equitable remedy and granted at the absolute discretion of the court.

The power to grant such an order in relation to the ownership of shares or debentures is encompassed in section 800 CA 2014. In accordance with this provision, on the application of any person who has a financial interest in a company, or the Director, the court may make a disclosure order, but only if the court considers that:

- it is just and equitable to do so; and
- in the case of an application made other than by the Director, the financial interest of the applicant is or will be prejudiced by the non-disclosure of any interest in the shares in or debentures of the company.

Types of disclosure order The court may make an order under section 800 requiring:

- any person whom the court believes has (or is able to obtain) information about the names and addresses of those currently (or previously) interested in the company's shares (or debentures) to disclose this information to the court;
- any person whom the court believes has (or is able to obtain) information about the names and addresses of people who currently act (or previously acted) for those currently (or previously) interested in the company's shares (or debentures) to disclose this information to the court;
- any person whom the court believes to be currently (or previously) interested, in the company's shares (or debentures) to confirm or deny that is the case. Where a person confirms their interest, they may be required to disclose any further information the court may require; or
- a person interested in the company's shares (or debentures) to disclose to the court in respect of those shares (or debentures) such information as the court may require (section 801 CA 2014).

In essence this means that, where shares or debentures are purchased as part of a share-acquisition agreement, or where they are being held in trust for a third party or where the applicant believes that the person named on the share certificate or debenture document is not the beneficial owner of the shares/debentures, then an application can be brought under section 800 to determine the true owner of the shares or debentures, as well as details of the trustees or representatives of these shareholders and debenture holders.

For the purpose of such a disclosure order, a 'share-acquisition agreement' means an agreement between two or more persons that includes provision for the acquisition by any one or more of the parties to the agreement of interests in shares comprised in the share capital of the company concerned, but only if the following two conditions are satisfied:

1. the agreement includes provisions imposing obligations or restrictions on any one or more of the parties to the agreement with respect to their use, retention or disposal of interests in that company's shares acquired in pursuance of the agreement; and
2. any interest in the company's shares is in fact acquired by any of the parties in pursuance of the agreement.

Such an agreement may arise where a group of friends decide to establish an investment group and they contribute a sum of money on a regular basis to invest in shares or debentures. One or more of the group may be authorised to purchase shares or debentures on behalf of the group and may be named on the share/debenture certificate as the owner of the relevant securities when in fact these securities are the property of the group, who are restricted based on the terms of their agreement in relation to dealings with respect to these securities. A disclosure order in these circumstances would identify all persons who are party to these share-acquisition agreements.

A person intending to apply for a disclosure order must give no less than 10 days' notice of the intention to apply to the company in respect of whose shares or debentures the order is sought, and to the person to whom the order is to be directed (section 10 CA 2014).

Scope of a disclosure order A disclosure order may require the person to whom it is addressed to give particulars of that person's own past or present interest in shares or debentures comprised in the share capital of the company or in debentures of the company held by that person at any time during the period specified in the order.

Such disclosures must include the following information:

1. the name and address of all persons who were party to the agreement for the acquisition of the relevant shares or debentures; and
2. the numbers of those shares.

Other additional powers of the court in relation to disclosure orders are as follows:

- it can discharge or vary a disclosure order;
- it can specify a person, group or class of persons to which the order applies;
- it can impose, for a specified period of time, such conditions or restrictions as it thinks fit on the rights or obligations attaching to the shares or debentures that are the subject of the order;

Furthermore, the party subject to such an order can apply to the court for relief from all or any of those conditions or restrictions mandated by that order. When this occurs the court may, if it considers it just and equitable to do so, grant such relief.

Notice of a disclosure order The notice of such an order can be sent to:

- the company (at its registered office);
- the Registrar;
- the registered holder of any of the shares or debentures; or
- any other person, as the court sees fit.

The notice should be sent by registered post and advertised in *Iris Oifigiúil* within seven days after the date of the making of the order.

Breach of a disclosure order Those subject to a disclosure order will not be entitled to enforce any of their rights or interests in respect of any shares or debentures of the company held by them where they either:

1. fail to comply with the requirements of the disclosure order within the period specified in the order; or
2. make a statement to the court in compliance with an obligation contained in that order, where they know that the statement is false or are reckless as to whether it is false.

If this occurs, the court may grant relief from these restrictions where it is satisfied that:

- the default was accidental or due to inadvertence or some other sufficient cause; or
- on other grounds it is just and equitable to do so.

The court may grant relief on the application of:

- the person in default; or
- any other person affected by the restriction.

Offences

As stated in the introduction to this chapter, the Companies Act 2014 has categorised certain breaches of company law as criminal offences.

These new offences are now classed in a hierarchical manner as category 1–4 offences – category 1 being the most serious and category 4 the most minor. This initiative under the new legislation facilities the standardisation of penalties for company law breaches.

Category 1 Offences

Section 871(1) Companies Act 2014 states:

> "A person guilty of an offence under this Act that is stated to be a category 1 offence shall be liable—
> (a) on summary conviction, to a class A fine [€5,000 (Fines Act 2010)] or imprisonment for a term not exceeding 12 months or both, or
> (b) on conviction on indictment, to a fine not exceeding €500,000 or imprisonment for a term not exceeding 10 years or both."

An example of a category 1 offence is fraudulent trading. Similarly, the failure by a company to maintain adequate accounting records or a breach of the rules regarding retention or access to these records, which results in liquidation or insolvency, is also classed as a category 1 offence.

Category 2 Offences

Section 871(2) CA 2014 states:

> "A person guilty of an offence under this Act that is stated to be a category 2 offence shall be liable—
> (a) on summary conviction, to a class A fine or imprisonment for a term not exceeding 12 months or both, or
> (b) on conviction on indictment, to a fine not exceeding €50,000 or imprisonment for a term not exceeding 5 years or both."

An example of a category 2 offence is providing false information, or failing to provide information when requested, to the Director of Corporate Enforcement regarding the identity of persons interested in the company's shares or debentures. Making a false or misleading statement to an auditor, knowing or being reckless as to the truth of the statement is also a category 2 offence.

Category 3 Offences

Section 871(3) CA 2014 states:

> "A person guilty of an offence under this Act that is stated to be a category 3 offence shall be liable, on summary conviction, to a class A fine or imprisonment for a term not exceeding 6 months or both."

An example of a category 3 offence is where a company fails to have at least one director for a period of 28 consecutive days. Similarly, the failure by a statutory (external) auditor to report to the Director of Corporate Enforcement any information that causes the ODCE to believe that the company or its officer or agents has committed a category 1 or 2 offence is classed as a category 3 offence.

Category 4 Offences

Section 871(4) CA 2014 states:

> "A person guilty of an offence under this Act that is stated to be a category 4 offence shall be liable, on summary conviction, to a class A fine."

An example of a category 4 offence is where a company fails to register a charge on its property (such as a fixed or floating charge) within 21 days of its creation or where a liquidator fails to send the Registrar within 14 days a copy of every resolution passed at creditors', contributories' or members' meetings or where a company or its officers fails to provide a copy of its constitution to its members upon request.

The categories of offences in company law are summarised in **Table 15.1**.

Table 15.1 Categories of Offences and Sanctions

Category of Offence	Conviction on Indictment	Summary Conviction
Category 1	Term of imprisonment not exceeding 10 years or a fine of up to €500,000 or both.	Term of imprisonment not exceeding 12 months and/or a class A fine.
Category 2	Term of imprisonment not exceeding five years or a fine of up to €50,000 or both.	Term of imprisonment not exceeding 12 months and/or a class A fine.
Category 3	Not applicable.	Term of imprisonment not exceeding six months and/or a class A fine.
Category 4	Not applicable.	Class A fine.

Class A fines are defined by the Fines Act 2010 as fines not exceeding €5,000.

Remedy

Where a company or its officers is convicted of a category 1–4 offence, in addition to the applicable criminal sanctions, the court may make an order requiring the company and its officers to undertake a specified course of action to remedy the breach. Such an action may include rectifying the breach, such as providing a copy of the company's constitutions to a member who has requested it, or making restitution of company money or property.

REVIEW QUESTIONS

(See Solutions to Review Questions at the end of this text.)

Question 15.1

Adler is the managing director and majority shareholder in Foster Recruitment Ltd. This company was incorporated in 2010 for the purpose of operating a recruitment consultancy business. Upon formation, the company borrowed €300,000 from the Prudential Bank of Ireland and in return the bank took a floating charge over the entire business of the company. In the last year, business has declined significantly and the company is haemorrhaging money. Following a review of the accounts two months ago, Adler decided to set up a business partnership with his wife and has transferred the accounts of the largest and most profitable clients of Foster Recruitment Ltd to this firm. The loss of these contracts now means that Foster Recruitment Ltd is on the verge of insolvency and the assets of the business will not be sufficient to cover the company's debts. Last month Foster Recruitment Ltd defaulted on a payment due to the Prudential Bank of Ireland and the bank had a receiver appointed to the company to recoup its debt.

Harrison, the receiver, has just reported back to the Prudential Bank of Ireland and outlined Adler's transfer of client accounts from Foster Recruitment Ltd to a partnership owned by him and his wife. In this report, Harrison stated that in his opinion the actions of Adler amount to fraudulent trading as they were intended to cause a loss to the creditors of the company.

The Prudential Bank of Ireland has initiated a legal action against Adler for fraudulent trading, but is concerned that he will remove his assets from the jurisdiction to avoid financial exposure. The bank is also unsure as to the sanctions that can be imposed upon Adler, both civil and criminal, if he is found guilty of fraudulent trading. It has contacted you for advice.

Requirement:

(a) Explain the procedure that should be adopted by the Prudential Bank of Ireland to obtain a court order restraining Adler from removing his assets from the jurisdiction. Your answer should comment on the requirements that must be complied with in order for the court to grant such an order.

(b) Outline both the civil and criminal sanctions that Adler may be exposed to if he is found guilty of fraudulent trading, pursuant to the provisions of the Companies Act 2014.

Chapter 16

INSIDER DEALING AND MONEY LAUNDERING

INSIDER DEALING

Insider dealing (sometimes referred to as 'insider trading') is where confidential, price-sensitive information (i.e. information that could affect the price of securities) is abused by a person connected to the company so as to make a profit for that person or a third party.

Insider dealing has been prohibited in Ireland since the Companies Act 1990 (CA 1990), which was inspired by an EC Directive. The CA 1990 provisions have subsequently been replaced by the Investment Funds, Companies and Miscellaneous Provisions Act 2005 (IFCMPA 2005), which gave effect to Directive 2003/6/EC.

The three main pieces of legislation that incorporate all the law on insider dealing are:

- Directive 2003/6/EC on insider dealing and market manipulation (commonly known as the 'Market Abuse Directive');
- Part 4 Market Abuse of the Investment Funds, Companies and Miscellaneous Provisions Act 2005;
- The Market Abuse (Directive 2003/6/EC) Regulations 2005 (S.I. No. 342 of 2005) (MADR 2005).

Chapter 2 of Part 23 of the Companies Act 2014 also regulates insider dealing in Ireland.

In order to bring an action for insider dealing, key requirements must be met. The information must:

1. be inside information of a precise nature;
2. not be in the public domain;
3. relate to the issuer of the financial instruments;
4. be used or disclosed by an insider; and
5. be price sensitive to the extent that its disclosure is likely to have a significant impact on the price of the financial instruments that are being traded.

Inside Information

Regulation 2 of the MADR 2005 defines 'inside information'. This includes:

> "information of a precise nature relating directly or indirectly to one or more issuers of financial instruments or to one or more financial instruments which has not been made public and which, if it were made public, would be likely to have a significant effect on the price of those financial instruments or on the price of related derivative financial instruments".

The MADR 2005 further states "'information which, if it were made public, would be likely to have a significant effect on the prices of financial instruments or related derivative financial instruments' means information that a reasonable investor would be likely to use as part of the basis of the investor's investment decisions".

Information of a Precise Nature

The MADR 2005 also states "'information of a precise nature' means information that–
(a) indicates–
  (i) a set of circumstances which exists or may reasonably be expected to come into existence, or
  (ii) an event which has occurred or may reasonably be expected to occur, and
(b) is specific enough to enable a conclusion to be drawn as to the possible effect of that set of circumstances or event, as the case may be, on the prices of financial instruments or related derivative financial instruments".

Financial Instruments

'Financial instrument' is defined to include 'transferable securities', which means shares in companies and other securities equivalent to shares in companies, bonds and other forms of securitised debt that are negotiable on the capital markets, and any other securities normally dealt in giving the right to acquire any such transferable securities by subscription or exchange or giving rise to a cash settlement.

In practical terms, 'financial instruments' include shares, stocks, bonds, debentures and derivative products, money market instruments, financial futures contracts, cash-settled instruments and forward rate interest agreements.

The 'right to acquire' means any product that gives the holder the ability to acquire financial instruments. For example, a convertible debenture would allow the holder to receive shares in a company in lieu of the repayment of a debt.

The regulation defines 'an issuer of a financial instrument' as an issuer of any financial instrument to which the terms of the regulation apply. This means that any person or body that issues stocks, shares, debentures, etc. is likely to be considered an issuer for the purpose of the law on insider dealing. The most obvious example of an issuer of a financial instrument is a public limited company that is listed on the stock market and is selling its financial instruments on that market.

Prohibited Actions

Regulation 5(2) provides that a person defined as an insider (defined below) shall not:

> "disclose inside information to any other person unless such disclosure is made in the normal course of the exercise of [the insider's] employment, profession or duties, or recommend or induce another person, on the basis of inside information, to acquire or dispose of financial instruments to which that information relates".

In real terms, the regulation prohibits the disclosure of inside information, the use of such information or inducing/encouraging another person to use or disclose this information.

Insiders

In accordance with the regulation, the following are considered insiders for the purpose of insider dealing:

1. a person who acquires inside information by virtue of his or her membership of the administrative management or supervisory bodies of the issuer of the financial instrument – this could include company officers or persons employed in brokerage firms or issuing houses;
2. a person who acquires inside information by virtue of his or her holding in the capital of the issuer – such as shareholders or debenture-holders;
3. a person who acquires inside information by virtue of having access to the information through the exercise of the person's employment, profession or duties – such as employees, persons working in the legal or accounting profession, persons employed with financial institutions or government workers; or
4. a person who acquires inside information by virtue of criminal activity – such as a person who hacks into a computer system or unlawfully accesses confidential information.

If the person who possesses the information is actually a company, then any person who carries out the transaction for the company is also considered an insider.

Furthermore, any person who acquires inside information and knows, or ought to have known, that it is inside information is considered a tipee and is classed as an insider for the purpose of the regulation. For example, if A is an employee of company X, which plans to merge with another company, and A tells B about the merger, who tells C, and all three of them buy shares in company X knowing that the information regarding the merger is price sensitive inside information, and that the shares are likely to increase in value when the merger is publicly announced, then A, B and C are guilty of insider trading. A is the tipper, B and C are the tipees, and they are all considered insiders. Even if A told B, and B told C, but only A and C purchased shares, B is still liable for tipping off C, as by doing so he or she disclosed inside information and induced C to acquire the shares.

Criminal and Civil Liability

Section 33 IFCMPA 2005 and section 1369 Companies Act 2014 create a civil liability for insider dealing, which means that a person can be made financially responsible arising from his or her actions. A person who breaches regulation 5 shall be liable to:

- compensate any other party to the transaction concerned who was not in possession of the relevant information for any loss sustained by that party by reason of the difference between the price at which the financial instruments concerned were acquired or disposed of and the price at which they would have been likely to have been acquired or disposed of in such a transaction at the time when the transaction took place if that information had been generally available, and
- account to the body corporate or other legal entity that issued the financial instruments concerned for any profit accruing to them from acquiring or disposing of those instruments.

In reality, what this means is that an insider may be obliged to compensate any party for losses that party incurred as a consequence of the insider dealing. In addition, insiders may also have to account for any profit they made from the transaction. For example, if insiders dealing artificially inflated a company's share price, which then dropped by 10% when the dealing was discovered, any party who purchased shares at the inflated price can sue the insider for that deficit (10% over-payment). In addition, if the company whose shares were the subject of insider dealing suffered a loss as a consequence of this dealing, then it too can sue the insider to recoup these losses. Finally, the insider may also be required to return any profit he or she made from the illegal transaction.

The statute of limitations to bring such a claim is two years from the date of the breach (section 1369(4) CA 2014).

Regulation 49 MADR 2005 and section 1368 of the Companies Act 2014 also make insider dealing a criminal offence. Regulation 53 provides that the offence of insider dealing may be prosecuted by the Central Bank in the District Court, in which case the penalty is limited to a class A fine and/or 12 months' imprisonment.

Section 32 IFCMPA 2005 and section 1368 CA 2014 also provide that the offence may be prosecuted on indictment (i.e. in the Circuit Court), in which case the penalty is a fine not exceeding €10 million, a term of imprisonment not exceeding 10 years, or both.

In addition, where a person is found guilty of insider dealing he or she may also be sanctioned by banning him or her from any dealings in financial instruments for 12 months from the date of their conviction.

The leading case in Ireland on insider dealing is *Fyffes v. DCC* (2007). This case was brought as a civil action and did not involve a criminal prosecution.

In *Fyffes v. DCC* (2007) Fyffes took legal action after DCC sold its stake in Fyffes a month before a March 2000 profit warning. DCC received €106 million for its Fyffes shares, yielding an €85 million profit. A director of DCC handled the sale of the Fyffes shares in February 2000. The same director also held a position as a director in Fyffes, which gave him access to information contained in Fyffes' trading reports for November and December 1999. This information was "generally unavailable". The High Court ruled against Fyffes, which appealed to the Supreme Court. **Held**: "the core issue was whether the information in the November and December 1999 trading reports was price sensitive"; in other words, that it "would be likely materially to affect the price of the shares if it were generally available". Once that information was made available to the markets in the form of a profit warning, issued on March 20, there was an "immediate drop" in Fyffes' share price. Thus, it was "an inevitable conclusion that the information was price sensitive".

The Supreme Court decision cleared the way for Fyffes to bring the case back before the High Court, but an out-of-court settlement was reached in April 2008 in which DCC agreed to pay Fyffes €37.6 million in damages, plus interest and costs, bringing the overall amount paid in the settlement to more than €40 million.

MONEY LAUNDERING

Money laundering is the process by which the proceeds of crime, either money or other property, are converted into assets that appear to have a legitimate rather than an illegal origin. The aim of the process is to disguise the criminal source of the money/property in order to allow the holder to enjoy it free from suspicion as to its source.

Money Laundering Offences

Section 7(1) of the Criminal Justice (Money Laundering and Financing Terrorism) Act 2010 states that a person commits an offence if he or she:

"(a) ... engages in any of the following acts in relation to property that is the proceeds of criminal conduct:
  - (i) concealing or disguising the true nature, source, location, disposition, movement or ownership of the property, or any rights relating to the property;
  - (ii) converting, transferring, handling, acquiring, possessing or using the property;
  - (iii) removing the property from, or bringing the property into, the State; and

(b) the person knows or believes (or is reckless as to whether or not) the property is the proceeds of criminal conduct."

Section 7(6) of the same Act states that a person handles property if he or she:

"(a) receives, or arranges to receive, the property, or

(b) retains, removes, disposes of or realises the property, or arranges to do any of those things, for the benefit of another person."

The offence provides that being reckless as to whether the property is, or represents the proceeds of, criminal conduct is a sufficient level of culpability to warrant conviction.

The process of money laundering usually involves three distinct phases.

- **Placement**, which involves the initial disposal of the proceeds of criminal activity into apparently legitimate business activity or property.
- **Layering**, which involves the transfer of money from business to business, or place to place in order to conceal its criminal source.
- **Integration**, which is the culmination of the previous procedures through which the money takes on the appearance of coming from a legitimate source.

Sanctions

A person who commits an offence under section 7 (1) is liable:

1. on summary conviction (see **Chapter 1**), to a class A fine or a term of imprisonment not exceeding 12 months (or both); or
2. on conviction on indictment (see **Chapter 1**), to an unlimited fine or imprisonment for a term not exceeding 14 years (or both).

Obligations and Designated Persons and Bodies

Section 33 of the Criminal Justice (Money Laundering and Financing Terrorism) Act 2010 imposes obligations on a wide range of persons and bodies providing financial services ('designated persons and bodies') to undertake certain measures ('customer due diligence') to prevent and detect money laundering.

The definition of a designated person or body is quite wide and includes the following:

- all credit and financial institutions, unless expressly exempted;
- an auditor, external accountant or tax adviser;
- a relevant independent legal professional;
- a trust or company service provider;
- a property service provider;
- a casino or a person who directs a private members' club at which gambling activities are carried out; and
- a person trading in goods in respect of transactions involving the receipt of cash of at least €15,000.

These designated persons and bodies are required, prior to: (1) establishing a business relationship with a customer, (2) providing a service to a customer, or (3) engaging in an occasional transaction with a customer valued in excess of €15,000, to undertake customer due diligence.

Customer Due Diligence

This customer due diligence requires these designated persons and bodies to:

- establish the identity of customers based on reliable documents or information (such as documents from a government source);
- identify any beneficial owner connected with the customer or service concerned (such as a company);
- obtain information in relation to the purpose and nature of the business relationship (such as where a person is acting as an officer of a company as well as the nature of the company's business);

- monitor dealings with a customer on an ongoing basis by scrutinising transactions and the source of wealth or funds for those transactions;
- determine whether or not the transactions are consistent with:
  - the designated person or body's knowledge of the customer and the customer's business and pattern of transactions, and
  - any knowledge that the designated person or body may have that the customer may be involved in money laundering.

Enhanced Customer Due Diligence

Enhanced due diligence is required where there is a higher risk of money laundering and terrorist financing. This would require designated persons and bodies to obtain additional information and undertake additional monitoring of certain customers including:

1. any customer (who is an individual) who was not physically present for identification purposes;
2. any non-domestic politically exposed person (PEP); and
3. when entering into a correspondent banking relationship with a non-EU credit institution.

These obligations also apply to the spouses, partners, children and the parents of spouses and partners and close associates of non-domestic politically exposed persons.

Exemption re Reporting and Customer Due Diligence

There are some limitations on the reporting of transactions by designated persons or bodies who are accountants, auditors, solicitors and tax advisors with regard to information they receive from, or in relation to, a client in some circumstances. These include where ascertaining the legal position for that client, or when defending or representing a client in, or concerning judicial proceedings, or when advising a client in relation to instituting, avoiding or defending judicial proceedings whether such information is received or obtained before, during or after such proceedings. In effect, where information is disclosed by a client as part of legal advice or proceedings and that disclosure is deemed privileged by law, then the aforementioned designated persons or bodies are not acting in breach of the legislation by their non-disclosure.

Miscellaneous Obligations Imposed on Designated Persons or Bodies

All designated persons and bodies are required to establish adequate procedures of internal control and communication in order to forestall and prevent operations related to money laundering. They are specifically required to maintain records for a period of five years in relation to customer due diligence and to provide relevant training of their officers and employees on the law relating to money laundering.

Failure to Report

Where a designated person or body has a suspicion that a customer is involved in money laundering, he, she or it is obliged to report that suspicion to An Garda Síochána and the Revenue Commissioners. If the designated person or body is subject to ethical regulation, such reporting is deemed not to breach any relevant code of ethics. Failure to report a suspicion is an offence and is punishable by a maximum of five years' imprisonment and/or a fine.

Tipping-off

A prohibition against tipping-off is contained in section 49, Criminal Justice (Money Laundering and Financing Terrorism) Act 2010. This provision makes it an offence for a designated person or body to disclose to a customer that they have reported them to An Garda Síochána and the Revenue Commissioners on suspicion of money laundering.

This tipping-off offence is punishable:

- on a summary conviction (see **Chapter 1**), by a class A fine or a term of imprisonment not exceeding 12 months or both;
- on conviction on indictment (see **Chapter 1**), by a fine (the Act is silent on the actual amount) or imprisonment for a term not exceeding five years or both.

REVIEW QUESTIONS

(See Solutions to Review Questions at the end of this text.)

Question 16.1

Buckley is the CEO of a waste management company, Premier Waste Disposal Ltd ('Premier'), which has contracts with a number of financial institutions around Ireland. Last year, a number of Buckley's collection drivers were unable to attend work due to heavy snow that had left a number of roads closed. Consequently, Buckley decided to complete a number of the collections himself. While collecting paper for shredding from the Bank of Cork, Buckley noticed a document in the shredding bag marked "Confidential – Department of Finance memo". Buckley took this document from the shredding bag and back in his office he opened the document and read its contents. The document stated that Balantine Pharmaceuticals Plc ('Balantine') was being investigated for Revenue fraud, and the document contained instructions to the bank granting the Department of Finance the right to review all of Balantine's bank accounts.

After Buckley read the memo, he contacted his accountant and asked him if any of his personal and pension investments included shares in Balantine. His accountant reviewed Buckley's investment portfolio and told Buckley that he had approximately €100,000 invested in Balantine. Upon hearing this, Buckley told the accountant to sell these shares immediately. When the accountant asked him why, Buckley stated that he had a bad feeling about Balantine. The accountant complied with Buckley's request and sold the shares.

Three months after selling shares in Balantine, the accountant saw a news story that Balantine was being investigated on suspicion of Revenue fraud. Following the disclosure of this story, the value of Balantine shares fell 48%. Upon hearing this news story, the accountant became suspicious about whether Buckley was engaged in 'insider trading' at the time he requested his shares be sold in Balantine.

Requirement:

(a) Define the term 'insider trading' and explain what is meant by 'inside information'.

(b) List the various classes of people who are considered 'insiders' for the purpose of the law regarding 'insider trading'.

(c) Outline the criminal sanctions that can be imposed where a person is found guilty of 'insider trading'. Comment also upon whether you consider Buckley to be guilty of this offence.

Question 16.2

Allen Enterprises Limited ('Allen') is an online gambling company. During an audit of this company, Paddisson, the auditor, discovered that a client, Mr Fit, made a €2,000 bet every month on a horse with long odds. Every month, Mr Fit's bet generated winnings in excess of €20,000. In 2014, Mr Fit, having not lost one bet, netted winnings of €263,000 from successful bets. Paddisson is now suspicious that Mr Fit may not be real and that the directors may be using Allen to launder money.

Requirement:

(a) Define the term 'money laundering' **and** explain any **two** ways in which this offence can be committed.

(b) Outline the legal obligations imposed upon auditors where a suspicion of money laundering occurs.

Chapter 17

THE REGULATION OF ACCOUNTANTS

Only those accountants who are members of a prescribed accountancy body (PAB) are regulated. Regulation in Ireland is through a two-tier system comprising regulation by professional bodies coupled with independent oversight.

- **Regulation by professional bodies** Nine PABs (including Chartered Accountants Ireland ('the Institute') are responsible for regulating their members in accordance with their respective rules. The regulation of accountancy services is not required by law and so is conducted on a voluntary basis. The regulation of audit and investment business, however, is required by law; the Institute is a competent authority under the relevant legislation.
- **Oversight** The Irish Auditing and Accounting Supervisory Authority (IAASA) is an independent state oversight body responsible for supervising the work of the PABs in regulating their members. The Central Bank of Ireland oversees the regulation of firms authorised to conduct investment business.

The Regulatory System of Chartered Accountants Ireland: CARB

Chartered Accountants Ireland regulates its members through the Chartered Accountancy Regulatory Board ('CARB'). This is an independent body established in 2007 to regulate the members of Chartered Accountants Ireland independently, openly and in the public interest in accordance with the provisions of the Institute's bye-laws. The Board has 12 members, seven of whom are not members of any accountancy body.

CARB's core activities include developing regulatory policy and professional standards, monitoring members and firms for compliance with those standards, authorising members and firms to carry on particular types of business, dealing with complaints and taking disciplinary action when appropriate.

Complaints and Discipline

Complaints against members, member firms, affiliates and students may be brought to the attention of CARB.

A member, member firm, student or affiliate may become liable to disciplinary action on several grounds including, but not limited to, the following.

- professional misconduct or incompetency;
- breach of a bye-law or regulation, e.g. a breach of the obligation to comply with the code of ethics or failure to comply with the requirements of the CPD regulations;

- bankruptcy or failing to pay a judgment debt;
- the imposition of a restriction or disqualification order against a member, student or affiliate;
- bringing discredit to themselves, the Institute or the profession of accountancy; and
- failure or neglect to respond to communications from the Institute or CARB.

Full details are included in disciplinary bye-laws 6 and 7.

Where a case has been found proven, the orders that may be made include, but are not limited to, the following:

- exclusion from membership;
- suspension of membership;
- severe reprimand;
- reprimand;
- remedial order;
- fine of up to €100,000 (or €100,000 per partner in a member firm);
- no further action; and
- costs.

Complaints are investigated by case managers under the direction of the head of professional conduct, who is appointed by CARB. A report is then prepared on each case for the consideration of the complaints committee.

In some cases, the head of professional conduct will decide that there is no *prima facie* case of liability to disciplinary action without referring the matter to the complaints committee. However, in such cases, the complainant can insist that the matter be referred to the complaints committee nevertheless.

Complaints Committee

The complaints committee, which comprises at least nine members, the majority of whom are not members of the Institute, decides whether there is a *prima facie* case of liability to disciplinary action. If it determines that there is no *prima facie* case to answer, then the committee will notify the complainant as well as the member, member firm, student or affiliate concerned, stating in writing the reasons for this decision.

Where it decides that there is indeed a *prima facie* case, the complaints committee must notify the relevant parties in writing, stating the action that it intends to take. These actions include:

- offering a 'consent order' (an order that the member, member firm, student or affiliate consents to, typically involving a sanction and a fine);
- deciding that the complaint should rest on the file of the member, member firm, student or affiliate concerned for a period of two years – subject

to obtaining the consent of the relevant member, member firm, student or affiliate (this is similar to a probation order, or a suspended sentence in criminal law as discussed in **Chapter 1**);
- deciding to take no further action; or
- in more serious cases, or where a consent order has not been accepted, referring a formal complaint for hearing before a disciplinary tribunal.

In addition, an order for costs can also be made against the member, member firm, student or affiliate.

If the complaints committee finds that there is no *prima facie* case, within three months the complainant may request to have the matter reviewed by an independent reviewer. If the independent reviewer disagrees with the complaints committee's decision, the complaints committee must consider the matter afresh in light of the independent reviewer's comments. The independent reviewers are neither employees nor members of the Institute.

Disciplinary Tribunal

Members of the disciplinary tribunal are drawn from a disciplinary panel comprised of at least nine members, of which: (1) at least six must be persons who are not members of the Institute, (2) at least two must be lawyers, and (3) not less than three must be members of the Institute.

Disciplinary tribunals are made up of three people appointed from the disciplinary panel. The chairperson of the disciplinary tribunal must be a lawyer and only one member of the disciplinary tribunal may be a member of the Institute. Hearings before disciplinary tribunals are generally held in public – although the respondent or the complaints committee can request that it is heard in private.

Respondents have certain rights to fair process when a case is being heard before the disciplinary tribunal. These rights include the right to:
1. attend and be heard at the hearing of the formal complaint;
2. be represented before the disciplinary tribunal by a practising lawyer or by a chartered accountant;
3. advance receipt of the material documents being relied on at the hearing, as well as the right to hear the evidence against them;
4. cross-examine witnesses called before the disciplinary tribunal;
5. adduce the documentary evidence;
6. call witnesses to give evidence on their behalf; and
7. make any submissions to the disciplinary tribunal that they desire.

The disciplinary tribunal will decide whether the formal complaint has been proven on the balance of probabilities and, where it has been found proven, the disciplinary tribunal will make whatever order it considers appropriate.

The sanctions that may be imposed by the disciplinary tribunal include: (1) expulsion, (2) suspension (for up to one year), (3) withdrawal of practising certificate, (4) a declaration that the respondent is ineligible for a practising certificate, (5) withdrawal of an insolvency licence, (6) a declaration that the respondent is ineligible for an insolvency licence, (7) withdrawal of any authorisation, licence or permit held by the respondent, (8) a reprimand or severe reprimand, or (9) a fine not exceeding €100,000.

In addition, if the respondent is a student, sanctions may include: (1) a declaration that he or she is unfit to become a member, (2) suspension of registration or training (for a period not exceeding two years), (3) a declaration of ineligibility to undertake Institute examinations (for a period not exceeding two years), and (4) disqualification from Institute examinations for a specified time period.

In addition, the disciplinary tribunal may make an order for costs against the member, member firm, student or affiliate.

Appeal Tribunal

Members of the appeal tribunal are drawn from an appeal panel that comprises at least nine persons, of which: (1) at least six must be persons who are not members of the Institute, (2) at least two must be lawyers, and (3) at least three must be members of the Institute.

Appeal tribunals are made up of three people appointed from the appeal panel. The chairperson must be a lawyer and only one member of the appeal tribunal may be a member of the Institute. Decisions of a disciplinary tribunal are subject to a member, member firm, student or affiliate's right of appeal within 21 days on specified grounds. These grounds include:

1. that the finding is wrong;
2. that the order is excessive;
3. that the finding and/or the order is flawed because of a serious procedural or other irregularity in the proceedings before the disciplinary tribunal; and/or
4. that the award of costs against the appellant is manifestly excessive.

Hearings before appeal tribunals are generally held in public – unless an application has been made by the appellant or the complaints committee to have the appeal heard in private.

Depending on the alleged breaches and the grounds upon which the appeal is sought, certain appeals may involve a rehearing of the case and are conducted and heard as though at first instance, whereas other appeals are held in a manner determined at the absolute discretion of the appeal tribunal.

Whatever the manner of the appeal, the appellant has the right to the same fair process as is afforded before the disciplinary tribunal.

An appeal tribunal may affirm, vary or rescind the disciplinary tribunal's decision; it may also substitute its own decision or order that another hearing be held before a different disciplinary tribunal.

In addition, the appeal tribunal may make an order for costs against the member, member firm, student or affiliate.

Note: CARB's disciplinary process does not in any way interfere with a complainant's rights in respect of a contract with an accountant. A member, or member firm, of the Institute may be sued in the courts for breach of contract or negligence, which could result in an award of compensation being made against the member or member firm.

New Disciplinary Process

From 5 October 2015, a new disciplinary process is due to come into force. This differs from the process outlined above in several respects, including:

- new grounds for liability to disciplinary action – in effect, the grounds will be reclassified and liability will arise in respect of misconduct, poor professional performance and failure to respond or co-operate with CARB or the Institute;
- new decision-making powers for the head of professional conduct – in less serious cases, the head of professional conduct is empowered to make a decision as to whether or not the member, member firm, student or affiliate has a case to answer in respect of the allegation. Such decisions will be subject to oversight by members of the conduct committee. Complainants will have the right to have findings of 'no case to answer' reviewed independently;
- a new order to be known as an 'unpublished caution' – this order can be imposed following a finding of 'case to answer' by the head of professional conduct or the conduct committee;
- the renaming of the complaints committee as the conduct committee, which will focus on more serious, higher-risk and complex cases;
- regarding sanctions, it will not be necessary to hold a hearing before a disciplinary tribunal where a member consents to the imposition of an order for exclusion or suspension from membership. The same applies in respect of suspension or removal of affiliate status;
- new provisions to allow cases to be resolved through settlement – parties will be entitled to seek to conclude proceedings by way of settlement agreement at any time prior to the final decision in a case. Details of settlement agreements will be published in all cases; and

- new provisions allowing orders to be made on an interim basis in matters of public concern – interim orders suspending membership or imposing conditions in public concern cases may be imposed in exceptional circumstances, where it has been established that it is necessary in the public interest to do so.

(*Note:* as these changes were not due to come into effect until October 2015, readers must consult their course co-ordinators and/or lecturers to establish when they will be examinable.)

Judicial Review

CARB's processes may be subject to judicial review. This means that a member or complainant can make an application for judicial review to the High Court in respect of failures to follow CARB's procedures or for acting without due regard to a person's constitutional rights and/or fair procedures and natural justice. The High Court will examine the decision and how it was reached and will **not** engage in an appeal on the merits of the case.

Questions of Public Concern

Where the complaints committee of CARB decides that a matter which has been brought to its attention gives rise to, or includes, questions of public concern, one of four approaches may be adopted:

1. if the case relates to a Republic of Ireland matter of public concern, the complaints committee will engage with the Irish Auditing and Accounting Supervisory Authority (IAASA) to determine whether the IAASA intends, under company law, to investigate the case itself;
2. if the case relates to a UK matter of public concern, the complaints committee will engage with the Financial Reporting Council (FRC) to determine whether it intends, under the provisions of the FRC scheme, to investigate the case itself; or
3. if neither IAASA nor the FRC undertake to investigate the matter, the complaints committee may arrange for the complaint to be investigated by a special investigator. The special investigator will report to the complaints committee whether or not, in his or her opinion, a *prima facie* case against the member or member firm exists. Where the special investigator certifies that a *prima facie* case exists, the complaints committee will immediately refer the matter by way of a formal complaint; or
4. if neither IAASA nor the FRC undertake to investigate the matter, the complaints committee may direct that the matter be investigated by a case manager under the direction of the head of professional conduct in accordance with the ordinary process.

Irish Auditing and Accounting Supervisory Authority (IAASA)

The Companies (Auditing and Accounting) Act 2003 established the Irish Auditing and Accounting Supervisory Authority (IAASA) as an independent regulatory body. Two of IAASA's principal functions are to strengthen the regulation of auditors, and regulate the methods by which supervisory bodies monitor their members. These powers are codified in Part 15 Chapter 2 of the Companies Act 2014. IAASA carries out these functions by regulating the prescribed accountancy bodies ('PABs').

Membership of IAASA

Section 6 of the Act provides that IAASA is to consist of the following members:

- each PAB that is a body corporate;
- in the case of a PAB that is not a body corporate, an individual or body corporate nominated by that PAB to be a member;
- each designated body that is a body corporate;
- in the case of a designated body that is not a body corporate, an individual or body corporate nominated by that designated body to be a member.

Each of the following is considered to be a designated body for the purposes of membership of IAASA:

- the Director of Corporate Enforcement;
- the Central Bank;
- the Irish Stock Exchange;
- the Revenue Commissioners; and
- any body prescribed by the Minister as a designated body.

Objects of IAASA

The principal objects of IAASA as per section 904(1) CA 2014, are to:

(a) supervise how the PABs regulate and monitor their members;
(b) promote adherence to high professional standards in the auditing and accountancy profession;
(c) monitor whether the financial statements or accounts of certain classes of companies and other undertakings comply with this Act; and
(d) act as a specialist source of advice to the minister on auditing and accounting matters.

Functions of IAASA

IAASA's overarching function is to "do all things necessary and reasonable to further its objects" (section 905(1) CA 2014). Specific functions are detailed in section 905(2). For example, IAASA:

- grants recognition to bodies of accountants for the purposes of the 2010 Audits Regulations;
- attaches terms and conditions to the recognition of PABs;
- requires that each PAB obtain IAASA's approval for:
  - its regulatory processes and annual reports of its regulatory plans, and
  - its constitution and bye laws, investigation and disciplinary procedures, and standards, as well as amendments to these;
- conducts inquiries into whether each PAB has complied with its approved investigation and disciplinary procedures;
- undertakes investigations into possible breaches of the standards of the PABs;
- imposes certain sanctions on PABs;
- supervises how each PAB monitors its members;
- undertakes certain reviews of the members of PABs;
- co-operates with the PABs and other interested parties in:
  - developing:
    - standards relating to the independence of auditors, and
    - auditing and accounting standards and practice notes;
  - monitoring the effectiveness of the
    - PABs' standards, and
    - provisions of the CA 2014 Act and the 2010 Audits Regulations relating to the independence of statutory auditors;
- supervises the investigation and disciplinary procedures of the PABs, including by requiring:
  - access to their records, and
  - explanations about the performance of their regulatory and monitoring duties;
- arranges for the regulation and supervision by PABs of certain statutory auditors; and
- performs the functions conferred on IAASA by:
  - certain transparency (regulated markets) law, and
  - the 2010 Audits Regulations, particularly the functions of public oversight.

As part of the recent EU audit reform measures, from May 2016 IAASA is due to be responsible for the inspection of the quality of audit work performed by the auditors of public interest entities.

REVIEW QUESTION

(See Solutions to Review Questions at the end of this text.)

Question 17.1

The directors of Lismount tell you that their finance director, Shane, a qualified accountant, has been making fraudulent travel claims against the company for the last six months. The amount fraudulently claimed has been in excess of €100,000. You tell the directors that they must now report this matter to the Chartered Accountant Regulatory Board (CARB) for investigation and that it is likely that Shane will be brought before the disciplinary committee of CARB.

Requirement:

(a) Explain the role of CARB and list any **two** grounds under which members and member firms become liable to disciplinary action by CARB.

(b) In the context of the disciplinary tribunal of CARB, outline its jurisdiction and composition, as well as the potential outcomes of a hearing before the disciplinary tribunal.

CHAPTER 18

CORPORATE GOVERNANCE

Updated by Shelagh McAlpine

What is Corporate Governance?

Corporate governance is a dynamic concept encompassing all aspects of the manner in which an entity is run, with a view to achieving an appropriate balance between the interests of its various stakeholders and ensuring that its management is held to account.

The term emerged in the early 1990s when a committee led by Sir Adrian Cadbury developed responses to a number of scandals (such as Polly Peck and BCCI), culminating in publication in 1992 of its report *The Financial Aspects of Corporate Governance* (usually known as the '*Cadbury Report*'), which defined corporate governance as "the system by which companies are directed and controlled."

In 1999, the World Bank's *Report on Corporate Governance* defined corporate governance as "a set of arrangements internal to the corporation that define the relationship between managers and shareholders." The Organisation for Economic Co-operation and Development (OECD), in its *Principles of Corporate Governance* issued in the same year and revised in 2004, takes a somewhat broader view by including a wider range of interested parties, stating that corporate governance "involves a set of relationships between a company's management, its board, its shareholders and other stakeholders".

The specific requirements of a system of corporate governance for an individual entity are determined by the nature of the entity and its purpose. Such a system includes, but is broader than, legal and regulatory requirements and includes codes of practice and self-regulatory arrangements. This combination is implicitly recognised in commentary from the Office of the Director of Corporate Enforcement (ODCE), which states that:

> "The principles underlying corporate governance are based on conducting the business with integrity and fairness, being transparent with regard to all transactions, making all the necessary disclosures and decisions and complying with all the laws of the land. It is broadly concerned with the relationships between company boards and the company's

shareholders, accountability and responsibility towards the stakeholders. Good governance should facilitate efficient, effective and entrepreneurial management that can deliver shareholders value over the longer term." (Source: www.odce.ie)

While this chapter incorporates comment on key aspects of corporate governance contained in Irish company law, its primary focus is on the codes of best practice, particularly as applied to listed companies.

The need for flexibility in determining specific approaches to achieving the aim of "efficient, effective and entrepreneurial management" that delivers shareholder value in the context of listed companies was recognised by the initial *Cadbury Report,* which sought to establish principles, rather than mandatory rules. This approach was reinforced when its recommendations were appended to the listing rules of the London Stock Exchange in 1994 and companies were required to state whether or not they had followed the report's recommendations, and if not to explain why. This '**comply or explain**' approach allows dialogue between management and shareholders as to how a company is managed and directed to best effect. The concept is also incorporated into EU law: Article 20 of Directive 2013/34/EU, dealing with annual financial statements and related reports of certain types of entities, requires public interest entities to disclose the corporate governance code(s) applicable to them and to explain any non-compliance. More recently, a European Commission recommendation has been issued to promote the quality of corporate governance reporting, with particular focus on 'comply or explain' (Commission Recommendation 2014/208/EU).

The Need for Corporate Governance

While focus on current concepts of corporate governance began in the early 1990s, the underlying issues predate that era and can be found in any form of organisation in which there is a separation of owners and managers. The emergence of companies and limited liability in the 19th century was accompanied by a need to ensure companies were run in a manner that had proper regard both to the expectations of investors not involved in day-to-day management and also to the rights of their creditors, a key stakeholder group.

Two key theories explain the need for and development of corporate governance for companies: agency theory and stakeholder theory:

- **agency theory** argues that those charged with the management of a company – its directors – act as agents to the shareholders of the company, and have a fiduciary duty to both the company and its shareholders. Therefore, the board of directors should act in the best interests of the shareholders when conducting the affairs of a company.

- **stakeholder theory** holds the view that the directors should act in the best interests of all with an interest in the company, for example: customers, suppliers, employees, the general public, etc.

Agency theory is considered to be a narrow view of corporate governance concerned solely with the relationship between the owners and managers of a company. Company law governance requirements focus primarily on this relationship, while including a degree of recognition of the interests of creditors and employees. The broader view, stakeholder theory, is concerned with all the relationships, both internal and external, formed by the company.

Both models suffer from potential complications arising from conflicts between the interests of the directors and the interests of shareholders and/or other stakeholders. The dynamics of the corporate structure, the motivations and expectations of investors, all contribute to the management of a company. For example, directors may be concerned only with their own bonuses based on the company's performance while they are in office, while shareholders have a longer term goal to generate wealth.

Corporate governance has evolved as a way of controlling such conflicts by a structure of regulations, legislation and a set of codes that attempt to affect the directors' management of companies, both by legal requirements and by focusing on the 'comply or explain' approach applied to an articulated set of principles, thereby allowing the directors flexibility to determine, within the framework of law, how best to meet the standards set out by those principles in the light of the company's particular circumstances. This allows, in the case of trading companies, a balance between prescriptive rules of behaviour for directors and the freedom to innovate in the specific way that they manage a company's affairs in the interests of its shareholders. As the Financial Reporting Council (FRC), the UK's and Ireland's independent regulator responsible for corporate governance and financial reporting, recognises: "Good governance can improve the board's ability to manage the company effectively to deliver long-term success as well as provide accountability to shareholders." (Source: *The UK Approach to Corporate Governance* (2010))

Legal Aspects of Corporate Governance

As noted above, company law incorporates elements of corporate governance, setting out shareholder rights and obligations of company directors, including matters such as holding meetings with shareholders and providing shareholders with an annual directors' report and financial statements that give a true and fair view. For Irish companies, these aspects are largely dealt with in Parts 4, 5 and 6 of the Companies Act 2014 (CA 2014).

Directors of larger private companies and public limited companies (PLCs) have additional obligations to:

- **establish an audit committee*** or explain reasons for not doing so in the annual directors' report (section 167 CA 2014, applying to private companies with a balance sheet total of €25 million or more and turnover of €50 million or more and applied to PLCs by section 1097 CA 2014). The audit committee should include at least one independent non-executive director and its responsibilities include monitoring of:
  - the company's financial reporting process;
  - the effectiveness of its systems of internal control, internal audit and risk management;
  - the statutory audit of the company's statutory financial statements; and
  - the independence of the statutory auditors, in particular the provision of additional (non-audit) services.

  (*This requirement is also applied to all 'public-interest entities' (regulation 91 of the European Community (Statutory Audits) (Directive 2006/46/EC) Regulations (S.I. No. 220 of 2010). For this purpose, 'public-interest entities' are those with securities admitted to trading on a regulated market of any EU Member State, credit institutions and insurance undertakings (regulation 3).)
- **include an annual compliance statement in the directors' report** (applying to private companies with a balance sheet total of €12.5 million or more and turnover of €25 million or more (section 225 CA 2014) and applying to all PLCs (section 1002)). In this statement, the directors are to acknowledge their responsibility for ensuring the company complies with its "relevant obligations"** and state whether:
  - a compliance policy statement has been prepared, setting out the appropriate policies concerning compliance by the company with its relevant obligations;
  - appropriate arrangements or structures exist that are, in the directors' opinion, designed to secure material compliance with the company's relevant obligations; and
  - a review of those arrangements or structures has been conducted during the financial year concerned.

  (**"Relevant obligations" consist of those provisions of the Companies Act where failure to comply would be a category 1 or 2 offence, or a serious market abuse or prospectus offence, and also tax law.)

Directors' duties and shareholder rights under the CA 2014 are considered in more detail in **Chapter 12** and **Chapter 13**.

Corporate Governance Statements

In the case of companies with shares or debentures listed on a 'regulated market'* within the European Economic Area, the directors' report required by company law must include a corporate governance statement identifying the corporate governance code that the company is either required to apply or has chosen to apply, together with:

- a description of the main features of the company's internal control and risks management systems;
- information on shareholder rights and arrangements for shareholder meetings; and
- information about the composition and operation of the board and its committees (section 1373 CA 2014).

(*The ISE Main Securities Market and LSE Main Market, but not ESM and AIM, are regulated markets for this purpose. A listing of such markets is maintained by the European Securities and Markets Authority.)

Oversight of Governance Arrangements

Additionally, company law provides for oversight of aspects of corporate governance, as set out in Part 15 of the CA 2014. Under this Part:

- the Director of Corporate Enforcement is responsible for encouraging and enforcing compliance with the Act, for investigating apparent non-compliance and taking steps to initiate prosecution of offences;
- the Irish Auditing and Accounting Supervisory Authority (IAASA) is responsible for monitoring whether financial statements of specified classes of companies comply with the Companies Act (and, where applicable, Article 4 of the IAS Regulation) and, in addition, for oversight of audit quality and for promoting adherence to high professional standards in the auditing and accountancy profession.

Corporate Governance of Listed Companies

In addition to the relevant provisions of company law, the governance of listed companies is determined within the framework of the listing rules of the Irish Stock Exchange and, for companies with a premium listing on the London Stock Exchange, the UK Listing Authority. The listing rules set a range of requirements, including those for admission to listing and continuing, subsequent obligations, that information which might affect the share price is made available to all investors at the same time and that reliable reports of financial results are released on a timely basis.

Both the Irish and UK Listing Rules require companies with securities listed on the Main Securities Market (Irish Stock Exchange) or having a Premium Listing (London Stock Exchange) to report on a 'comply or explain' basis on their application of the recognised code of corporate governance, currently the *UK Corporate Governance Code* (2014) ('the Code') as issued by the FRC. This is achieved by requiring the annual report to include:

- a statement of how the listed company has applied the main principles set out in the *UK Corporate Governance Code* in a manner that would enable shareholders to evaluate how the principles have been applied;
- a statement as to whether the listed company has:
  - complied throughout the accounting period with all relevant provisions set out in the *UK Corporate Governance Code*; or
  - not complied throughout the accounting period with all relevant provisions set out in the *UK Corporate Governance Code* and if so, setting out:
    - those provisions, if any it has not complied with;
    - in the case of provisions whose requirements are of a continuing nature, the period within which, if any, it did not comply with some or all of those provisions; and
    - the company's reasons for non-compliance.

The Irish Stock Exchange listing rules also require the same disclosures regarding compliance with the Irish Stock Exchange, *Main Securities Market Listing Rules and Admission to Trading Rules*, Appendix 4, "Irish Corporate Governance Annex" issued in 2010, which sets out a number of additional requirements concerning remuneration and audit committees (Irish Stock Exchange, *Main Securities Market Listing Rules and Admission to Trading Rules*, Appendix 4).

Development of the UK Corporate Governance Code and the "Irish Corporate Governance Annex"

The *Cadbury Report* represented the first step towards development of the current *UK Corporate Governance Code*. It was prepared by a committee chaired by Sir Adrian Cadbury, set up by the Council of the London Stock Exchange (LSE) and the accountancy professions in 1991 in response to concerns relating to standards of practice in a number of major companies, including Polly Peck, which collapsed in 1990.

The resulting report recommended that the boards of public companies should be required to apply a code of best practice (i.e. the principles set out in the *Cadbury Report*, known as the 'Cadbury Code') as a condition of continuing to be listed on the LSE. This recommendation was put into effect by the LSE in 1994, from which date listed companies were required to confirm in their annual reports that they had conformed to the Cadbury Code or set out instances of non-compliance and the reasons for them. The Irish Stock Exchange (ISE) introduced an equivalent requirement in 1999.

The Cadbury Code recommended that:

- the roles of chairman and chief executive officer be separated;
- independent non-executive directors should be appointed to the boards of listed companies;
- executive directors should not be offered service contracts of more than three years unless approved by the shareholders at a general meeting; and
- all listed companies should have an audit committee, whose members should be non-executive directors.

These recommendations of the *Cadbury Report* formed the foundation of what is regarded today as best practice and good corporate governance. They have been updated and extended at regular intervals as a result of recommendations from various committees.

- In 1995, the *Greenbury Report* set out recommendations on the remuneration of directors. In 1998, the *Hampel Committee* reported on its review of the way in which recommendations of previous reports were being implemented, following which the existing reports were brought together in the *Combined Code on Corporate Governance* (the 'Combined Code'), applying to UK listed companies from 31 December 1998 and to Irish listed companies one year later.

- In 1999, a committee established by the Institute of Chartered Accountants in England and Wales, chaired by Nigel Turnbull (director of Rank plc) issued guidance for company directors regarding the Combined Code's provisions relating to internal controls and setting out best practice on internal control for UK listed companies. In October 2005, the FRC issued an updated version of the guidance with the title *Internal Control: Guidance for Directors on the Combined Code*. In September 2014, this was superseded in light of work following the financial crisis of 2008, by the FRC's guidance *Risk Management, Internal Controls and Related Financial Reporting*.

- Following the collapse of Enron in 2001, two committees were established to consider the effectiveness of non-executive directors (the Higgs Committee, which reported in 2003) and the independence of auditors (the Smith Committee, which also reported in 2003). Findings from both were incorporated into the 2003 version of the Combined Code. Though the *Higgs Report* introduced a number of changes regarding the way boards and directors operated, it supported, in overall terms, the approach to corporate governance taken in previous Codes. Given the different direction taken in the US in response to Enron, this was a significant decision. The US Sarbanes–Oxley Act of 2002 introduced prescriptive requirements for procedures and controls to support financial reporting and for auditors to report on the effectiveness of those procedures and controls. It did not, however, address wider issues of governance. The *Smith Report* provided guidance for boards to assist in making suitable arrangements for audit committees and their interaction with the external auditor.

- At this time the UK Government also decided that the FRC was to take responsibility for publishing and maintaining the Combined Code. Two further revisions of the Combined Code were undertaken in 2006 and 2008 as a result of routine reviews of effectiveness.

- A more fundamental assessment was undertaken in the wake of the financial crisis of 2008. The FRC commenced this assessment in March 2009, shortly after the UK Government launched a review of corporate governance in UK banks, led by Sir David Walker, with the purpose of recommending measures to improve corporate governance practices, in particular with regard to risk management. This focus accords with the conclusion of an equivalent review by the OECD, whose paper *Corporate Governance and the Financial Crisis* (February 2010) notes that "boards' responsibility for defining strategy and risk appetite needs to be extended to establishing and overseeing enterprise-wide risk management systems ... in some important cases the risk management system was not compatible with a company's strategy and risk appetite".

  The FRC's review resulted in an updated and renamed code, the *UK Corporate Governance Code,* issued in 2010 alongside a new code setting out responsibilities of institutional investors, the *UK Stewardship Code.* Institutional investors who become signatories to this code are required to report on their policies for monitoring and engaging with the companies in which they invest.

- During 2009, the Irish Stock Exchange and the Irish Association of Investment Managers initiated a review of the quality of Irish listed companies' application of the Combined Code. This work was undertaken by a committee chaired by Professor Niamh Brennan, whose resulting *Report on Compliance with the Combined Code on Corporate Governance by Irish listed Companies* made a number of recommendations to support improved workings of boards and audit committee and greater transparency in reporting. Consultation based on its recommendations was undertaken by the ISE during 2010, following which the ISE confirmed that it would require application of both the *UK Corporate Governance*

Code and a new Irish Corporate Governance Annex, setting out requirements for additional disclosures relating to board appointments and their operation, audit committees, and remuneration.

- Since 2011, the FRC has issued annual assessments of the impact of the *UK Corporate Governance Code* and the *UK Stewardship Code*. Work prompted more specifically by the financial crisis also continued, with a number of new requirements introduced in 2012 and through an inquiry led by Lord Sharman, commissioned by the FRC in the same year to identify steps to improve consideration by companies and auditors regarding going concern and liquidity risks, and to recommend measures necessary to improve the existing reporting regime. The final *Sharman Report* was issued in 2013, its main conclusion being that both directors and auditors need to put greater focus on robust management of risks to going concern and in doing so consider the full business cycle of the company concerned. Consequential changes were introduced in the *UK Corporate Governance Code* of 2014 and supplementary guidance, introducing new requirements relating to risk assessment and mitigation, and the monitoring of internal controls and assessing going concern. This was matched by new disclosure requirements setting out the board's views on the longer-term viability of the company and the period they have considered for this purpose.
- Auditing standards in the UK and Ireland have also been updated to complement and support developments in governance practice and reporting – requiring auditors to provide commentary on major risks affecting the audit and to report by exception if information regarding governance given in the company's annual report is not consistent with information obtained during the audit.

Principles of the UK Corporate Governance Code

The *UK Corporate Governance Code* sets out the principles of good governance under five headings as shown in **Table 18.1**.

Table 18.1 The Main Principles of the *UK Corporate Governance Code*

Section A: Leadership

1. Every company should be headed by an effective board which is collectively responsible for the long-term success of the company.
2. There should be a clear division of responsibilities at the head of the company between the running of the board and the executive responsibility for the running of the company's business. No one individual should have unfettered powers of decision-making.

Table 18.1 ***(Continued)***

3. The chairman is responsible for leadership of the board and ensuring its effectiveness on all aspects of its role.
4. As part of their role as members of a unitary board, non-executive directors should constructively challenge and help develop proposals on strategy.

Section B: Effectiveness

1. The board and its committees should have the appropriate balance of skills, experience, independence and knowledge of the company to enable them to discharge their respective duties and responsibilities effectively.
2. There should be a formal, rigorous and transparent procedure for the appointment of new directors to the board.
3. All directors should be able to allocate sufficient time to the company to discharge their responsibilities effectively.
4. All directors should receive induction on joining the board and should regularly update and refresh their skills and knowledge.
5. The board should be supplied in a timely manner with information in a form and of a quality appropriate to enable it to discharge its duties.
6. The board should undertake a formal and rigorous annual evaluation of its own performance and that of its committees and individual directors.
7. All directors should be submitted for re-election at regular intervals, subject to continued satisfactory performance.

Section C: Accountability

1. The board should present a fair, balanced and understandable assessment of the company's position and prospects.
2. The board is responsible for determining the nature and extent of the principal risks it is willing to take in achieving its strategic objectives. The board should maintain sound risk management and internal control systems.
3. The board should establish formal and transparent arrangements for considering how it should apply the corporate reporting, risk management and internal control principles and for maintaining an appropriate relationship with the company's auditors.

Section D: Remuneration

1. Executive directors' remuneration should be designed to promote the long-term success of the company. Performance-related elements should be transparent, stretching and rigorously applied.

Table 18.1 ***(Continued)***

2. There should be a formal and transparent procedure for developing policy on executive remuneration and for fixing the remuneration packages of individual directors. No director should be involved in deciding his or her own remuneration.

Section E: Relations with Shareholders

1. There should be a dialogue with shareholders based on the mutual understanding of objectives. The board as a whole has responsibility for ensuring that a satisfactory dialogue with shareholders takes place.
2. The board should use general meetings to communicate with investors and to encourage their participation.

These main principles of the *UK Corporate Governance Code* are designed to achieve:

- well-directed and balanced activity by the board, with clear leadership by the board's chairman, focussed on the long-term success of the company;
- the contribution of appropriate skills, knowledge and time to achieve that success;
- effective identification and management of risks together with clear and understandable reporting;
- safeguards on remuneration so as to ensure alignment of executive directors with the company's long-term success;
- meaningful dialogue with shareholders.

Each of the main principles is supported by specific provisions setting out the steps ordinarily required to achieve the aim of the principle concerned. Key provisions of the code can be summarised as follows.

Leadership (Section A) The board's role consists of entrepreneurial leadership within a prudent framework of controls, ensuring appropriate resources are available. The board is also to set the company's values and standards and ensure that its obligations to its shareholders and others are understood and met. Steps to achieve this include ensuring that:

- the board meets sufficiently regularly to discharge its duties effectively;
- there is a formal schedule of matters reserved for its decision;
- the annual report provides information to shareholders (and others) on how the board operates; and
- appropriate insurance cover for directors is in place.

In addition, the *UK Corporate Governance Code* stresses the importance of a clear division between responsibility for the operation of the board and responsibility for the running of the company's business. To this end, the code both requires an appropriate balance between executive and independent non-executive directors (setting out criteria for determining independence) and states clearly that responsibility for running the board lies with the chairman, who is to be independent on appointment and who should not combine the role with that of chief executive. Specifically, the chairman is responsible for:

- setting the board's agenda;
- ensuring there is adequate time for discussion, in particular of strategic issues;
- encouraging openness and debate; and
- ensuring that directors receive accurate, timely and clear information.

Non-executive directors, for their part, are to bring appropriate scrutiny to bear on the performance of management and reporting of performance. As part of doing so, one of the independent non-executive directors is to be appointed as the '**senior independent director**' and in that role should:

- act as a sounding board for the chairman;
- be available to shareholders who wish to raise concerns.

Effectiveness (Section B) The board is to be of a size sufficient to meet the needs of the business (without becoming unwieldy) and is to include an appropriate combination of executive and non-executive directors such that no individual or small group can dominate its decision-making. In support of this aim:

- shareholders (and others) are to be provided with information as to which directors are considered independent, together with explanatory information for that conclusion in circumstances in which contraindications exist, such as recent employment by the company, close family ties with the company's advisor, directors or senior employees, or when a director represents a significant shareholder;
- at least half the board is to consist of independent non-executive directors and the code sets out criteria against which independence is assessed;
- there should be a nomination committee (with a majority of independent non-executive directors) to lead the process for board appointments, which are to be made on merit, against objective criteria and with due regard for diversity (including gender) as a safeguard against inappropriate 'group think', with regular opportunities for re-appointment;
- terms and conditions of appointment of non-executive directors are to be made available for inspection (and thereby comment);

- directors are to update their skills and knowledge on a continual basis, with review by the chairman as to their training and development needs;
- new directors are to be given a full, formal and tailored induction, including opportunities to meet major shareholders;
- directors are to have access to independent professional advice;
- the chairman is to act on the result of the required annual evaluation of board performance, both by recognising strengths and addressing weaknesses, including, if appropriate, making changes in board membership;
- in the case of larger companies, an external facilitator should be involved at least every three years ('larger' companies are those within the London FTSE 350 and those listed on the Irish Main Securities Market and having a market capitalisation of €750 million or more);
- the non-executive directors are to evaluate performance of the chairman.

Accountability (Section C) The board's overall responsibility is presentation of the "fair, balanced and understandable assessment of the company's position and prospects". In doing so, each annual report of the company is to contain:

- a confirmation from the directors that they consider the standard of "fair, balanced and understandable" has been met;
- an explanation of how the company generates or preserves value over the longer term (taking into account the direction given by the FRC's *Guidance on Risk Management, Internal Control and Related Financial and Business Reporting* (2014)) in addition to a statement as to whether the directors consider it appropriate to adopt the going concern basis of accounting in preparing the company's financial statements;
- a confirmation from the directors that they have carried out a robust assessment of the principal risks facing the company, together with a description of those risks and how they are being managed or mitigated; and
- an explanation of how the directors have assessed the longer term prospects of the company, the period they have considered for this purpose (which the FRC guidance indicates is likely to be considerably in excess of a year), and whether they have a reasonable expectation that the company will be able to continue in operation and meet liabilities over that period.

In addition, the 2014 version of the *UK Corporate Governance Code* also introduced a requirement for ongoing monitoring of risk management and internal control systems, supplementing the requirement of earlier codes for an annual review of those systems.

On these points, the external (statutory) auditors of the company also have a part to play. All information published alongside audited financial statements must be considered by the auditors, in compliance with International Standard on Auditing ('ISA') (UK and Ireland) 720 – Section A *The Auditor's Responsibilities relating to Other Information in Documents containing Audited Financial Statements,* and any inconsistencies with the information they have obtained during the audit must be highlighted in their report. More specifically, ISA (UK and Ireland) 700 *The Independent Auditor's Report on Financial Statements* was revised in 2012 and 2014 to require that auditors report by exception if they consider that the board's statement that the annual report is fair, balanced and reasonable is inconsistent with knowledge acquired in the course of the audit (paragraph 22B). Additionally, ISA (UK and Ireland) 700 requires auditors to provide an independent commentary on risks from an audit perspective – describing those that had the greatest effect on the audit, how the concept of materiality was applied and how both were reflected in the scope of the audit (paragraph 19A). In relation to the statements on going concern and longer term viability, ISA 570 (UK and Ireland) *Going Concern* requires auditors to consider those statements and report whether they consider further information should be provided (paragraph 17-2).

Section C of the *UK Corporate Governance Code* also establishes that companies should establish an audit committee of at least three independent non-executive directors (or two, for smaller companies), with at least one member having recent and relevant financial experience, and with written terms of reference covering at least the matters set out in **Table 18.2**. In addition, it requires the committee:

- to review arrangements for staff of the company to raise concerns in confidence regarding possible improprieties, whether regarding financial reporting or other matters; and
- if there is no internal audit function, to make an annual assessment of whether this is appropriate.

Table 18.2 Role and Responsibilities of the Audit Committee

The *UK Corporate Governance Code* (paragraph C.3.2) indicates that the audit committee's terms of reference, which are to be in writing and available on the company's website, should include:

- to monitor the integrity of the financial statements of the company and any formal announcements relating to its financial performance, reviewing significant financial reporting judgements contained in them;
- to review the company's internal financial controls and, unless expressly addressed by a separate board risk committee composed of independent directors, or by the board itself, to review the company's internal control and risk management systems;

Table 18.2 *(Continued)*

- to monitor and review the effectiveness of the company's internal audit function;
- to make recommendations to the board, for it to put to the shareholders for their approval in general meeting, in relation to the appointment, re-appointment and removal of the external auditor and to approve the remuneration and terms of engagement of the external auditor;
- to review and monitor the external auditor's independence and objectivity and the effectiveness of the audit process, taking into consideration relevant UK professional and regulatory requirements;
- to develop and implement policy on the engagement of the external auditor to supply non-audit services, taking into account relevant ethical guidance regarding the provision of non-audit services by the external audit firm; and to report to the board, identifying any matters in respect of which it considers that action or improvement is needed and making recommendations as to the steps to be taken; and
- to report to the board on how it has discharged its responsibilities.

How the audit committee discharged its responsibilities is to be set out in a separate section of the annual report, which is to include:

- significant issues considered in relation to the financial statements and how these were addressed;
- the committee's assessment of the external auditor; and
- if the external auditor provides non-audit services, an explanation of how auditor objectivity and independence are safeguarded.

Again, while not set out in the *UK Corporate Governance Code* itself, the auditor has a role and is specifically required by the revised ISA (UK and Ireland) 700 to comment if this section does not appropriately address matters communicated by the auditor to the audit committee.

Remuneration (Section D) The board is to establish a remuneration committee with a majority of independent non-executive directors which is responsible for setting the remuneration of executive directors and the chairman. The committee is to use careful judgement to determine remuneration levels, with the aim of promoting the long-term success of the company. Performance-related elements are to be transparent, and the code indicates that the remuneration arrangements should also:

- include provisions to enable the company to recover sums paid or withhold payment in specified circumstances;
- avoid termination payments that reward poor performance and take a robust line regarding directors' obligations to mitigate loss; and

- in the case of non-executive directors, exclude share options or other performance-related elements (unless shareholder approval is obtained in advance).

To help support appropriate decisions, the chairman should ensure that the remuneration committee chairman keeps principal shareholders informed regarding remuneration, and that shareholders are invited to approve all new and amended longer-term incentive schemes.

Relations with shareholders (Section E) As can be seen, a number of elements in earlier sections of the code are designed to support an open and effective dialogue with shareholders. The final section of the code underpins these by requiring that:

- the chairman ensure that views of shareholders are communicated to the board as a whole;
- non-executive directors are provided with opportunities to attend meetings with major shareholders;
- the annual report sets out steps taken by board members to develop an understanding of the views of major shareholders;
- arrangements for general meeting include clearly set resolutions and appropriate arrangements to facilitate proxy voting;
- when a significant proportion of votes is cast against a resolution, the company explains what actions it intends to take to understand the reasons behind that result; and
- the chairmen of the audit, remuneration and nomination committees are available to answer questions at the annual general meeting.

The UK Stewardship Code

The term 'stewardship' is used in a wide range of contexts to indicate the proper use of resources. In the context of commercial enterprises, effective stewardship involves acting to promote long-term success in such a way that companies, investors and the economy as a whole benefit. The term was used in the *Cadbury Report* primarily in describing the duties of directors to act as good stewards of the company's resources; however, while primary responsibility lies with the company's board, which oversees management, investors also have a part to play in publicly-listed companies by holding the board to account for the fulfilment of its responsibilities.

The *UK Stewardship Code* aims to support constructive involvement by institutional investors, such as pension funds, insurance companies, investment trusts and asset managers, in supporting effective governance by holding the board to account for the fulfilment of its responsibilities. While following the

UK Stewardship Code is voluntary, the FRC encourages institutional investors to become signatories of this code and to publish on their website a description of how they have applied its principles or, if the *UK Stewardship Code* is not fully applied, disclose reasons why.

Principles of the UK Stewardship Code The *UK Stewardship Code* sets out seven principles, requiring institutional investors to:

1. publicly disclose their policy on how they will discharge their stewardship responsibilities;
2. have a robust polity on managing conflicts of interest;
3. monitor their investee companies;
4. establish clear guidelines on when and how they will escalate stewardship activities – these include (but are not limited to) circumstances in which investors have concern about the company's strategy, performance, governance, remuneration or approach to risks;
5. be willing to act collectively with other investors where appropriate;
6. have a clear policy on voting and disclosure of voting activity; and
7. report periodically on their stewardship and voting activities.

Steps by which institutional investors may monitor investee companies are also set out in the code and include: keeping abreast of the company's performance and factors that could affect that performance; considering whether the company adheres to the spirit of the *UK Corporate Governance Code*; and attending general meetings. Investors should also endeavour to identify at an early stage any issues that may result in a significant loss in investment value, raising concerns as appropriate with the company's board.

Corporate Governance in Other Types of Organisations

The *UK Corporate Governance Code* reflects governance practices that are relevant in the context of larger listed companies. However, the concepts underlying its principles, or those set out in the OECD's *Principles of Corporate Governance,* can be used for other types of entities, such as a private company limited by shares. The issues arising from agency and stakeholder theory, outlined above, apply in enterprises of all types and size; hence, though the specific provisions of the *UK Corporate Governance Code* may not be necessary in the context of, for example, smaller or non-profit entities, the code may be used to help inform development of governance structures that respond to the expectations of finance providers and stakeholders, either in a particular entity or a particular class of entity.

Any entity may choose to apply the *UK Corporate Governance Code* on a voluntary basis (as is done by a number of Irish State bodies, such as the ESB).

Voluntary application may be considered appropriate in cases where there is a wide base of shareholders or other finance providers, such as holders of listed debt. Full application on a voluntary basis would, however, be relatively unusual. More commonly, the boards of other types of entity that wish to comment on governance matters provide descriptive commentary without claiming application of the code or, if an alternative code for their sector has been develop by a relevant industry or government body, will benchmark their governance arrangements against that 'industry' code. Such codes include the following.

1. **Smaller listed companies** The Quoted Companies Alliance, a UK-based organisation representing the interests of small to mid-size quoted companies, has developed and issued a code for smaller listed entities, *Corporate Governance Code for Small and Mid-Size Quoted Companies 2013*, which provides a governance framework consistent with the *UK Corporate Governance Code* principles but takes into account the context in which such smaller listed companies and their shareholders operate. For boards of companies with securities listed on the Emerging Securities Market (ESM) in Dublin or the Alternative Investment Market (AIM) in London – many of which comment on the governance practices they apply – it provides an alternative recognised framework against which to benchmark those practices.
2. **Irish State bodies** The term 'State bodies' in Ireland refers to enterprises that are beneficially owned, either completely or mostly, by the Irish Government. State bodies may be incorporated under company law or under specific applicable statute. Each body has a sponsor minister who acts as shareholder, either independently or together with the Minister for Finance.

   The Department of Finance has issued guidelines for State bodies in its *Code of Practice for the Governance of State Bodies* (2009) which sets out provisions covering internal governance practices of such bodies and their external relations with the Government, relevant departments and ministers. The Department's stated purpose is to give a structure that supports proper management of State bodies which "must serve the interests of the taxpayer, pursue value for money in their endeavours (including managing risk appropriately), and act transparently as public entities".

   All State bodies – both commercial and non-commercial – are required to apply the *Code of Practice for the Governance of State Bodies* and the chairman of each body is required to make an annual report to the relevant minister confirming compliance with this code. Unlike the *UK Corporate Governance Code*, the State bodies must apply the *Code of Practice for the Governance of State Bodies* in full unless they agree variations with the minister; there is no application of the 'comply or explain' concept.

As noted above, some State bodies have opted to apply the *UK Corporate Governance Code* in addition to the *Code of Practice for the Governance of State Bodies*. Such bodies are generally those operating as commercial entities, e.g. the ESB.

3. **Financial institutions** The Central Bank of Ireland has issued corporate governance codes applicable to:
   - credit institutions and insurance undertakings; and
   - captive insurers and reinsurers.

   These codes take account of provisions of EU Directives applicable to such institutions and include a requirement for them to make an annual statement of compliance with their requirements directly to the Central Bank, noting any material departures. The auditors of such institutions are not required to review or report on these statements.

   Additionally, the Irish Funds Industry Association (IFIA) has developed and issued the *Corporate Governance Code for Collective Investment Schemes and Management Companies* that, though voluntary, is strongly recommended by the IFIA. Collective investment vehicles listed on the ISE's Main Securities Market, and therefore required to disclose details of the corporate governance applied, generally report on their compliance with the IFIA's code.
4. **Charities** Charities in Ireland are not required to apply or report against a corporate governance code. However, a *Code of Practice for Good Governance of Community, Voluntary and Charitable Organisations in Ireland* has been developed on a voluntary basis by a grouping of charities. Charities are encouraged to apply this code, which has been developed with the specific expectations of charity stakeholders in mind, particularly donors of funds. The code follows the 'comply or explain' approach.

   In the UK, an equivalent grouping of charity organisations issued *Good Governance: a Code for the Voluntary and Community Sector* in 2005 with support from the charities regulator, the Charity Commission. A revised version was issued in 2010.

Future Developments

As noted at the start of this chapter, corporate governance is a dynamic concept. Factors likely to result in further changes to the principles discussed here include:

- the continuance of FRC's annual assessments of corporate governance;
- the conclusions of the OECD's consultation on revisions to its principles, launched in 2014, and continuance of its monitoring of global developments in the governance arena; and

- alignment of best practice across the EU, as the European Commission progresses its *Action Plan: European company law and corporate governance* (issued in 2012) and considers the effectiveness of actions taken following its *Commission Recommendation on the quality of corporate governance reporting* ('**comply or explain**') (2014/208/EU).

However, it is unlikely that this brief summary will prove complete with hindsight. We can anticipate that there will be continual further improvement and refinement in the articulation of relevant corporate governance principles and practices in the light of experience.

REVIEW QUESTIONS

(See Solutions to Review Questions at the end of this text.)

Question 18.1

Define and explain corporate governance.

Question 18.2

The Department of Transport, Tourism and Sport announced last week that the activities of Vehicle Testing Ireland (VTI), which is responsible for the road testing of all vehicles in the country as required under legislation, are to be transferred immediately to a new company, Vehicle Testing Ireland Limited (VTIL). VTIL is not a government department but is instead a single-member company, the single member being the current Minister of Transport, Tourism and Sport. The current board of VTIL consists of five senior civil servants from the Department of Transport, Tourism and Sport, VTI's general manager and its financial controller; the secretary of the Department is the chairman.

All five of the senior civil servants from the Department have been appointed to each of the audit, nomination and remuneration committees, with one of them (other than the chairman of the board) taking the chair of each of these committees. All five plan to step down next month and have already produced a shortlist of potential board candidates (see table below).

Name	Current Position	Background	Role Envisaged in VTIL
Dan Maguire	General manager and director of VTIL	15 years in VTI	Managing director
Peter Patterson	Financial controller of VTIL	12 years in VTI	Director of finance and human resources
Sharon Hughes	General Manager of State Vehicle Procurement Office	24 years in State Vehicle Procurement Office, worked in motor industry prior to that	Non-executive director and member of audit and nomination committees; chair of nomination committee
Neil Marsden	General manager of State Information Technology Lab	8 years in State Information Technology Lab, prior to that 20 years in IT industry in USA	Non-executive director and member of audit and nomination committees; chair of audit committee
Pat Porterhouse	Secretary of Department of Transport, Tourism and Sport and chairman of VTI	30 years in public service	Chairman of VTIL and remuneration committee; member of audit, nomination and remuneration committees
Elizabeth O'Connor	Assistant Secretary in Department of Transport, Tourism and Sport; responsible for HR in VTI	26 years in public sector	Non-executive director and member of audit, remuneration and nomination committees

Name	Current Position	Background	Role Envisaged in VTIL
Mark Wilson	Recently retired as CEO of major vehicle importer; appointed to a number of State boards	40 years in motor trade	Non-executive director and member of audit and remuneration committees
Monica O'Brien	International business consultant and member of a number of State boards	25 years in business consulting	Non-executive director and member of nomination and remuneration committees

Requirement Assess the plans of VTIL in the context of its desire to achieve the highest standards of corporate governance.

SOLUTIONS TO REVIEW QUESTIONS

Question 1.1

An important distinction must be drawn between the areas of criminal and civil law. A crime is conduct prohibited by law, for example larceny under the Larceny Act 1916. Criminal prosecutions are generally brought by the State, but in rare cases an individual can maintain a private prosecution. An Garda Síochána or the Director of Public Prosecutions (the DPP) will take the initial decision to prosecute. The State prosecutes because it is notionally the community as a whole that suffers when the criminal law is infringed.

Civil proceedings have as their object the resolution of disputes between individuals and the compensation of those who have been wronged under the civil law. The main areas of civil litigation comprise the law of contract, torts, employment and family law.

Question 1.2

Jurisdiction of the High Court in Ireland The following is a summary of the jurisdiction of the High Court:

- this court can award unlimited damages – in general it deals with civil law cases claiming damages in excess of €75,000 (personal injury €60,000);
- it has supervisory jurisdiction over inferior courts, administrative bodies and persons with quasi-judicial functions by way of judicial review;
- it deals with cases challenging the validity of any laws or legislation vis-à-vis the Constitution of Ireland;
- it also deals with succession, trusts, wardships/wards of court, company law, defamation cases, bankruptcy, judicial separation and divorce matters (where matters are complex and involve considerable assets or income); and
- it also has appellate jurisdiction in relation to cases referred from the Circuit Court and certain tribunals – it can give rulings on questions of law referred from the District Court.

Question 1.3

Precedent A precedent can be defined as a judgment that is cited as an authority to justify a similar decision in a later case involving similar legal issues. In relation to the hierarchy of the courts, the precise rules of precedent are:

- a decision of a superior court is binding upon an inferior court,
- a decision of an inferior court will not bind a superior court,

- courts of similar authority have neither the power to bind or over-rule each other, and
- a decision of a foreign court will not bind a national court although it may act as persuasive authority.

Question 1.4

(a) *Commercial Court* The High Court operates a commercial list – known colloquially as 'the Commercial Court'. This court has the jurisdiction to deal with
  - current commercial disputes where the claim, or counterclaim, is not less than €1 million,
  - any application or proceedings under the Arbitration Acts where the value of any claim or counterclaim is not less than €1 million,
  - any legal dispute relating to patents, trademarks, copyright, industrial designs or a case relating to 'passing off', and
  - any appeal or application for a judicial review of a previous decision or determination that a judge considers suitable for admission to the Commercial Court.

(b) *Conclusion* As Dylan Accounting College's action is for passing-off it can be heard in the Commercial Court.

Question 1.5

EU Directive This is a guideline/instruction to Member States as to how they should standardise legislation in a particular area (within a particular time-frame in which to achieve this standardisation). It is binding as to the result to be achieved and is not directly applicable, i.e. an EU Directive gives the individual Member States the choice as to the form and method of implementation. In Ireland, EU Directives become part of Irish law through either an act of the Oireachtas (where it involves a substantive issue) or a statutory instrument (where it involves a more technical issue). The idea embodied in the Directive is enacted as legislation, but the exact particulars are at the discretion of the Member States. Examples include the Organisation of Working Time Act 1997 and the National Minimum Wage Act 2000. All affected parties must comply with a Directive when it is enacted into Irish law.

Question 1.6

Distinction between Civil and Criminal Law

- Definitions: civil law is deemed to be private law and it generally concerns disputes between individuals, where one person sues another person for a wrong, whereas criminal law is deemed to be public law, which involves the State imposing codes of conduct and prosecuting an individual for breaching that code.

- Title of the proceedings/parties: a civil claim is called an 'action' and the parties are known as the 'plaintiff' and the 'defendant'; whereas a criminal case is called a 'prosecution' and the parties are known as the 'prosecution' and the 'defence (accused)'.
- Objectives: the main objective of civil law is compensation and ceasing the unwanted conduct; whereas criminal law's objective is punishment (as well as incapacitation, retribution, deterrence and rehabilitation).
- Tests: for a civil court to find a defendant liable the test is 'the balance of probabilities'; whereas for a criminal court to find a defendant guilty the test is 'beyond all reasonable doubt'.
- Commencement of proceedings: in civil law, an action is initiated by way of pleadings, whereas in criminal law a prosecution is initiated by the State/People/DPP either through a summons or an indictment.
- Representatives: the representative of the State in civil cases is the Attorney General, whereas the representative of the State in criminal cases is the Director of Public Prosecutions.
- Remedies: the main civil remedies are damages, injunctions, court orders, an account for profits, etc., whereas the main criminal remedies are fines, imprisonment, probation orders, community service orders, etc.
- Courts: there are different hierarchies of civil and criminal courts – the main civil courts are the District Court, Circuit Court, High Court, Court of Appeal and the Supreme Court, whereas the main criminal courts are the District Criminal Court, Circuit Criminal Court, Central Criminal Court, Special Criminal Court, Court of Appeal and the Supreme Court.

Question 1.7

Civil Law and Criminal Law (**Six** differences are explained here – only **four** are required by the question.)

1. Objectives: the main objectives of civil law are compensation and ceasing the unwanted conduct, whereas criminal law's objective is punishment (as well as incapacitation, retribution, deterrence and rehabilitation).
2. Tests: for a civil court to find a defendant liable the test is 'the balance of probabilities', whereas for a criminal court to find a defendant guilty the test is 'beyond all reasonable doubt'.
3. Commencement of proceedings and representatives: in civil law an action is initiated by way of pleadings, whereas in criminal law a prosecution is initiated by the State/People/DPP either through a summons or an indictment.

4. The representative of the State in civil cases is the Attorney General; whereas the representative of the State in criminal cases is the Director of Public Prosecutions.
5. Remedies: the main civil remedies are damages, injunctions, court orders, an account for profits, etc., whereas the main criminal remedies are fines, imprisonment, probation orders, community service orders, etc.
6. Courts: there are different hierarchies of civil and criminal courts. The main civil courts are the District Court, Circuit Court, High Court, Court of Appeal and Supreme Court, whereas the main criminal courts are the District Criminal Court, Circuit Criminal Court, Central Criminal Court, Special Criminal Court, Court of Appeal and Supreme Court.

Special Criminal Court This court is reserved for cases involving scheduled offences (usually involving dangerous criminals and terrorist cases). There is no jury, but three (rather than the usual one) judges preside. This court is not a permanent court but is established as necessary to deal with cases that cannot be properly heard in the other courts.

Question 1.8

Delegated Legislation This is a secondary law made by an executive authority under powers delegated by primary legislation. The purpose behind this legislation is to administer and implement the terms of primary legislation. Delegated legislation was used to implement the provisions of the Health and Safety Act 2005 regarding the testing of employees to ensure compliance with the obligation not to be under the influence of an intoxicant while at work. There are various pieces and classifications of delegated legislation, including ministerial orders, regulations, bye-laws or schemes, and rules or independent support of legislation.

The main advantages of delegated legislation are as follows:
1. it allows flexibility;
2. it ensures access to particular skills and expertise; and
3. it saves time.

Question 1.9

Offences A summary offence is a less serious offence than an indictable offence. It is normally tried in the District Court without a jury. The penalty is normally not more than 12 months in prison or a fine of not more than €1,905 (with limited exceptions).

Indictable Offences are more serious offences – they are generally heard in jury courts (with the exception of cases heard before the Special Criminal Courts). They are heard either in the Circuit Court, the Central Criminal

Court or the Special Criminal Court – depending on the nature and seriousness of the offence. They generally carry the option of a term of imprisonment as a potential punishment.

Question 1.10

(a) The Circuit Court is comprised of eight courts, a president and 37 ordinary judges with two permanent courts in Dublin and Cork, and six movable courts, which travel throughout the country and sit in various locations.

(b) In the case of civil law, most of the work of the Circuit Court involves disputes in contract and tort. The maximum quantum of damages that can be awarded is €75,000, or €60,000 where the case involves personal injuries. The Circuit Court will also hear disputes in relation to:
- the recovery and title of land;
- equity matters, such as trusts;
- other matters including the granting of liquor licences; and
- some family law matters, such as divorces.

In the area of criminal law, the Circuit Court has the jurisdiction to hear all indictable (non-minor) offences except murder and rape, aggravated sexual assault, treason and piracy.

The court also hears appeals from the District Court and certain quasi-judicial tribunals.

Question 1.11

Quasi-judicial Tribunals These are specialist tribunals, permitted by Article 34 of the Irish Constitution, established to deal with civil matters.

The main **advantages** of these tribunals are: (**Seven** advantages are explained here – only **three** are required by the question.)

1. speed – they usually deal with matters more expeditiously than the courts;
2. informality – these are less formal, less intimidating and the stricter rules of evidence do not apply;
3. flexibility – they are not absolutely bound by the strict rules of precedent,
4. privacy – cases before these tribunals tends to be heard in private; in certain situations, the identities of the parties are undisclosed;
5. cost – tribunals are generally a much cheaper procedure than taking a case to the normal courts;
6. expertise – the use of specialist tribunals ensures that the person deciding the case has expert knowledge of the practice within the area under consideration and can form his or her conclusion in line with accepted practice; and

7. finality – appeals on decisions are limited and, once the tribunal has reached a decision, the parties may be bound by it and any award can be enforced through court action.

The main **disadvantage** of tribunals is that they generally do not make an award for costs.

Question 2.1

If a negligence action is taken against Martin, the following essential elements must be established:

- duty of care,
- breach of that duty; and
- damage resulting from the breach.

In this situation, and in order to establish negligence, you must first establish a duty of care from Martin towards Acme. Obviously, in this case there is a duty as he was hired to perform a task for Acme. He should regard Acme as a neighbour, as defined in the case of *Donoghue v. Stevenson* (1932), in that he should be aware that his activities will affect the wellbeing of Acme. Thus, there is a duty of care, and if Martin fell below the standard of a reasonable professional auditor, then there is a breach of the duty of care. To fall below the standard of a reasonable auditor would mean not abiding by current practices and recommendations of the professional body. For example, not attending a stocktake for five years is a clear breach of the professional bodies' regulations and, thus, he has fallen below the standard of a reasonable auditor.

The next question to ask is whether the negligent act of Martin has had a negative effect on Acme. This is the issue of causation. One can safely say that "but for" the negligent act of Martin not attending the stocktake for five years, the directors' actions would have been noticed, so there is a link between the negligent act and the loss suffered; therefore causation has been proved.

In terms of the issue of remoteness and whether the damage caused was foreseeable, it is fair to say that the loss was foreseeable and that a reasonable auditor would know that not attending a stocktake for five years could facilitate a fraud by the directors and, therefore, Martin is responsible for all economic damage suffered by the company.

Question 2.2

Duty of Care The original test to determine whether a duty of care exists is based on the decision of Lord Atkins in *Donoghue v. Stevenson* (1932) and is known as the 'neighbour principle'. The current test was established in *Caparo Industries plc v. Dickman* (1990) and is a three-part test that asks: (1) was the harm reasonably foreseeable?; (2) was there a relationship of proximity between the parties, *Ward v. McMaster* (1988)?; and (3) considering the circumstances, is it fair, just and reasonable to impose a duty of care?. This test was endorsed in Ireland in *Glencar Exploration plc v. Mayo County Council* (2001).

Question 2.3

Contributory Negligence This arises where a person contributes to his or her own injuries by failing to exercise reasonable care in relation to his or her own personal safety or the safety of property – the court views it as a breach of duty of care towards oneself. The defence is governed by the Civil Liability Act 1961, which allows for the apportionment of damages where contributory negligence arises, based on the degree of fault of the respective parties. The defence may also arise by a failure to mitigate damages, such as in *Jones v. Livox Quarries* (1952), and in *Froom v. Butcher* (1976). In allowing a defence of contributory negligence, the court will take into consideration the age and experience of the person, as well as the actions of a reasonable person, such as in *Hegarty v. Donegal County Council* (1998) and *Raleigh v. Iarnród Éireann* (2003). In our scenario, the defence may apply and reduce Peter's compensation if his failure to wear the regulation work boots, as required by health and safety law, exacerbated his injuries.

Question 2.4

Remoteness of Damage This is a device used by the court to determine whether or not the level of damage caused by the breach could have been reasonably foreseen. If the courts determine that the level of damage caused by the breach was too remote and could not have been foreseen by a reasonable person, they will not hold the defendant liable. This means that although the defendant's breach may cause the damage, the defendant will not be held accountable for all of the damage. This is because the damage resulting from the breach is so unexpected or 'remote' that the court considers it unfair to hold the defendant accountable for a level of damage he could not have foreseen. This test is known as the 'reasonably foreseeable' test and was developed in *The Wagon Mound (No 1)* (1961).

Conclusion Bluesky Ltd is obliged to compensate Denis for his injuries as it owed him a duty of care (employer–employee) but breached the standard (storing the printer dangerously on an overhead shelf), thereby causing his injuries, which were foreseeable.

Question 2.5

Standard of Care The standard of care of a financial controller or any professional is based on the standard of a reasonable man. The court will look at how a reasonable financial controller would have acted. The court will assume that the individual has all reasonable common sense and common knowledge, together with the reasonable amount of knowledge that a financial controller would be expected to have. The test is a subjective one that is modified according to personal characteristics. In this situation, we are talking about a reasonable financial controller and not, for example, a reasonable window cleaner. The financial controller is presumed to have the necessary skill that a financial controller would have. In determining whether a reasonable man would act in a certain manner, the court reviews various factors including the:

- probability of the accident – the greater the probability, the higher the standard required;
- gravity of the threatened injury – the more grave the potential injury, the higher the standard required;
- social utility of the defendant's actions – this may mitigate against a deviation from the behaviour of a reasonable man; and
- costs and practicalities of eliminating the risk – this weighs up risk versus cost and practical issues.

In this situation, it is clear that the financial controller's actions amount to a breach of standard by under-insuring the gems.

Question 3.1

There are three main factors necessary to create a contract:
1. offer;
2. acceptance; and
3. consideration.

1. One party makes an offer. An offer may be described as the terms and conditions on which the offeror is prepared to enter a contract. An offer is clear, complete and final.
2. The second party must accept the offer (as made by the offeror). Acceptance is the unconditional agreement to all the terms of the offer communicated to the offeror.
3. Exchange of consideration: consideration is something of value in the eyes of the law, e.g. money or money's worth.

Furthermore, there must be an intention to create legal relations, and the parties to the contract must have capacity to enter into the contract, e.g. have the appropriate intellectual capacity and have reached the age of majority.

All of these factors must be met for the contract to be enforceable, i.e. recognised by a court as giving rights and obligations to the parties to the contract.

Question 3.2

(a) *Contractual Capacity and Minors* In accordance with the Age of Majority Act 1985 a minor is defined as any person under the age of 18 and who has never been married. Under contract law, minors have limited contractual capacity. Certain contracts made by a minor are valid, but some are void and others are voidable.

Valid contracts are contracts for necessaries and beneficial contracts of service. 'Necessaries' are defined by the Sale of Goods Act 1893 as "goods suitable to the condition in life of such ... minor ... and to his actual requirements at the time of the sale and delivery". The test for determining whether the goods are necessaries is subjective in nature. In *Nash v. Inman* (1908), 11 fancy waistcoats purchased by an Oxford undergraduate were not classed as necessaries, as the minor's father convinced the court that his son already had sufficient clothing. In contrast, in *Soon v. Wilson* (1962), the court ruled that a contract for the purchase of books by a minor for his studies was valid, as the books were necessaries.

A beneficial contract of service is one where the minor provides a service for which he obtains a benefit, for example, contracts of apprenticeship, training and education. In *Shears v. Mendeloff* (1914), a minor boxer entered into a management contract. The terms of the contract provided that: (1) there were no obligations on the manager to arrange matches for the boxer; (2) the boxer had to cover his own expenses; but (3) if the minor earned any fees, he had to pay his management 25% of these fees. The court ruled that, as there was no substantial benefit to the minor in this contract, it was not a beneficial contract of service and it was void.

(b) *Conclusion* Anton and Aaron are under 18 and are therefore minors. As this contract is not for necessaries and is not a beneficial contract for service, it may be voidable at the option of the minors when they attain the age of majority.

Question 3.3

Elements of a Valid Contract The main elements of a valid contract are as follows:

1. *Offer* An offer is a clear and unambiguous statement of the terms and conditions under which the parties are willing to contract and often needs to be distinguished from an invitation to treat, which is merely an invitation to make an offer. The offer must be met by a valid acceptance.

2. *Acceptance* This can be defined as the 'final and unequivocal agreement to the terms of the offer'. The acceptance must be communicated to the offeror although, in the case of unilateral offers, it may be deemed accepted by performance.
3. *Consideration* Consideration must bind the offer to the acceptance – this is defined as 'mutuality of agreement', the 'price you pay for an offer', or '*quid pro quo*'. Consideration may be executed (a promise for an action of a thing) or executory (a promise for a promise).
4. *Intention* The parties must also indicate an intention to be legally bound; this is presumed in commercial agreements but not presumed in social agreements, unless the parties demonstrated intention by their actions.
5. *Capacity* The parties must also be capable of creating a contract and must not be incapacitated by age, mental incompetence, intoxication etc.

Conclusion An offer has been made and accepted between BCG Ltd and Mr Elis; the consideration is executory and is the purchase price in return for the land. As this is a commercial contract, intention is presumed and there is nothing to indicate that the parties are incapacitated. Therefore, as all elements are present, a valid contract exists between the parties.

Question 3.4

(a) *Methods of Contractual Discharge* Contractual discharge can arise in the following ways: (**Five** methods are discussed here – only **four** are required by the question.)
   1. performance of contractual obligations – the general rule is that contractual obligations are only discharged by complete and exact performance,
   2. agreement – this may arise pursuant to a condition precedent or subsequent, or where neither exist, the agreement must be supported by consideration,
   3. notice – this may arise as per the terms of the contract, subject to minimum notice being prescribed by legislation, or based upon what the court considers reasonable in the circumstances,
   4. breach of a contractual condition – the breach may be anticipatory or actual, and
   5. operation of the law – this may arise upon
      - death,
      - bankruptcy,
      - insanity or
      - frustration.

(b) *Conclusion* Bella's contract has been discharged by either (1) operation of the law based on a frustrating event – where government intervention has prevented performance of the contract (the fire inspection report preventing use of the premises as a bakery in their present condition) or (2) by breach of an implied term regarding fitness for purpose.

The legal consequence of a frustrating event is that the loss lies where it falls **or** the legal consequences of a breach are damages and/or rescission.

Question 3.5

Contract Formation To create a contract an offer must be met by acceptance and supported by consideration. In reviewing this case, it is clear that an offer was made by the CEO of the college to all of the lecturing staff. An offer can be defined as 'a clear and unambiguous statement of the terms and conditions under which the parties are willing to contract'. In this scenario, the offer can be classified as a unilateral offer (where the promise is made 'in return for' the doing of the act). When an offer is made, it must be accepted to create a valid contract – acceptance can be defined as the 'final and unequivocal expression of agreement to the terms of an offer'. To constitute a valid acceptance, the response must be a mirror image of the offer. In the case of a unilateral offer, acceptance can take place by performance. Relevant case law relating to unilateral offers and acceptance by performance include *Billings v. Arnott* (1945), and *Carlill v. Carbolic Smoke Ball Company* (1893).

It is obvious from the scenario that both Anne's and Frank's actions constitute acceptance by performance to the offer. However, as the offer was only made to the lecturing staff, Frank's actions cannot be classified as valid acceptance as his actions do not mirror the offer.

Conclusion The only valid contract that exists is between Dylan Accounting College and Anne, and the CEO cannot revoke the offer as performance has already taken place.

Question 3.6

(a) *Frustration* This is where a contract cannot be completed as agreed due to some unforeseeable factor outside the control of the contracting parties. The circumstances where a claim of frustration will be upheld include:

1. when the subject-matter of the contract is destroyed – in *Taylor v. Caldwell* (1863), the destruction of a music hall by a fire four days before a performance was due to take place was held to amount to frustration;

2. where government interference prevents performance of the contract – in *Ross v. Shaw* (1917), a contract to purchase yarn from a mill in Belgium could not be lawfully performed once the mill was occupied by German troops during World War I and the contract was deemed frustrated;
3. where performance of the contract becomes illegal – such as the sale of certain substances by head shops following the enactment of the Psychoactive Substances Act 2010;
4. in contracts of personal service, the death or incapacity of one party will amount to frustration – in *Flynn v. Great Northern Railway Company* (1953), the employment contract of a van driver was deemed frustrated when medical evidence proved that he would not be able to return to his job;
5. an inordinate delay or interruption of the contract – such as the contract for the construction of the M50 motorway following the delays caused by the discovery of an old Viking burial site;
6. commercially different circumstances (this scenario arose in a number of coronation cases, including *Krell v. Henry* (1903), when the coronation procession of Edward VII had to be cancelled due to the illness of the king – consequently many arrangements made in which persons obtained the right to view the procession from hotels and rooms overlooking the route came before the English courts, which ruled that the contracts were frustrated); and
7. where a particular event, which is the sole reason for the contract, fails to take place.

(b) *Conclusion* The contract is frustrated because government intervention has prevented the performance of the contract.

Question 3.7

(a) *Restraint of Trade Clause* This is a clause where one party to the contract agrees to restrict his liberty in the future to carry on trade with other persons, not parties to the contract. Generally these clauses arise in the context of: (**Three** examples are given here – only **two** are required by the question.)

1. employment contracts – in order to protect employees from using trade secrets/confidential information in future employment,
2. contracts with vendors of businesses – to protect the goodwill that has been purchased by the vendor, and
3. *solus*/distribution agreements – to guarantee exclusivity of supply in exchange for a benefit.

(b) *Validity* This clause may be classified as invalid – it is protecting a legitimate interest and is not excessive in terms of time, but the geographical restriction is quite wide.

(c) *Injunctions* These are court orders requiring a person to do something (mandatory) or to refrain from doing certain actions (prohibitory). They are generally awarded prior to a full hearing on an interlocutory basis, or after a full hearing on a permanent basis.

Question 3.8

Contractual Frustration This occurs, for example, where a valid contract is discharged by operation of the law – an unforeseen event arises that prevents completion of the contract. The crucial point is that this unforeseen event is outside the control of the contracting parties.

Circumstances where a claim of frustration will be upheld are as follows: (**Seven** circumstances are explained here – only **four** are required by the question.)

1. substantial delay or interruption of the contract that makes its performance impracticable,
2. where the subject matter of the contract is destroyed,
3. where the performance of the contract becomes illegal,
4. where government interference prevents performance of the contract,
5. the death or incapacity of one party (where the contract is one of personal service),
6. commercially different circumstances (including coronation cases), or
7. where a particular event, which is the sole reason for the contract, fails to take place.

Question 3.9

(a) Restraint of trade clause: this is a clause where one party to the contract agrees to restrict his liberty in the future to carry out trade with other persons, not parties to the contract. It is normal for such clauses to be included in employment contracts, but they also arise in relation to contracts with vendors of businesses and *solus* agreements (exclusive distribution agreements).

(b) The courts tend to the view that they are appropriate and will allow them when they are: (1) protecting a legitimate interest (such as confidential information and/or trade secrets); (2) deemed reasonable between the parties both in terms of geographical and time restrictions; and (3) not classed as contrary to public interest.

(c) *Conclusion* Based on the information provided it is reasonable to assume that the clause may be valid as: (1) Downey Investment Advisors is protecting a valid interest (confidential information and trade secrets); (2) the restraint is not unreasonable in terms of time, being only six months, nor in terms of geography (50 kilometre radius of Downey's offices in Galway and Limerick); and (3) there are no public policy reasons to prohibit it (abuse of monopoly, manipulation of a dominant market position, etc.).

Question 3.10

Contractual Condition A contractual condition is regarded as a vital or a prime contractual term that goes to the root of the contract. Contractual conditions are regarded by the courts as being responsible for inducing the contractual party to create the contract. Breach of a contractual condition equals a breach of contract and gives the injured party the right to terminate the contract and to claim for damages. An example of a breach of contractual condition arose in *Poussard v. Spiers and Pond* (1876) and in *Re Moore & Co Ltd and Landauer & Co* (1921).

Warranty A warranty is regarded as being less significant than a condition. Warranties are generally not the basis of the contract but peripheral to the overall agreement. Where a breach of warranty arises, it allows a claim for compensation only and generally does not facilitate the rescission of the contract. An example of a breach of warranty arose in *Bettini v. Gye* (1876).

Question 3.11

Order for Specific Performance This is where the court orders the defaulting party to perform specific obligations under the contract on the terms agreed.

The court will never grant an order for specific performance in the following contracts:

1. contracts for personal services (including employment contracts, contracts to perform at a specific concert/event or to take part in a film or television project). The rationale behind this exclusion is that such an order would be analogous to forced labour and is futile where the other party simply refuses to perform or performs to an inadequate standard;
2. contracts to advance money;
3. where the court cannot supervise performance of the contract (where constant supervision by a court is required);
4. where one of the parties is an infant/minor;
5. when damages are adequate compensation;

6. where the order would cause undue hardship on the party in breach; and
7. where the contract is neither fair nor just or where the conduct of the party seeking specific performance is questionable.

Conclusion It is unlikely that the court will grant the order as this is a contract for normal goods that are not in any way unique and damages will compensate adequately in this situation.

Question 3.12

For there to be a valid contract, three main elements need to be present:
1. offer,
2. acceptance and
3. consideration.

Together with these three main elements, there also must be capacity by the parties concerned to enter into the contract, and there must also be an intention by both parties for the contract to be legally binding.

An offer can be defined as a clear and unambiguous statement of the terms and conditions under which the parties are willing to contract. In return, there must be acceptance, which must be deemed valid. For there to be valid acceptance there must be a final and unequivocal agreement to the terms of the offer – therefore there must be no difference between the terms offered and the terms accepted. This acceptance must be communicated to the offeror.

The third element is 'consideration', which can be defined as 'money or money's worth'. Consideration can also be deemed to be the price paid for the offer. Consideration may be either executed, i.e. a promise to do something, or executory, i.e. a promise for a promise. The parties must also indicate an intention to be legally bound. In social relations there is no presumption that the parties intend to be legally bound and therefore it has to be explicitly stated. However, in commercial agreements, it is presumed that there is an intention to be legally bound by any agreement.

Finally, all parties to the contract must have the necessary legal capacity to enter into the contract and must not be incapacitated by reasons such as being under 18 years old, lacking the necessary mental competence or being intoxicated.

Question 3.13

The postal rule holds that a letter of acceptance is validly communicated when it is posted, as opposed to when it actually arrives and is received by the recipient. This rule has been applied in several cases, the most famous one being *Adams v. Lindsell* (1818). However, it must be remembered that this rule can be expressly excluded by the parties to the contract; it can specifically be provided that the postal rule is not to apply to their particular agreement. To be able to invoke the postal rule, it must be agreed, or must be seen as being a reasonable approach, given the contract between the parties. Obviously, correspondence must be properly addressed, stamped and posted. In this case the statement made by Gerard to Mark was **not** an offer but a statement of information; consequently the response by Mark is the offer and therefore, as there is no acceptance, there is no valid contract. If it was found by a court that the statement by Gerry was to be deemed an offer, then Mark's response would be deemed to be acceptance. However, in this particular situation, it is questionable as to whether the postal rule applies as the original offer was made by e-mail and the response was by post; therefore it would seem the response by post is not reasonable. Section 19 of the Electronic Commerce Act 2000 provides that acceptance of an offer by e-mail or any related communication may, unless otherwise agreed by the parties, be communicated by means of an electronic communication. In this case, such communication would be the reasonable means of responding.

It is also important to remember that the offer could be revoked prior to acceptance whereas, if the postal rule applies, there is a valid contract from the date of posting.

Question 4.1

(a) Steps Mary must take in applying for full planning permission:
- Valid notice of intention to apply for planning permission. The application for planning permission must be made within two weeks of publication of the notice. Mary should draw up an advertisement conforming to the regulations in a local newspaper and erect a notice on the site that is clearly visible and legible to passers by.
- Mary must then make an application for planning permission to her local planning authority. The application must be submitted to the relevant planning authority. The applicant should also submit copies of the public notices, as well as the necessary documents, particulars, plans, drawings and maps.

(b) Jim will need to apply for a retention permission. Retention permission is applied for in circumstances where an unauthorised use or works has been carried out on the land. An example is where someone builds a structure such as a house without first applying for planning permission. Jim will, in making an application for retention permission, be subject to a high fee and will face enforcement proceedings should retention permission be denied.

Question 4.2

Application Process for Planning Permission (**Six** steps are identified here – only **three** are required by the question.)

1. Notice: a notice of the application must be placed in the newspaper and a site notice at the location of the development two weeks before the application is made and must stay in place five weeks after the application is lodged.
2. Application: an application must be submitted to the planning authority, including detailed drawings and maps and cannot be in contravention of the development plan. The application must also state the type of permission being sought.
3. Inspection: the relevant planning authority will inspect the land and consider whether the requirements regarding the site notice have been complied with.
4. Public participation: any person/body can make a submission/observation in relation to the planning application within five weeks of the application being received.
5. Decision: the planning authority will issue a decision within eight weeks as to whether to grant/refuse the planning application (with or without conditions).
6. Appeal: the applicant can appeal a rejection to An Bord Pleanála.

Consequences of Proceeding without Planning Permission (**Three** consequences are given here – only **two** are required by the question.)

1. A warning letter may be issued against the unauthorised use of the land.
2. An enforcement notice may be issued requiring the developer to discontinue the unauthorised use of the land.
3. A planning injunction may be granted to ensure that an unauthorised development does not commence or continue.

Question 5.1

(a) Important terms in a lease include:
- identity of the parties;
- date of commencement of the lease;
- a clear and exact description of the premises;
- the rent payable; and
- length of the term being granted.

(b) Three typical covenants that bind tenants include:
- covenant to pay service charges;
- covenant to permit landlord to enter at reasonable times for purposes of inspection and repair; and
- covenant to pay rent in full and on time.

Three typical covenants that bind the landlord include:

- covenant to allow the tenant quiet enjoyment of the premises (implied by law);
- covenant that the landlord has the right to let the premises (implied by law); and
- covenant to maintain and repair structure.

Question 5.2

Terms in a Commercial Lease (**Nine** terms are listed here – only **five** are required by the question.)

1. the name and address of the parties to the lease,
2. the date the lease commences,
3. a description of the premises,
4. the amount of rent payable,
5. the period of the lease,
6. a clause detailing the consequences of a breach of the lease,
7. rent review clause,
8. service charge clause, or
9. alienation/sub-letting clause.

Question 5.3

Rent Review Clause The right to review rent is exercisable by the landlord of any commercial premises. It normally allows the landlord to review the level of rent every three to five years. Within the ambit of this right, there is also a right of the tenant to ask that an independent person review and determine the new level of rent. The clause does not usually provide for a downward variation.

Question 6.1

As a consumer, James can take advantage of the terms of the Sale of Goods and Supply of Services Act 1980. This Act is a comprehensive statement of the law regarding the basic features of consumer sale transactions. It is intended to protect parties, especially parties in unequal bargaining positions, from unfair advantage being taken of them when a purported choice is forced upon them.

For the Act to apply, the contract must have as its objective the transfer of property in goods, the contract must be for a sale and the goods to be sold must be given a price tag or a price.

With every contract, certain terms are implied. The first of these implied terms is that the seller should have good title to the product and the right to sell the product. The next implied term is that goods sold by description must correspond to the description. Thirdly, under section 14, it is implied that goods are of merchantable quality and are fit for the purpose or purposes intended. It is also presumed and implied that they are as durable as one can expect having regard to description, price and all other relevant circumstances.

The requirement of merchantable quality does not apply to goods whose defects are brought to the attention of the buyer before the contract is made. Nor does this requirement apply in a situation where the defects, if examined by the buyer before the contract was made, would have been obvious to the buyer or a reasonable person in the circumstances. In these instances, the doctrine of *caveat emptor* applies.

James needs to be aware that there is an absolute prohibition on any attempt to exclude the terms of the Sale of Goods Act in consumer contracts.

In this situation, James is entitled to a remedy, be it a repair, replacement or refund, as it was obvious that the book was not of merchantable quality.

Question 6.2

(a) *Definition of a Defective Product* A defective product is defined by the Liability for Defective Products Act 1991 as a product that fails to provide the safety that a person is entitled to expect, taking all circumstances into account, such as the presentation of the product, the intended use of the product and the time the product was put into circulation.

Definition of a Producer This includes any person who:

- manufactures a finished product or a component part, the producer of any raw material or component;
- has carried out the initial processing of products of the soil, stock-farming, fisheries and game;
- presents himself as a producer, for example, where a person puts a trade mark on a product or uses some distinguishing feature of his business in connection with the product;
- imports the product into any Member State from a place outside the EU; or
- the supplier or importer, when the producer or importer cannot be identified by reasonable steps, upon the request of the injured party, within reasonable time of the injury being incurred.

(b) *Defences* The main defences given in the Liability for Defective Products Act 1991, section 6, are as follows: (**Six** defences are given here – only **three** are required by the question.)
1. the product was not put into circulation by the producer;
2. the defect did not exist when the product was put into circulation;
3. the circulation of the product was not for economic purposes and was not supplied in the course of a business;
4. the product was produced in compliance with mandatory regulations;
5. development risk defence – this defence asserts that the state of scientific and technical knowledge at the time when the product was put into circulation was not such as to enable the existence of the defect to be discovered;
6. the defence for a producer of parts – if the party is being sued because it manufactured a component, that the defect is a defect within the finished product, and came about because of the way the finished product was designed or because of instructions given by the manufacturer of the finished product.

Question 6.3

(a) *Merchantable Quality* Section 14 of the 1893 Act states that goods must be fit for the purpose for which they are supplied and as durable as one can expect, taking account of price, description and all other relevant circumstances (time of sale, changing standards), as per *Egan v. McSweeney* (1956). Goods are not of merchantable quality where the performance of the product is prejudiced and the defect cannot be easily remedied or repaired without expense or taking some time to perform. The only exception to this rule is any defect brought to the attention of the buyer before the contract is made, or defects obvious to a reasonable person.

Fitness for Purpose Section 14(3) states that, where the seller supplies goods in the course of business and the buyer makes a particular purpose known to the seller, then there is an implied condition that the goods are fit for that purpose.

(b) *Conclusion* The actions of Premier Kitchen Supplies are in breach of the Sale of Goods legislation as the product sold was not fit for purpose, and this purpose was specifically brought to its attention. The main remedies available to Bella are a repair, replacement or refund of the cost of the machine (the latter being the most appropriate remedy in this situation).

Question 6.4

Functions of the Competition and Consumer Protection Commission (**Seven** functions are given here – only **three** are required by the question.)

1. Investigating and challenging practices that are damaging to consumers and/or the wider economy.
2. Bringing anti-competitive behaviour and practices that are harmful to consumers to an end, where necessary via court actions.
3. Providing information to consumers to help them make informed decisions.
4. Examining certain mergers and acquisitions to ensure that there is not a substantial lessening of competition in Ireland.
5. Advising policy-makers in relation to consumer protection and competition matters.
6. Promoting compliance with a new regulatory regime in the grocery sector aimed at ensuring balance and fairness in commercial relationships.
7. Responsibility for market surveillance in relation to the safety of products covered by a number of EU Directives, including monitoring and processing non-food product recalls in Ireland.

Question 7.1

(a) Section 6(4) of the Unfair Dismissal Act lists a number of circumstances that render a dismissal fair. These are:

- the capability, competence or qualification of the employee to perform the kind of work that he or she was employed to do;
- the conduct of the employee, e.g. being drunk on duty, or being violent. In *Murray v. Meath County Council* (1978) a dismissal was deemed to be fair where the employee assaulted his superior;
- redundancy of the employee: an employer is entitled to dismiss an employee on the grounds of redundancy. Redundancy is defined by the Redundancy Payments Acts 1967–2012. However, it will not be a fair ground where a selective redundancy is made;
- where continuation of employment would result in contravention of the law;
- the dismissal of a civilian from the Defence Forces for the purpose of safeguarding national security.

(b) Constructive dismissal occurs where the employer is in serious breach of an express or implied term of the contract, and the employee is entitled to terminate the contract. This amounts to constructive dismissal by the employer and entitles the employee to leave the job without giving notice and sue for wrongful dismissal.

In *Liz Allen v. Independent Newspapers* (2001), the Employment Appeals Tribunal (EAT) accepted that the plaintiff had been isolated at work, and had had her confidence and health undermined. This had left her with no option but to resign. She won her constructive dismissal case, and was awarded €70,500.

Question 7.2

Terms to be included in Statement of Employment In accordance with the provisions of the Minimum Notice and Terms of Employment Act 1973–2001, a written statement of employment should provide the following details. (**Nine** terms are listed here – only **five** are required by the question.)

1. The proper names of the employer and employee.
2. The address of the employer and the principal place of business or, if there is no fixed/main place of work, a statement that the employee is required/permitted to work at various places.
3. The title of the job or the nature of the work.
4. The date of commencement of employment and, in the case of a temporary contract, the duration of the contract/date that the contract expires.
5. The particulars of pay, the rate and method of calculation, frequency of payment, overtime, commission, bonuses and their method of calculation.
6. The particulars concerning hours of work and holiday entitlements.
7. The particulars concerning incapacity, sick pay arrangements and pension schemes.
8. The period of notice that must be given by both the employer and the employee for the termination of the employment contract.
9. A reference to any collective agreement(s) that directly affects the terms and conditions of the employment.

Question 7.3

(a) *Redundancy* Section 7(2) of the Redundancy Payments Act 1967 defines a redundancy as arising where the employer has ceased, or intends to cease, to carry on the business for the purposes of which the employee was employed by him, or has ceased, or intends to cease, to carry on that business in the place where the employee was so employed, or where the requirements of that business for employees to carry out work of a particular kind, or for employees to carry out work of a particular kind in the place where they were so employed, has ceased or diminished or is expected to cease or diminish.

(b) *Eligibility Requirements* The following are eligibility requirements to make a claim for redundancy payment: (**Three** eligibility requirements are listed here – only **two** are required by the question.)

1. the worker must be over 16 years old,
2. the worker must be employed under a contract of service, and
3. the worker must have been employed by the employer for at least two years after his or her 18th birthday.

(c) *Conclusion* Porter is not entitled to a redundancy payment in these circumstances as his position is still available. Therefore this is not a genuine redundancy – in reality he has been dismissed for gross misconduct.

Question 7.4

Tests to Determine the Distinction between an Employee and Contractor (**Four** tests are given here – only **two** are required by the question.)

1. *Control Test* This test questions whether the employer controls all aspects of the employee's work – in effect, has he or she control over the work done, the method of completion, the means employed to achieve the result and the time and place the task is to be done? There are inherent problems with the test in the context of certain workers who are subject to limited control, such as in *Tierney v. An Post* (2000).
2. *Integration Test* This test asks whether the worker is employed as part of the business, and whether the work done is integral to the business. The application of this case was illustrated in *Re Sunday Tribune (in Liquidation)* (1984) and in *Kelly v. Irish Press* (1985) in the context of journalists/editors who were described as contractors but integrated into the business. The main problem with the integration test is the difficulty in its application to small businesses.
3. *Enterprise Test* This test questions whether the person has engaged himself or herself to perform services as a person in business on his or her own account. It asks whether the worker has made a financial investment in the work, whether he or she can reap a reward/profit from effective performance of the job, and whether there is a financial risk in undertaking the work. It was applied in *Mahon v. Henry Denny & Sons Ltd* (1997) and in *McDermott v. Loy* (1982), wherein the lack of entrepreneurship indicated an employee relationship. Problems with the enterprise test arise in the context of employees paid on a commission basis.
4. *Mixed/Reality Test* In this test, all factors are considered equally (more focus on control in the mixed test) and an overview is taken. Relevant factors include: method of pay, right to select and dismiss, ability to delegate performance of duties, provision of training and equipment, level of financial risk undertaken by the worker, whether the worker has the opportunity to profit from effective management of the task. The application of this test was seen in *ÓCoindealbháin (Inspector of Taxes) v. Mooney* (1990) where the worker was classified as an employee by taking a holistic view of all aspects of the working relationship.

Conclusion It is more likely that Mary will be classified as an employee as:

1. she is controlled (attending all meetings);
2. she is integrated (attending social functions connected with employment, and she has been provided with her own office); and
3. there is no evidence of entrepreneurship, as there is no financial investment/risk involved in her performance of the job.

Therefore, in reality, she is likely to be classified as an employee (the issue of statutory deductions is irrelevant in making this determination).

Question 7.5

Duties of the Employer (**Eight** duties are given here – only **three** are required by the question.)

1. To provide a safe place of work (including entrances and exits).
2. To provide a safe system of work.
3. To provide employees with proper training.
4. To provide employees with proper equipment.
5. To provide employees with protective clothing (where it is not possible to control or eliminate hazards in a place of work).
6. To prevent any improper conduct or behaviour likely to put the safety, health and welfare of employees at risk.
7. To have necessary emergency evacuation plans.
8. To provide competent co-workers.

Conclusion Regal has breached its duty by not providing the injured employee with protective clothing.

Question 7.6

Health and Safety Authority Sanctions (**Five** sanctions are given here – only **two** are required by the question.)

1. Improvement notices.
2. Prohibition notices.
3. An on-the-spot fine of €1,000.
4. On summary prosecution, a fine of up to €3,000 and/or six months' imprisonment.
5. On prosecution on indictment, a fine of up to €3 million and/or two years' imprisonment.

Question 7.7

Grounds for Fair Dismissal (**Six** grounds are given here – only **two** are required by the question.)

1. Lack of competence
2. Lack of capability
3. Lack of qualifications
4. Redundancy
5. Misconduct
6. Illegality.

Procedures to Effect a Fair Dismissal
The employer must:
1. tell the employee of any allegations against him or her;
2. give the employee a copy of any evidence;
3. give the employee a right to respond and make representations;
4. allow the employee to bring a witness/representative to the disciplinary meeting;
5. give the employee the right to address a adjudicating body and make any pleas in mitigation; and
6. give the employee a statement of the reasons for the dismissal.

Question 7.8

(a) *Procedures Outlined in the Code of Practice on Grievance and Disciplinary Procedures* (**Six** procedures are given here – only **four** are required by the question.)
   1. Employee grievances must be examined and processed fairly.
   2. Details of any allegations or complaints must be put to the employees involved.
   3. The employee(s) must then be given the opportunity to respond fully to the allegations or complaints.
   4. The employee(s) must be offered the right to be represented during the procedure.
   5. The employee(s) has a right to a fair and impartial determination of the issues.
   6. The employee(s) has the right to be penalised in a manner that is proportionate to the gravity of the offence committed.

(b) *Conclusion* The actions of Fiona's employer are likely to be classified as unfair, given that there was no notification, representation or right to reply, and the penalty was disproportionate to the offence.

(c) *Conclusion* The actions of Fiona's employer are likely to be classified as grounds for a claim for constructive dismissal, as it is attempting to penalise Fiona for a failure to alter her contract.

Question 7.9

Constructive Dismissal This is where the employee terminates the contract under which he or she is employed because of the conduct of the employer. The conduct of the employer must be sufficiently serious as to entitle the employee to resign from the employment. In this instance, the onus lies on the employee to prove that what has happened amounted to a dismissal.

Question 7.10

Prerequisites to bring a Claim for Constructive Dismissal (**Nine** prerequisites are given here – only **two** are required by the question.)

1. An employee must have a minimum of one year's continuous service (except where dismissal results from maternity, trade union membership or exercising the right to minimum wage).
2. The worker must be employed under a contract of service.
3. The employee cannot have reached normal retiring age.
4. An employee cannot be a member of the Defence Forces or the Garda Síochána.
5. The employee cannot be employed by a family member in his or her home or farm.
6. The employee cannot be employed at sea.
7. The employee cannot be employed on a probationary period.
8. The employee cannot be working illegally within the State.
9. The employee cannot be employed in certain public servants' positions.

Question 7.11

(a) *Prerequisites to Claim Unfair Dismissal* (**Three** prerequisites are given here – only **two** are required by the question.)
   1. The worker must be an employee, employed under a contract of service.
   2. The worker must have been in continuous employment for at least one year with the employer (subject to limited exceptions).
   3. The worker must not be employed in a excluded profession (such as members of An Garda Síochána, or persons employed by VECs, etc.).

(b) *Tests to Determine the Status of a Worker*
   1. *Control Test* This test questions whether the employer controls all aspects of the worker's work – whether he or she has control over the work done, the method of completion, the means employed to achieve the result and the time and place the task is to be done. There are inherent problems with this test in the context of professional workers who are subject to limited control, such as in *Tierney v. An Post* (2000).
   2. *Integration Test* This test asks whether the worker is employed as part of the business, and whether the work done is integral to the business. The application of this test was illustrated in *Re Sunday Tribune (in Liquidation)* (1984) and in *Kelly v. Irish Press* (1985) in the context of journalists/editors who were described as contractors but were integrated into the business. The main problem with the integration test is the difficulty in its application to small businesses.

3. *Enterprise Test* This test questions whether the person has engaged himself or herself to perform services as a person in business on his or her own account – it asks whether the worker has made a financial investment in the work, whether he or she can reap a reward/profit from effective performance of the job, and whether there is a financial risk is undertaking the work. In *McDermott v. Loy* (1982), the lack of entrepreneurship indicated an employee relationship. Problems with the enterprise test arise in the context of employees paid on a commission basis.
4. *Mixed/Reality Test* In this test, all factors are considered equally (with more focus on control in the mixed test) and an overview is taken. Relevant factors in determining status under this test include: method of pay, right to select and dismiss, ability to delegate performance of duties, provision of training and equipment, level of financial risk undertaken by the worker, and whether the worker has the opportunity to profit from effective management of the task. This test's application was seen in *Mahon v. Henry Denny & Sons Ltd* (1997) where the worker was classified as an employee by taking a holistic view of all aspects of the working relationship.

(c) *Conclusion* Sarah is likely to be classified as an employee as she is controlled in terms of hours/days of work, teaching and syllabi, etc., and integrated in terms of attendance at exam boards. There is no evidence of entrepreneurship, therefore in reality, when all factors are balanced, the likelihood is that she will be classified as an employee.

(d) *Quasi-judicial Tribunals* These are specialist tribunals, permitted by Article 34 of the Irish Constitution, established to deal with civil matters. The main **advantages** of these tribunals are: (**Seven** advantages are given here – only **three** are required by the question.)

1. speed – they usually deal with matters more expeditiously than the courts;
2. informality – these are less formal, less intimidating and the stricter rules of evidence do not apply;
3. flexibility – they are not absolutely bound by the strict rules of precedent;
4. privacy – cases before these tribunals tend to be heard in private. In certain situations, the identities of the parties are undisclosed;
5. cost – tribunals are generally a much cheaper procedure than taking a case to the normal courts;
6. expertise – the use of specialist tribunals ensures that the person deciding the case has expert knowledge of the actual practice in the area under consideration and can form a conclusion in line with accepted practice; and

7. finality – appeals on decisions are limited and, once the tribunal has reached a decision, the parties may be bound by it and any award can be enforced through court action.

The main **disadvantage** of these tribunals is that they generally do not make an award for costs.

Question 7.12

Duties of the Employer (**Seven** duties are given here – only **four** are required by the question.)

1. To pay wages – and comply with the requirements of the National Minimum Wage Act 2000.
2. To provide work (in certain situations).
3. To indemnify employees against expenses arising in the course of employment.
4. To treat the employee with respect.
5. To provide annual and public holiday entitlements – as well as all other statutory entitlements.
6. To provide a safe work environment.
7. To provide a reference.

Question 7.13

Main Sources of Implied Terms of Employment Contracts (**Four** sources are given here – only **two** are required by the question.)

1. Custom and practice.
2. The Constitution.
3. Legislation (both Irish and EU – and both primary and delegated).
4. The courts.

Question 7.14

(a) *Information Required to be Included in a Statement of Employment*
Irrespective of whether the employment contract is in writing or otherwise, there is a statutory requirement imposed upon the employer to provide certain information to employees by virtue of minimum notice in the Terms of Employment Act 1973 as amended by the Terms of Employment (Information) Act 1994 to 2001. The legislation requires the employer to give detailed written information to employees with regard to the terms of their employment. An employee must, within two months of the commencement of employment, be supplied with a written copy of the following information:

1. the full names of the employer and employee;
2. the address of the employer and the principal place of work or, if there is no fixed/main place of work, a statement that the employee is required or permitted to work at various places;
3. the title of the job or the nature of the work;
4. the date of commencement of the employment;
5. the particulars of pay, rate and method of calculation;
6. the particulars concerning the hours of work, holiday entitlements; and
7. the particulars concerning sick pay, incapacity and pension schemes.

(b) *Implied Duties of an Employer in an Employment Contract*

1. To provide work – the **general** view is that an employer is **not** under any legal obligation to provide work for an employee; in effect, no breach of duty will occur provided the employee continues to be paid, even though there may be no work available. The **general** rule however might not hold true where the employee is employed on a piecemeal or commission basis, or the employee is a skilled employee, or where the need to work on a regular basis is required in order to maintain skills.
2. To ensure safety – the employer has a duty to take all reasonable care to ensure the safety of the employee. Most of these duties are contained in various pieces of legislation.
3. To provide paid holiday leave – this provision of holidays is generally a matter of contractual agreement between the parties although statute provides minimum holiday periods for all employees regardless of status or service.
4. To treat all employees with respect – the foundation of the employment relationship is presumed to be a mutuality of respect, trust and confidence and the employer must not act in any way calculated to damage such mutuality. Consequently, employers cannot treat their employees in an abusive manner and must be prepared to address any grievance they may have.
5. The right to receive a reference. It was decided in *Lint v. Johnson* that no action can be brought against an employer for failure to furnish a reference. However, the decision is not so definitive – it now seems to be the case that an employer is obliged to confirm that the employee worked for the employer, detailing what position he or she occupied, his or her main duties and responsibilities and the date of commencement and cessation of service. Additional information or the failure to provide a reference may lead to a claim for discrimination under the terms of the Equality Acts. There is no legal obligation to provide an account of the employee's behaviour and performance during the period of employment.

(c) *Implied Duties of an Employee in an Employment Contract*

1. To be available for work – the employee has a duty to be available for work for the hours agreed. These are usually specified in the contract of employment.
2. To obey lawful orders – the employee has a duty to obey all reasonable lawful orders given to him by his employers. However, the employer has no right to give orders that are manifestly unreasonable or not wholly connected with the employee's duties.
3. To exercise care and skill – the employee has a duty to exercise all reasonable care and skill in the performance of his or her work.
4. To act with trust and confidence and good faith – the employee is obligated to act in good faith in dealing with the business of his or her employer. Essentially, this requires the employee to act honestly in the interests of the employer.
5. Duty to disclose breaches of duty – depending upon the status or position of the employee, he or she may be obliged to report breaches of duty by fellow employees. In general, the higher position the employee holds, the great the burden placed upon him or her.

Question 7.15

(a) Redundancy is defined in section 7(ii) of the Redundancy Payments Act 1967 as being dismissal attributable wholly or mainly to: (1) the fact that an employer ceased, or intends to cease to carry on the business for the purpose of which the employee was employed, or has ceased, or intends to cease, to carry on that business in the place where the employee was so employed; or (2) the fact that the requirements of that business for employees to carry out work of a particular kind, or for employees to carry out work of a particular kind in a place where they were so employed, has ceased or diminished, or is expected to cease or diminish.

(b) Key requirements in order to obtain redundancy are: (1) the worker must be over 16 years old, but employed for two years after his or her 18th birthday; (2) the worker must be employed under a contract of service; and (3) the dismissal must be as a consequence of a redundancy.

(c) Statutory redundancy payment is two weeks' pay for every year of service. This is no longer linked to age. In addition, there is an additional payment of one bonus week. There is also a maximum ceiling of €600 per week – although an employer may choose to pay more.

Question 8.1

(a) Brian exceeded his actual authority to sell the goods to Paula. By merely entrusting Brian with the goods, Alan does not represent that Brian has apparent authority in excess of his actual authority. Where there is no such representation, the sale is made without authority and is void. Paula must return the goods to Alan but can claim damages for breach of warranty from Brian.

(b) Brian owes Alan a duty not to allow a conflict of interest situation to arise. Brian will be accountable to Alan for the secret profit that he made as a result of his position as Alan's agent.

Question 8.2

Agency by Estoppel This is where the principal allows a third party to believe that the person is his or her agent, or where the actions of the principal have suggested this fact. This situation may arise where a person acted as the agent in the past and continues to act as such after the agency relationship has been terminated. It may also arise by a course of dealing, such as in the case of employees, or by virtue of the position they hold. Case examples include *Panorama Developments (Guildford) Ltd v. Fidelis Furnishing Fabrics Ltd* (1971), and *Freeman & Lockyer v. Buckhurst Park Properties (Mangal) Ltd* (1964). In these circumstances the agent does not have actual authority, but instead the agent has apparent or ostensible authority.

Conclusion Cupcake and Coffee Ltd is legally obliged to pay the €3,000 due to the Aromatic Coffee Company. As Porter acted as an agent of Cupcake and Coffee Ltd, the Aromatic Coffee Company had no reason to believe that he was acting outside the scope of his duties and for his own personal interest. The only option available to Cupcake and Coffee Ltd is to seek recompense of this €3,000 from Porter.

Question 8.3

Agency In this situation it would be fair to say that Rose did have the capacity to create the contract. She is a director of the company and therefore should have the actual authority (either express or implied) to create such a contract on behalf of the company. Even if she did not have such authority or where she exceeded her authority, this contract will still be binding based on agency estoppel or ostensible authority. In these situations, if a principal allows a third party to believe that the person is his or her agent or the actions of the principal have given the impression of this fact, then agency by ostensible authority applies.

This may arise where a person has acted as an agent in the past and continues to act as such after the agency relationship has been terminated. It may also arise by virtue of a course of dealings in the past. Relevant case law includes *Panorama Developments (Guildford) Ltd v. Fidelis Furnishing Fabrics Ltd* (1971).

Conclusion In this situation it would be fair to say that any third party would assume that a company director has the customary authority to create contracts on behalf of the company. In these circumstances, the contract arose in the normal course of dealings, therefore Daffodils and Dandelions Ltd is estopped from denying that Rose had the power to create the contract. In this situation the contract is binding and enforceable.

Question 8.4

Agency The main issue in relation to the contract between Edward and Fairways Fabrics is the issue of agency. Normally an agent has the authority to bind its principal to any contract that it engages in. Therefore normally Edward, as a director of Giselle Ltd, would be an agent of the company and would be entitled to bind Giselle to the contract for Fairways Fabrics. It could be argued that an executive director, such as Edward, would have actual authority to create a contract on behalf of Giselle Ltd.

In this situation he was not acting in the interests of Giselle Ltd nor on its instructions. He acted in his own self-interest and therefore he did not have actual authority to create a contract on behalf of Giselle Ltd. However, he did have ostensible authority to engage in this contract. Ostensible authority is the idea that a principal allows a third party to believe that the person is his agent, or where the activities and actions of the person (Edward) in the past have created the belief on the part of the third party that he is an agent of the company. Obviously Edward has entered into contracts with Fairways Fabrics for several years and it is entitled to presume that, due to his behaviour in the past, he has the authority to bind Giselle Ltd to the contract.

This gives protection to third parties who could not possibly know whether an agent, such as Edward, is acting on actual authority or acting outside the scope of his authority. This has been seen in previous cases such as *Panorama Developments (Guildford) Limited v. Fidelis Furnishing Fabrics Limited* (1971).

Conclusion In this case, Giselle Ltd is obliged to pay for the fabrics supplied by Fairways Fabrics as Edward made a representation that he was Giselle's agent and Fairways relied upon the statement and created a contract. Giselle Ltd could seek to sue Edward (for acting outside the scope of his authority) for the amount of money that it has had to pay Fairways Fabrics for the materials.

Question 9.1

Advantages of Operating as a Sole Trader

1. no formal permission or licence is required to trade as sole trader; there are no registration or filing requirements,
2. a sole trader is the only person who has a say in the running of the business – not accountable to shareholders or partners,
3. good for small businesses as the sole trader personally owns all of the business assets, so extremely flexible, and
4. there are no specific legislative formalities regarding the operation of the business form.

Disadvantages of Operating as a Sole Trader

1. difficult to raise capital – cannot issue shares or bring in an additional partner and must rely on own funds, profits from business and personal borrowing from banks,
2. a sole trader has unlimited personal liability for the debts of the business. If the business owes money to a third party, the third party can pursue the sole trader's personal assets e.g. home. If the business of a sole trader fails, the sole trader may face personal bankruptcy,
3. it can be difficult to sell all or part of the business; the sole trader must sell each individual asset, e.g. premises, client list, goodwill, and
4. the business lacks perpetual existence and comes to an end on the death of the sole trader.

Question 10.1

The duty that the members of a partnership owe to one another is the general duty to act in good faith, owing to the fiduciary relationship.

In addition, specific duties of partners are set out in sections 28, 29 and 30 of the Partnership Act 1890:

- duty of disclosure;
- duty to account; and
- duty not to compete.

Duty of Disclosure

Section 28 of the Partnership Act 1890 provides that partners must render true accounts and full information in relation to all things affecting the partnership to the other partners or their legal representatives.

In *Law v. Law* (1905), one partner accepted an offer from the other to buy his share of the firm. At a later date, he discovered that certain partnership assets had not been disclosed to him, and he sought to have the contract set aside. **Held**: as the purchasing partner had breached the duty of disclosure, the agreement could have been set aside. This order was not necessary on the facts as the parties had come to an arrangement.

The Duty to Account

Section 29 of the Partnership Act 1890 provides that partners must account to the firm for any benefit obtained, without consent, from any transaction concerning: the partnership; its property, including information derived from membership of the partnership; its name; or its business connections. This provision only applies to secret profits. A partner must make full disclosure, or he or she will have to account to the partnership for the profit made.

The Duty not to Compete

Section 30 of the Partnership Act 1890 provides that, where a partner competes with the partnership business without the consent of the other partners, then that person shall be liable to account to the partnership for any profits made in the course of that business.

In *Pathirana v. Pathirana* (1966), the plaintiff and defendant were partners in the selling of Caltex petrol and kerosene oil from a service station belonging to Caltex Ltd. After the termination of the partnership by due notice given by the defendant to the plaintiff, the defendant continued to carry on business on the premises in his own name and did not account to the plaintiff for his share of capital or any profits. The court **held** that section 42(1) of the Partnership Act entitles a partner to claim such share of the profits made since the dissolution of the partnership as the court may find to be attributable to the use of his share of the partnership assets:

- that, under section 29 of the Partnership Act, a partner must account to the firm for any benefit he may derive which is obtained by him (without the assent of the others) through a partnership transaction;
- that goodwill of a business may exist "notwithstanding that it is incapable of being ascertainable in pounds, shillings and pence";
- that where a partner who manages the business fails to produce books of account, the court may assess the profits of the business in a practical way upon the evidence.

Question 10.2

Deed of Partnership This is the partnership agreement and is in reality a contract between the partners. It outlines rights, duties and obligations. A deed of partnership generally includes the following terms: (**Twelve** items are given here – only **four** are required by the question.)

1. the nature of the firm's business, the name of the firm and its principal place of business;
2. the capital and property of the firm and the proportion contributed by each partner;
3. the date of commencement and the intended duration of the partnership;
4. provision for the payment of salaries, if any, to the partners;
5. rights, obligations and duties of each individual partner, i.e. the legal relationship between the different partners;
6. provision for audits and accounts, partner drawings and partnership meetings.
7. division of profits and losses;
8. the procedure to be adopted on the death, retirement or bankruptcy of a partner;
9. the procedure for the valuation of the goodwill and assets on the sale of the partnership or on the death of a partner;
10. provision for the dissolution of the partnership;
11. provision for the admission of an additional partner or the expulsion of an existing partner; and
12. an arbitration clause setting down the procedure to be used in solving disputes.

Question 10.3

Limited Liability Partnership This is a partnership whereby one/some of the partners have limited liability. This liability is limited to the amount of capital that they have contributed to the partnership. To create a limited liability partnership, at least one of the partners must have unlimited liability and the partners with limited liability must be inactive and registered with the Companies Registration Office (CRO) as having limited liability pursuant to the Limited Partnership Act 1907. The main limitation is that a limited liability partner cannot be an active partner in the firm – he must be a silent/sleeping partner. Therefore, it may not be a viable option for Bertie and his children if they all want to be actively involved in the running of the firm.

Question 10.4

Dissolution of a Partnership The three main provisions of the Partnership Act 1890 governing the termination of a partnership relate to causes of dissolution. This may arise:

1. by agreement of the parties (section 32) – through the expiration of its term or by the giving of notice,
2. by operation of law (section 33 and 34) – through death, bankruptcy, illegally, or a change of a partner's share in the partnership, or
3. by order of a court (section 35) – through insanity, incapacity, conduct prejudicial to the business, breach of duties; or in any circumstances that the court considers just and equitable.

Question 10.5

(**Two** advantages and disadvantages are given here – only **one** of each is required by the question.)

The main **advantages** of a partnership as opposed to a company are that there are no obligations to file accounts with the Companies Registration Office (CRO) and therefore there is greater privacy. There is less regulation and formality surrounding the setting up of a partnership – therefore it is also cheaper to establish.

The main **disadvantage** of a partnership is the fact that it has no separate legal existence. This means that the partnership's assets are completely vulnerable should creditors wish to sue the partnership. A second disadvantage of a partnership is that, once one of the partners dies, the partnership may be brought to an end; this is not the case with a company, which has perpetual existence.

Question 10.6

No formalities are required to form a partnership. However, the relationship may come into existence when the parties make an express contract, which is known as a deed of partnership. Most partnerships are created by prior written agreement in the form of a deed of partnership. This deed will usually provide for the following matters:

1. The nature of the firm's business, the name of the firm and its principal place of business.
2. The capital and property of the firm and the proportion contributed by each partner.
3. The date of commencement and the intended duration of the partnership.
4. Provisions for the payment of salaries, if any, to the partners.
5. Rights, obligations and duties of each individual partner.
6. Provisions for audits, accounts, etc.

7. An arbitration clause setting out the procedures to be used in solving disputes.

Question 10.7

Partners' Statutory Duties

1. *Duty of Disclosure* (Section 28 of the Partnership Act 1890) This duty provides that partners are obliged to give full information about all aspects of the partnership to any partner or his or her legal representative. In *Law v. Law* (1905), one partner accepted an offer from another to buy his shares in the firm. He later discovered that certain assets belonging to the business had not been disclosed to him and he took action to have the contracts set aside. The court complied with his request as the failure to disclose amounted to a breach of duty.
2. *Duty to Account* (Section 29 of the Partnership Act 1890) This duty provides that the partners must account for all profits made by them in the use of the firm's property, name or business connections without the consent of the other partners. In *Bentley v. Craven* (1853), the defendant bought sugar on his own account and later sold it to the firm without declaring his interest to the other parties. The court ruled that this action amounted to a breach of section 29.
3. *Duty Not to Compete* (Section 30 of the Partnership Act 1890) This duty states that, where a party carries on his own business in competition with the partnership without the consent of the partnership, he is liable to account to the partnership for all profit made in the course of that business.

Question 10.8

Dissolution of a Partnership Dissolution is a procedure whereby a partnership is brought to an end and may be specifically provided for in the deed of partnership. Where there are no express provisions, the Partnership Act 1890 applies. Dissolution will occur by: (1) mutual agreement between the parties; (2) operation of the law; or (3) by an order of the court.

The following are grounds upon which a partnership will dissolve by operation of the law.

1. By retirement/notice given by the partners in a partnership at will; this can only be done where all the partners concur.
2. By efflux of time where the partnership is formed for a specific purpose, or is a venture for a predetermined period.
3. By the death or bankruptcy of any of the partners. This is because a partnership is not a distinct or separate legal person and therefore cannot exist apart from those members who compose it.
4. By an intervening illegality.

In addition, the court can order the dissolution of a partnership where a partner becomes mentally ill, insane or incapable of managing his own affairs. The court will order the dissolution of the partnership to preserve the incapacitated partner's interest, but may also grant this order if a partner suffers a permanent physical incapacity or if a partner wilfully and persistently breaks the partnership agreement. It will also grant this order if the business of the partnership can only be carried on at a loss, or where a partner breaches the agreement or where it is deemed just and equitable to do so.

Question 11.1

(a) **Types of Companies**

The various options available to Jane are as follows: (**Five** options are given here – only **four** are required by the question.)

Public Limited Company This type of company has the following characteristics:

1. in order to be incorporated, this type of company is required by law to register a Memorandum and Articles of Association, which state that it is a public limited company;
2. it is required to have a nominal share capital of at least €25,000 on incorporation;
3. it must have a minimum of one shareholder, with no maximum number;
4. there is no restriction on the transfer of its shares, and it may be listed on the stock market;
5. it requires a trading certificate in order to commence trading;
6. it must have at least two directors; and
7. it is required to state its objectives upon incorporation – and act within the parameters of these objectives.

Private Company Limited by Shares This type of company has the following characteristics:

1. it must have a minimum of one and a maximum of 149 shareholders;
2. there is no minimum share capital threshold, and it can choose not to have an authorised share capital on incorporation;
3. there is a restriction on the transfer of shares;
4. the liability of shareholders is limited in respect of fully-paid shares – therefore shareholders are liable to pay the unpaid portion of partly-paid shares in the event of the liquidation of the company;
5. it must have at least one director;
6. it can commence trading on receipt of a certificate of incorporation;
7. it has no limitation on its business activities;

8. it is incorporated by the registration of a single document constitution; and
9. in certain situations it can dispense with the requirement to hold an annual general meeting.

Company Limited by Guarantee This type of company has the following characteristics:

1. it does not issue shares or have a share capital, and therefore it does not have shareholders;
2. the membership is by subscription and the members agree upon incorporation to contribute a pre-determined amount to the assets in the event of insolvent liquidation;
3. it is the most common form of entity used by charities, sports and social clubs and management companies;
4. it is incorporated by the registration of a Memorandum and Articles of Association;
5. it is required to have an objects clause;
6. it may opt to have just one member;
7. it will be eligible to avail of the audit exemption;
8. its name must include the words "Company Limited by Guarantee" or "CLG";
9. it must have at least two directors, and retirement by rotation will apply in respect of these appointments; and
10. it has an exemption from filing financial statements with the Registrar where it is a charity or where it has an exemption given by a relevant authority.

Unlimited Liability Company This type of company has the following characteristics:

1. the members agree that, upon winding up, they will be liable, without limit, to contribute to the assets of the company a sufficient amount for the payment of the company's debts and liabilities;
2. certain companies of this type are exempted from many financial disclosure requirements imposed upon limited companies;
3. it is formed by the registration of a Memorandum and Articles of Association;
4. it is required to have an objects clause stating the purpose for which the company was established;
5. it may opt to have just one member;
6. its name must include the words "Unlimited Company" or "UC";
7. it must have a minimum of two directors;
8. where it is a single member company, it does not have to prepare a director's compliance statement, or hold an annual general meeting; and
9. this type of company may be a private unlimited company (ULC), a public unlimited company (PUC), or a public unlimited company that has no share capital (PULC).

Designated Activity Company This type of company has the following characteristics:

1. it is incorporated through the registration of a Memorandum and Articles of Association;
2. the DAC is a private limited company, which can be limited by shares or guarantee having a share capital;
3. it is required to have an objects clause stating the purpose for which the company was established;
4. the name of the company must end in DAC or its equivalents;
5. it must have a minimum of two directors;
6. it can have from one to 149 members;
7. it will not be prevented from having its debentures admitted to trading or listed on the Stock Market; and
8. it can dispense with the requirement to hold an annual general meeting, where it is a single member company.

(b) **Company Name**

(i) *Registration of Business Names Act 1963* A name is automatically disallowed if it is considered undesirable by the Registrar (section 26(5) Companies Act 2014); names considered undesirable include:

1. offensive, immoral or blasphemous names;
2. names suggesting a connection with any government department, local authority or State agency, where no such connection exists;
3. a name that uses "bank, society, co-operative or insurance", unless it has obtained the appropriate permission from the minister;
4. a name that includes a registered trademark, without production of the consent of its owner;
5. a name regarded as being misleading or confusingly similar to a registered name; or
6. a name of an existing company.

(ii) *Conclusion* The likelihood of John obtaining an injunction to prevent Jane's use of this name is high, as the names are confusingly similar and there is a strong likelihood of passing-off.

(c) ***Ultra Vires***

(i) A PLC has the capacity to do any act or thing stated in the objects set out in its Memorandum of Association (section 1011(1) CA 2014). The concept of *ultra vires* covers a situation where a public limited company or designated activity company acts outside its objectives, as stated in its Memorandum of Association. When we say that the company is acting outside its objective, we mean that it has created contracts for an activity or for a product that has not been sanctioned by the objectives clause in its Memorandum of Association.

(ii) *Ultra vires* contracts are generally void and unenforceable by the company. However, while they may be unenforceable by the company, they can be enforceable by a third party provided he or she is dealing in good faith with the company (section 1012). This is because a third party is not bound to enquire as to whether the transaction is permitted by the PLC's objects. Any action beyond the PLC's capacity may only be ratified by the company by special resolution. In addition, a member of a PLC can bring proceedings to restrain a PLC from entering into an *ultra vires* contract. Acting beyond capacity would also amount to a breach of directors' duties.

Question 11.2

Advantages of a Public Limited Company vis-à-vis a Partnership (**Four** advantages are given here – only **three** are required by the question.)

1. Separate legal entity: a PLC is a separate legal entity from its members (it can contract in its own name/sue or be sued in its own name, etc.).
2. Perpetual existence: because a PLC is a separate legal entity, this allows it to have perpetual existence, which means that a PLC will only cease to exist when it is struck off the Register of Companies.
3. Liability: PLC shareholders have limited liability, i.e. on liquidation they are not required to make a contribution towards company debts where their shares are fully paid.
4. Taxation: partnership profits are assessed for income tax purposes whereas company profits are assessed for corporation tax (which is significantly less).

Disadvantages of a Public Limited Company vis-à-vis a Partnership (**Four** disadvantages are given here – only **three** are required by the question.)

1. Formation: a partnership can be created by an oral or written agreement (known as the 'deed of partnership' or the 'partnership agreement'), whereas a company must be registered with the Companies Registration Office (which is a more arduous procedure).
2. Publicity requirements: PLCs have significant publicity obligations in return for separate legal existence (such as statutory registers, constitutional documents, certain resolutions, etc.), whereas partnerships are more private entities (the only publicity obligation arises if there is a limited liability partner).
3. Regulation: companies are subject to much more regulation than partnerships, under the Companies Act 2014.
4. Filing obligations: PLCs are required to file annual accounts and returns with the CRO every year.

Question 11.3

(a) *Private Limited Company's Constitution* This document must contain the following information in accordance with section 19:
   1. the company name;
   2. a statement that it is a private company limited by shares registered under Part 2 of the Companies Act 2014;
   3. a statement that the liability of its members is limited;
   4. a statement regarding its share capital, containing either: (i) the amount of share capital with which it proposes to be registered ("its authorised share capital"), and the division of that capital into shares of a fixed amount specified in the constitution, or (ii) without stating such amount, that the share capital of the company will, at the time of its registration, stand divided into shares of a fixed amount specified in the constitution;
   5. a statement of the number of shares (which shall not be less than one) taken by each subscriber to the constitution; and
   6. if the company adopts supplemental regulations, a copy of those regulations outlining the rules governing the internal management of the company.

(b) *Alteration of the Constitution* In order to amend a company's constitution, a meeting of the shareholders must be held (the shareholders must be given 21 days' clear notice of this meeting), a special resolution must be proposed, and the members must vote either in favour or against this resolution to amend the constitution. If this resolution is passed, the CRO must be notified of the alteration.

Question 11.4

Distinction between a Public Limited Company and Private Limited Company

(**Eight** differences are given here – only **three** are required by the question.)

1. Capital – there is no minimum capital requirement in a private limited company, whereas there is a minimum nominal value of the issued share capital in a public limited company of €25,000. In addition, a PLC must have an authorised share capital, whereas a private limited company can choose not to have an authorised share capital.
2. Members – membership in a private limited company is restricted to a minimum of one and a maximum of 149 shareholders, whereas in a public limited company there must be a minimum of one shareholder but there is no maximum limit.
3. Shares – there is a restriction on the transfer of shares in a private limited company, whereas shares are freely transferrable in a public limited company and may be listed on the stock exchange/market.

4. Trading – a private limited company can commence trading upon receipt of its certificate of incorporation, whereas a public limited company can only commence trading on receipt of its trading certificate.
5. Directors – a private limited company may operate with a minimum of one director, whereas a public limited company must have a minimum of two directors.
6. Annual General Meetings – a private limited company can dispense with this requirement in certain situations, whereas a public limited company cannot.
7. Formation – a private limited company is formed by the registration of a single constitutional document, whereas a public limited company is formed by the registration of a Memorandum and Articles of Association.
8. Corporate Capacity – a private limited company has no limitation on its business activities, whereas a public limited company is limited by its objectives clause, and any contract in contravention of this clause is classed as *ultra vires*.

Question 12.1

(a) *Executive Directors* These are directors who are involved in the operational management of the business. They provide continuous attention to the affairs of the business and are generally employees of the company, for example, the managing director. They usually hold important positions in the day-to-day running of the business.

Non-executive Directors These are directors appointed to manage the business on a transient basis. They are more involved in strategic management at board level, and not involved in the operational running of the business. They are appointed due to their expert knowledge, experience, attainment or skills. Their role is to act as monitors of the executive directors (by ensuring that they are acting within their powers and the company's objectives) and to provide the board of directors with additional expertise and an objective view point.

(b) *Appointment of Directors* The procedure for appointment of directors after their initial appointment is contained in the Companies Act 2014. This is done by the passing of an ordinary resolution of the shareholders of a company at a general meeting. These appointments are made individually. The board of directors can also appoint a person to act as a director where a casual vacancy arises. However, at the next AGM, any person so appointed would have to resign and, if he or she desires to be re-elected and is eligible to be re-elected, then he or she can ask the shareholders for re-election at the AGM.

(c) *Resolutions* The main differences between **ordinary** and **special** resolutions are:

	Ordinary	**Special**
How they are passed	This is defined as a resolution passed by a simple majority of the votes cast by members of a company or their proxies.	This is defined as a resolution passed by not less than 75% of the votes cast by the members of the company or their proxies.
Notice to members	No specific notice except to remove a director or auditor, which requires 28 days.	Always requires 21 days' notice.
Registration with the CRO	Do not need to be registered (with limited exceptions).	Must be delivered to the CRO within 15 days, otherwise the company is liable to be fined.

Question 12.2

Memo on Disqualification Orders:
To: Porter
From: A. Body
Date: May 2015
Subject: Disqualification Order

Porter,

Following your receipt of a letter from the Director of Corporate Enforcement notifying you that an application has been brought to the High Court seeking your disqualification as a company director, you requested advice regarding this. I have detailed below the areas you requested advice on.

(a) *Effect of a Disqualification Order* A disqualification order is an order brought against directors, auditors, company officers, liquidators or receivers, which disqualifies them from taking part in the promotion, formation or management of any company, either directly or indirectly for up to five years, or any other such period (longer or shorter) as the court may direct.

(b) *Grounds for Imposing the Order* The grounds can be automatic or discretionary and may be summarised as follows: (**Fourteen** grounds are given here – only **six** are required by the question.)

Automatic grounds – a director will be automatically disqualified:

1. where a person is convicted of an offence under the Companies Act 2014, or convicted of any offence involving fraud or dishonesty;
2. where a person is convicted of acting while restricted, except in the limited circumstances permitted by company law;
3. where a person is convicted of acting while disqualified;
4. where a person is a director of a company and there has been a failure to notify the Companies Registration Office, either at the time the company's constitution was being registered or when there was a change in the register of directors, that the person was disqualified in another jurisdiction, and a failure to provide the requisite details.

Discretionary grounds occur as follows:

1. where a person is found guilty of fraud while acting as a company promoter, officer, auditor, receiver, liquidator or examiner;
2. where a person is found guilty of a breach of duty while acting as a company promoter, officer, auditor, receiver, liquidator or examiner;
3. where a person is guilty of fraudulent or reckless trading;
4. where a person is unfit to be involved in the management of a company by reason of their past conduct as a company promoter, officer, auditor, receiver, liquidator or examiner;
5. where a person is unfit to be involved in the management of a company, following an inspector's report under the Companies Act 2014, by reason of their past conduct as a company promoter, officer, auditor, receiver, liquidator or examiner;
6. where a person is persistently in default of the filing requirements of the Companies Act 2014 (three or more defaults in a five-year period prior to the application);
7. where the person is disqualified under the law of another state from being appointed or acting as a director or secretary of a body corporate or an undertaking, and it would have been proper to make a disqualification order against the person based on his or her conduct or the circumstances that gave rise to the foreign disqualification if it had occurred or arisen in Ireland;
8. where a person commits two or more offences in respect of failing to keep proper financial records;
9. where he or she has been the director of a company that has been struck off the Register of Companies for failure to submit one or more annual

returns, unless the company had no liabilities at the time of strike-off, or where the liabilities have since been fully discharged; and

10. where the High Court, in its absolute discretion, considers that such disqualification is fair and equitable and in the best interests of the company.

(c) *Effect of Acting in Breach of a Disqualification Order* A person who acts while disqualified faces the following consequences:
   1. being guilty of a category 2 offence;
   2. having the period of disqualification extended for a further period of 10 years; and/or
   3. incurring personal liability for the debts of the company if it becomes insolvent at the time of, or within 12 months of, the disqualification order.

If you have any further questions please contact me.

Regards
A. Body

Question 12.3

(a) *Disclosure Obligations and Contracts* Section 231 of the Companies Act 2014 requires directors to disclose any direct or indirect personal interest they have in company contracts at the first directors' meeting at which the contract is discussed or at the next meeting after which they become aware of the conflict. This disclosure must be made to a properly convened board meeting, where the disclosure is recorded and minutes are taken. In addition, within three days of the disclosure, details of the disclosure must be entered into a book kept by the company for that purpose – this book must be available for review by company officers, members and the ODCE. In accordance with section 232, default of this provision will result in the company director being obliged to account to the company for any gain that he or she makes directly or indirectly from the breach of duty, and/or indemnify the company for any loss or damage resulting from that breach. Equitable relief may also be available to the company.

   Conclusion In this scenario Sam has breached his statutory duty as he failed to disclose a substantial conflict and used his power as a director to ensure that the contract was awarded to his sister's company.

(b) *Removal of a Director* In accordance with section 146 of the Companies Act 2014:
   1. a director can be removed from office by the passing of an ordinary resolution at a general meeting;
   2. extended notice of 28 days or more must be served by the company on the shareholders indicating the intention to remove the director;

3. a copy of the resolution proposing to remove the director must be given to the director concerned;
4. the director has a right to make written representations and have them circulated by the company to all the members before the general meeting;
5. if the representations are not sent, they must be read out at the general meeting;
6. the director has the right to speak at the meeting; and
7. a vote is taken and, if passed by a majority of those present, the CRO must be notified.

Question 12.4

(a) *Auditor's Role* An auditor is an independent, professional expert appointed by a company to prepare an independent report on the financial affairs of the company (i.e. appointed to audit the company), and to present this report to the shareholders at the annual general meeting. To be qualified to act as an auditor, a person must be:
   1. a member/qualified by a recognised accountancy body;
   2. registered with the CRO; and
   3. independent.

(b) *Powers of the Auditor* Sections 386–388 outline the rights of the auditor, which include: (**Five** powers are given here – only **three** are required by the question.)
   1. the right of access at all reasonable times to the company's accounting records;
   2. the right to ask questions of relevant persons (e.g. company officers and employees) in the company and to receive explanations and information as required to perform the duty as auditor;
   3. the right to information and explanations concerning subsidiary companies;
   4. the right to attend any general meetings of the company and to receive all notices and communications regarding the general meetings; and
   5. the right to speak at the company's general meetings on matters concerning the auditors.

(c) *Removal of the Auditor* Sections 394–398 CA 2014 provide that an auditor may be removed from office by an ordinary resolution, requiring 28 days' extended notice to members. A copy of this resolution must be sent to the CRO within 14 days and to the auditor whose removal is intended. The auditor has the right to contact the company and shareholders for the purpose of canvassing for his re-appointment, and may attend the relevant company meeting or make a representation in writing to the company.

If this representation is received in advance of the meeting then it should be circulated to all members at the company's expense.

Question 12.5

(a) *Annual Return* The general information included in the annual return is: (**Eight** pieces of information are given here – only **four** are required by the question.)

1. the name and registered number of the company;
2. the address of the registered office of the company;
3. the financial period covered by the return;
4. details of all shares issued for cash or other consideration, any calls made on shares that have been received or remain unpaid, any commission paid or discounts given on shares or debentures;
5. particulars of the total amount of indebtedness of the company that is secured by mortgages or charges, which are required to be registered;
6. a list of all persons, including names and addresses, who are members of the company, and of persons who have ceased to be members since the date of the last return;
7. details of shares held by each of the existing members, specifying the shares transferred since the date of the last return; and
8. particulars of the directors and secretaries to be entered in the company's register of directors and secretaries.

Documents that must be annexed to the annual return are:

1. a copy of the statutory financial statements of the company;
2. a copy of the directors' report; and
3. a copy of the auditor's report.

(b) *Annual Return Date* Every company has a fixed annual return date (ARD). On the commencement of the Companies Act 2014, all existing companies retained their existing ARDs. Companies incorporated after this Act came into existence are allocated an annual return date six months after their date of incorporation and, in each subsequent year the ARD will be the anniversary of its first annual return date. The annual return, together with the statutory financial statements of the company, directors' report and auditor's report, must be delivered to the registrar within 28 days of the annual return date.

Non-compliance Failure to file an annual return is an offence and, as a consequence, the company: (**Four** consequences are given here – only **two** are required by the question.)

1. may be fined,
2. may be issued with penalties,
3. risks losing its audit exemption, or
4. risks being struck off the register.

Question 12.6

(a) *Eligibility* The following people are ineligible to act as a company director: (**Six** people are given here – only **four** are required by the question.)

1. the company's auditor;
2. an undischarged bankrupt;
3. a company;
4. a restricted person (subject to limited exceptions);
5. a disqualified person; and
6. a minor (a person under the age of 18 years).

Under Irish company law, all private limited companies must have a minimum of one director.

(b) (i) *Substantial Transaction in Respect of a Non-cash Asset* Section 238 of the Companies Act 2014 defines this as the purchase by a company of a non-cash asset from a company officer/connected person or acquisition by a company officer or a connected person of a non-cash asset from the company, whose value exceeds €65,000 or 10% of the company's net assets; a transaction of less than €5,000 falls outside this definition. Where such a transaction arises, before the acquisition can take effect, the company must obtain approval to proceed with the transaction by way of a resolution of its shareholders at a general meeting.

(ii) *Duty of Proper Care, Skill and Diligence* Section 228(g) of the Companies Act 2014 requires directors to exercise reasonable skill, care and diligence in the performance of their duties. The guidelines in relation to exercising this duty were laid out in *Re City Equitable Fire Insurance Company Ltd* (1925) and have been reinforced by legislation, as follows:

1. the director must exercise his or her duty to a standard reasonably expected from a person of his or her knowledge and experience;
2. the director is not bound to give continuous attention to the affairs of the company and need only attend meetings when he or she can reasonably do so or at least regularly;
3. the director can delegate the duties of the company to the management provided it is normal business practice and there are no suspicious circumstances, although the director still has a duty to supervise the discharge of the delegated function, as per *Re Barings plc (No 5)* (2000). The test to determine liability is a subjective standard test and the court will examine what is reasonable for that particular director – the more qualified the director, the higher the standard will be expected, as per *Dorchester Finance Co Ltd v. Stebbing* (1977).

(iii) *Fiduciary Duties of a Company Director* These can be summarised as follows: (**Six** duties are given here – only **three** are required by the question.)

1. directors must exercise their powers *bona fide* in the best interest of the company as a whole;
2. directors must exercise their powers for the purposes for which they were conferred, in furtherance of the company's constitution and for lawful purposes;
3. directors have a duty to avoid conflicts of interest between themselves and the company;
4. directors are required to act honestly and responsibly in relation to the conduct of the affairs of the company;
5. directors are prohibited from using company property, information or opportunities for their own personal benefit or for any other person's benefit; and
6. directors have a duty to maintain independent judgement in the performance of their duties, except where otherwise permitted by the constitution of the company or where it is approved by an ordinary resolution of the members in a general meeting.

Question 12.7

Indoor Management Rule In advising Ryan, the liquidator, on the validity or otherwise of this contract, the issue revolves around the application of the indoor management rule. Under this rule, where a third party contracts with a company, he or she is entitled to presume that things done in a company are done according to correct procedures, as required by the company's constitution. In other words, an outsider is entitled to presume that issues of internal management have been transacted in a procedurally correct manner. This rule originates from the case of *Royal British Bank v. Turquand* (1856). However, it is important to note that the indoor management rule does not apply in cases where the facts should make the outsider enquire further – for example, where there are suspicious circumstances, such as arose in *AL Underwood Limited v. Bank of Liverpool & Martins* (1924) where a company director lodged cheques payable to the company into a personal bank account.

Alternatively, the contract may also be enforceable where Ethan is a registered person in accordance with section 40(1) of the Companies Act 2014. If Ethan is a registered person, then he automatically has the power to bind the company in contract, irrespective of whether he exceeds the actual authority bestowed upon him by the company's constitution.

Based on the application of either of these rules the contract created by Ethan on behalf of Arlington Enterprises Ltd is valid and the liquidator must rank this debt as an unsecured debt. However, the liquidator may take an action against Ethan for breach of his fiduciary duties (not acting in good faith and in the best interests of the company/not acting within his powers). This may result in an award of damages against Ethan for losses sustained by the company.

Question 12.8

Directors' Loans The issue of directors' loans is covered by section 239 of the Companies Act 2014. This section contains a prohibition against loans, quasi loans, credit transactions and guarantees from a company or subsidiaries to a director or any connected person. Although there is a prohibition at the start of this section there are also exceptions to this prohibition. These include situations where:

1. the value of the transaction is less than 10% of the value of the company's net assets (section 240(1));
2. the summary approval procedure has been applied (section 242);
3. intragroup transactions (section 243); or
4. the advancing of money to the directors for reasonable expenses (which must be vouched expenditure) incurred on behalf of the company in the performance of duties (section 244).

In addition, where the company enters into the transaction concerned in the ordinary course of its business, for example, where the company is a bank or financial/credit institution that lends monies in the normal course of business, then this transaction is permissible (section 245). In this situation the transaction must be the subject of normal standard business terms.

Where a director is aware that the value of the transaction is greater than 10% of the company's relevant assets, he or she is required to amend it to bring it within this 10% limit within two months of becoming aware, or when he or she should reasonably be aware, of this situation. If this does not happen, the transaction may be voidable at the instance of the company.

In addition, a breach of any of these rules may result in:

1. the restitution of monies or assets;
2. where the transaction affects the solvency of the company, the person benefitting from the transaction may be exposed to personal liability for the debts of the company arising therefrom; and
3. any officer of the company who acts in default of these obligations will be guilty of a category 2 offence.

Loans to directors must also be properly documented (section 236). If they are not, then they are deemed repayable on demand and with interest. Loans by directors to their companies must also be in writing or they will lose interest and lose priority if the company later goes into liquidation.

In conclusion, in this scenario, I would argue that the proposed loan is not permissible under company law as it does not fall under any of the stated exceptions.

Question 13.1

(a) *Share Premium* A share premium is where a company issues shares above their par/nominal value – the excess in value is known as the 'premium'. This capital is also known as undenominated capital – this is defined as the excess of company capital over the nominal value of issued shares.

In relation to the company accounts, this premium must be lodged into the share premium account, which is part of the undenominated capital. This account can be utilised for the payment of any premium due on the redemption of redeemable shares or debentures, and for the issuing of bonus shares.

(b) *Pre-emption* A pre-emption right is an obligation on a company when allocating shares. The pre-emption right means the company must allot ordinary shares to existing shareholders in proportion to their existing shareholding before offering them to third parties (section 69(6) – private limited company, and section 1022 Companies Act 2014 – public limited company). This pre-emption right allows shareholders to keep their level of shareholding constant. Where shares are issued in accordance with the pre-emption provisions of CA 2014, the issue is commonly known as a 'rights issue'.

Question 13.2

(a) *Characteristics of Ordinary Shares* The owners of these shares are classed as the equity shareholders of the company as they bear the burden of the company's performance. These shares have the following characteristics: (**Four** characteristics are given here – only **three** are required by the question.) (1) their owners are risk-takers as they are the last to be paid upon the liquidation of the business and, if there are no funds available on liquidation, they receive no return on capital; (2) they have the possibility of capital growth in that their owners have a right to a share of any available assets/funds upon winding up if funds are available; (3) their owners receive a return called a dividend, but its payment is dependent upon company performance – if profits are available for distribution and the directors declare a distribution then they may receive a dividend; and (4) the owners of ordinary shares can generally influence company policy by exercising voting rights at meetings (both AGMs and EGMs) relating to company business.

(b) *Partly-paid Shares* These are shares issued where the total nominal value is not paid upon subscription and where the unpaid sum is required at either a pre-agreed future date or upon the liquidation of the company (whichever arises first). The paid-up amount is reflected on the balance sheet as paid-up/called-up issued share capital – the unpaid portion is reflected as unpaid capital/reserve capital (where the unpaid portion is reserved exclusively for liquidation purposes).

(c) *Mark's Liability upon Liquidation* As Mark purchased partly-paid shares, he is obliged to pay the unpaid balance when called (depending upon the terms of the issue) or upon liquidation (whichever occurs first) – therefore he is obliged to pay the balance (300,000 × €0.50 = €150,000) if the company is put into liquidation.

Question 14.1

(a) *Grounds for Compulsory Liquidation* (**Numerous** grounds are given here – only **two** are required by the question.) This may arise where the court considers it just and equitable to liquidate the business (section 569(e) CA 2014). This is the most dynamic ground for petitioning to have the company wound up. This has occurred in the following circumstances: (1) where there has been a deadlock in the corporate management of the company; (2) where there is failure in substratum; (3) where the company has illegal/fraudulent objectives; or (4) where the company is a corporate instrument of fraud.

In addition, section 569 of the Companies Act 2014 also lists the following as grounds for an application for compulsory liquidation: (1) where the company has passed a special resolution to liquidate; (2) where the company has not commenced trading within 12 months of its incorporation or it has ceased trading for a period of 12 months or more; (3) if the members of the company are all deceased or no longer exist; (4) where the company is unable to pay its debts as they fall due; (5) where the court is satisfied that it is in the public interest that the company be liquidated; and (6) where the court considers it necessary to protect the interests of minority shareholders who are being treated in an oppressive manner.

Furthermore, a company may also be subject to compulsory liquidation arising out of failed examinership. This can occur where an examiner is unable to secure agreement or formulate proposals for compromise or a scheme of arrangement (section 535) or where the court refuses to confirm proposals (section 542(5)).

(b) *Alternatives to Compulsory Liquidation* There are **three** (only two are required by the question) main alternatives to compulsory liquidation:

Examinership This is the process whereby a company is placed under the protection of the court for a period of 70 days. The purpose of an examinership is to allow the company a period of time to determine whether its continued existence is a possibility without fear of legal action. In effect an examiner is appointed to investigate the company's affairs and to report to the court on its prospects for survival. Relevant cases are: *Re Atlantics Magnetics Limited* (1993) and *Re Holidair Limited* (1994).

Members' Voluntary Liquidation of the Company This requires that either the summary approval procedure is followed or alternatively, that: (1) the company is solvent; (2) a declaration of solvency has been made by the directors; (3) this resolution is corroborated by a report of an independent accountant; and (4) a resolution has been passed by the members to liquidate.

Creditors' Voluntary Liquidation This arises where the company is not solvent. In this situation: (1) the directors decide that the company is insolvent; (2) a resolution of the shareholders to liquidate the company is effected; (3) the directors then ask the creditors to agree to a creditors' liquidation; and (4) a creditors' liquidator and a committee of inspection oversee the liquidation of the company.

Question 14.2

(a) *Reasons to effect a members' voluntary liquidation* (**Three** reasons are given here – only **two** are required by the question.) In general, a company may be wound up voluntarily by its members: (1) when the period, if any, fixed for the duration of the company by its constitution expires; or (2) if an event occurs that the constitution specifies will result in the dissolution of the company; or (3) if the company in a general meeting passes a resolution that the company be liquidated.

(b) *Prerequisite to effect a members' voluntary liquidation* In order to liquidate by a resolution of the members, the pre-requisite is that the company is solvent.

(c) *Procedure in accordance with the summary approval procedure* This procedure requires: (1) the directors to make declaration of solvency; (2) the passing of a special resolution or a written resolution to liquidate the company within 30 days of the declaration of solvency; (3) a report by a person qualified to act as a statutory auditor confirming that the declaration is not unreasonable; (4) a copy of the declaration to be delivered to the CRO within 21 days of the commencement date of the members' voluntary liquidation; (5) if this resolution is passed, a voluntary liquidator is appointed to sell off the assets, pay the company debts and distribute the residue in accordance with the terms of the company's constitution and company law; and (6) when this is effected, the liquidator will then instruct the CRO to strike the company off the register and effectively bring it to an end.

Question 14.3

Creditors' Voluntary Liquidation (1) a company unable to make a declaration of solvency because of insolvency may initiate a creditors' voluntary liquidation; (2) the members of the company must pass a resolution to liquidate the company; (3) the company must then call a meeting with the creditors – this meeting usually takes place on the same day or the next day after the resolution is passed to effect a creditors' voluntary liquidation (creditors must be provided with at least 10 days' written notice of this meeting. Notice of the meeting must also be advertised in two daily newspapers circulating in the area. This notice must state who the proposed liquidator is, and must be accompanied by a list of creditors or notification of where this list is available for their review); (4) at the creditors' meeting, the directors must produce a statement of affairs showing particulars of the company's assets, debts and liabilities, as well as a list of the creditors and the debts owed, and explain to the creditors that the company is insolvent and cannot pay its debts; (5) a vote is then taken by the creditors to agree to a creditors' voluntary liquidation, and a liquidator will be appointed; and (6) a committee of inspection may also be appointed to assist the liquidator (this committee may be made up of a maximum of eight creditors. The committee will monitor the liquidator and his exercise of his powers in winding up the company).

Question 14.4

The following should be included in a memo.

(a) *Floating Charge* (1) this charge is created when a company borrows money and secures that borrowing on a non-specific company asset – the charge was defined in *Re Yorkshire Woolcombers Association Ltd* as a charge on an asset both present and future, which changes in the ordinary course of business; (2) a floating charge does not attach to the asset until the charge crystallises. Crystallisation can arise by default on the debenture/loan, company liquidation, receivership or the cessation of business; or, alternatively, on a pre-determined future date. Upon crystallisation, the floating charge becomes fixed to the charged asset over which it previously floated; (3) when a floating charge is created, the borrower retains the ability to deal with the asset in the normal course of business; and (4) the priority of floating charge upon crystallisation is that it is only paid after the fixed charges and the preferential debts have been discharged.

(b) *Liquidation* Upon liquidation, the debts of the company are paid in the following priority: (1) costs of liquidation; (2) debentures secured by fixed charges; (3) preferential debts; (4) debentures secured by floating charges; (5) unsecured creditors; and (6) return to shareholders.

(c) *Application* The listed debts will be paid as follows: (1) fixed charges: €165,000 mortgage in favour of Trinity Bank Plc; (2) preferential debts: Revenue debts of €20,000 and four months of the six months' unpaid salaries of €30,000 (up to a maximum of €10,000 per employee); (3) floating charges: the loan of €100,000 in favour of Fern Bank of Galway and then the €40,000 in favour of Russet Provincial Bank (as they are paid in order of registration, not creation – subject to the requirement that they are registered within 21 days); and (4) unsecured debts: €40,000 to trade creditors' two months of the six months' unpaid salaries of €30,000 and €30,000 unsecured loan from James's father.

Question 14.5

Liquidators and the Director of Corporate Enforcement

- Section 682 of the Companies Act 2014 provides that a liquidator of an insolvent company must, within six months after the date of his appointment, and at intervals as required by the ODCE, report to the Director of Corporate Enforcement on the affairs of the company and the conduct of the company's officers for the purpose of determining whether restriction/disqualification (Part IV CA 2014) proceedings are justified. Where they are justified, the liquidator is obliged to bring proceedings unless excused by the ODCE (section 683).
- The liquidator also has a duty to report any suspicion of criminal offences committed by a company, or its past or present officers to the ODCE and the DPP, and may be required to provide information to the DPP and assist him or her by giving access to facilities for inspecting and taking any copies of any company documents required (section 723).
- The liquidator has a duty to produce books and records for examination to the ODCE, and to answer any questions of the ODCE concerning the conduct of the particular liquidation (section 653).

Question 14.6

The memo to the shareholder should include the following paragraphs:

(a) *Fixed Charge* A fixed charge is a charge that attaches to the fixed asset from the moment it is created. It normally attaches to assets such as land or machinery. A fixed charge ranks in priority to other charges, such as floating charges.

When the fixed charge attaches to the asset, the company cannot deal with the asset without the consent of the charge-holder. In this context 'dealing' includes selling or re-financing the asset or creating other charges on the same asset.

(b) *Receiver* A receiver is appointed when the company defaults on payments of a debt. The receiver will go into the company and sell the charged asset in order to repay the debt and return any surplus funds to the company. The receiver has the power to sell the charged asset for the best possible price.

Effects of Appointment of a Receiver (1) all floating charges crystallise and become attached to the assets over which they previously floated, (2) directors are prohibited from making management decisions in relation to the charged assets, and (3) the company may continue trading.

(c) *The Distinction between Receivership and Liquidation* A receiver's job is to repay the debt of the debenture holder by selling the charged asset. It does not necessarily involve bringing the company to an end. It may bring the company to an end if the asset is critical to continuing the business, but that is not the case in all situations. In contrast, the objective of a liquidator is to bring a company to an end by selling off all of its assets and repaying the total debt due by the company in the order of priority set out under the Companies Act 2014.

Question 15.1

(a) *An Order Restraining the Removal of Assets* This type of order is known as a freezing order as it restrains a company officer from removing assets from the State or reducing the value of assets below a specified amount. The procedure to bring such an application is that an application must be made to the court under section 798 CA 2014. The requirements are that: (1) the applicant must be a relevant person and (2) the claim must be a qualifying claim.

The following are relevant people for the purpose of this application: (1) the company itself, (2) a director, (3) a member, (4) a liquidator or receiver, (5) a company creditor or (6) the ODCE.

For the purpose of this application, a qualifying claim is one where the person against whom the order is requested may be exposed to significant personal financial liability arising out of his or her actions while acting as an officer of the company.

In this scenario, the receiver or the Prudential Bank of Ireland (as a creditor of the company) may make the application for the order, and the action for fraudulent trading would constitute a qualifying claim for the purpose of this application.

(b) *Sanctions* From a criminal perspective, the Companies Act 2014 classifies fraudulent trading as a category 1 offence. In accordance with the legislation, a category 1 offence carries a class A fine and/or a maximum term of 12 months' imprisonment on summary prosecution, and a €500,000 fine or a maximum term of 10 years' imprisonment or both, where prosecuted upon indictment. The civil sanctions that are imposed for this offence are personal liability without limit for the debts of the business arising from the fraudulent act.

Question 16.1

(a) *Definition of 'insider trading'* This is where confidential, price-sensitive information is abused by a connected person to make a gain/avoid a loss (whether for themselves or someone else). This area is regulated by the Investment Funds, Companies and Miscellaneous Provisions Act 2005 and Chapter 2 of Part 23 of the Companies Act 2014. The legislation defines 'insider information' as: (1) information of a precise nature relating directly or indirectly to one or more issuers of financial instruments or a financial instrument, which has not been made public and which, if it were made public, would be likely to have a significant effect on the price of those financial instruments or on the price of related derivative financial instruments; (2) information that a reasonable investor would be likely to use as part of the basis of the investor's investment decisions; or (3) information of a precise nature that: indicates (i) a set of circumstances which exists or may reasonably be expected to come into existence; or (ii) an event which has occurred or may reasonably be expected to occur, and is specific enough to enable a conclusion to be drawn as to the possible effect of that set of circumstances or events, as the case may be, on the prices of financial instruments or related derivative financial instruments.

(b) *Definition of an 'insider'* A person may be defined as an insider as a consequence of: (1) his or her membership of professional bodies (especially those who issue financial instruments); (2) by virtue of his or her capital holding; (3) through employment or professional duties; or (4) through criminal activity. An insider may also be a company or a person who received a tip with information that they knew, or ought to have known, was inside information.

(c) *Criminal Sanctions for Insider Trading* (1) on summary conviction, a term of imprisonment not exceeding 12 months and/or a class A fine; (2) on indictment, a term of imprisonment not exceeding 10 years and/or a fine not exceeding €10 million; and (3) a prohibition from any dealing for 12 months from the date of conviction.

Conclusion It is likely that Buckley will be found guilty as he was aware of (1) the price-sensitive nature of the information, and (2) that it was confidential – and nonetheless used it to avoid a loss. He is an insider through employment.

Question 16.2

(a) *Money Laundering* Money laundering is the way in which criminals attempt to turn cash and other assets obtained from criminal activities into genuine assets through the financial services system and through established businesses. Money laundering is an offence under the Criminal Justice (Money Laundering and Terrorist Financing) Act 2010. Under this Act, an offence is committed where a person engages in any of the following acts in relation to property that is the proceeds of criminal conduct: (**Three** ways are given here – only **two** are required by the question.) (1) concealing or disguising the true nature, source, location, disposition, movement or ownership of the property, or any rights relating to the property; (2) converting, transferring, handling, acquiring, possessing or using the property; or (3) removing the property from, or bringing the property into, the State.

Section 7(6) defines handling as arising where a person receives, or arranges to receive, the property, or retains, removes, disposes of or realises the property, or arranges to do any of those things, for the benefit of another person.

The offence requires knowledge or a belief or reckless disregard that the property is, or probably is, the proceeds of criminal activity.

The offence may occur by: (1) placing (into an apparently legitimate business activity or property); (2) layering (moving funds to conceal their initial source); or (3) integrating criminal funds into a legitimate business.

(b) *Auditor's Reporting Obligations:* (1) the auditor is legally obliged to report any suspicion of money laundering to the Garda Síochána and the Revenue Commissioners; (2) the auditor is obliged to report any suspicion that a company officer has committed a category 1 or 2 offence (such as money laundering) to the Director of Corporate Law Enforcement (failure to do so is classified as a category 3 offence); (3) a member/student member of Chartered Accountants Ireland should report any suspicion to the Institute; and (4) it is an offence to notify (tip-off) any person/body that they have been reported on suspicion of money laundering.

Question 17.1

(a) *Role of CARB* CARB is an independent body established to regulate the members of Chartered Accountants Ireland in accordance with the provisions of the Institute's bye-laws, and to take disciplinary action where required.

Grounds for Disciplinary Action by CARB These include: (**Three** grounds are given here – only **two** are required by the question.) (1) breach of a bye-law or regulation; (2) failure to comply with standards of professional conduct; and (3) bringing discredit on themselves, the Institute or the accounting profession.

(b) *Jurisdiction of the Disciplinary Tribunal of CARB* This tribunal has the jurisdiction to hear cases referred to it by the complaints committee of CARB; in general, all cases are heard in full and in public.

Composition of the Disciplinary Tribunal This tribunal consists of three persons appointed by the chairperson of the disciplinary tribunal, who are drawn from the disciplinary panel, to hear the case; only one can be a member of the Institute.

Outcomes of a hearing of the Disciplinary Tribunal This Tribunal can suspend or exclude a member, withdraw licences or practising certificates – or declare ineligibility to hold these, impose a reprimand or a severe reprimand, or levy a fine not exceeding €100,000. If a member is not happy with the outcome of a hearing of the disciplinary tribunal, he or she can appeal any finding of the disciplinary tribunal to the appeal panel of CARB.

Question 18.1

Corporate governance refers to the system by which companies are run and operated by their boards of directors, which are responsible for the governance of their companies. Corporate governance has become an increasingly important issue for companies worldwide in the wake of such scandals as Enron and WorldCom.

Corporate governance has been described in many ways, two such examples include:

- The *Cadbury Report* in 1992 defined corporate governance as: "The system by which business corporations are directed and controlled."
- The World Bank's *Report on Corporate Governance* (1999) defines it as: "A set of arrangements internal to the corporation that define the relationships between managers and shareholders."

In order to ensure an effective corporate governance structure, defined rules and regulations have been developed, including voluntary codes.

Question 18.2

The first point to note is that it is not appropriate for existing directors to select candidates for the board of directors. Under section B of the *UK Corporate Governance Code* (the Code), widely regarded as representing the highest standards of corporate governance, the nomination committee should propose candidates for the board. Candidates will ultimately be subject to review and approval by the members of the company (in the case of VTIL, the only member of the company is the current Minister of Transport, Tourism and Sport). It is useful that the existing board has produced a shortlist, but it is important to recognise that it is not final and candidates can be added (or removed).

Secondly, under section B of the Code, VTIL would be regarded as a small company (as it clearly would not qualify for inclusion on the FTSE 350 if it were listed) – it should therefore have at least two 'independent' non-executive directors (NEDs).

In assessing individual candidates, the following points can be made:

1. Executive candidates (the current general manager and the current financial controller) – it is common in commercial organisations and in smaller companies, for the highest ranked operating manager and the most senior financial manager to be members of the board. Of course, just because it is **typical** does not mean it should necessarily be so.
2. Non-executive candidates – it is important to identify whether they qualify as 'independent' under the Code. The VTIL board should set out in its annual report those NEDs it considers to be independent (as per the criteria outlined in the Code) – although the final decision rests with the board.

Applying the Code's independence criteria, Pat Porterhouse and Elizabeth O'Connor would not qualify because of their links to the sole member of the company; Mark Wilson may not qualify due to his involvement in a party that has major commercial transactions with VTIL. Therefore only Sharon Hughes, Monica O'Brien and Neil Marsden appear to qualify as independent under section B of the Code. Sharon Hughes' industry experience offers her a clear advantage over the other candidates. However, none of the three 'independents' appear to have recent and relevant financial experience as required under section C of the Code – that at least one member of the audit committee has such experience. Ultimately, the appointments will be decided by the sole member of VTIL.

It is also important to note that the Code does not seek to limit the number of NEDs (except that the board should not be so large as to be unwieldy (section B)). On that basis there would be no prohibition in appointing some, or indeed all, of the candidates – all appear to have valuable experience. In particular, Mark Wilson's industry experience might be particularly useful especially as customer focus is likely to be a major consideration.

The role of chairman is probably the single most important role in corporate governance and, under section A, the chairman should be independent on appointment. Therefore the candidacy of Pat Porterhouse, the incumbent chairman of VTIL, does not meet these criteria – as Secretary to the Department of Transport, Tourism and Sport, he is clearly linked to the sole member. On this basis, only Sharon Hughes, Monica O'Brien and Neil Marsden appear to qualify as independent (under section B) and would therefore qualify to be chairman. Of course, someone else could be appointed as chairman. Although Pat Porterhouse is ineligible to remain as chairman, given his experience it would be sensible for him to remain on the board in a transition role. If he is not available (or willing) to fulfil this role, one of the other current board members could do so.

Based on the above, if the new board were to consist of the three independent NEDs, plus an additional independent NED with relevant financial experience, an independent chairman and Pat Porterhouse and two other executive directors, then the board would consist of eight people, which would not be excessive.

If the committee responsibilities were allocated as set out in the question, then:

- The audit committee would have two independent NEDs, as required by the Code; NEDs who would not qualify as independent (Elizabeth O'Connor and Mark Wilson) should **not** be appointed (sections C and D); and the issue of an independent NED with relevant financial experience needs to be considered;
- The nomination committee would also have two independent NEDs, plus one non-independent NED (Elizabeth O'Connor) – in line with the Code's provision (section B) that non-independent NEDs be in the minority;
- The remuneration committee would have only one NED likely to be regarded as independent (Monica O'Brien); again, non-independent NEDs should **not** be appointed under sections C and D.

It is also important to consider the board's gender balance in order to encourage diversity in the board's activities (section B).

When the board does take office it will have to consider its strategic and legal responsibilities. As VTIL does not have a primary listing on the Irish Stock Exchange the "Irish Corporate Governance Annex" does not have any direct impact.

Index